Cultural Heritage of Assam

Cultural Heritage of Assam

Editors

Sarit K. Chaudhuri

Mini Bhattacharyya Thakur

Indira Gandhi Rashtriya Manav Sangrahalaya
(National Museum of Mankind Bhopal)

GYAN

First Published, 2017

Published by

Gyan Publishing House
5, Ansari Road
Daryaganj, New Delhi-110002
Phone: 9811692060
E-mail: books@gyanbooks.com

and

Indira Gandhi Rashtriya Manav Sangrahalaya
Shamla Hills, Bhopal
Phones: 0755-2661290, 2661319
Fax: 91-755-2661458

Printed at: G. Print Process, Delhi.

Cataloging in Publication Data—DK
Courtesy: D.K. Agencies (P) Ltd. <docinfo@dkagencies.com>

Cultural heritage of Assam / [editors], Sarit K. Chaudhuri, Mini Bhattacharyya Thakur.
pages cm
Contributed articles.
Includes bibliographical references.
ISBN 9788121213424

1. Cultural property—India—Assam. 2. Assam (India)—Social life and customs. I. Chaudhuri, S. K. (Sarit Kumar), editor. II. Thakur, Mini Bhattacharyya, editor.

DS485.A852C85 2017 DDC 363.690954162 23

Contents

List of Tables

List of Figures

List of Contributors

— **Aparna Goswami,** Department of English D.K. College, Mirza.

— **Archana Barua,** Department of Humanities and Social Sciences Indian Institute of Technology Guwahati, Assam.

— **Archana Kalita,** Research Sholar, folklore Research Department, Gauhati University, Guwahati.

— **Binita Devi,** Junior Fellowship Award, Ministry of Culture, India.

— **Birinchi K. Medhi,** Formerly Professor, Department of Anthropology, Gauhati University, Guwahati-781014, Assam.

— **Chandana Sarma,** Assistant Professor in Anthropology, Cotton College, Guwahati.

— **Christene Bora,** Senior Research Fellow, Department of Anthropology, Cotton College, Guwahati-1, Assam.

— **Gangotri Bhuyan,** Research Scholar, Department of Anthropology, North-Eastern Hill University, Shillong-793022.

— **Gitika Saharia,** Post Graduate teacher, Khetrihardia H. S. School, Kamrup (Rural).

— **Gulrukh Begum,** Associate Professor Dept of Anthropology, Gauhati University, Guwahati.

— **Jilmil Bora,** Associate Professor, Department of English, Dakshin Kamrup College, Mirza 781125, Kamrup, Assam.

— **Kunal Choudhury,** Research Scholar, Department of Anthropology, Gauhati University, Guwahati.

— **Lipika Sarmah,** Programme Associate, SRC Dispur Guwahati-6.

— **Mini Bhattacharyya Thakur,** Professor and Head, Anthropology Department, Gauhati University, Guwahati.

— **Mondira Boruah,** Assistant Commissioner, SDO (C), Dhakuakhana, North Lakhimpur.

— **Monimugdha Bhuyan,** Lecturer, Department of Anthropology, North Lakhimpur College (Autonomous), North Lakhimpur - 787031, Assam.

— **Mridutpal Goswami,** Assistant Professor, Dept. of History, Dudhnoi College, Dudhnoi.

— **Moushumi Dutta Pathak,** Associate Professor Department of History, Arya Vidyapeeth College.

— **Mridul Das,** Assistant Professor, Pandu College, Guwahati-12.

— **Nancy C Malsawmtluangi,** Senior Research Fellow of Anthropology Department, Gauhati University.

— **Pankaja Dutta,** Research Scholar, Department of Anthropology, Gauhati University, Guwahati.

— **Paramita Kakati,** Dept. of Architecture Girls Polytechnic and Principal Assam Textile Institute, Guwahati.

— **Parismita Saikia,** Research Scholar, Department of Anthropology, Gauhati University, Guwahati-14, Assam.

— **Paromita Das,** Professor and Head, Department of History, Gauhati University, Guwahati.

— **Purabi Baruah Talukdar,** House No. 20 Neer Mahal, Bye lane 3-bir lachit path, Survey-Ajanta Path, Guwahati-28, Assam.

— **Ritu Geu Goswami,** National Institute of Public Cooperation and Child Development, Khanapara, Guwahati.

— **Rupa Barman Borgohain,** 33, Kharghuli, Guwahati-781004.

— **Rupashree Hazowary,** PhD student, Dept. of Folklore Research, Gauhati University, Guwahati.

— **R. P. Athparia,** Senior Fellow, Jagriti (2nd Floor), North Eastern Social Research Centre, Guwahati-5.

— **Sangeeta Kakoty,** Associate Professor (History), Arya Vidyapeeth College Guwahati-16.

— **Shabeena Yasmin Saikia,** Associate Professor, Department of Sociology Gauhati University.

— **Simanta Sarma,** HOD and Asstt. Professor, Department of Computer Science, SBMS College, Sualkuchi, Assam.

— **Tharsush K. Sangma,** Researcher, Don Bosco, Damra.

— **Tiluttoma Baruah,** Associate Professor, Department of Anthropology, Cotton College, Guwahati-1, Assam.

1

Introduction

— Sarit K. Chaudhuri, Mini Bhattacharyya Thakur

On a daily basis there has been a progressive loss – throughout the world by communities – of languages, knowledge, customs, and ideas, leading to a gradual impoverishment of human society. In August 2004, at a meeting organised by UNESCO in Tokyo, the Minister of Culture, Education, Science, and the Church of Greenland, stressed that in her country they 'have dozens of names for snow and ice because it is important to the hunters to differentiate them, but many children today know only a few of these names'(Lenzerini 2011). There are multitudes of such examples where communities lament the loss of their precious folktales, songs and dances, traditions, ritual practices and material artifacts. The Greenland example only epitomises our contemporary world, in the context of which the larger societies globalise. The obvious fear that globalisation will obliterate cultural boundaries and hence loss of ethnicity has been playing in the minds of communities and North-East India is no exception to it. In cultural terms, uniformity means not only loss of cultural heritage – both tangible and intangible–but also standardisation of the different peoples of the world and of their social and cultural identity into a few stereotyped ways of life, of thinking, and of understanding the world. Diversity of cultures reflects diversity of peoples; this is linked to Cultural heritage, especially Intangible Cultural Heritage, because such a heritage found in its folklore represents the living expression of the different communities.

An understanding of the cultural heritage of different communities is essential; it helps with intercultural dialogue, and encourages mutual respect for other's ways of life thus paving pathways toward inclusive participation, dispute prevention or resolution, peace building, and stability. This is critical to the situation of North-East India who has a long history of ethnic strife and cultural struggles in the region.

Cultural heritage also has an important role to play with regard to environmental sustainability. Traditional knowledge, values, and practices accumulated and renewed across generations as part of intangible cultural heritage have guided human societies in their interactions with the surrounding natural environment for millennia. Today, the contribution of intangible cultural heritage to environmental sustainability is recognised in many fields such as bio-diversity conservation, sustainable natural resource management, and natural disaster preparedness and response. The body of knowledge, values, and practices of intangible cultural heritage related to the environment has the capacity to evolve and adapt for more sustainable use of natural resources, enabling communities to better face natural disasters and the challenges of climate change.

UNESCO declaration has called for urgent action for safeguarding and preserving both tangible and intangible heritage. Cultural heritage as popularly understood does not end at monuments and collections of objects. It includes traditions or living expressions inherited from our ancestors and passed on to our descendants, such as oral traditions, performing arts, social practices, rituals, festive events, knowledge and practices concerning nature and the universe or the knowledge and skills to produce traditional crafts.

Keeping the above considerations in mind a three-day National seminar on Cultural heritage of Assam was organised in the Department of Anthropology, Gauhati University in collaboration with Indira Gandhi Rashtriya Manav Sangrahalaya, Bhopal, a national institute which has redefined the notion of museum in India. This seminar envisaged deliberating on some of the core components of the tangible and intangible cultural heritage of the state-Assam. It also includes traditions or living expressions of different ethnic communities living in Assam such as oral traditions, performing arts, social practices, rituals, festive events, knowledge and practices. According to Chutia (1984), " The credit for the first attempts towards bringing to light the rich cultural traditions of Assam and unraveling its significant and glorious past must go to a number of well-meaning British civil and military officers aided by some local people whose enquiries yielded astounding results. The attention of indologists was gradually drawn to this part of the country as a hidden treasures of antiquities, in the form of relics of ancient monuments, sculptures of the fine workmanship, epigraphs, coins, hoards of manuscripts, etc. bearing on the culture and ancient civilisation that existed in Assam and her neighborhood started coming to light by chance discoveries or by strenuous efforts of a few individual antiquarians."

The state of Assam in the north-east of India is a couldron of rich heritage of cultural and natural resources. It is one of the few places bestowed with remarkable diversities. It is the abode of good number of ethnic groups beside the caste and religious communities who have distinct linguistic and socio-cultural characteristics. Before coming of the Aryans, Assam was mostly inhabited by numerous tribes both in the hills and in the plains in different parts of the valley.

As time passed by, these tribal communities came closer to the Aryanised society mainly due to socio-economic and political reasons. But they retained their respective customs, traditions and practices (religious) along with their respective languages or dialects.

This plurality in the cultural heritage of Assam can be sensed in its history, archaeology, art, architecture, performing arts, oral tradition and numerous tangible and intangible aspects of the culture to mention few. The Neolithic and early cultural beginnings as evident from the findings from the erstwhile North Cachar hills and foothills of Assam-Meghalaya border that continued to that of megalithic and early historic traditions flourished to a phase of artifactual grandeur indicated by the famous Ambari site of ancient city of Guwahati. This unique cultural heritage of Assam having its root in the prehistoric past regained vitality in the ancient Kamrupa and in the subsequent period with the advent of the Ahom kings. The cult of the *shakti* and the tenets of *tantricism* which was in vogue in early Assam have its vivid reflections in the *Puranic* literature and traditions embedded in numerous shrines, monuments and temples scattered throughout the region. The germination of the geo-cultural concept of Assam is considered as a contribution of the long six hundred years of existence of the Ahom monarchy. The iconic saint Srimanta Sankardeva in the fifteenth century medieval Assam refurbished this legacy of the tradition with a touch of eternal retouching through the propagation of the doctrine of neo Vaishnavism. The mainstream socio religious life of the region was shaped by this historic event which culminated in the establishment of the significant cultural institutions surrounding neo Vaishnavite dormitories- the *sattra* in the largest river island Majuli being its focal seat. According to Neog (1959:31),"The great-neo-Vaisnava movement of Assam of the sixteenth century brought about a new and comprehensive outlook on life, a distinctly healthy tone to social behaviour with an all- pervasive organisational set-up, and accelerated the pace of literature and the fine arts like music and painting."

The state is endowed with palpable natural diversities that as understood anthropologically have its impact on the manifestation of multiple ethnographic entities. The hills and the valleys, the floodplains and the plateaus, the forests and the wetlands each endowed with distinct cultural entities speaks of the oft-quoted phenomenon of nature- culture relationship. This further exemplifies the biocultural significance of the region. The ethno diversities of the region can hardly be separated from the faunal and floral diversities that need to be understood in its totality for a meaningful reconstruction. A large number of tribes, each unique in their tradition, culture, dress and exotic way of life have inhabited varied ecological niches. Diverse tribes like Bodo, Kachari, Karbi, Miri, Mishimi, Rabha, etc co-exist in Assam. Most tribes have their own languages though Assamese is the principal language of the state.

In Assam, the caste system, although it exists, is not as prominent as in other parts of India. Other religions such as Buddhism, Christianity, Hinduism, Sikhism and Islam are also practiced in Assam. The national festival of Assam is the Bihu, which is celebrated three times during a year with great pomp and grandeur by all Assamese, irrespective of caste, creed or religion.

Muslims represent the largest minorities, followed by Nepalis and populations from neighbouring regions of India. From time immemorial, the people of Assam have traditionally been craftsmen, artists, sculptors, masons, weavers, spinners, potters, goldsmiths, artisans of ivory, wood, bamboo and cane to mention a few.

Weaving is one traditional craft that every Assamese woman takes pride in. The Assamese women produce silk and cotton clothes of exquisite designs in their looms. Assam is renowned for its exquisite silks namely Eri, Pat and the world famous Muga silk. The textile as an aspect of tangible heritage often joins the body and culture together (Sarmah, 2009). It reflects the cultural need of people at any given space and time. Here ecology has a great role to play as it determines the growth, development, form and function of textile and other items of material culture. The costumes, designs, motifs and hue symbolise the cultural identity of different ethnic groups since each group shows leaning towards certain colour and design in their clothes. The differences in the form of textile and motifs are the result of interaction among different culture, environment and technology. The type of costumes, their wearing style, colour and motifs identify the ethnic group, marital status, age and sex of a person. Most importantly it expresses the cultural aesthetics and mind of an individual. So, one group may easily be identified from other on the criteria of their dresses.

In rural area, the textile has not yet lost its traditional existence. It continues more or less unchanged albeit with some urban influence. Before it completely dies, it is the need of the hour to preserve the indigenous traditional textile and design, as they constitute the base of Assamese culture and society.

Modernisation in designs and technological change has been achieved in the handloom sector in Assam. The traditional throw-shuttle looms are now replaced gradually by improved type of fly-shuttle loom. On the other hand, the imagination and creativity of the weaver is gradually lost and depends totally on professional designer who break and alter the traditional motifs without any hesitation. Due to emergence of synthetic dyes, the traditional practice of dyeing, using natural ingredients are gradually vanishing. Moreover, the women-folk today find sericulture work laborious and time consuming. They used silk yarn imported from outside. The traditional practice of making various loom and accessories is also disappearing. Due to long co-habitation with diverse ethno-cultural groups various tribal elements come into Assamese costumes as well as in design. Different geometrical motifs of tribal costumes are now used as fashionable design on Assamese costumes (ibid.)

Metal craft comprises of one of the oldest cottage industries of Assam. Unique artistic skills of local artists and craftsmen of the state are mainly involved in designing brass and bell metal utensils. Sarthebari is famous for this craft specialisation. Wood carving, ivory work and jewellry making are some other crafts of Assam.

Assamese culture is laden with a vast repertoire of folklore comprising of oral folklore or folk literature which includes folk poem/song or oral/ verbal song- ballad, religious song, love song, working song, etc. Prose narratives in the form of myth, legend and folktale; proverb, saying, and maxim. Material culture includes folk crafts, folk art, folk architecture, folk costume and folk cookery. Performing folk art includes folk drama, folk music and folk dance. Festival and celebration, recreations and game, folk medicine, folk belief and religion constitute rich segments of culture. Looking at the wider canvas we like to mention clearly that a single volume is not enough to weave the complete picture of cultural heritage of a state like Assam. There are large number of books and alternative literature published in English, Assamese and other languages cutting across the disciplinary boundaries. Naturally, we tried to deal with its different core domains as reflected by various contributors of this volume, which may add value to our existing understanding on the variegated issues concerning the cultural heritage of Assam.

Aparna Goswami has dealt with one of the distinctive and popular performing tradition of Assam that are prevalent in the region of Lower Assam, known as Ojâpâli . She added that in this performance, the performers narrate a story with the accompaniment of music and dance along with a personal commentary. However, the main story which is traditionally narrated is highly flavoured with the present day context as the artists, 'Ojâ' and 'Pâli' comment on many socio-political issues in course of performance. The main story serves as the plot or framework around which the artists 'Ojâ' and 'Pâli' build a subtext depending upon the context and the socio-cultural milieu of their audience. She tried to reflect on how this art- form prevailed as a tool for creating social awareness though it is gradually becoming an endangered art form as younger generation not taking much interest.

Archana Barua primarily made an attempt at re-defining Caste, Tribe and Gender in 15th century Assam from the Neo-Vaishnavite Bhakti perspective of Mahapurush Srimanta Sankaradeva. She argued that the *Bhakti movement* in Medieval India was conspicuous by its plurality in which various forces, both conservative and radical authoritarian and protesting co-existed. But all of them gave new impetus to the *bhâsa* and none of them felt problem within the existing linguistic hierarchy. She tried to reveal how the leaders, irrespective of their lineage and social connections, made significant effect on the life of the common man in varying degrees for their concerns about religious institutions and the basic existential problems.

Archana Kalita focused on the richness of Assamese cuisine through exploration of various genres of folk literature and finally tried to deal with the question of women empowerment issue by linking it to diverse culinary heritage of the state.

Binita Devi and Simanta Sarma tried to deal with the puppetry of Assam by locating their functional utility in developing communication skill of the children. According to them puppetry is not merely an act of entertainment, rather it serves as an applied art, conveying meaningful messages of various art forms. Their contribution underscores how puppetry show may educate children through moral and historical stories enacted out by the puppets through various modes of communication.

It is a well-known fact that Bamboo is an integral part of Assamese socio-cultural life. Its multifarious uses as food, fuel, housing and building material, furniture, utensils and decorative items, fishing and weaving implements etc., have made it an indispensible material trait of the Assamese society. It has been rightly termed as 'cradle to coffin timber' and regarded as a cultural symbol of the Assam in specific and North-East as a region. Birinchi K. Medhi and Jilmil Bora tried to narrate the sacredness of this 'Green Gold' in the context of the Assamese society by focusing on the diverse ways of worshipping bamboo with causal explanation with special emphasis on *Bhatheli*.

The notion of 'Sacred complex' has a central place in Indian anthropology while dealing with Hinduism. A Hindu desires to visit some of the temples and shrines during his lifetime, which are distributed in various regions of India. Among such sacred complexes some occupy central places in the Hindu religion. There are some important religious centres of the Hindus in Assam that are integrally related to the nucleus of the Hinduism. Basistha is such a temple of Assam devoted to Lord Shiva, the most popular and widely worshipped Hindu god of India. This temple is situated in the capital city Guwahati of Assam. In different Holy Scriptures of the Hindus mention of Basistha is conspicuous and each year a good number of pilgrims and tourists visited the temple. Through their writing, Birinchi K. Medhi and Kunal Choudhury tried to examine the mythological, historical and contemporary importance of the Basistha temple in the context of Assam.

The Kaibartas, one of the Scheduled Castes of Assam, practice fishing as their primary occupation. On the basis of five village studies, Chandana Sarma tried to understand the relationship between economy and society of the Kaibartas in the context of normative coherence.

Through the village based empirical study, Christene Bora and Tiluttoma Baruah tried to show that the Sarania Kachari people of Kaljhar village belief in Hinduism. By reflecting on various rituals and festivals, such as, Baa Gosain festival; Gossainghar; Bambol pita puja; Moh Kheda festival; Chidra Gossain puja; Jaikuwari puja; Sop Bhanga puja; and Hunkar puja, they tried to establish the importance of the sacred domains to preserve these invaluable traditions for the coming generation so that they may have the same opportunities to learn about the past and also understand their own roots of identity.

Gangotri Bhuyan's paper discusses the issues of preserving cultural heritage for posterity, since the people, of the people and for the people, built the heritage of a place or community. Based on the study carried out especially in the museums and the monuments surrounding the Guwahati city he tried to understand the levels of awareness of the population towards places of heritage, and its conservation and finally gave stress on the importance of involvement of public for policy formulation.

Gitika Saharia wrote on the institution of Satra, a unique feature of Vaishnavism in Assam which was established by Sankardeva, the father of Satriya culture which are like medieval monasteries. Khatara Satra is one of the blessed sacred institutions having positive influence on religious and cultural aspects of Assam. In fact, his paper attempts to study the cultural tradition of Khatara Satra of Darrang District giving stress on the various performing traditions by locating its far- reaching impact on Vaisnavite culture.

Moushumi Dutta Pathak has dealt with partition-displaced Bengali Hindus in the context of post 1947, which witnessed the Sylhet Referendum over the question of the identity of Sylhet. Leading to the migration of population identified as the Partition-Displaced from Sylhet and other districts of East Pakistan to various parts of India. Obviously, Assam was once such province wherein large groups of such migrants came in. She has focused on this group of migrants as a part of the larger Bengali community having a distinctive culture.

Her paper seeks to explore into the level of cultural assimilation and integration of the displaced with the 'host' society. She tried to narrate the process of adaptation and assimilation that led to formation of Bengali 'ghettoes' or cultural islands and enclaves and finally has shown how they existed within the host society but were insular in their thoughts and practices.

Taking cue from the concept of 'Cultural Ecology', Mondira Boruah tried to underscore how the people of flood prone villages namely Chamarajan and Ujoni Kekuri in Assam negotiate their life through the year.

Monimugdha Bhuyan made an attempt to examine the dimensions of the village level Vaishnavite religious institution *namghar* of Majar Chapari Village and its impact among the Deori, a Scheduled tribe of Assam.

Mridul Das, made an attempt to write on the myths and other integrated dimensions of Kherai, one of the important festivals of the Bodos of Assam. He has tried to deal with the emerging dimensions of such performing tradition from contemporary perspective.

Mridutpal Goswami wrote on historicity of silk industry of Assam during colonial time, which is very central to understanding cultural heritage of Assam even in contemporary time.

Nancy Malswmtlungi and Mini Bhattacharyya Thakur have dealt with the rich festive heritage of the Kuki in Assam before the advent of Christianity. These festivals are no longer celebrated in Assam except *Chavang Kut* (post harvest festival), which is the only existing festival today.

Paramita Kakati seeks to demonstrate how strategies of orientation were inscribed in the folkloric tradition of Assam by bringing together architectural knowledge and vernacular oral heritage. She categorically mentioned that in historical literature on 'sciences' like architecture, as part of a 'rational' tradition, has tended to discredit vernacular modes of engaging with scientific manipulation of the environment as inferior and lacking the ability to use 'reason'. She attempted to question this basic assumption, and ultimately opined that there may be more 'reason' to the rhyme.

Based on both primary and secondary database, Parismita Saikia tried to highlight the variegated traditional food items and their method of preparation among the Mising community of Majuli. She also attempted to highlight the medicinal value of the food items.

Paromita Das as a historian has dealt with archaeological heritage of Guwahati city that stand mute witness to its history and culture since pre-colonial days. She revealed that while the Archaeological Survey of India and the Directorate of Archaeology have preserved many of these remains in the Assam State Museum and at designated protected sites, others have been partially or wholly destroyed by the actions of time, nature and man.

As we know that folklore is an indispensible part of culture and it represents what people preserve in their culture throughout the generation by words as well as customs. Therefore, Folklore is important at least for those who create it and also who transmit it. Purabi Barua Talukdar adds that the lore of folk people is transmitted through orally by means of folk tales or narratives over generation after generation without knowing the authorship. That is how a knowledge structure continues and binds a group socially. According to her, most of the oral forms incorporate performances or some activities to get more connected. *Ojâ-pâli*, an epic singing performance of Assam is such an example of performance to reach the public. It basically recites or narrates traditional verse along with rhythmic movement. In the paper, Purabi Barua Talukdar, has been dealt with a case study of variant of *Ojâ-pâli* prevalent among Rabha tribe of Assam whose transmission of orality is found in indigenous religious faith. Author believed that such research findings might lead to the preservation and promotion of community culture.

Ritu Geu Goswami and Mini Bhattacharyya Thakur presented a discursive narrative of food habit and indigenous cuisines of the Karbi tribe of Assam based on empirical study.

On the basis of fieldwork among the Bodos located under three out of the four districts of BTAD, namely, Kokrajhar, Chirang and Udalguri, R P Athparia tried to deal with matrimonial laws and their impact on their women.

Rupa Barman Borgohain tried to look at the distinctive customs as well as tradition of the Bodos of Assam to evaluate the importance of their rootedness and also harped on the recent history of the Bodos and the role of the state to understand and evaluate the precise nature of the problems they are facing.

Rupashree Hazowary tried to explore the origin and dances of the *Kherai* and different aspects of such performance in the traditional context and the changing trend of such combination of dances among the Bodos of Assam.

Sangita Kakoty's paper is a humble attempt on the part of the scholar to investigate what space has been allocated to women in the scenario of Theater in Assam. It is an accepted fact that it was Srimanta Sankardeva who gave birth to drama in Assam in the 15th Century though even before that, from times immemorial semi- dramatic folk performances like *Ojapali, Kushangaan, Bharigaan, Posoti* etc have enriched the cultural arena of Assam. She added that young males in Sankardeva's unparalleled creation, Ankiya Bhaona, enacted female roles and even the *Jatra* that came in from Bengal had the same story. In the context of the patriarchal society she raised certain basic questions linked with such cultural heritage of Assam.

Shabeena Yasmin Saikia explained that the Karbis of Guwahati although shares a number of cultural/ethnic markers with the other Karbis of the plains of Assam and to a certain extent with the hill Karbis, these elements of cultural heritage are undergoing transformation within the fast changing context of urbanisation of Guwahati in the past four decades. In his paper he attempted to comprehend the nature of these changes as well as their identity maintenance processes.

The Garos are one of the tribal communities living in the state of Assam though they are the dominant tribe of Meghalaya.The Garo people generally observe number of traditional festivals and ceremonies though they have abandoned many due to multiple reasons. Tharsush K. Sangma tried to give a quick overview on those fast disappearing social and religious festivals of the Garos living in Assam.

References

Chutia,D. (1984) Preface, in *Readings in the History and Culture of Assam*, Kamrupa Anusandhana Samity, Guwahati.

Lenzerini, F(2011) Intangible Cultural Heritage: The Living Culture of Peoples. Eur J Int Law (2011) 22 (1): 101-120.

Neog,M. (1959) *The Vaisnava Renaissance in Assam, Aspects of the Heritage of Assam: A souvenir*, Indian History Congress, Gauhati, pp. 31-49.

Sarma, Jayanta Deva(2009) *Changing perspectives of textiles of Assam with special reference to Kamrup District* (Unpublished Ph.D thesis) Department of Folklore, Gauhati University, Guwahati-781014.

2

The Role of Ojãpãli in Creating Social Awareness and the Need to Reinstate it in the Modern Assamese Society

— *Aparna Goswami*

Introduction to the North-East: Land and People

North-East India, geographically and topographically distinct from the mainland India has a peculiar identity of its own. It is a region of myriad variety of cultures as it has settlers from diverse parts of the land as some are from the regions like Kanouj in central India while some are from the ancient Mongol regions. All have contributed in building the composite culture of the region by adding to it the nuances of their respective traditions. While the earliest inhabitants were supposed to be different indigenous tribes of the Mongoloid stock like the Boros, Rabhas, Tiwas, Lalungs, Garos, Khasis, Hazongs, Tai-Turungs, Madahis, some Sonowal Kacharis etc., the coming of the Aryans in historical times and the resultant intermix gave the area the demographic character it has today. Today these indigenous communities, the non-tribal Hindus of different castes, some people subscribing to Islam and Buddhism and some other groups, inhabit the region. It is largely due to this, that the caste or community division in this area is not as rigid as in other parts of India. (Goswami: 2013)[1] The region has always been looked upon as 'An anthropologist's paradise' for its rich diversity of ethnic culture and is also considered 'A linguist's paradise' due to its multilingual continuum. Around forty five different languages are spoken by different communities in and around this area which is the meeting place of three different language families as per the available data: Austro-

Asiatic (5), Sino-Tibetan (24) and Indo-European (12). Out of these different languages, Assamese has been performing the role of the lingua franca among the different indigenous communities (Goswami: 2013)[1]. Well-known anthropologists like Verrier Elvin made this land their abode in order to study the reflection of this diversity in the lifestyle of the countless tribes belonging to the region. Each of the tribes has its distinctive traditional attire, weaving patterns, dwelling structures, folklore, legends, art forms, and material aspects of culture in form of various artifacts which have always attracted scholars from worldwide to undertake research.

Introduction to the Performing Art Form Ojāpāli

Each of the North-Eastern state has its distinctive dance form along with some unique performing art forms Ojāpāli is a popular performing art form in the lower Assam. In its performance, some interconnected stories are narrated with the accompaniment of music and dance along with a personal commentary by the performers. There are five to six performers in a troop in which Ojā the leader is accompanied by his 4-5 pālis.The term Ojāpāli consists of two words, 'Ojā' and 'Pāli'. The word 'Ojā' emanates

from the Sanskrit term Upādhyāya and connotes the chief singer of the Ojāpāli chorus. The word 'Pāli' is a Sanskrit term suggesting the assistant of the 'Ojā'. (Sarma: 2011:46)[4]. At times the dialogues between the 'Ojā' and 'Pāli' give the audience a feel of watching a drama. In a way, Ojāpāli can be considered as an antecedent of the mobile theatre of Assam. There are seven types of Ojāpāli performance based on the thematic differences. *Vyāsa Ojāpāli* also known as *Vyās Sāngeet* is considered as the original classical form from which the other variations are believed to have emanated. The *Vyās Ojāpāli* uses classical ragas. Tradition goes that this art form uses six *ragas* and thirty six kinds of *raginis*. (Sarma: 1988: p. 32)[5] In the performance of it the leader Ojā narrates the stories from the famous epics of Bhāgvata, Mahabharata and Harivansa; following the Vaishnava cult of Assam, while interacting with Pāli who accompanies him with the help of cymbals, also known as bhor-tāl. Beside the Vaishnava tradition, in Assam there is Sākta tradition too which believes in the worship of female deities like Manasā as presented in Sukanāni form of Ojāpāli. The main story which is narrated in traditional form is highly flavoured with the present day context as both 'Ojā' and 'Pāli' comment on many socio-political issues in their interaction in the course of performance. The main story serves as the plot or framework around which the artists 'Ojā' and 'Pāli' build a subtext depending upon the context and the socio-cultural milieu of their audience. This is how the art-form prevailed as a tool for creating social awareness and is still functioning mostly in villages even in the age of improved modern information technology.

Manner and Mode of Presentation

Though the art-form Ojāpāli was initially associated with various religious rituals or with certain rituals to be performed for the appeasement of deities like goddess Manasā, its performances took a secular tone as well as subject matter to fit into the change in social order. The decline in the stronghold of religion in Assamese society can be traced to some extent by the growing secular notes in the dialogues in a performance. Therefore, we can make two broad divisions of the art-form: One that is based on the epics; while the other that is not based on epics and has rampant folk elements in it. In ancient times the performances were held in the premises of the temples and the plot of the performance was based on the stories of the epics interspersed with personal interpretations. The performances based on epics have further variations on the basis of religious sects like Sāivas (the worshippers of Lord Shiva) following the Sākta tradition and Vaishnavas (the worshippers of Lord Vishnu/Krishna) following the Vaishnava tradition. Then as far as the stylistic elements are concerned, we find some more variations in it on the basis of geographical regions namely, Darrang, Nalbari and Kamrup districts. Irrespective of these differences at thematic as well as stylistic level the basic norms of the performance are common for all the types. The performance combines narrative singing and dancing interspersed with dramatic dialogue and action. The Ojā is the main narrator-singer and is regarded as the head artiste while the pālis are his assistants in the performance. One of the Pālis is regarded as the chief assistant Daina Pāli (right-hand assistant) who initiates the dialogues by asking the Ojā various questions on different matters. The primary goal of any Ojāpāli performance is the narration of a story and the recitation of songs and verses with pleasurable association of dance and music. Differences in terms of narration, recitation of songs or verses and the style of presentation are but quite natural in different Ojāpāli performances based on varied contexts. Such variations have resulted in the growth and development of different forms of Ojāpāli. (Paraphrase from: Sarma: 1996)[3]

Importance of the Dress Code

The performers of an Ojāpāli troop follow a peculiar dress code which sets them apart from the spectators and helps in creating a distancing effect. As the Ojā and his assistants appear before the audience in their traditional dress the air of familiarity or former acquaintance vanishes and the mood of the gathering is set for receiving the message of the performers. Abhinaya or acting is an inevitable part of the performance along with the other arts like singing, dance and accompaniment of music. The Pālis accompany the Ojā's song with khutitāl or bhor-tāl. The dress code that they follow has a symbolic significance. The turban that the Ojā wears represents Vishnu; the tilaka that beautifies his forehead is believed to be the dwelling place of Mother-Bhakti. He puts the silk-coat (chāpkan) on the outer part of the S′iva-mûlādhāra. Māyā resides in his ear-rings and in his bangle. Brahma Prājapati dwells in the scarf that hangs on the either side of his neck. Goddess Ganga appears in the form of anklet and Goddess Saraswati reveals herself in the form of the girdle. Thus, the Ojā (especially the Vyāsa Ojā emerges in the form of a Gandharva. (Sarma: p. 36)[5] The spectators, mainly the village folk, believe that divine performers have come down to the earth. The message imparted by them then becomes more effective as the spectators listen to them more attentively.

Secular Elements in the Art Form

As stated earlier, Ojāpāli performances started from the temple premises but in the due course of time they reached out to the masses as the performances were later held even outside the temples in open spaces where the subject matter tended to be more and more secular. In the initial stage, in Vyās-Sangeet or Vyās-Ojāpāli, Ojā was selected from the Brahman community and therefore the descendants of a Brahman family could function as Ojās. This fact can be validated through the copper plates issued by kings to the representatives of distinguished Brahman communities. The language of discourse in the initial stage of the art form was Sanskrit. However, in later times such norms were slightly relaxed and persons from other communities could also become Ojās provided that they possessed necessary skills for the performance and the language used by the common people became the medium of communication. Though the form of Vyās-Ojāpāli is prevalent in the district of Darrang, some uncommon sub-types like Dhepadhûl also emerged at various points of times. The subject matter of these performances commemorates various historical occasions such as the peasants revolt during the British reign that took place in various places in the later part of the nineteenth century. In a field-study undertaken by the investigator in Darrang district near Sipajar in an interior place called

Dhokapara, informants Balaram Deka (aged 75) and Lohit Saharia (aged 74) revealed the fact that the details of the peasant's revolution that took place at Patharughat in the later part of the nineteenth century are incorporated in the Ojāpāli songs of the region. The pathetic story of the merciless firing by the British on the revolutionaries near the river Digaj and the hopeless attempts of their escape by jumping into the river are recorded in the songs and are consequently transferred from one generation to another. Thus, in this particular context, Ojāpāli serves as the medium of transmitting historical events from the local history of a relatively small region to the masses who might otherwise remain ignorant about the historical background. In the course of dramatic dialogues, Ojā and Dainapāli might interact on the importance of fighting for one's rights and thereby sensitise the people about their rights. Though the context changes, it is often said that 'history repeats' and it is likely that the people of the present times might need to face the similar problems that their forefathers faced years back. In such eventualities, it is always better for the people to know how their ancestors reacted to various social issues like invasion, immigration, exploitation and many other challenges of their times.

Function of Social Awareness

The above cited example of the reference to the exploitation of the farmers during the British reign that appears in the Ojāpāli songs focuses on the role of the art-form in creating public awareness. The secular nature of the art form permits it to include contemporary issues as part of its subject matter so as to suit to the taste of the audience as well as to the need of the time. It however depends upon the awareness of the Ojā about the currents of thoughts running in his society. If the contemporary problems are handled well and some kind of message can be imparted to ensure harmony in the society, the purpose behind the performance gets fulfilled in the real sense of the term as the audience gain information or knowledge along with entertainment. Sometimes, at the time of social unrest it serves as a tool to bring back harmony in society. Some interviews taken by the investigator at a place called Jagara in the district of Nalbari revealed the role of Ojāpāli as a social stabiliser during the time of Assam Movement, a very powerful movement fought for the identity of the Assamese race that had caused a considerable havoc as the sentiments of the activists went out of control thereby causing a threat to the law and order in the state.

Apparently a performance meant for solemnising certain religious rituals, for appeasing deities or used as a form of entertainment in social gatherings it served to calm down the public sentiment through its philosophical discussions and ensured peace in the society. The interviews of people in Nalbari district also revealed a custom of organising an Ojāpāli performance to solemnise the *Shradhhās* (rituals to be performed in the honour of the dead). The stories narrated by the Ojā on such occasions deal with the inevitability of death, the fact of mortality, divine justice, well wishes for the departed soul etc. so as to console the members of the family through philosophical exchanges. This information proves that Ojāpāli performances are not meant only for the festivities like the onset of the New Year (*Bohāg Bihu*) or festivals like *Durga Puja* or *Ras* but they also serve the purpose of consoling the distressed people in the community.

Ojāpāli as an Agent of Social Change

The above discussion on the role of Ojāpāli art form in the lives of the people of Assam (especially lower Assam) has many dimensions besides entertainment. It helps in strengthening the bond between people in the society through the social interchange that is facilitates during the performance and ensures harmony. In spite of the growing web of connectivity and the spread of audio-visual media; people, especially the village-based people, look upon this art form as a source of 'edutainment' for it educates the masses along with the entertainment. On the backdrop of the present social unrest caused by the sensitive matters like demands of separate territories by certain communities or various demonstrations by some groups fighting for their identity, people can again rely upon this age old art form to bring back the sense of stability and security in the mindsets of the masses through the effective preaching of the Ojās.

Problems Faced by the Performers

However, a painful truth about the plight of the performers came to light in the course of some interviews conducted by the investigator in Darrang district. These performers do not seem to get much recognition or financial aid by the government though they admitted having received some accessories required for their performance from Srimanta Sankardev Kalakshetra. Perhaps this feeling of negligence appears to have dissuaded the youths from joining the troops as it may not bring much dividends nor will guarantee strong public acclaim. Some veteran members of the Dhepadhûliya Dal in Dhokapara run by Mr. Bipin Deka (aged 76) complained of the lack of interest that the younger generation showed towards the art as their efforts of training the youths in the art that they themselves have been performing since over five decades were met with reluctance. They feared that the art form might be extinct if the members of the greater community do not take any note of the receding interest among the budding performers who actually should mold the art form to suit the needs of the time and help in its continuation. This younger generation needs to be trained in order to ensure the preservation of this art form on the face of various changes brought in the society as a part of modernity. If proper incentives are given and if the troops get sufficient limelight though media like television, the art form can get its lost glory back as it will get a broader avenue.

Comparison of Ojāpāli with Keertan, a Performing Art Form of Maharashtra

Though in the North East India, Ojāpāli is a unique art form as far as its manner, mode and style of presentation is concerned, surprisingly it has its kin art form in the western parts of India, in the state of Maharashtra known as Keertan. Irrespective of the socio-economic as well as political diversity and the geographical distance and diversity between the two regions namely, Assam and Maharashtra, the two art forms bear a striking resemblance in their context, manner and mode of presentation. Not only do their thematic and stylistic aspects match but the evolutions that the art form faced in the course of various social upheavals also follows a similar graph except for the fact that Maharashtrian art form Keertan is a little less secular than its Assamese counterpart Ojāpāli.

A Brief Description of *Keertan as a Performing Art Form*: *Keertan* as a performing art form mainly intends to undertake spiritual teaching through story-telling which is typically performed by one or two main performers called *'Keertankar'* along with the accompaniment of harmonium and *Tabla* musicians. It involves singing, acting, dancing and story-telling. It stands out among other performing arts by the virtue of its pure glorification of God and godly acts. *Keertans* are traditionally performed at the temples and other holy places. However, the changing trends have brought it out in the public forum as a result of wide popularity and circulation. If we consider the history of *Keertan* as a performing art form as practiced in the last four hundred years, we find it being used as a tool for mass education. Apart from its status as an age-old form of devotion, we often find its performers using it as a medium to reach out to the masses and to keep them updated about the things happening around them and train them in good values of life. The themes of *Keertan* are often philosophical and certain existential questions like the purpose of human life are addressed in its purview. {Paraphrase from Pathak, Y.(1980)}[2]

Thus, we can safely say that both the forms bear a strong likeness. However, in the course of time *Keertan* has got a wider scope and has reached even abroad. There are institutions for the purpose of training youths in this traditional art form. In order to gain such a wider currency, the art form has enhanced its flexibility by introducing a few changes suiting to the changing times. It has come out of its orbit of male dominion and has included female '*Keertankars'* with an equal zest. This feature is not perceived in Ojāpāli as female performer in the role of the Ojā is a rarity.

Female Participation in Ojāpāli Performance: In an Ojāpāli performance females generally perform shamanistic dances beside the Ojā in an accompaniment of his narration. Although womenfolk are not allowed to act as Ojā and Pāli and present performances, in the context of Manasā worship celebrated privately or publicly, they can sing songs from the *Padmapurana* in the context of the *Manasā Vrata* in the sitting position without cymbals or drum. The leader of the troop is called *Ojeni* and her assistant is known as *Dhareti.* Normally men folk do not participate in such performances. Even the spectators of these performances are exclusively women. (Sarma: 2011: p. 50)[4] If the upcoming generations of Ojāpāli overcome this gender bias they will get a broader choice about the possible performers.

Conclusion

In view of the above deliberation, it appears to be our foremost responsibility to reinstate the diminishing status of our valuable art form *Ojāpāli* by taking some concrete steps to preserve this heritage of ours. If we gauge the status of its parallel art form *Keertan* mentioned above, we get a quite heartening picture. In case of Maharashtrian art form *Keertan*, attempts on the part of performers as well as connoisseurs have come to fruition and as a result many universities in Maharashtra have started offering courses in *Keertanshastra* (a systematic study of Keertan as an art-form). Therefore, it is possible for one to make career in the art form irrespective of gender. This folk art form which was limited to the state alone has reached out at an international level. If we can take our art form Ojāpāli to a similar status it will be a great honour for the Assamese identity as well as for Assam at large.

Though the initial wave of modernism caused disintegration or dislodgement of traditional cultures, there has also been a reaction by many social groups to retain their identity which has been termed as contra-acculturation by some anthropologists. Such groups have been frantically searching for their roots which they have generally discovered in their folk traditions. If the same happens with Ojāpāli, the age-old art form of Assam it will be a great contribution towards preserving the identity of Assamese community on the face of the changes brought about by the era of globalisation.

References

Goswami, B.J. (2013), *A Semiotic Study of Assamese Folktales from Lower Assam:* (PhD Thesis) ch. 4.3, pp. 144, 145.

Pathak, Y. (1980), *Nachu Keertanache Rangi:* Continental Prakashan Pune.

Sarma, N.C. (1996), *Ahomor Parivesyākala Ojāpāli*: publised by Bani Prokash Ltd., Guwahati.

Sarma, N.C. (2011), *Introduction to the Folklore of North-East India*: pub by Bani. Prokash Ltd., Guwahati, pp. 46, 50.

Sarma N.C. (1988), *Essays on the Folklore of North Eastern India:* Arunoday Press, Silpukhuri, Guwahati, pp. 32, 36.

3

An Attempt at Re-defining Caste, Tribe and Gender in Fifteenth Century Assam from the Neo-Vaishnavite Bhakti Perspective of Mahapurush Srimanta Śankaradeva and its Emphasis on Democratisation of *Bhakti*

—*Archana Barua*

Mahapurush Srimanta Śankardeva inspired the Bhakti movement in Assam just as Guru Nanak, Ramananda, Kabir, Basava and Chaitanya Mahaprabhu inspired it elsewhere in the Indian subcontinent. Even among these giants of men, Śankaradeva stands apart if only because of his versatility, he is a poet, a musician, an artist, a dramatist, an admirable producer-director of plays and stage decorator, and of course a great scholar in Sanskrit who chose to write in the vernacular medium so that the masses are benefitted by these works that depict the glory of *bhakti* and *bhakta.* In the words of the celebrated Oriental scholar Dr Suniti Kumar Chatterjee: "Śankaradeva gave to Assam a new discipline of faith in a single divinity, and helped Assam to break away with a past with its complicated esoteric doctrines and unmeaning practices and gave to the people something simple and straightforward, divested of all questionable associations or implications. He was the greatest builder of Assam by bringing in a purer spiritual life, and although circumstances prevented his influence from being spread into other parts of India, as a religious leader he is unquestionably one of the greatest India has produced, and he deserves to be mentioned with Sankaracharya, Ramanujācharya, Basavappa, Ramananda, Kabir, Chaitanya, Mira Bai, Guru Nanak and Tulsidas. Unlike Basavanna,

Chaitanya, Tulsi or Narsimehta, all of whom were Brahmins. Kabir belonged to the lower strata of the society, like Kanakadasa, theVaishnaba poet of Karnataka whose initiation by Vyasa Ray created a furore among the Brahmins or like Tukaram, or Dadu or Nam-alwar, the great Tamil Saint poet. He was truly the medium through whom the spiritual light of Medieval India as a whole shone upon the life of Assam."[1]

The *Bhakti movement* in Medieval India was conspicuous by its plurality in which various forces, both conservative and radical authoritarian and protesting coexisted. But all of them gave new impetus to the *bhāsa* and none of them felt problem within the existing linguistic hierarchy. But all the leaders, irrespective of their lineage and social connections, made significant effect on the life of the common man in varying degrees for their concerns about religious institutions and the basic existential problems. Despite limitations and contradictions in their life and action the Bhakta reformers remain a source of hope and courage and comfort to the millions. In Śankaradeva it was his way of transcending the barriers of the givens, of caste, class and gender, by transforming oneself to devotee, a *bhakta*, who can even purify *mantra, murti* and *tirtha*, and above all, who can re-discover his true essence as a *bhakta* of the One compassionate Isvara. Sankaradeva thus left behind him a section of dignified humans, the select group of *úaraniyābhakats*, religious heads mostly from the aboriginal tribes of the communities such as *Nagas, Garos* and from some underprivileged castes like *Hiras, Kaivartas*, *Bhutias* who were thus placed on equal footing with other high-caste leaders of the community. Sankaradeva even admitted Muslims into his sect, like Jayhari, who became *Atoi* (religious head) of his Muslim converts. Śankaradeva is thus closer in spirit with other *bhakta saints* of India who sang the glory of man while singing the glory of God. Ramananda declared thus *: Jāti- pātipuchahunāhi koi, Harikobhajai so Hariko hoi*! But in real life these remain as ideal teachings as the followers soon fall prey to the existing patterns of caste, creed, and the discriminations. Assam proved an exception in this regard that the *sattra* institution, attached with Vaishnavism, did not acknowledge caste hierarchy till some *sattras* succumbed to feudal pressures at a later time. For the first time the tribes and the ethnic communities in Assam had a taste of free and dignified life with a strong sense of belongingness to a community in which they all were treated alike.

Introducing Mahapurush Sankaradeva in the Context of Assam and its Place in India

Although it is a common approach to Hinduism as a juxtaposition of opposing elements, variously seen as the great and the little traditions, an explanation of change in terms of the interaction of two disparate traditions ignores the internal dynamic of the Hindu tradition itself (Cantlie : 1984).[2] It is a truism of some kind that we try and understand the cultural scene in India by using the two supposedly dichotomous notions of 'main stream' and 'marginality', that since India is a nation, then in some, as yet, invisible, but profound sense, it must also be uncultured. Noted scholar Mrinal Miri observes: 'It is inappropriate and potentially dangerous to understand cultural Indian terms of the metaphors of 'mainstream' and 'marginality'. In the case of the main stream and the tributaries which flow into it, the latter's place of origin does, in fact, literally make a great deal of difference to their natures, and when they do flow into the main stream, the main stream is not what it was before either. Take the marvellously different natures of the tributaries of the great river Brahmaputra and the difference which is made to them by the sources which keep them running, and the difference each of them makes to the nature of the great river itself. The river Brahmaputra would certainly not be what it is, but for its tributaries.' The scholar submits: "Diversity does not, as I have tried to suggest at various points, imply mutual exclusion. Our cultural boundaries are fluid and 'messy'."[3] The main stream and its margin metaphor works in a manner that many of us are not aware of the great contributions made by this great son of mother India, and of Assam and the entire Northeast, once known as *Bor Axom, Mahapurush Srimanta* Sankaradeva, who, for the people of this part of the world, is the father figure, the friend, philosopher and the spiritual guide of the people that he is not only the Mahapurush for these people irrespective of caste, creed and religion, but is still the revered "great – grand father", "*Eebudhou –Shankerdev*"[4] for the people of Manipur as well. "The Bhagavatic religious movement he started, Ekasarana Dharma and also called Neo-Vaishnavite movement, influenced two medieval kingdoms—Koch and the Ahom kingdoms—and the assembly of devotees he initiated evolved into Sattras over time, which continue to be important socio-religious institutions in Assam and to a lesser extend in North Bengal. His influence spread even to some kingdoms as the Matak Kingdom founded by Bharat Singha, and consolidated by Sarbanda Singha in the later eighteenth century endorsed his teachings."[5]

In the words of Dr R. K. Dasgupta: "If any great religious leader and poet has received much less attention than he deserves, he is Sankaradeva (1449–1568), the founder of Assamese Vaishnavism and one of the finest writers of devotional verse in Indian literature. It is indeed very curious that J. N. Farquhar's *An Outline of the Religious Literature of India* (1920), a work of four hundred and fifty pages, which is a sourcebook of our sacred literature, does not mention Sankaradeva either in the text or in its long, descriptive bibliography of Vaishnava writings. No less curious is the fact that Estlin Carpenter has no occasion to refer to him in his *Theism in Medieval India* (1921). When eight years later, Ksitimohan Sen gave his lectures on medieval mysticism of India in Calcutta University, he ignored the great Assamese mystic, and there is not a word on him in the English version of the lectures published in London in 1935."[6] Failing to understand why it is so, Dr Dasgupta finally submits: "But our indifference to the great Vaishnava poet of Assam remains. There is not a line on Sankaradeva in the *Penguin Anthology of Indian Literature* (1971) of more than six hundred pages, and very rarely do we see any verse of this poet in the works on Indian literature that we read. Dr V. Raghavan has drawn our attention to the Assamese poet by including three of his fine lyrics, two *Bargits* and a *Kirttana-Ghosa*, in his *The Great Integrators* (1965), and he has taken care to mention him as "a predecessor of Chaitanyadeva of Bengal." It is reassuring to see that Dr Dusan Zbavitel does not say anything more about Sankaradeva's links with Chaitanya than that he met him at a theological discussion."[7] The usual way is to look for a possible *Guru-sisya* link between Brahmin *Bhakta Saint* Sri Chaitanya Mahaprabhu and *Sudra Guru* in Assam, Mahapurush Śankaradeva!

Sankaradeva and his Assam: Tribes, Castes and Beyond

Born in the *Āhin* (September-October) month in 1371 S*akābda* (1449 AD) at *Ali Pukhuri* near Bordowa, the present-day Nagaon district of Assam, Sankaradeva, who would one day bar idolatry from his religion, had himself grown up in a Tantricism mixed Shakta environment that demanded the offering of blood to the Devi (Goddess). The Saint lost both his father Kusumvara Bhuyan and his mother Satyasandhya Devi at a very tender age and was raised by his grandmother Khersuti. He married his first wife Suryavati when he was in his early 20s. Soon after his daughter was born his wife died and Sankaradeva's encounter with the tragic and the apparently meaningless sense of life is complete.

"...Wealth and family are illusory,
so are life, youth, and this our world.
Wife and children are all insubstantial,
Whom shall I rely upon?
This my soul is as fickle
as the water on floating lotus leaves,
and never at rest for a moment.
Immersed in the enjoyment of worldly pleasures,

I feel no direct touch of Thy Supreme Feet..."
(Sankaradeva's Bargeet: Songs celestial)

Few years later, after finding a suitable match for his daughter, as requested by his dear departed wife, he set out, like Buddha, to find out the answer. For twelve long years he roamed around India, meeting scholars, holy people, musicians and the like trying to find how the wise and the creative people find meaning in life and try to link with God. Sankaradeva completed his pilgrimages to the holy places of the land and he found that the true India resides at the heart of the devotees, he saw the humanitarian aspect of the lived dimension of religiosity, across all external boundaries, to be deeply imbibed in the deeper psyche of the land: the land sanctified by the humblest of the humble devotees of God and of men, and how the common masses were inspired by the devotional songs of Kabir, Nanak, and others, and their humanitarian zeal...And he re-discovered the soul of this holy land in religiosity, in devotional hearts of the multitudes. Śankaradeva re-discovered the *Bharatvarsha* of his quest and sings her glory and the glory of the present *Iron Age*, although the most corrupt and condemned by all, it too has a little saving grace of its own. In this age, in this holy land, anyone who sings the glory of God is liberated if one has a mind steadfast in God, and sees God in all! What else one aspires for? Why one needs to be a Brahmin then, he wonders? And he sings the glory of his wonderful motherland, the land of *Bharatas*, the holy land of the '*bhaktas*' at heart: "Glory to be born as man in *Bharatvarsha* in the *Kali* age!" From Sankaradeva onward the poets of different ages have been singing the glory of India. Madhavadeva sings.

Dhanya Dhanya Kalikal Dhanya Naratanu Bhal
Dhanya Dhanya Bharatvarisha[8]

Śankaradeva thus found the true essence of this pious land that could nurture all differences in a spirit of love and tolerance and he also found the true essence of all religions that is based only on one principle, the principle of love and tolerance. His *Eka Sarana Naama Dharma* could proclaim this truth to his lost countrymen that "devotion to God was not a business transaction, where one invested pragmatically with many gods to harvest rich dividends in return. Instead, true devotion was total submission to the Supreme God with deep and absorbing love.[9] A true devotee is one who takes utmost refuge at God's feet, *kāya-bākya-mané*, and leads a dutiful life with a sense of complete dedication to the Lord. In similar vein Sant Tukaram sang the glory of *bhakti* and *bhakta* thus: "Worthy of worship is the family and sacred is the land where are born true devotees of the Lord."

In order to give voice to the voiceless Sankaradeva opted for a softer and a tolerant version of Hinduism. On account of such liberal attitudes it could make itself acceptable to the various indigenous tribal communities of region. The basic spirit of *Ek Sarana Nām Dharma* is to reaffirm and to firmly re-assert the centrality of the path of *bhakti* and of *bhakta*, and to be firmly rooted in the unvitiated and at the same time exclusive devotion to the One. Sankaradeva prescribes the supremacy of the *Bhakti Path* and of *Bhakti-Dharma* not only as a means to an end, but also as the end in itself, and that, he says, is the true essence of the Bhagavata. "People interpret the *Bhagavata*," says Sri Krishna, according to their own whims. They find sanction for everything except Bhakti. Some make it out that the Vedas inculcate ceremonials, sacrifices, gifts, and oblations; others that the Vedas prescribed the worship of smaller gods, pilgrimages and bathing in sacred waters; others again, that the supreme bliss comes through knowledge. Their interpretations are coloured by the dominant attributes of their minds. But, know thou this, my friend, I am not accessible through knowledge nor through penance, nor through renunciation, nor through gifts, I am not accessible by Yoga nor by knowledge, I am accessible by *Bhakti* alone."[10] The essence of the teachings of Śankaradeva as contained in his *Kirtana-ghosa*, *Bhakti-ratnakara*, and those of his spiritual successor, Madhavadeva, is devotion to *Harinama.* That *bhakti* alone is the means and the end that keeps no room for any other means of God realisation other than *bhakti.* Rather *bhakti* alone is the means and the goal, while other means of God realisation remain incomplete unless *bhakti* complements these paths.

One of the prime objectives of *Ek Sarana Dharma* is to reverse the existing norms of social hierarchy by opening the path of *bhakti* to one and all, especially the left out and the neglected ones in a Hindu society. In his scheme of *bhakti,* it is the *Bhakat* (a devotee*),* even from low caste, is superior in status than any one born in high caste but who is not a devotee of the Lord. Śankaradeva was a revolutionary in the true sense of the term when he boldly declared that everyone has a right to enter the path of *bhakti. Abhakta* is the one who can purify *tirtha, murti* and even *mantra* [*Udaracaritanaamtuvasudhaivakutumbakam* (*Vishnu Purana*)]. With the introduction of the institutions of Nāma-ghar and Satra the 'temple culture' almost came to an end in Assam and Assam has produced a culture in which the dividing line between the tribes (plains tribes) and the non-tribes is rather thin. Śankaradeva writes in the Kirttana:

> 'Who understand the words of Krishna'
> What need no be by birth a Brahman?

Let him only remember Hari by day and by night,
Bhakti does not care if he has a caste or not'.[11]

Bhakti Democratised: *Eka Śarana Nām Dharma* and its Compassion for the *Sudra* and *Stree*

Many scholars have noticed a striking similarity between the techniques of propagation of ideas and Sankaradeva in his fight against the reigning orthodoxy. As against the *Brahminical* orthodoxy and conservatism, neo-Vaishnavism advocated simplicity and liberalism in religious practice. Sankaradeva's life provides a fine example of this power equation. He had invited opposition of the *Shakta-Tantrikas* by his vigorous rejection of the *Tantric* mode of worship and the magic and sexual perversion and human sacrifice associated with it. He also incurred the wrath of the Brahmins by his criticism of many Hindu rituals, and more particularly by his assertion of the spiritual equality of man. The trial that he had faced in the court of the Ahom king Suhummung is an indication of the collaboration of the vested interest with the ruling power against the forces of non-conformism. Sankaradeva's son-in-law Hari was beheaded and his disciple Madhavadeva was kept under detention for several months. Sankaradeva had to leave the Ahoms kingdom and settled in Barpeta. Not all the Saints of this period had to undergo similar political persecution but most of them had to negotiate with the dominant religious trends and potential powers patronizing them and when one takes these factors into consideration. Audrey Cantlie comments: "The growing movement incurred the hostility of the Brahman priesthood who complained against him before the Ahom kings and Shankara was forced to flee from place to place to avoid persecution. He finally found refuge near Barpeta in the Koch kingdom of Naranarayana where he died in A.D. 669 after a long life of 118 years, 10 months and a few days.[12]

Liberalisation of the Bhakti Path and some Distinctive Features of Tribe-Caste Continuum in the Context of the Bhakti Movement of Srimanta Śankaradeva

If there could be any question of mutation or affiliation still, it could have been with the Gita and the Bhagawat direct which Sankardew read and interpreted in his own way, at once original and new" (Neog 1963, p. 4). Haladhar Bhuyan, the founder of the Sankar Sangha, a modern sect of Ekasarana concurs: "Sri Neog now definitely shows that Sankardew's philosophy is his own and that his religion is as original as that of any great preacher of the world" (Neog 1963: vii). For example, "the Chapters of the Bhagavata Purana, where the Pancharatra theology is discussed, have been omitted by Assamese translators because the *Vyuha* doctrine finds no place in the theology of Assamese Vaishnavism." (Sarma 1966, p. 27); "the highly philosophical benedictory verse (*mangalacarana*) of Book I of the *Bhagavata-Purana,* which has been elaborately commented upon by Sridhara from the monistic stand-point, has been totally omitted by Sankaradeva in his rendering." Whereas, "Kapila of *SaC khya* is an incarnation of God" in the original, *SaC khya* and *Yoga* are made subservient to *bhakti* (Neog 1980, p. 235). Furthermore, "Where Sridhara's commentary appears to them in direct conflict with their *Ekasarana-dharma,* they have not hesitated to deviate from Sridhara's views." (Sarma 1966, p. 48).[13]

The poets therefore adopted various media of transmission without depending on the written or the spoken words alone but what Marshall McLuhan calls the hybridisation of media. Sankaradeva is widely credited with building on past cultural relics and devising new forms of music (Borgeet), theatrical performance (Ankia Naat, Bhaona), dance (Sattriya), literary language (Brajavali). Besides, he has left an extensive literary oeuvre of trans-created scriptures (Bhagavat of Sankardeva) poetry and theological works written in Sanskrit, Assamese and Brajavali. *Bhagavatapurana*, a work composed in Sanskrit in the tenth century emerged out of the spiritual experience of about three centuries as a part of the process of codification and Sanskritisation. This itself is an evidence against the chronological development of Bhakti from Sanskrit to *Bhasa* or from the restrained devotion of the Upanishadic text into a popular emotional upsurge. While in the Sanskrit Bhagavata speaks of the tribes like Abhiras, Kiratas, Hunas, Pulindas etc., quite unfamiliar to Assamese readers and listeners, Sankaradeva substituted these words with names of familiar tribes in Assam like Kiratas, Kacharis, Khasi, Garo, Miri and others.

Sankaradeva was particularly concerned for providing a secure shelter to these particular communities along with other discriminated ones like women and Sudra in general. In his translation of the *Bhagavata* into Assmese verse we find the additional names of tribes and communities from the region thus:

Kirāta Kachāri Khāsi Gāro Miri
Yavana Kanka Gowāla
Asama Muluka Dhobāje Turuka
Kubācha Mlechcha Chandāla[14]

J.P. Rajkhowa comments: "Sankaradeva named a number of *'impure'* people in consideration of the existing tribes who were outside the pale of Hinduism in his own days. [Comment: Sankaradeva called those people 'pure' who became devotees of his faith '*Eka-saran naam dharma*' or monotheism. The others are called 'impure'] ...."[15]

Dr Satyandra Nath Sarma comments: "The references here are not only to the so called lower castes within the Hindu fold but also to the tribes of the region as well as to the *Yavanas* and *Turukas* (Muslims) who are outside the pale of Hinduism. As is well known, the north-eastern region is dominated by various groups of *Kirata* affiliation and Sankaradeva's particular mention of many of them– the *Kacharis,* the *Khasis,* the *Garos,* the *Miris* (*Mishings*), the *Ahoms* and so on - not only speaks of his knowledge of the ethno-social background of the region but is also a measure of his genuine concern for its people."[16] Sharma continues: "There is reason to believe that one of the motives of Sankaradeva, in keeping his religion so simple, was to keep the door open for all 'non-believers' including the tribal who had no organised religion and who might otherwise be scared away by excessive organisational rigours. Sankaradeva also took a soberly tolerant view of the customs of the tribal, normally frowned upon by orthodox Hindus and this is brought out in the following piece of his writing:

kukurakokhāyhenayaCandalúuddhahayāatiúaya
somapānakarejitomahāajñatārapratitustahaya

(Even the *Candala* who eats dog meat becomes highly clean, and the utterly ignorant one who drinks liquor pleases God when *His Name* is remembered, sung, heard or respected by them). (*Kirtana Ghosa*).

The spirit of *Ek Sarana Nām Dharma* and its centrality of Bhakti and Bhakat is definitely captured in that said portion of the *Pāsanda Mardan* that itself is a post-pilgrimage period composition of the Saint and above any kind of idolatry of any sort, be it *murti-puja* to ceremonial celebration of rituals just for the sake of doing so. Sankaradeva would rather salute the *bhakta* from the so-called 'untouchable' of the orthodox Hindu sects than paying visits to temples that would restrict the entry of such *bhakta* devotees for the sake of safeguarding the purity of temple rituals. Because of Sankaradeva's influence there is practically no problem of untouchability in Assam and this land is comparatively free from caste prejudices, religious and communal fanaticism.[17]

The North-East India was known for different ethnic conflicts when Srimanta Sankaradeva was born here in the fifteenth century. Those ethnic groups were *Karbi, Ahom, Kachari, Chutiya, Naga, Manipuri Meitei, Koch, Mising, Jaintia, Tipra, Khasi, Barahi, Moran, Matak, Deuri, Rabha, Tiwa, Kalita, Kayastha, Bodo, Hajang, Garo, Dimasa, Brahmin, Kaivarta, Daivajnya, Kumar, Bonia, Adi, Khamti, Luchai, Kuki, Dafala, Serdukpen,*

Mech, Misimi, Monpa etc. Among these tribes and castes, *Bodo, Koch, Mech, Garo, Rabha, Tiwa, Dimasa, Tipra* and *Kachari* have anthropological and linguistic similarities. So these nine *Tibeto-Mongolean* tribes are called the *Bodo* group. All other social groups in the above list are called tribes. Ahoms conquered the north-eastern part of Assam in the first half of the thirteenth century. Since then many other Shan tribes, all affiliated to Buddhism in some manner, came to Assam. "These are the Khamtis, Phakiyals, Aitaniyas, Turungs and Khamjangs."[18] In the *Uresha-Varnana* section of Kirttana-Ghosa, Sankaradeva mentions some of the professional castes of Assam– The Baniyas (goldsmith), the sutras (carpenters), the Carmakaras, the Candalas, the Kamaras, the Kumbhakaras, the Natas, and others. Vaishava following of Sankara and Madhava were Kamalapati and Krishna who was oilman. Haridasa was a Baniya." Apart from that we find some castes like Maralas, Kamaras, Camars Hiras and Kumars, Kaivartas, Dhobas, Napits or barbers, Salais, Tantis (weavers), Nadials (fishermen), Haris (scavengers), etc. The professions of these people became the marker of their castes. "There were other professionals, who were not caste marked–the ploughmen, boatmen, fuel sellers, Alkali sellers or Khariyas."[19] It is said in the histories that gold was washed from the sand of the Brahmaputra. Overall combination is such that there is now found a small portion of exterior castes (*Hira, Kaibartta, Brittial, Bania, Namasudra*), and still smaller of twice - born, the *Brahmans*, and *Ganaks*. The Brahmins did not involve themselves in the cultivation. They were in the same positions of priests. They run the school of Sanskrit learning which is called the *tolas,* and enjoyed important position in administration. Apart from Brahmins there were other non-Brahmins such as Kayastha, Ganaka and Kalita who were working as accountant, astrologer and traders respectively. All people were directly or indirectly involved to it. Rich people engaged the poor for their work.

The Ahom king Sukapha had an immense contribution to the agricultural sector of Assam. He had great knowledge over *panikheti.* He saw that the Bara Bhuyans of the western part of Assam ploughed their land with cow for *panikheti* and the *Moran* and *Barahis* did not even know the system of ploughing land with cow. So Sukapha taught them to plough their land with buffalo. Cultivation was the main occupation of the people. The Ahoms themselves patronised an extensive network of Vaishnavite monasteries (*satras*), whose monks played a key role in the reclamation of wastelands for rice cultivation throughout the Brahmaputra Valley. Great Kalitas are the highest Sudra caste in Assam ranking only below Brahman, Ganak and Kayastha, the agricultural core of the Kalita caste remains. All of them encouraged congregation.Neo-Vaishnavism in Assam was based on a wide network of *Satras* (monasteries), headed by a Guru.

By taking *œarana* (religious shelter) under a *Guru* through a very simple procedure anyone could enter into the fold of neo-Vaishnavism. Satras in which the principal preceptors lived, or which preserve some of their relics are also called *than.* Numbering in the hundreds, these centres are generally independent of each other and under the control of individual *adhikaras* (or *satradhikars*), though they can be grouped into four different *Sanghatis* (orders). These centres, in the minimum, maintain a prayer house (Namghar), initiate lay people into the Ekasarana tradition and include them as disciples of the Satra. By undergoing a process of 'renunciation' (of certain erstwhile tribal customs) and 'enunciation' (of certain Hindu customs), the neophytes could move to higher stages. In the process, in a matter of a few generations it even became possible for many tribal neophytes to enter into the coveted fold of the caste system. When the tribes enter into caste system as *œaraniyā* or *bhakatiyā* they do not enter it at the bottom, nor as untouchables, but as *shudra* caste or sub castes to be promoted or demoted as per life style, *madhyam, uttam* etc. the majority of castes remain *Shudra,* and purity is ascertained gradation wise and from some such promoted devotee class to an extent that Brahmins and upper caste in society open up by adopting a policy of taking water from some of them. Upward mobility of the tribal neophytes did not stop here. By undergoing a process of 'renunciation' (of certain erstwhile tribal customs) and 'enunciation' (of certain Hindu customs), the neophytes could move to higher stages. In the process, in a matter of a few generations it even became possible for many tribal neophytes to enter into the coveted fold of the caste system.

Bhakti *appears* to be a heterogeneous and polyphonic movement. The caste hierarchy and the ritual complexities of Brahminic Hinduism enjoyed little significance in neo-Vaishnavism. In Assam a non-Brahman Vishanava Guru could initiate Brahmanins (Harinaryan Datta Buara: Srimanta Sankardev, p. 38). Later this democratic spirit of the *Mayamora Sattra* made people elected 'Sudra' Guru more popular than the powerful Ahom monarchy. There is vast difference between the systems of the two religions in terms of beliefs and practices. The Brahmaputra valley of Assam constitutes a distinct regional unit within which the different indigenous castes are related to form a system. It is interesting to note that Sanskritisation and Aryanisation in the plains of Assam followed a different pattern from the other parts of the country as in the absence of the notion of a dominant caste in the context of Assam; there was no need for a tribe to emulate a high caste to achieve an enhanced status. The following interesting observation is made in the Census report of Assam 1891 (pages 233, Vol. 1, chap 8).[20] But the Sankaradeva's Movement in this respect went a little further so as to raise the people from the lower strata of the caste hierarchy to the position of apostolate or pontifical order. And in the *Charit-puthis* we have several examples how Sankaradeva and Madhavadeva, Aniruddhadeva, Srirama Ata brought up devotees from among the tribes who were considered even outside the traditional caste hierarchy and raised them to the stature of chief apostles. Thus, we have Govinda of the Garos, Paramananda of the Miris (Misings), Narottam of the Noctes, Chandsai and Dhyanpati of the Muslims and all of them were endearingly called as Atas. Again there were disciples of Gopaladeva who was authorised to establish satras for proselytising people in upper Assam embracing the Misings, the Sonowals, the Barahis, the Marans and the Deuris. Thus, satras like Gojala, Ceca, Budbari, Dihing, etc. have large number of Misings, Sonowals and Deuris as their laity. Simultaneously the Chaliha Bareghar Satra of Nazira of this sect went to the hills in today's Arunachal Pradesh to proselytise the Noctes and King Lakha Khunbao of the Noctes became one of the principal devotees of the satra. In the same way, Aniruddha, one of the principal apostles of Gopaladeva proselytised mostly among the Morans, the Barahis, the Chutiyas, etc. and brought into fold one Muslim tailor Dheli. The descendants of this devotee belonging to the Dheli Gaon are still among the prominent disciples of the Mayamara Dinjaya Satra of Chabua. The Nikamul Satra of Purussamhati and the Gharamara Satra of the Brahmasamhati sects, also proselytise among the Akas, Dafalas and Hill Miris of the Arunachal Pradesh.

The Satras of Kalasamhati including Dihing, Cesha, Katoni rendered a great service for these deprived sections of the people by guiding them to a path of spiritual and cultural development under the guidance of a patron figure, the Guru. Noted historian Dr S. K. Bhuyan states thus: "In other parts of India, the humiliation to which these unfortunates were subjected drove them to the bosom of other religions; in Assam the liberal policy of the *Kālasamhati* (Mayamarā and Dihing being the most leading ones) endowed them with a sense of self-respect and individual value.[21] Unfortunately, instead of earning appreciation of this liberal policy of *Mayāmaria Satra,* it was looked down by rival Sattras and they did no keep relation with them and started using the name Mayāmara in a derogatory sense.[22]

"A Candala who remembers Hari is much superior to a Brahman observing religious vows (Sankaradeva: Bhagavata X 12622-3). Mullan coins the term exterior caste to denote those beyond the social pale of Hindu society and he comments: "...the word "depressed" is not, in my opinion, suitable as a description of the status of any caste in Assam." As he finds no such degree of depression in Assam as elsewhere and "an unapproachable caste is unknown here." not associated with degradation as all castes are freely admitted to schools and drawing water from wells and tanks.[23] Cantlie comments: "the proportion of exterior castes is not only small as compared with the position elsewhere, but the disabilities attached to their status are less severe. Exterior castes in Assam are not landless labourers employed in estates owned by higher caste but mostly independent fishermen, small artisans often owning or cultivating in addition a little land."[24]

The process of initiation is the first step in this regard and it is described in a number of Census reports: I quote Cantlie : "The Miris, like other wild tribes, are distinguished by the Assamese into *bhakatiya* and *abhakatiya*, according as they are or are not followers of a Goshain...Their connection with Goshain, however, is rather temporal than spiritual. It is worth their while to secure him as their friend by presents of a few *annas* yearly and a portion of mustard and pulse according to each man's means and inclination: but they have no Brahmins, nor do they adore any idol. In some places, however, I found that they had been prevailed option to leave off buffalo's flesh' (R.C.A.1881:87-8). The scholar continues: "In the Brahmaputra valley it is hard to say when the new converts definitely became Hindus, especially as many of them cling to their old habits of eating and drinking. I remember meeting some Miris in the east of Darrang, who told me that they continued to eat fowls and to drink liquor, though they had come under the tutelage of a *Goshain*, but were careful to avoid these infringements of his precepts in his presence : when I questioned them as to why they became *bhakats* of a Hindu Goshain if they did not obey him in matters of food and drink, they said that they were strangers in a strange land, and unless they made some arrangement with the gods of the place or their representative, there was no knowing what evils might befall them ; hence they placed themselves under the care of the *Goshain* and paid him his annual fee in order to be on the safe side. No doubt in a few generations these people will have attained recognition as orthodox Hindus, but it is impossible to define the border line which they must cross. Amongst such people as these the missionary efforts of the Vaishnava Gosains of the Brahmaputra valley have been very successful..." (R.C.A. 1911:41).[25]

The Sonowal Kacharies accepted dual religious system. They are 'Kirata dharma' and 'New-Vaishnavism' or '*Eaka Saran Namdharma*'. But there is vast difference between the systems of the two religions in terms of beliefs and practices. Though they have faith in *Namdharma*, which is against the worship of any other god or goddess with or without sacrifice, yet they can't abolish their traditional religious system. So they still continue to hold sacrificial worship to their traditional deities Homs, Morans, Mataks, Chutias, etc. came to fold of Hinduism, yet they retained some of their distinct identities and this helped in asserting in the modern period as ethnic communities as against caste identities. If it is accepted that social mobility and rearrangement have remained a feature of caste despite the idea of caste as a closed group prevails. When Arunachal was within the map of Assam, Shri Ramadev Gossain, Satradhikar of *Chaliha Bareghar Satra,* a dynamic personality, initiated Lotha Khon Bao and renamed him as Narotom. Therefore, the kings of Loptang and Namchang were initiated to Vaishnava sect along with thousands of Noctes. The *Garamur Satra* of North Lakhimpur took similar steps among the *Abors*. All of these communities were from the hills, which now come under present Arunachal Pradesh.

Sankaradeva selected religious heads mostly fromthe aboriginal tribes of his community such as Nagas, Garos and from some underprivileged castes like Hiras, Kaivartas, Bhutias who were thus placed on equal footing with other high-caste leaders of the community. Sankaradeva even admitted Muslims into his sect, like Jayhari, who became *Atoi* (religious head) of his Muslim converts. For the first time the tribes and the ethnic communities in Assam had a taste of free and dignified life with a strong sense of belongingness to a community in which they all were treated alike. They saw in Sankaradeva a deliverer from their economic oppression and social degradation under the Brahmins and Ahom rulers, and hoped that Sankaradeva would inaugurate a new era in Assam in which they too would have a claim to honour and wealth, and a heaven after death. In the process of upward mobility, most of the indigenous communities retained some of their beliefs and practices and refused to fully conform to the highest cost codes and regulations on.

Later this democratic spirit of the Mayamora Sattra could pose threat to the powerful; Ahom monarchy at one time of its history. The Bhakti Movement which swept north India, sowed seeds of democracy as it asserted the dignity of the human soul, raised the socially underprivileged to give them equal share of the religious activities. One of the prominent *sishyas* of Gopal Ata was Aniruddhadeva who played a very significant role specially working among the deprived and socially backward classes of the society in upper Assam in the post-Sankaradeva period. Because of his genuine effort actual social reform could be made to break caste-creed barrier when the guru himself took initiative to cook food for all and sharing meal with all the devotees sitting together and also expelling a devotee from the Sect in case of refusal to inter-dine with others and he was courageous enough to meet the challenges.[26]

Sristidhar Dutta describes how Aniruddhadeva's farsightedness has made *Moran-Mataks,* the first Assamese tribe in eastern Assam to be Vaishnava devotees of *Mahapurushiya dharma* and how the other tribes, finding their disciplined life style and codes of conduct under Guru's guidance, and their access to a new way of life as ploughing was introduced, certain crafts and industries were taught and how their existing community bond could act as a strong impetus to act for development under the able guidance of the *Sattra* and *Gurus*. These have made a great impact among other tribes like the Barahis, the Kacharis, the Chutiyas to accept the new creed and all the newly initiated ones started identifying them as M*ataks*. "As a result, the term Matak was no longer confined to the Matak-Moran people alone, but was extended to include the other tribal members as well. Padmeswar Gogoi found that even the Ahoms, who became disciples of the Mayamara Satra, had identified themselves with the *Mataks* and preferred to be called *Matak* to Ahom. In course of time attracted by the scholarly qualities of Aniruddhadeva and the liberal democratic nature of the satra, some Brahmin, Kalita and other people also became disciples of the satra and they too came to be identified as *Mataks.*" Interestingly the original identity of the tribe was kept at time as a suffix to the term *Matak*, for example, *Matak-Chutiya, Matak-Ahom,* a practice that was abandoned during the time of *Matak* rebellion when all members preferred to identify themselves with a larger identity, namely '*Matak'*. The Census Report, 1881 mentions that "a follower of one of these Gosains, would call himself *Matak Moran*, but the distinction is one neither of caste nor nationality."[27]

As the prime Guru of the Mayāmara community of upper Assam, he tried his best to uplift their status. The Mayamara devotees follow the *Bhakti Mangal Ghosha,* popularly called by them the *Bhagavata Sāstra* written by their Guru Sri Aniruddhadeva. What role these Gurus have played in spreading the liberal ethos of Sankaradeva's *Ekasarana Dharma* with its centrality of *bhakat* (devotee) over *mantra, murti* and *tirtha,* etc. is evident in Aniruddhadeva's catholicity for the downtrodden and the deprived ones." Apart from converting out castes into Hinduism through the new channel of the Vaishnavite faith as in the case of Dheli tailor, he played a prominent part in assimilating different groups into the mainstream of Assamese society. The different ethnic groups with their respective dialects, culture and tradition when embraced the new faith came within the Mayāmara Vaishnava community and gradually got themselves completely assimilated with the greater Assamese society. From a state of unsophistication they were uplifted, given status and rights equal with others. There are innumerable instances of upgradations among the Myamara Vaishnavas which were done mostly by Aniruddhadeva. Some such examples worth mentioning are the families of Nagagharia, who originally hailed from the Nagas Kacharigharia, originally Kachari, Khamtigharia and Chowkhamgharia, originating from the Khamtis, Mirigharia, originating from the Mishings, etc. They got assimilated to such an extent that unless on their own they reveal their original identity, there is no other way to distinguish them from the rest of the members of the Mayāmora or Assamese society."[28]

The Gender Question: Stree and Sudra

শ্লোকসংস্কৃতেআমি/লিখিবাকভালজানিতথাপিকৰিবোপদবন্ধ
স্ত্রীশূদ্রআদিযত/জানোকপৰম-তৎৰগ্ৰবণতমিলয়আনন্দ ||[29]

With the spread of Neo-Vaishnavite ideals of advanced humanism and of human dignity irrespective of sex, gender or class and caste, educated women came forward to break taboos of inter-caste marriage. Women in general, inspired by the Neo-Vaishnavite movement, got more in touch with her subtle side paving way for finer expressions of her being in the form of poetry, music, art and learning. In fact, so inspired was she that she broke down earlier shackles and bondage and dared to give expression to a mind of her own. The *Brihat Rajavamsavali* holds that the ladies of the Bhuyan families were well educated. Pratap Bhuyan's daughter Bhanumati who was given in marriage to Koch king Naranarayana, later took the name Ratnamala, inspired great Sanskrit scholar Purusottam Bhattacharya to write the Sanskrit grammar *Prayog Ratnamala*. The *Katha-Guru-Charit* mentions that Dayal, the wife of Teli-Krishna Ataoi was appointed Medhi who taught the procedure of the recital of God's name at different intervals of the day and the reading of the holy books such as *Ghosā, Kirttana*, *Bhagavata,* etc. Bhubaneswari, daughter of Vaishnava preacher Harideva, was conferred the headship of his satra and Dharma-mala, even when Harideva was alive. She was the first woman to become the head of a religious institution in Assam. Chandari, the nurse of Sankaradeva, was quite acquainted with the teachings of the *Gita* and the art of painting and could also take part in theological discussions.[30]

In his attempt at re-defining the worth and dignity of a *bhakta* at heart, who stands over and above any kind of "ism", be it Brahmanism, casteism, feminism, or any other group loyalty of any kind just for the sake of belonging to a group biologically, genetically or otherwise, it encouraged re-defining hierarchies in terms of virtues, worth, and dignity, and a condemned low caste woman suddenly found herself elevated in some other manner. *Sati Radhika*, a pious and dutiful housewife and a fisher woman, could be elevated to a higher status because of her acquired virtues. If class and rank are decided by one's innate qualities then Sati Radhika would rank higher than those boasting of that status or rank just by birth without actually possessing any of those virtues. Not only that, it re-opened the door of woman to be able to shine also as a poet and a writer, an intellect of some kind, a now forgotten but once glorified Vedic woman of enlightenment, Gargi, Maitreyi, and some others ! Bhakti also produced the first Asasmese woman poet of a kind, Ai Padmavati. Āi Padmavati, daughter of Gopal Ata, the founder of *Kāla Samhati*, stands unique as the first poetess in the Assamese language that composed the devotional lyric in the seventeenth century. The first line is: "*Gurupadanubhulibi mon toi, (don't forget the feet of the Guru, Oh mind!.*"

Concluding Remarks: Need for Re-Discovering Sankaradeva in Our Midst and to Creatively Re Visit the Path of Bhakti in the Contemporary Time

At a later time the outlook of the *Sattras* toward women reflected orthodox and conservative attitude and women were not allowed to enter many *Satras* although such rigidly is now greatly diminishing. However, at a later time some Brahminical *Sattras* started re-discovering their Hindu-Brahminical roots. The elitist attitude which emerged out of united growth under the royal patronage of the Brahminical sect of Neo-Vaishnavism and Shakta Brahminicalism from Bengal proved detrimental to the subaltern communities which had experienced upliftment and relief from social suppression during the Vaishnava movement of Sankaradeva. As the existing religious order instead of becoming an instrument of social change became ritual-oriented and a tool for perpetration and perpetuation of the existing dominant order, its potency to stimulate social progress also declined and the process of formation of a broad-based society in the valley was faced with a serious crisis. It is very significant that prior to the introduction of "Namghar" set-up the self-governed tribal societies both in hills and plains had "*Deo-Ghar*" etc. and in such tribal societies the community head was called *Gaon–burā* or Rāja, although here the *rāja* is controlled by the commune. Leela Gogoi finds not much difference between the pre-Vaishnavite and the Vaishnavite set-ups. The social set-up of these tribal villages have retained the age old structurally without much change. Before it has "*deo-ghar*", now it is '*nam-ghar.*"[31] The basic different between the *Deo-ghar* centric and later Buddhist –Vaishnavite centric *namghars* retained democratic values in Assam while in neighbouring Bengal it became caste-rigid feudal society. Contrary to the ethos of "*rajjei raja*" (people are the real king) it gave the artisans, agriculturists etc. low caste" status. Along with Namghares 'Sarana" rather than *diksa* saved Assam from the dominance of *Brahmin-Kayastha* centric priest oriented social set-up. It could make innovative ways for continuing that dialogue further in a Bhakti centric way that all can overcome limitations of caste, class and gender by taking refuge at the shelter. The Bhagavat Gita *sarvadharmānparityejyamāekam-saranahaja*" is reflected in the spirit of *Ekaœarana*, and the *Śabda Brahma, the Bhagavata* as the *ISVARA RUPA,* is placed in the altar.

Like the Buddhist *samghas*, the *sattras* were modelled on egalitarian ideals. There was no division of rich and poor, high and low castes and nor was there any system. At a later time the development of education and the spread of Gandhian values among one and all have acted favourably for strengthening reform movements under the banner of *Srimanta Sankar Sangha* sought to restore the true significance of Śankaradeva's writings in an unadulterated manner Implication of caste in devotion. Interestingly, many Brahmin Vaishnavas identified themselves with the reform initiatives taken by the Sangha for restoring the humanitarian ideals of Sankaradeva and Madhavadeva and the initial steps taken by the Brahmin followers of Sankaradeva for spreading the humanitarian ideals of the Bhakti Renaissance. Pitambar Dev Goswami, the then Sattradhikar of *Garamursatra* came forward for supporting Gandhian call for eradication of untouchability and other caste prejudice thereby re-discovering Sankaradeva's spirit at the heart of the caste centric *Brahminical satras* that ironically stood on the way of bridging the gap between man and man and between man and God. The dialogue continues between the forces of conservatism and of reform and in this interesting movement it is not absolutely a situation that the two remain completely in opposite positions. Mrinal Miri comments: "some of them, miraculously perhaps, have retained a sense of both functional and moral-spiritual autonomy which provides, as it were, the springs of action."[3] Rather than being dictated by others, these newly convert devotees started dictating their own terms as pre-requisites for meaningful dialogue that would be mutually beneficial to both. Sankaradeva made provisions for safeguarding their rights at all costs. In no other period of our cultural history so many figures from the lower-strata of the society were empowered in such a manner to assert against the Brahmanical and feudal hierarchy. Perhaps even now the gap between the ideal and the actual remains and it will be explored and re-explored time and again and questions will be asked again and again because those very people who use to remain blind followers of any creed or caste, have now learnt to ask questions and to remain explorers for their own sake.

References

1. Quoted in Jyoti Prasad Rajkhowa. *Sankaradeva: His Life, Preachings and Practices,* (Guwahati, B.S. Publications, Guwahati, 2003), p. 2.
2. Cantlie, Audrey (1984). *The Assamese.* London.
3. Miri, Mrinal. *Community, culture, nation,* Seminar No. 550, June 2005, pp. 54-68.
4. Mahapurush Sankaradeva is worshipped as a deity, a patron saint and a Lai in Manipur and there is a temple "Eebudhou–Shankerdev" in which vegetable offering is made before the deity, a grand father Shankaradeva, whose idol is decorated with an orange colour robe befitting a monk and there is a turban as well. Scholars in Assam and Manipur like Birendranath Datta, E. Nilmani Singh and others talk about a long association of Assam with Manipur and followers of Sankaradeva may have introduced worship of Sankaradeva that later became associated with a deity (Patron Saint), a Lai.
5. "Sankardev's Religion – Mah′purusis." Retrieved 27 October 2012.
6. 'Sankaradeva: The Founder of Assamese Vaishnavism in *Sankaradeva Studies in Culture*' ed. By Bhaba Prasad Chaliha, pp. 160-164.
7. Dasgupta, RK, "Sankaradeva : The Founder of Assamese Vaisnavism", (online : http://www.atributetosankaradeva.org/Sankaradeva_%20Founder_of_Assamese_Vaisnavism.pdf, accessed January 2011).
8. *Kaliyuga* is to be praised, human life is to be praised and *Bharatavarsha* is to be praised.
9. Sitocandālakagaristhamāni
   Yārajihbāgrethāke Hari vāni.
   SehisékulinVedakbujé
   Yāhāramukhé Hari Nāmbijé."
10. D. Neog, Jagat Guru Sakardew, pp. 23-24. (Second Edition 1998. Published by Srimanta Sankaradeva Sangha, Nagao, Assam).quoted in Jyoti Prasad Rajkhowa, *Sankaradeva: His Life, Preachings and Practices*, Guwahati, B. S. Publications, Guwahati, 2003, p.79.
11. Shankaradeva, Kirrtan.
12. Cantlie, p.153.
13. Neog, Dimbeswar (1963). *Jagat-Guru Sankardew*. Nowgong: Haladhar Bhuya. Sarma, S N (1966). *The Neo-Vaisnavite Movement and the Satra Institution of Assam*. Gauhati University.
14. Bhāgavata/2/53).
15. Rajkhowa, J.P. (2003). SANKARADEVA : HIS LIFE, PREACHING (B.S. Publication, Guwahati), p. 24.
16. Sarma, S.N. The Neo-Vaishnavite Movement and the Satra Institution of Assam. (Guwahati: LBS, 1999), pp. 30-52.
17. *Ibid.*
18. Neog, Maheswar, *Early History of the Vaishnava Faith and Movement in Assam* (LBS: Guwahati, 2008 reprint), pp. 30-70.

19. *Ibid*. 235.
20. Census of India : Assam 1891, Vol. 1, chapter 8, p. 67.
21. Quoted in *ibid,* p. 73.
22. Dhekial Phukan, Haliram, Assam Buranji Guwahati 1996, p. 96.
23. Quot can 247.
24. *Ibid.*
25. *Ibid.,* p. 237.
26. Summary of Barua, Swarnalata (2002). 'Preface', in Swarnalata Barua (ed) Life and Teachings of Sri Sri Aniruddhadeva (Sri Sri Aniruddhadeva Chair, Dibrugarh University), pp. 4-5.
27. Report on the Census of Assam for 1881, op. cit., pp. 98 f. quoted in *ibid.* p. 69.
28. Dutta, Sristidhar, (2002). "Origin of the Names 'Matak', 'Moamariai' and 'Mayamara' and their Historical significance", In Swarnalata Barua (ed) *Life and Teachings of Sri Sri Aniruddhadeva* (Sri Sri Aniruddhadeva Chair, Dibrugarh University), pp. 60-61.
29. Canto X, Middle, vv. 3096. *Srimad-Bhagavata,* Srimanta Sankaradeva Sangha, p. 1228.
30. *Ibid.*
31. L. Gogoi, p. 143.

4

Assamese Cuisine in Folk Literature and Economic Empowerment of Women through Assamese Cuisine

— Archana Kalita

Introduction

Folk literature is also known as oral literature and verbal art. It is transmitted orally from generation to generation. Folk literature reflects the culture of a society. Folk literature includes folk song, prose narrative, proverb, riddle and folk speech. Under prose narrative folk tale, myth and legend are included.

Folk cookery of Assam has a rich tradition. Since time immemorial folk cookery or Assamese cuisine has a special place in the society. During the season of festivals and ceremonies Assamese people arrange feast and prepare delicious meal. The women of Assam cook delicious food and serve the family members and guest. Several instances found on Assamese cuisine in folk literature. In Yogini Tantra and Kumara Harana there are descriptions of various *vyanjanas* i.e. special dishes made from vegetables, pulses, fish and meat.

During bihu (a festival associated with the agricultural cycle) and other festivals women folk make different types of traditional foods like *pitha, laru, sandah* etc. for the family members and guest.

Nowadays various self-help groups, NGOs and entrepreneurs are trying to focus Assamese cuisine in national and international level.

Assamese Cuisine and Folklore

Assam has a rich tradition of folklore. Folkore may be the cultural heritage of any community. There are various folk items scattered throughout Assam. Every community has their specific food habit and specific cuisine. Assamese cuisine also has an unique identity. There are special method of cooking and preparing Assamese cuisine. Many beliefs and practices are related to folk cookery among the women folk in Assam. While they are ready to prepare rice, in some places mainly in lower Assam they tell a chant-

Emuthisaolaredumuthihoba
Sakalokeati-juriemuthiroba.

The contextual meaning is that women are very conscious about the availability of rice for every member so that each member can enjoy the food. Here is some examples of folk literature which reflects the richness of Assamese cuisine.

Proverb

Proverbs are fixed phrase genre of oral literature. In Assamese language proverbs are generally known as *jojana, prabachan, prabadvakya, lokakti* etc. Dakar bachan or speeches of Dak also fall under the ambit of proverb. There are various proverbs related to Assamese cuisine. Though the contextual meaning is different but from such proverbs we are able to know how some special meal are important in Assamese society. The main dish of Assamese people is rice. So there is a proverb '*aakalarbhatnidanarmaat*' i.e. rice is famine is like a word in helpless situation. Another one is '*bhatartitakhabapari, maatartitasahibanowari*'. Assamese people like to enjoy 'paitabhat' or 'pantabhat' which is made from cooked rice soaked overnight. People say *'magharpantabagharbal.'* i.e. who eat paitabhat in the month of Magh, he will be strong as like as Tiger. The Duck meat is very popular among Assamese people. That is why there is a proverb- *'Haahemaahesaman'* or '*Haahereorajimahereoraji.*' i.e. one can be pleased with duck's meat and with *maatimaah*. Urad bean or maatimaah has an unique place in Assamese cuisine. If duck meat is prepared with urad bean it is become tasteful. Another proverb is *'kina haharthotaloikemangah'*. i.e. duck meat bought from the market is considered very valuable. As Assam is a land of rivers and ponds, there are availability of fish, tortoise etc. So, fish and tortoise also have a place in Assamese cuisine. One popular proverb in Assamese is *'maasegarakaanjakhabasahuegarakabowari baba'* i.e. curry with fish is tasteful. Likewise daughter-in-law trained by mother-in-law is efficient in every work. Assamese women use mustard oil for fish fry. After frying the fish the remaining oil again use by them. So there is a saying *'maasarteledimaasbhaja'*. The fish curry made with aari and chital fish is popular in Assamese society. To mention the importance of such curry there is a proverb *'aarirmurachitalargadatakjanobapa hen halionera'*. i.e. do not give the head of Ari fish (Giant river catfish) and the back of Chital fish (Humped feather back) to others even if he is your own child. One of the stalwarts of folklore study Dr Birinchi Kr. Baruah divided the Assamese curries taken with rice into three categories- sour, bitter and alkaline i.e. *tenga, tita* and *khar* (Baruah:2009:142). Alkaline curry is very popular among the Assamese people which are very unique. That is why there is a saying- *'Kharkhowa Assamiya'*. There is a popular proverb related to khar- *'kabulibanajane Ratnavalisai, pasalakhararjutinejanebhojrandhibaloi jai.'* i.e. who doesn't know how to prepare pasalakhar (alkaline curry of banana plant) he is not an efficient cook. In Assamese cuisine, people use leafy vegetables also as side dish. With the leafy vegetables like *manimuni, bhedailata, tengeshitenga* they make such items which are not only tasteful but they have medicinal value also. When someone is suffering from diarrhoea and loose motion they make items from such plants and serve the patient. To make availability of milk for the lactating mother women prepare dish with jaluk or black pepper. *'Lon jalukerekhuabajaaltebestanrash-hoibebhal'*. (The meal with salt and black pepper increases mother's milk). To prepare the sour items Assamese people use *outenga i*.e. Elephant Apple, *thekera, tengamora or noltenga*, lemon etc. Outenga with dhekia leaf is an enjoyable side dish with rice. There is a popular saying- *'outengadhekiasaakjibharpaniparithak'*. i.e. Elephant Apple cooked with Dhekia leaf is very tasteful and that is why mouth-watering. Pitika or mashes also important dish for Assamese people. People say *'saakatnakhailonpitikat jai tinigun.'* (though salt is not taken with herbs yet three times salt is taken with mashes, the contextual meaning is that whenever a person tries to safe money yet the cost is three times of his earning.) There are some instructions on cooking in Assamese cuisine. In Nalbari district of Assam people say- *'jeitaidiba noon, juidibatini gun.'* i.e. whenever the cook pour salt to the dishes maximum level of fire should be applied. Without salt cooking is not completed. Proper salt makes an item delicious. So there is a saying- *'haladhi masala dilobatilonnahoikarilemaati.'* i.e. though turmeric and spices are added but due to unconsciousness salt is forgotten for which the food is not tasteful.

Dakar Bachan

Dakar bachan or speeches of Dak has important place in Assamese society. It is believed that there was a person namely, Dak who was born in Lehidongora village of Barpeta district of Assam. He mentioned different rules and regulations on various items associated with Assamese society. In Dakar bachan also there are some instances on cuisine and cooking. There is an instruction how maagur (cat fish or magur) and kaoi fish (climbing perch) can be prepared.

'Magurmaasakkasikutiahaladhimarishhingakdiyatoilalon di karibapaakeivyanjansar bole Dak.' Regarding the cuisine of Kaoi fish Dak says *'Kaaoimaasakkasikutiahaladhimarishhingakdiyaolatpalatkaribapithi-khaipaibatebetusti.'*

Regarding Preparation of Rice Dak says

'saoldibajatekapanidibatinitateka.' The literally meaning is that if there is one cup of rice then water must be three cup. Sour items have important place in Assamese cuisine. Assamese people make sour dish with Tamarind (teteli) also. Dakar bachan says- *'pakateteliburhabaralibistarkaridibaha jail. Barhidibatengarjhol, khabarbelamundanotol.'* Literally meaning is that if Barali fish is prepared with tamarind in maximum heat it becomes so tasty that everyone should enjoy the delicious dish.

In this way proverbs and Dakar bachan reflect the Assamese cuisine.

Folk Song

In bihu geet, biyanaam we find different types of Assamese cuisine. The male folk recite in huchari- 'eta batitnaharu, eta batitpanaru, eta batitkhuturasaak. Murarsulisingiashirbadkarisogrihasthakushalethak.' i.e. in one pot there is garlic, in one pot there is panaru and in one pot there is khuturaxaak or leaf and the dancers wish that the whole year will be fine for the family. From this huchari song we can get an idea about the importance of garlic, khuturasaak in Assamese society. During Bohagbihu there is a tradition of saatsaaki where seven types of herbs and leafs collect by the women folk which has medicinal value also. In some places women folk collect fourteen types of herbs and in some places they collect hundred and one types of herbs. Assamese jalpan is very popular in the society. So in huchari there is mention about *'bakulbaradhanarkarai', 'dewabhajachira'* etc. In bihugit we find about *Pabha fish, kharisa* (mashed fermented bamboo shoot). For instance- '*Gadhulibazararpabhamaaskinilo:*

Kharisatenga di randho.
Khabarsamayattoloimanat pare
Bhatarpatatbahiloikando.'

i.e. in the evening market the male folk has bought the Pabha (Pabo cat fish), fish and made curry with *kharisa* (Bamboo shoot). During the time of eating his lover is not with him.

There is a reflection of society and culture in the biyageet. Biyageet are part and parcel of women folk's life. There are various steps in marriage ceremony and there is biyageet related to each and every step of the marriage ceremony. Household works, cuisine also mentioned in biyageet. For instance,

'Saolcharipurakotenoerilachiracharipurapatra oi ripalpalRukunirkapal-bhal.'

Teasing song or khisageet also is a part of biyageet. Here also there are some mentioning of Assamese food. For instance-

'bokasaolbhijaloadhaphuta, lighte o jalalonaikaphita'. i.e. bokasaol is not fully absorbed in water for which it is not tasteful.

In the historical ballad like 'Manikonwarargeet' we find 'Aamguri-khatarsukankharisabalamabilarmaas, tumieahisasonabar TamuliMani-dharkimanarpaas. Opar Dikhour Silgharia Barpatharar Joha, rajbharalar son-kharahirediyabailungakbata.'

Folk Tale

In 'Burhiaair sadhu' compiled by Sahityarathi Lakshminath Bezbauah we find some tales where Assamese delicious meal is mentioned. For example, in sarabjan we get the instance of komalsaol, doi, gur. In Tula and Teja there is a mention of Tortoise meat.

Assamese Cuisine and Women Empowerment

For the development of a society both male and female should be equally empowered. Women empowerment is a concerning issue nowadays. Women should be empowered politically, economically, socially and educationally. Economic empowerment is an essential factor for development of society. If women are economically empowered they become self-dependent. Assamese cuisine may be one of the important mediums for women empowerment. Nowadays the NGOs, SHGs are trying to give a platform to the women for their own products. Through exhibitions and expo women folk are now selling their hand-made products including handicrafts and Assamese traditional food items. It is a positive issue for their uplift in economic field. Though nowadays due to impact of globalisation many national and international food come to our families still traditional food have high value in Assamese society. Women folk can make different breakfast items like *pitha, laru, sandah* etc. and they are able to cover the market for such delicious items. Scientifically packaging the home made traditional items can be exported to other part of India and world. Proper training should be given to the women folk regarding the making and manufacturing the items. The government should take initiative in this issue. With the help of NGOs and SHGs and Rural Development Departments Government should give training to the women folk. Our Assamese cuisine may able to make a place like lijjat papad and Amul which are maintained only by female folk. Nowadays some women have able to focus Assamese cuisine by their writings on Assamese cuisine. A few books on Assamese cuisine have been published. Jyoti Das, Dr Mridushmita Phukan etc. published books on Assamese cuisine. Assamese cuisine has a rich tradition. So women folk should give emphasise on establishing restaurant on Assamese cuisine. Presently some women have come up to Assamese cuisine business with their male counterpart. Assamese cuisine may be one of the important factors for rural tourism. Tourist can be attracted by the Assamese delicious meal which help to earn money.

Summing up

Assamese cuisine is a mixture of different indigenous styles with considerable regional variations and some external influences. A traditional meal of Assam ends with offering betel nut. People able to enjoy sour, bitter and alkaline taste in Assamese cuisine. For the development of a society both male and female should be empowered and Assamese cuisine may be one of the mediums of women empowerment in economic field. Assamese cuisine may be the factor of rural tourism. The rural development department as well as tourism department of Assam can take proper initiative to develop this field as Assam is still rich in traditional dishes.

References

Baruah, Dr Birinchi Kumar. *A Cultural History of Assam* (Early period) (Bina Library, Guwahati, 2003).

Baruah, Dr Swarnalata, Bargohain Dr Mamani. *Assamiya Nari Atit Aru Bartaman* (Bani Mandir, Guwahati, 2010).

Bhattacharya, Dr Basanta. *Assamiya Lokagit Samikhya* (Chandra Prakash, Guwahati, 2007).

Datta, Birendranath. *Folkloric Foragings in India's North-East* (Guwahati: Anandaram Borooah Institute of Language, Art and Culture, Assam 1999).

Datta Birendranath (ed). *A Handbook of Folklore Material of North-East India* (Guwahati: Anandaram Borooah Institute of Language, Art and Culture, Assam, 1994).

Dutta, Sujit Kumar, Ghosh Dilip Kumar. *Empowering Rural Women* (Akansha Publishing House, New Delhi, 2002).

Dorson, R.M. Folklore and Folklife: An Introduction (London: The University of Chicago Press Ltd., 1972).

Sarma, Dr Nabin Chandra. *Dakar bachanaru Dak Prabachan* (Banalata, Guwahati, 2010).

Dr Ananya Baruah, Dr M. Gopal Singha, Bhupati Das, Rajlakshmi Hazarika (ed). *Empowerment in Independent India* (Assam Book Hive, Guwahati 2012).

Gurdon Captain P.R. *Some Assamese Proverbs* (Lawer's Book Stall, Guwahati, 1998).

Gogoi, Dr Lila. Bihugitaru Banghosha (Banalata, Dibrugarh and Guwahati, 2008).

Sen, Soumen. *Folklore in North East India* (Omsons Publication, New Delhi, 1985).

Sinha, Harendra, J. Zorema (ed). *Empowerment of Women in North- East India Socio-Economic Perspectives* (Concept Publishing Pvt. Ltd., New Delhi, 2012).

Website- www.en.wikipedia.org/assamese cuisine.

5

Role of Puppetry in the Development of Communication Skills in Children

— *Binita Devi, Simanta Sarma*

Introduction

India is a home of folk culture. India have various forms of folk culture which have been used from the ancient times to till today includes different combination of dance, drama, song, mime, puppetry, storytelling etc. Those folk culture always provides moral, religious and social message, folk forms are based on religion community, caste, culture and language. There are significant regional differences in the style of presentation, crafting of puppets manipulation technique and repertoire. The earliest reference to puppetry in India is in the epic Mahabharata's Jana Parba and Udyog Parba, dating back to around the ninth century BC, and Patanjali, the author of Yogasutra, mentioned puppet in their works; so did Tiruvalluvar, the Tamil poet of second century BC, who wrote: 'the movement of a man who has not a sensitive conscience are like the simulation of life by marionettes moved by string'.

The Aims and Objectives of the Study

- To study the inception of puppetry as a form of folk art.
- To find out the techniques and types of puppetry in Assam.
- To study its importance.

Inception of puppetry as a folk art form

It is not possible of demarcate exact time of the birth of puppetry in Assam. According to Katha-guru-charitra (early eighteenth century), puppetry was a popular and influential art form at the time of Sankardeva the great social reformer of Assam was born. First, there is a direct reference to a shadow puppet show, performed at the residence of Sankardeva's father (Kusumber Siromoni Bhuya) on the 22nd day of the saint's birth. Sri Sankardeva evolve Bhaowna, the Traditional theatre of Assam by fusing elements from the Sanskrit theatre and prevent performance forms which included puppetry so it can be said that puppetry theatre was a popular pre-Sankara performing art form. The string puppet of Assam are known as Putul Nach, Ptul Bhaowna and Putula Bhaowria. However, some contemporary group also use the term Puppet theatre, Putula theatre which is a popular folk entertainment medium in the plains of Assam. Puppet show in Assam started from September at the time of Bishwakarma Puja and continued till Bohag Bihu i.e. the month of April. The shows are organised during the festive season because of the optimum audience participation at that timeframe.

Techniques and types of puppetry in Assam

Mainly there are four types of traditional puppetry string, rod, shadow and glove.

- **String:** The string puppets movements are controlled by strings attached to different part of its body i.e. hand, head and leg etc. string puppets can do many actions and need special skills to operate them.

Figure 5.1: String Puppet, Photographer: Authors.

String Puppet Making

In traditional, the puppets are made of solapithor some soft wood by joining together different parts forming the head, torso and limbs with the help of cloth. They cover the head and hand with a paste of clay and cow dung, and colour them. Some puppets have joints in elbows but no legs. The lower portion is normally covered with cloth so that, while manipulated, the figures glide smoothly along the floor of the stage. The size of the puppets varies from one foot to three feet. Now we make puppet through thermocol, play board, paper, hard board, cloth etc.

Figure 5.2: Puppet making, Photographer: Authors.

String Puppet Stage Making

The stage is small and simple. A frame is put up with a few bamboo posts. Within this frame, a small platform, measuring about 10 to 12 feet in length and three to four feet in breadth, is raised on one side at a height of about three feet from the ground. Three sides of the frame are covered other than the platform side. Upper and lower portions are covered with screens, leaving a space of about three to four feet open along the length of the platform. At the back of the platform is another screen, normally black, standing about four feet, behind which the manipulators stand either on the ground or on a low bench and are not visible.

A manipulator can easily manipulate two puppets with two hands, but an expert player can handle up to four to five puppets at a time! The speeches are made in a high-pitched, squeaking sound by a Pyapa (whistle) made of bamboo frame with a leaf or rubber membrane. The leader enters into a conversation with the characters speaking in a shrill voice in a skilful manner.

Figure 5.3: String Puppet of Nalbari, Photographer: Authors.

- **Rod:** Rod puppets are manipulated by the rod. The puppets body is securely tied to the rods or sticks. The rod puppet is popular in West Bengal and Odisha.

Rod Puppet Making

Rod puppets are an extension of glove puppets but often much larger. They are fixed to heavy bamboo sticks which are tied to the puppeteer's waist. These are three-dimensional moving figures that are manipulated with the help of rods. The rod puppet in Assam called *mariputola.* The face

Figure 5.4: A set of Rod Puppet. Tejimola and Mahimak (stepmother) from the famous folk tale of Assam Tejimola, Photographer: Authors.

of rod puppet made by paper match and the body are made by ply board or thermocol. These rod puppets can be up to 1.25 meters in height and about 5 to 10 kilograms in weight. One puppet can manipulate by one or two manipulator.

- **Glove:** Glove puppets are manipulated by the puppetries hand. The presenter's hand become the puppets body. Puppeteers wear them on the hand and manipulate their heads and arms with their fingers.

Glove Puppet Making

The face of glove puppet made by socks and cotton. The body of this puppet made by cloth and cotton. The glove puppet can be up to one foot in height.

Figure 5.5: Glove Puppet of Assam, Photographer: Authors.

- **Shadow:** Shadow puppets are operated on a white screen with a light behind or above the screen so that audience can see only shadow of the puppets. In this form, shadows of puppets are used in black and white or in colour. The flat figures, usually made of leather, are lightly pressed on a transparent screen with a strong source of light behind. The screen thus forms the barrier between the audience and the puppet, creating the projection of image. The impact on the audience, surrounded by darkness all around, is quite dramatic. The screen in India is a simple sheet stretched on an adjustable frame. Perhaps one of the oldest forms of puppetry, shadow puppets are found in the states of Andhra Pradesh, Karnataka, Kerala, Maharashtra, Odisha and Tamil Nadu. Ravan

Chhaya from Odisha and Tholpavai Koothu from Kerala are the two prominent shadow puppet theatre traditions of India.

Figure 5.6: Shadow Puppet, Photographer: Authors.

Those entire four kind of traditional puppet only string puppet is widely popular in Assam. Below we mention the puppetry group of Assam who perform string puppet:

1. "Moukhuli Putula Nach Samiti" Nalbari, Chief Puppeteers: Banikanta Barman.
2. "Sagorika Puppet Theatre" Kamrup, Chief Puppeteers: Monoranjan Roy.
3. "Assam Puppet Theatre" Nalbari, Chief Puppeteers: Narayan Deka.
4. "Sri Gobinda Putula Samitee" Auniatisatra Majuli, Chief Puppeteers: Budhindra Pathak.
5. "Ma Bhabani Putula Theatre" Drang, Chief Puppeteers: Krishna Das.
6. "Rubi Puppet Theatre" Kamrup, Chief Puppeteers: Abani Sarma.
7. "Nataraj Puppet Theatre", Nalbari Gandhia.
8. "Nataraj Puppet Theatre" Darang.
9. "Basudev Putula Theatre" Gandhia.

10. "Nabaratna Ptula Theatre" Morigaon Bhalukmari.
11. "Panchratna Pyula Theatre" Morigaon Bhalukmari.

Only three puppets groups of Assam perform string, rod and glove puppets.

1. "Mukak Puppet Theatre", Assam Engineering College Campus, Guwahati-13.
2. "Surojit Academy", Assam Engineering College Campus, Guwahati-13.
3. "Srimanta Sankaradeva Kalakhetra Society puppet Section", Punjabari, Guwahati.

Importance of Puppetry

(i) Puppetry as a medium of communication to children:

Puppetry, the popular folk form, attracts the audience irrespective of age group, race, sex etc. it is serving as an ideal medium of communication. Children connect with puppet in a variety of ways. Children listen to what the puppet say, children are remarkably willing to change their behaviour to keep the puppets happy. So puppetry is a very effective way to communicate with child. Puppets to teach children physiology, hygiene, civics, history, geography, poetry and storytelling for an effective way.

Puppets are being used in education for children promotion of latest farming tools and handling social issues, cultural affairs, song and drama division uses puppets extensively use puppet shows for the campaigns various government programmes. Hence, this medium is apt for wide variety of communication.

(ii) Positive social/emotional development:

Puppets provide a sense of security that makes it easier for children to express thoughts and feelings. Talking through a puppet allows children to explore feelings, freely and exact situation in a way that they are familiar with, for example, we frequently see that if a adult man and woman asked question to child they are simply feel shy and fear and not give any reply if the same question will be asked by a puppet children happily talk with it. This provides excellent opportunities for teaching positive social skills. The process also allows for children to develop empathy for others.

This medium also proved effective to bring about positive changes in disable children behaviour and to develop their talent capacities.

Puppets will be not only to import education to children, but the children were encouraged to make the puppets of their own. This activities gave these children an opportunity to express their feelings, to learn skills like drawing, stitching and to function in a group. As a result of these activities, the level of confidence, skills and happiness of these children was enhanced.

(iii) Puppetry develops child imagination capacity:

When Children are able to play with puppets a new world opens up where they can be the role of any one they want. Their puppet might be a doctor, police man, teacher, post man who always help others. The roles are endless and it is helpful to brainstorm with children ideas they might use when playing with puppets to help expand imagination and motivate new learning.

Puppetry is an important characteristic to develop children interpersonal intelligence which is important in the learning process. Those who have strong interpersonal intelligence good at understanding and interacting with other people and are able to assess to emotions, motivations, desires and intentions of those around them.

Puppet can develop child creative imagination. Puppet can paint with children or introduce a new craft to the children. Give them the opportunity to make their own individual puppets out of socks or brown paper bags, sticks, spoons, balls, glove etc, encourage the children to be as creative as possible. Need voice, acting, music, dance, expressions, emotions, characters, good script. A good mixture of all those component makes puppetry.

(iv) Puppetry as a medium of quick learning:

Puppets give children valuable learning opportunities in many developmental areas. When puppets telling stories, singing songs and rhymes child listen very attentively. Children can sometimes be intermediate when learning new vocabulary and expressions. Sometimes its became they don't understand, and sometimes they simply feel shy. Puppets help with both of these situation. Puppet support oral language skills and communication, social, emotional development and also help children learn and understand the world around them through imaginative play and character observation.

Learning through Play

Learning through play is fundamental to our children education, helping them to develop the necessary skill of life. Puppet can stimulate children imagination encourage creative play and discovery. Puppet can be effectively used in stories and dramas which have imaginary events, places and characters. Parables and historical stories depict puppet as their main characters. Active and attractive puppets can turn any topic into an interesting one. Any story, poem or drama given in the textbooks can be effectively explained to the students through puppets. Puppets can also be used to explain certain scientific principles. Children learn quickly through learning by doing method (hands on experience). Puppet convey message through its tragic and comic theme and we accept the message without even realising that we are learning. Lesson learned in this way are more likely to be remembered and to become part of our solid stock of knowledge.

Research Methodology

For the collection of primary data, here the researcher has adopted a qualitative research methods in which personal interviews and focused groups discussions to assess the impact of puppetry as a means of children communication development. The research has interviewed various puppeteers from Assam Chabin Rajkhowa retired from Cultural Affairs (Puppetry Section), Archana Talukdar work on Cultural Affairs (Puppetry Section), Banikanta Barman and Radha Kanta Barman, Chief Puppeteers of "Maukhuli Putla Nach Samitee, Nalbari." Interviewed on Gauhati University Professor from Education Department Dr Dulumoni Goswami and Dr Mayri Sarma. Group discussion with the student and guardian of folk cultural institution of Assam "Surojit Academy" and audience of puppet play have been addressed in course research, various sources from books, magazines, journals, the internet has used for the collection of secondary data.

Findings and Analysis

Nowadays Assam puppet group face various threat for the advent of new media and the mobile theatre industry incorporating modern technology for making its performance more attractive so the popularity of the puppet shows started declining. What was earlier an indispensable component at the fairs and festivals Raas, Paal Nam, Janmastami, started losing ground because of public apathy. And another important point of declining the popularity of puppet show in Assam that many puppet group in Assam use traditional puppet for show in where there are no development like dress, makeup, figure of puppet etc. so in age of globalisation people would like to see technological development. Today, puppet associate with children entertainment. On television, programmes like Gali Gali Sim Sim use brightly coloured puppet to make learning fun and the series continues to six years.

Suggestions

So to the development and to engage new generation in this folk culture the department of puppet section which was form in the year 1987 through the Government of Assam under the Directorate of Cultural Affairs must be start more and more training, workshop (to make puppets with waste products such as glove, shoes boxes, paper bags etc.) holding festivals and seminars. Through inviting experts of Assam and other state and taking keen interest in the popularisations of this art form and awareness programme among the parents that how puppet can develop child communication skill, creative art etc.

As the visual arts, theatre and literature, puppetry in India today is expressed to international treads and modern influences. As a result, a new kind of puppetry, amalgamated various forms, has emerged. There is now a considerable body of experimental work, some interacting with traditional forms and others with contemporary theatre, music and dance.

The puppet has been called a mask through which the nuances of emotion and the mundane realities of life can be suggested. Threatened, as it is, by technology and mass media, this fragile art needs our nurture and support for it to remain a part of our imaginative experience.

Puppets can provide a useful mechanism to enhance children's engagement and to promote talk involving reasoning in primary science lessons. There is evidence that when teachers use the puppets children talk more readily about scientific problems and higher-order thinking is promoted. They can be particularly significant in engaging reluctant speakers, such as shy children, and promoting greater involvement in scientific discussion with these children. The puppets appear to be effective in providing an interactive narrative which sets a context for learning and provides a purpose for children's talk and follow-up activity. In Puppet dance is refreshment of human life. Puppet dance is most important in educational courses. Many universities introduced puppetry chapter in higher education course (i.e. Mass Com, Folklore, Literature Subject etc). Film Maker introduced in his film. Now Puppet maker scientifically developed of puppet making. All puppet dances are mostly attractive to new generation in world.

Today, while puppetry has made its way into the cities, traditional puppetry is dying a slow death. Modern puppetry on the other hand, is gaining momentum, albeit slowly, and is often used as a tool for imparting social messages. Puppeteers now tell stories on everything from medieval kings, "Phulan-Devi", "Aladin", "Tejimala", "Witch-Craft" to AIDS because to survive in this digital world, revolution has become a necessary component for this centuries old craft.

Acknowledgments

At first the authors would like to express his praise to god that the article was completed within perfect time. The authors expresses the profound gratitude and heartiest thanks to the honourable teacher Prof Mini Bhattacharyya Thakur, HOD, Department of Anthropology, Gauhati University, Assam and Indira Gandhi Rastriya Manav Sangrahalaya, Bhopal for organising national seminar on Cultural Heritage of Assam. The authors tenders his regards and profound complement to puppet groups of Assam for the valuable suggestion and esteemed co-operations at different stages of the research. Finally authors like to express his appreciation and heartily thanks to others who have directly or indirectly helped them for this exclusive work.

References

1. Arthur, G., (1975, September). *Rough Theatre Serves Literacy in Jamaica: Instructional Technology Report*, Jamaica.
2. Baran, S. J. (1999). *Introduction to Mass Communication: Media Literacy and Culture.* Mayfield Publishing, California.
3. Bordoloi Nirmalbprabha, (1972). *Asomor Lokosanskriti*, Bina Library, Assam.
4. Dutta, Dr Birendra, (1986). "Folk Toys of Assam", Directorate of Cultural Affairs, Assam.
5. Kumar, K. J. (2010). *Mass Communication in India*, Jaico Publishing, Mumbai.
6. Learning and teaching through puppets, (1995), CHETNA, Ahmadabad.
7. Meher, K. C. (1970, January-March). *The Role of Puppetry in Contemporary Education*. Sangeet Natak, No. 15.
8. "Putulayatra", (2011). An exhibition of Indian Puppets, Songeet Natak Akademy, Assam.
9. "Putulayatra", (2003). An exhibition of Indian Puppets, Songeet Natak Akademy, New Delhi.
10. Sarma, Dr Nabin, (2013, January). *Lokosanskriti,* Chandra Prakash, Guwahati, Assam.
11. Sarma, Dr Nabin, (2012). *Bharator Uttar Purabanchalor Lokosanskriti,* Bani Prakash, Guwahati, Assam.
12. Talukdar Nagen, (2014, July). *Barnaoy Silpisangrami Silpi,* Ankita Computer press, Nalbari, Assam.

6

Appeasing the Bamboo Deity in Assam: A Study with Special Reference to Bhatheli

— *Birinchi K. Medhi, Jilmil Bora*

Introduction

Bamboo occupies an indispensable place in the socio-cultural life of the Assamese since time immemorial. It is highly auspicious for the people of Assam and it can be understood from its usage in most of the day-to-day affairs, especially in the Assamese folk life. When we look into the annals of history, we find that bamboo was regarded as a rich natural resource, as the forests of Assam were full of different species of bamboo. Almost all the Assamese people residing in the villages or rural areas have bamboo plantations at their backyards. This reflects the close association of the Assamese people with bamboo. There is a popular Assamese proverb in this regard:

Jar nai bah tar naisah i.e. one who does not possess bamboo, does not have courage also.

The typical pattern of a rural Assamese compound is as follows:

Pube hah
Pachime bah
Uttareguwa

Daksinedhoua, i.e., ducks or the tank in the east, bamboo plantations in the west, areca palms in the north and open space in the south. This indigenous compound pattern is very scientific. The eastern side is kept open for the passage of air and for the morning sunlight which are considered to be good for health. That is why water bodies or the pond with domesticated ducks is placed in the eastern side. Moreover the weaving loom, which is an indispensable part of an Assamese household, is also placed in this direction for light. To provide safeguard to the house from the westerly winds of the monsoons and to give respite from the summer sun the bamboo plantations are there in the west. The areca palms are in the north because the southern direction is kept open for light and air.

Literature is a reflection of society and hence many write up on Assam or about Assam do focus on the importance of bamboo upon Assamese life. This is because bamboo occupies a pedestal position in the Assamese society. Various authors have highlighted about the role and importance of bamboo in Assamese culture. Eminent writers like Datta (1980), Bordoloi (1991), Bordoloi (1991), Neog and Gogoi (2003), Baruah (2005), Chetia (2008), Medhi *et al* (2009) and Gogoi ((2009) all wrote about the various usages and influences of bamboo in life of the Assamese. They all opined that bamboo is used for various purposes by the Assamese society like for construction, making different type of agricultural, fishing, hunting and weaving implements besides handicraft items and in almost all the major religious and social functions.

Bamboo is the fast growing woody plant and it can grow up to 250 centimetres or 98 inches per day depending on the local soil type, climatic conditions and species. Bamboos grow 3-10 centimetres daily in temperate climates. Some species of bamboo can grow more than 30 metre or 98 feet in height with a diameter of 15-20 centimetres or 5.9-7.9 inches. In freezing temperatures many tropical bamboo species die while some so called hardier or temperate bamboos can survive even in as low as 29^{0}C or 20^{0}F temperatures also. With 1250 species in 75 genera worldwide and 136 species in India, the Northeast has 58 species belonging to 10 genera. Next to China and India, Assam has a rich repository of bamboo with 42 species belonging to 10 genera growing abundantly in her hills and plains (Bhagabati, 2006). Some of the common bamboo varieties in Assam are *Bhaluka* (*Bambusabalcooa*), *Jati* (*Bambusatulda*), *beti* (*B. mastersii*), *mokal* (*B. nutans*), *kak* (*Dendrocalamusgigenteus*), *dalou* or *deu* (*Phyllostachysmannii*), *bajal* (*Saccharumpolymorphum*), *bijuli* (*Bambusa pallida*), *kotoh* (*Bambusabambos*), etc. (Das, 2006). Bamboo prefers slightly acidic nitrogen rich soil. In terms of soil texture it prefers loam. Bamboo needs a well drained soil. It cannot grow in swampy water logged soil. It also grows well in sandy soil and red clay (www.bamboobotanicals.ca/html/bamboo-care/soil-for-bamboo.html). The climatic condition and soil composition of the Northeast India and that of Assam is suitable for bamboo cultivation.

Assam lying in the regime of monsoon climate has a hot and wet summer, cool and dry winter, high humidity and relatively low temperature during the year. The marked variation in its climatic pattern is due to the peculiar location, natural vegetation and the presence of water bodies including rivers in the state. Assam experiences an annual rainfall of less than 1000 mm to more than 6000 mm; the temperature is between 7°C – 36°C and the relative humidity between 60 to 85 per cent. Assam have four soil types, out of which the alluvial soil is mostly composed of sandy to silt loams and is slightly acidic in reaction; the hill soil is rich in nitrogen and organic matters while the lateritic soil have heavy loams (Bhagawati, 2006). All these soil types are perfect for bamboo cultivation.

Bamboo and Assamese life, especially rural or folk life are so inter-dependent that daily life without bamboo is unthinkable. Bamboo has many practical uses like fencing, making agricultural implements, fishing implements, weaving implements, musical instruments, ornaments, traditional headgear *japi*, furniture, decorative items, mats, baskets, house building purposes etc. (Chetia, 2008). In short, Assamese culture can be called as bamboo culture (Hakacham, 2008, p.162/Sarma, 1995). Because of its affinity with Assamese life, bamboo has found a place in the folk lore, ballads, folk beliefs, folk festivals, sculpture, folk performing arts, indigenous games, food and folk songs. The following is such a Bihu folk song:

Aagalibaharelahorigagana
Bahitatorpatitbao,
Ahekinahe oi morenocenaidhan
Chiripatimangalkhancao

It means that the bamboo musical instrument *gagana* is being played while sitting in the loom. The weaver, generally a girl, waiting eagerly for her beloved wants to confirm his arrival by taking recourse to the superstitious process of looking at the *mongal* (divination) (Das, 2006). The song reflects the unsteady mental condition of the weaver during the spring time Bihu festival.

There is the mention of bamboo in another folk song:

Bahoreaagoloi chai pothialo
Baharkondalipon
Chenairemukhaloi chai pothialo
Jen purnimarejon

It means that the tip of the bamboo in a grove decides which one is straight and beloved's face is like a full moon when looked upon. Here the beauty of the beloved's face is compared with the beauty and height of a bamboo pole. This song reflects the love of the beloved for his sweetheart with a covert element for desire.

Again in the following lyric, the relationship and position of bamboo for an Assamese is reflected:

Barirepicharejati bah ejupi
siomorsodararbhai
Jiaithako mane karokathi-kami
Marileolagate jay

It means that the bamboo plantation in the back of the compound is like ones brother. Till life exists, we keep on doing bamboo works and it ends with parting of the soul.

Bamboo has many medicinal and nutritional properties and hence it is also consumed as a delicacy by the Assamese people. For this purpose the bamboo shoots are used. The people of Assam either eat it raw, cooked or in dried form. It is used for flavouring dishes and as pickle also. Thus, bamboo is a part of Assamese ethnic food culture (Das, 2006). Bamboo as a medicinal ingredient has been in use from centuries. It is extensively used in Ayurveda for curing both minor and major ailments.

Moreover, bamboo is associated with folk beliefs. Ghosts are believed to reside in bamboo thickets and plantations. Bamboo grooves are the houses of malevolent ghosts like *deu* or *deula, pikhas, jokhini, bira, kandha* etc. according to local folk beliefs. It is believed that when one passes through a bamboo plantation at night then ghosts residing there stops him/her by lowering bamboo plants thereby blocking the way and then suddenly lifting the bamboo plant. If one sets foot on such a bamboo plant then he/she is also lifted up with it and might get killed in the process. Bamboo plants are not felled or cut on Saturdays, *amabaishyas* - the last lunar day of the dark fortnight and *ekadashis* - the eleventh day of a lunar fortnight according to folk beliefs. Bamboo flowering is believed to be a fore warning of misfortune, evil omen and natural calamity (Das, 2006).

Bamboo is so much closely associated with Assamese culture that right from birth till death its role is indispensable. A new born baby is separated from its mother with a sharp bamboo split to cut the umbilical cord in rural areas. Again a dead body is carried in a bamboo byre to the cremation ground for its last rites according to folk customs. Thus, its necessity is felt in every step. It has been appropriately termed as 'poor man's timber', 'green gold', 'friend of the people' and 'cradle to coffin timber' (Medhi *et al,* 2009).

The object of this paper is to focus on the ways of worshipping bamboo and to find out the reasons behind it with special reference to Bhatheli.

Bamboo Worship and Fertility Cult

It is a common practise in Hinduism to worship nature and inanimate objects by personifying them. This is the reason behind the worship of stones and various trees and plants by the Hindus. To the ancient people birth of animals and plants were a mysterious aspect. But they knew that reproduction involved biological process. So they created a culture which was potent for biological activities of human beings. The ancient cave paintings bear proof to such facts.

Worshipping the human sexual organs is a part of fertility cult. Failing to unearth the mystery of birth, it is not surprising that the people started worshipping the sexual organs in ancient times. The act of reproduction by both human and nature is beyond their comprehension. But they found a similarity between the reproductive instincts of humans and nature. Hence they started regarding the earth as mother and worshipped her (Borgohain, 2004). Similarly the motive behind bamboo worship is birth- the carving for male inheritors in the family to carry on the family legacy and the growth of plants or increased production for the better sustenance of the family. When and how the practise of bamboo worship came to Assam, there is no acceptable statement available. According to Hakacham its prevalence might be due to the cultural synthesis, acculturation and cultural diffusion of the different colourful indigenous tribes residing in Assam and their social structures (Hakacham, 2008).

Types of Bamboo Worship

In many parts of Assam especially in middle and lower Assam, in the districts of Darrang, Goalpara, Barpeta and Kamrup bamboo is worshipped in various forms. Paura Tola, Bah Puja in Goalpara district, Bhateli in North Kamrup district, Suweri in South Kamrup and Barpeta district, Dohor Ghuruwa, Deol in Darrang district, Lamja Kora, Putalar Biya (puppet marriage), Bah Gushaier Puja (worship of the bamboo lord) and Suree in Goalpara district are some forms of bamboo worship ((Das, 2006). It is to be noted that the different tribes residing not only in Assam but the entire Northeast region also worship bamboo. For example, we see the Tiwa tribe celebrating Jongkhong, the Rabhas celebrating Hachimaranga and Paroba, Bashpuja of the Hajongs and Koch-Rajbongshis and Paboni or Bauch of the Koch community (Hakacham, 2008). To put it plainly bamboo worship is the worship of two decorated bamboo poles which is believed to symbolise the bride and the groom.

(a) **Paura Tola** of Goalpara, is a form of bamboo worship where two decorated bamboo poles with a fly-flicker made from the hair of a yak tied at the top of the poles, believed to symbolise the bride and the groom, are worshipped at a public place. The taller pole is called the *matapaura,* i.e., the male pigeon, and the shorter one is called the *maikipaura,* i.e., the female pigeon. Nearby the poles a house is constructed with bamboo and the dried leaves of banana plant. It is called as the bhatheli house which is later demolished at night after a mock argument between two groups of people. The winning group demolishes the house and take away the cash inside it which has been offered by the devotees during the worship at daytime. As bamboo is a symbol of reproduction, this folk festival symbolises the worship of the phallus according to some scholars (Das, 2006).

(b) **Bah Puja** or bamboo worship is celebrated in Goalpara district on Madan Chaturdashi in the Assamese month of Chot, i.e., mid-March to mid-April. It is also called as Madan Kamdeva Puja or worship. It is supposed to be a localised version of the Madan festival celebrated in some parts of ancient India. But there is no history how and when this festival spread over a huge area of Kamrup district. According to stories Kamdeva, the god of love got his second life in Kamrup. So the worship of Kamdeva in Kamrup looks quite natural. Traditionally the worship of Lord Vishnu, Lord Krishna and Lord Kamdeva are same. But how bamboo worship came to be related with the worship of Madan Kamdeva or how and why the two bamboo poles came to represent Lord Madan Kamdeva and his wife goddess Rati are really thought provoking. Madan Kamdeva worship is celebrated for three to five days by men only. An interesting aspect of this celebration is that women and children are not allowed to take part in the worship proceedings though they can watch the celebrations. Moreover, an important feature of this worship is that Brahmin priests are not allowed to perform the religious ceremony (Borgohain, 2004). The Hazong and the Rajbongshi communities of Goalpara, unlike the Assamese of Kamrup, plant three bamboo poles representing the lord Madan, goddess Rati and lord Gopal. For decorating the poles different coloured cloth are used – white for the first and red for the second. The third is decorated with *zakoi,* i.e., bamboo scoop used for catching fish, creel or a bamboo basket used for keeping fish (*khaloi)* and a half broken plough. Two whisks of yak tail hair are tied at the top of the first two poles which are erected side by side, while the third pole is erected at a little distance. People give sacred offerings, sing and dance playing musical instruments to satisfy the Bamboo Lord (Das, 2006). Singing of ballads which are descriptive in nature is a part of this celebration. The subject matter of such ballads include the birth of Madan Kamdeva; birth of cotton and the process of weaving cloths; birth of bamboo; selection of the right variety of bamboo from amongst different varieties; mystery behind the creation of opium and stories related to opium eaters; stories associated with the tradition of gifting to brides, etc. Eminent folklorist Goswami (Borgohain, 2004, p. 116) mentions that the ballads sung by the Hajongs in this celebration are not only appealing in nature but also full of pangs for not attaining their desired beloveds. The presence of sexual content in some of the current songs indicates the association of fertility cult with this celebration. A further proof of this association is the union of the first two bamboos symbolising the bride and the groom. The decoration of the third bamboo pole indicates the wish of the people for better production or productivity (Borgohain: 2004, pp. 115-116).

(c) **Suweri** celebration of Barpeta district on the fourth day of Holi festival is different from that of South Kamrup. In Barpeta, bamboo is not worshipped but used as a barrier for Lord Krishna who is believed to return to his wife goddess Lakshmi's house on this day after visiting Princess Ghunucha. The Lord married Ghunucha secretly and spent the night with her. The devotees bring the deity of the Lord out of the *Kirtanghar,* the worshipping house of the Vaishnavites village lord on this day and takes out a procession in a palanquin playing coloured powder around the place to mark the return of the Lord to His house. On their return they find their entrance blocked with four big bamboo poles by the loyalists of the goddess Lakshmi. The devotees of the Lord ask for forgiveness for the Lord's act but the party representing the goddess refuse to give way. Then a mock debate ensures. At last He is allowed to enter only after reasoning with the loyalists. He takes seven rounds around the *Kirtanghar* and rests for a while. Again a debate takes place and this time the Lord looses. So the devotees of the Lord have to pay in cash to enter the main temple (Das, 2006).

(d) **Suweri** and bamboo marriage function is also celebrated in South Kamrup. In this celebration unlike *Bhatheli* no tall bamboo plants are planted, instead bamboo poles having leaves at the top are planted. Under the poles the deities brought from the neighbouring *namghars* or community prayer halls of the Vaishnavites are placed and worshipped. In the evening the deities are taken back to their village *namghars* and the returning party divides into two groups – one carrying the deity and the other obstructing them in their journey. This leads to a mock fight and the first party is made to enter each household in the village. The people welcome the deity and the processing party in front of their gates by lightning earthen lamps and taking His blessings. Goswami (cited in 'Suweri Aru Bah Biya Anusthan', Boragohain, 2004) mentioned that earlier buffalo fights, elephant fights etc. were also a part of this celebration. In some places of South Kamrup there is a custom of blocking the way of the procession party. The party then have to break the blockade and move forward (Bhattacharya, 2013).

(e) **Deol** celebration of Darrang district is not exactly bamboo worship. It is celebrated throughout the Assamese month of *Bohag* i.e. in mid-April and mid-May in different parts of the district. The scholars see a similarity between Bhatheli, Suweri, Bah Puja and Deol festivals because in the ancient times during the reign of the Bhuyans in Darrang, Vishnu worship became synonymous with bamboo worship. Bamboo symbolises procreation. This festival is based on the acts performed on a mound of earth (deol). There are seven storeys in the mound which symbolises the seven heavens. Four *jati* bamboos (Bambusatulda) and four banana saplings are planted in the four corners around the earthen mound. A stone is placed at the seventh floor and at the middle of the *deul,* a throne is placed with fishes and two *magars,* a Hindu mythological imaginary aquatic animal with an elephant's trunk in the body of a fish. An altar is made around the *deul* where four banana saplings are planted. Here Lord Vishnu is worshipped by the priest. But before that the Brahmin priest carries the throne on his head and goes round the seven stories. On reaching the top he places the statue of Lord Vishnu on the throne and carries it back. Then the throne is placed at the altar and the worship commences. It is interesting to note that the beard of a he-goat is burned on the previous day of the festival in a house constructed with dried bamboo leaves nearby the *deul.* This function is known as *Meha Dahan* (the burning of the goat). *Ojapali* and other cultural items of Darrang are performed in this function (Das, 2006).

(f) **Bah Riya** or **Bash Biya** means marriage of bamboos. It is interesting to note that this celebration is prevalent among certain sections of Muslims residing in Kamrup district. Like their Hindu counterparts they also regard the two bamboos erected during the festival as bride and groom. Nobody knows how this celebration, which is purely a Hindu celebration, came into the Muslim community. It is assumed that may be due to assimilation or may be due to conversion of some Hindus into Muslims. Bah Biyais celebrated by a certain section of the Muslims (Borgohain: 2004).

Bhatheli in the Context of Assam

Bhatheli is a very ancient agricultural festival. Most of the people agree that it is a worship of Lord Madan Kamdeva, the god of love in Hindu mythology. According to Banikanta Kakoti (cited in 'Bhatheli', Borghain, 2004), the two bamboo poles erected in Bhatheli called as *mataparo* or *paura,* i.e., a male pigeon and a *maikiparo* or *paura,* i.e., a female pigeon, might be the indigenous versions of *indradhwaj,* i.e., the flag posts planted in the honour of Lord Indra, the god of sky and clouds in the Hindu mythology, and the king of the gods and goddesses. He further compared Bhatheli with the worship of Lord Indra prevalent during the *Mahabharata* period. These flag posts were then planted seven days before full moon and earlier it was an agricultural festival. Bamboo is regarded as a symbol of fertility. Hence the two bamboo poles erected in Bhatheli festival brings together the sky and the earth resulting in rain quickening the growth of plants and crops.

It is clear that this was basically an agricultural festival as the growth of agriculture and cattle were associated with it. But still a question arises regarding the celebration time of Bhatheli. The worship of Lord Indra in the rest of India is traditionally done during the autumn season while Bhatheli is celebrated in the spring season in Assam. If Bhatheli is considered to be the localised version of the worship of Lord Indra then why is it not celebrated in the autumn season like the rest of India? Moreover, when was there the prevalence of Indra worship in Assam? When we arrive at the correct answer to these questions then only we can be assured that the worship of the Lord Indra of the earlier times maybe present in a corrupted form or localised version in Assam.

There is mention of the presence of Indra worship in the *Kalika Puran* which was composed in the tenth century. Moreover, Goswami (cited in 'Bhatheli', Borghain, 2004) gives another proof of Indra worshipping in Kamrup district of Assam as seen in a stone inscription of Balobarma. If we consider Bhatheli to be the same as Indra worship then there cannot be such a vast difference between the celebration times of the two. Maybe we can assume that in Assam from early times Indra worship is done in the beginning of the Assamese New Year in the month of *Bohag* (mid-April-May), in the spring season. After the passing of many centuries maybe Indra worship is saved through Bhatheli festival. But the point to be noted is that in Indra worship Lord Indra is worshipped while in Bhatheli Lord Vishnu or his full incarnation Lord Krishna is worshipped. Hence at the present prevalent form there seems to be no connection between Indra worship and Bhatheli as suggested early by Banikanta Kakoti.

That Bhatheli was an agricultural festival there is no doubt, but at the same time it is also associated with fertility cult. The reason behind this is the mock marriage between the two bamboo poles representing the bride and her groom. The marriage ceremony is conducted basically for fulfilling the purpose of reproduction and growth. There is, however, no proof in history from when this festival is celebrated. Hence it can be assumed that Bhatheli was there from very early times. Though in the early period Lord Indra or bamboo was worshipped, in the latter period the worship of Lord Krishna and Lord Vishnu has taken over his place. The significance of this festival is the fertility cult on one hand and the power of the god on the other hand (Borgohain, 2004).

Bhatheli is a very popular, seasonal, daylong folk festival of Kamrup. There is no fixed date for this festival. It is celebrated in any date in the Assamese calendar month of *Bohag*. Some scholars opine that it is a kind of bamboo worship. It is known by various names in different parts of Kamrup like Bhatheli in the north and Suweree or Shori in the south; Bishuba in Goalpara district and Deol in Darrang district. It is interesting to note that it is also celebrated in our neighbouring state of West Bengal. Early morning on the day of the festival the youths of the village take bath and according to folk the customs cut two bamboo poles, cleans them by removing the green outer layer, wash them, dry them, wrap them in cloth and dress them with garlands. A fly-flicker made from the hair of a yak's tail is tied at the top of the poles. All this work is done in the house of a wealthy person of the village. The people, young and old alike carry the dressed bamboo poles in a procession to the place of celebration by singing, dancing and playing religious musical instruments like conch, drum, *khol* - an elongated drum, *kali* – a clarion, *borkah* – a gong and *uruli* – a shrilling sound produced repeated movements of the tongue by the women on auspicious occasions. Normally two bamboo poles are erected in this festival but sometimes three or four poles are also planted giving instance of the pride and prosperity of the area (Bhattacharya, 2013). The bamboo poles are erected either at the courtyard of the community prayer hall/*naamghar* or in an open space amidst a lot of merry making. These two bamboo poles symbolise the bride and her groom according to folk belief. The bamboo symbolising the groom is called *daraparo* and the bride is called *kainaparo*. Generally the hoist village plants the *daraparo* and the *kainaparo* is planted by the youths of another village. A mock marriage ceremony is conducted between these two bamboo poles. People sing and dance merrily around the poles in a daylong celebration. A gateway is also constructed by planting a bamboo pole and a banana plant (Chetia: 2008). In this festival Lord Krishna and Lord Vishnu are worshipped. The deities are placed in a throne in the middle of the field or open space. The deities are later taken out in a procession. Bhatheli celebrations do not have any religious implications as there is no special worship or fasting in this festival.

The main object of Bhatheli festival is '*paro*' or the decorated bamboo flags (poles) which fly beautifully in the sky. During the Vedic *jagyas* or sacrifices the priest performing the *jagya* used to plant bamboo poles. Such poles were also planted at the beginning of the Shiva festival of the ancient Dravidians, during the time of dramatist Bharata. This pole was called as *jorjor* (anguished) pole or as *indradhawaj*. Erection of such poles was considered to be auspicious. In Charak worship of the tea tribes and after funeral rites there is a tradition of planting such poles in the Arya Hindu society. On the other hand there is a close relationship of the Kirata culture with bamboo. Late Sarat Ch. Goswami (compared the plantation of *paro* in Bhatheli festival with *hokrothan*- victory celebration of the kings. But Bhatheli is celebrated in the Assamese month of *bohag* while *hokrothan* is celebrated in the month of *Bhadra* (mid August-September). It is assumed that the tradition of Bhatheli is the result of the collective influence of the spring time festival Bihu, the use of bamboo by the Kiratas, the Vaishnavite religion and the *indradhawajs* of Shiva festival of Assam and the North East India. Though there is a slight colouring of the spring time festival Bihu and fertility cult upon Bhatheli festival, there is no sign of open sex appeal in it (Bhattacharya, 2013).

Nearby the poles a Bhatheli house is constructed with banana leaves where cash and sacred food are placed. Both the poles are devotedly worshipped throughout the day. It is the tradition of this festival to demolish the Bhatheli house in the evening. Generally the young boys of the village demolish the house by shouting and declaring that Bhatheli is over. They then share whatever is inside the house amongst them. Sometimes mock fights also take place in this function. When boys from the neighbouring villages arrive to destroy the house, then the boys of the hoisting village enacts to prevent them (Borgohain, 2004). Bhattacharya (2013) compares the demolition of the Bhatheli house with the clearing of the blockade by the procession party in *Suwori* celebration of south Kamrup. In both the occasions the parties displays their physical strength over the other party.

A significant part of this celebration is the fair held simultaneously. Clay toys specially made by the women folk and children of the area for the occasion are displayed in the fair. In some places the youngsters perform *dadhimanthana* dance (churning of milk and curd to produce butter, the favourite food of the Lord, by Yashodha, the foster mother of Lord Krishna). Though the organisers of the festival are Hindus, other religious groups also partake in it and enjoy the festival (Das, 2006).

Genesis of the Word '*bhatheli*'

Different scholars have given different opinions regarding the genesis of the word '*bhatheli*'. According to some scholars the word '*bhatheli'* has been derived from the Sanskrit word *'bhanthalika'*, which means 'the sky'. Maybe, therefore, the sky towering bamboo poles symbolise the sky. Another group of scholars opine that these bamboo poles symbolise the phallus. Thus, this festival is phallus-centric and is associated with fertility cult. The bamboo poles are believed to connect the sky and the earth. The sky is imagined to represent the male and the earth the female (Chetia, 2008). Bhattacharya (2013) disagrees with the opinion of Goswami regarding the origin of the word *'bhatheli'*. Goswami believes the origin of the word '*bhatheli'* is '*bhathi,* which in the colloquial language of Kamrup and in the dialect of an elephant caretaker means the ejaculation of a young elephant. But Bhatheli is a spring time festival so he hinted at the presence of the element of desire in it and associated the origin of the word '*bhatheli'* with '*bhathi'*. But Bhattacharya points out that at present there is no such indication and hence such an explanation cannot be accepted. Another group of scholars believed the word '*bhatiyali'* to be the root word of '*bhatheli'*. If this is true then it can be assumed that '*bhatiyali'* became '*bhaitheli'* or '*bhatheli'* in the colloquial language of Kamrup. But '*bhatiyali'* of *Padma Purana* cannot be linked and associated with '*bhatheli'*. Bhattacharya as a linguist further disclaims the association of '*bhatheli'* with the Sanskrit word '*banti'* – lamp and '*upastha'* – penis. Poet Choudhary said that '*bhatheli'* originated from the Assamese word '*bhuinthali'* and the word '*bhuin'*- land means paddy field. Linguist Banikanta Kakoti is of the opinion that the origin of the word '*bhatheli'* is the Sanskrit word '*bhasthali'* or '*bhosthalica'* where '*bha'* means sky and '*sthali'* means place.

The origin of the word '*paro'* is also mysterious. This word can be associated with the Sanskrit word '*parawat'* – pigeon. But then what are the similarities between a '*parawat'* and a '*mata'* or '*maikiparo'* of Bhatheli. How the word '*paro'* got such an important position in bhatheli requires research. Goswami tried to establish a relation between the word '*paro*' and the Bhutanese word '*porosa*' (Bhattacharya: 2013).

Conclusion

Bamboo is the most commonly grown plant in the villages of Assam. Each household possesses a bamboo plantation at their backyards. They feel incomplete and weak without such a plantation. They cannot imagine a life without bamboo. Hence they grow it in abundance. Its multifarious use has made the socio-cultural life of the Assamese rich. It is cultivated for food as well as social, religious and economic purposes. It has a close association with most of the rites of Assam. No *pandal* whether religious or social is complete without bamboo poles. Many customs and belief systems came to be associated with bamboo. Moreover, it is regarded as sacred and believed to be associated with fertility among the Assamese Hindus. It is worshipped in diverse ways in the agricultural-based economy by the village folks. Bhatheli is one such folk festival where people of all castes and religion are seen to participate openly in large numbers.

The Muslim community of Hajo in Kamrup district are seen to celebrate this festival. They call it as Bah Riya or Bah Biya which means bamboo marriage (Chetia: 2008). There is no proper document explaining how, why and from when they celebrate this festival. The only acceptable assumption is that maybe it is the result of their assimilation with the Assamese Hindu community and customs.

Bamboo-based-festivals in Kamrup Rural district of Assam are seen to have undergone changes in the present time due to the invasion of the electronic media in the form of private Assamese news channels. In order to attract the electronic media the local organisers compete with the celebrations of other places and incorporate extra elements into the function. This leads to the loss of the actual gravity of the celebration to some extent. Moreover, such festivities have turned into tourist destinations for the urban folks who are always in search of respite from their busy schedules. As a result, urban elements have entered into these celebrations. The fairs, for example, are invaded to a great extent by the established business organisations resulting in the loss of the rustic ethnic flavour. Again the main celebration or bamboo worship has also become glamorous or grandiose. All these changes have affected the festivities positively and negatively also. In the positive aspect it has helped in boosting the rural economy besides been successful in letting the young urban generation to know and learn about their culture. It is, therefore, the need of the hour to preserve and at the same time promote such culturally rich bamboo-based folk festivals for the posterity in their original flavour.

References

Baruah, B.K. (2003), *Bihugeet at Asomiya Jibonor Chitra*. In Asamiya Sanskriti, 4th ed. (ed.) Hariprasad Neog and Lila Gogoi, —, Dibrugarh: Assam Sahitya Sabha.

Baruah, B. K. (2005), Asamar Loka Sanskriti, 8th ed., Guwahati: Bina Library.

Bhagawati, A.K., M.C. Kalita and S. Barua (2006), *Status of Biodiversity*. In Biodiversity of Assam Status Strategy and Action Plan for Conservation (ed.) 9-10, 36, Guwahati: EBH Publishers (India).

Bhattacharya, P.C. (2013), *Asamar Loka-Utsava*, 38, 40-42, Nalbari: Journal Emporium.

Bordoloi, N. (1991), *Asamar Loka Sanskriti* (4th ed.), Guwahati: Bina Library.

Borgohain, J. K. (2004), *Asamar Utsava aru Puja*, 75-77, 104-109, 114-116, Guwahati: Student Store and Jyoti Prakashan.

Chetia, U. (2008), *Asamar Loka Sanskritir Ruprekha*, 120-121, 265-266, Dhemaji: Kiran Prakashan.

Das, N. (2006), *Khoricha (Bah Gaj)*. In Asamiya Sanskritir Kanika (ed.) N. Das and P. Rajbongshi, 93, Guwahati: Chandra Prakash.

Das, N. (2006), *Bah Puja*. In Asamiya Sanskritir Kanika (ed.) N. Das and P. Rajbongshi, 248, Guwahati: Chandra Prakash.

Das, N. (2006), *Suweri*. In Asamiya Sanskritir Kanika (ed.) N. Das and P. Rajbongshi, 312, Guwahati: Chandra Prakash.

Datta, B. (1980), *The Assamese Folk Mind*. In Assam and the Assamese Mind (ed.) Nagen Saikia, 60-70, Guwahati: Assam Sahitya Sabha.

Dutta, P. (2006), *Asomiya Sanskritit Bah*. In Asomiya Sanskritir Konika (ed.) N. Das and P. Rajbongshi, 34-35, Guwahati: Chandra Prakash.

Gogoi, Chow Lokeswar (2009), *Asamar Loka –Sanskriti,* 2nd edition, Bhopal, Debajit Barua and Nang Bandana Barua, Madhya Pradesh.

Hakacham, U. R. (2008), *Bar Asamar Barnil Sanskriti,* 162-167, Guwahati, Bina Library.

Medhi, B. K. and K. Jose SDV (2009), *Indigenous Resource Management among the Tribes of Northeast India*. In Tribes of North-East India Issues and Challenges (ed.), B.K. Medhi and K Jose SDV, 95, New Delhi, Omsons Publications.

Rajbongshi, B. (2006), *Bhatheli*. In Asamiya Sanskritir Konika (ed.) N. Das and P. Rajbongshi, 264, Guwahati: Chandra Prakash.

Rajbongshi, H. (2006), *Darrangar Deul*. In Asamiya Sanskritir Konika (ed.) N. Das and P. Rajbongshi, 182-183, Guwahati: Chandra Prakash.

Rajbongshi, P. (2006), *Paura Tola*. In Asamiya Sanskritir Konika (ed.) N. Das and P. Rajbongshi, 219-220, Guwahati: Chandra Prakash.

Rajbongshi, P. (2006), *Gagana*. In Asamiya Sanskritir Konika (ed.) N. Das and P. Rajbongshi, 100-101, Guwahati: Chandra Prakash.

Sarma, N. C. (1995), *Asamiya Loka Sanskritir Abash,* 31, 33, 225

www.bamboobotanicals.ca/html/bamboo-care/soil-for-bamboo.html, Retrieved on 2-4-2015.

7

An Exploration of the Sacred Complex of Vasisthasrama of Assam

— *Birinchi K. Medhi, Kunal Choudhury*

I

Assam is situated in the tropical latitudes 24.3° N and 28.0° N and latitudes 89.5° E and 96.1° E. Among all the states of North East India Assam is the most populous state. The Vasisthasrama, popularly known as the Vasistha, is an immensely revered temple located in Guwahati, the capital city of Assam. 'Assam is an ancient land and it has a thought provoking history. In the epic period the land was referred to as Pragjyotishpura (the land of eastern light) and in the *Purana* and *Tantra* periods it acquired the name Kamrupa (where the god Kamadeva regains his physique). The name Assam is an anglicised formation of the Sanskrit term '*asama*', which means 'unparallel' or 'peerless' (Medhi, 2008:91). Assam is a place of temples and shrines. Guwahati being the capital of the state for prolonged period and because of this place is booned by picturesque beauty with Brahmaputra and other rivers, serpent like green hillocks and mesmerising plain areas, a good number of temples and shrines are established here. TheVasisthasrama (hermitage of Vasistha), is a renown temple situated at a distance of about 11 kms in the southern direction from the centre of Guwahati city. According to the *Kalika Purana*, due to the penance of sage (*rishi)*Vasistha divine river Ganga came as three rivulets, viz., the Sandhya, the Lalita and the Kanta, to the Sandhyachala hillock of Guwahati, and the confluence of these three rivulets is known as the Vasistha Ganga. The Ahom king Rajeswar Singha had constructed a temple nearby this water source during AD 1751-1769. In the temple wall there is an inscription on stone of the time of the

Ahom king Rajeswar Singha, which was inscribed in 1686 *saka.* Inside the temple there is a pair of foot marks and the Hindus believe that these are the foot prints of the great *rishi* Vasistha (Neog, 2008:263).

It should be noted here that amidst the overwhelming majority of the Siva temples only a few religious centres devoted to the other gods and goddesses are located in Guwahati. The principal deity of the Vasisthasrama is also Lord Siva known as Golokeswara Siva ('Golok' means 'Vaikuntha', a place in heaven, the abode of Lord Vishnu) and *'iswara'* means 'authority', that means authority of Goloka. 'The name Siva is unknown to *veda*, but Rudra, another name of the deity, and almost equally common, occurs in the *veda* both singular and plural, and from these the great deity Siva and his manifestation, the Rudra, have been developed. In the *Yajur-veda* there is a long prayer called *Satarudriya* which is addressed to him and appeals to him under a great variety of epithets....In *Upanisadas* his character is further developed....In *Ramayana,* Siva is a great god, but the references to him have more of the idea of a personal god than a supreme divinity....The *Mahabharata* also gives Vishnu and Krishna the highest honour upon the whole. But it has many passages in which Siva occupies the supreme place, and receives the homage and worship of Vishnu and Krishna (Dowson, 1987: 296-297).

Siva, the dissolver and reproducer, is the third deity of the Hindu triad, the other two are Brahma, the creator, and Vishnu, the preserver. Lord Siva is generally imagined as garbing by a tiger skin, body is smeared with ashes, bearer of divine river Ganga (Gangadhara), having matted hair *(*Jatadhara), wearing in neck a garland of human skull (Kapalmali) and a serpent with conspicuous hood (Phanidhara), moon crested (Chandrasekhara), blue-throated (Nilakantha), three eyed (Trilochana, Trinayana, Tryambaka) and so on, and having a trident *(trishula*) called *pinaka* and a *dambaru*, a kind of musical instrument, in his hands. He is habituated to consume regularly thorn apple fruit *(dhatura*) and *bhang* (*Canabis Sativa L.*). Like other Hindu gods and goddesses Siva also have a good number of names and epithets, some of which are: Aghora (the terrible), Bhairava (the terrible destroyer), Chandradhara, (middle of his forehead is surmounted with a creseant of moon), Dhurjati (loaded with matted hair), Digambara (the naked one), Girisha (mountain lord), Hara (the seizer), Ishana (the ruler), Mahadeva (the great god), Mahakala (the great time), Mahesha (the great god), Mahayogi (the great ascetic), Maheswara (the great god), Mrityunjaya (vanquisher of death), Panchanana (five faced), Pashupati (lord of animals), Pinakpani (who holds a *pinak,* i.e., a trident), Rudra (from the Sanskrit root 'rud', means 'to weep'), Sadasiva, Sambhu, Sankara and Siva (the auspicious), Ugra (fierce), and so on.

Like almost all the Hindu gods and goddess lord Siva does not live in heaven, but resides at the Kailasa hill. He also sometimes lives in the cremation ground along with the ghosts and imps (*bhuta*), for which he is known as Bhutanatha and Bhuteswara. Siva moves around riding on a milky white healthy bull known as Nandi. It is a paradox that he is the lord of the universe (Viswanatha), but lives on begging. In an Assamese folk song this character of Siva is depicted in a conspicuous manner:

'O Siva Bholanatha he
Tomar shire jata
Jagataka bar diya
Apuninangatha.'

The broad meaning of the song is : O Siva Bholanatha, you have matted hair in your head, you offer boons to all, but you are naked.

II

In Assam, Siva is a immensely popular god and generally known as Bholanatha, Mahadeva, Sadasiva or Siva, but most popularly revered as Burha Gosair (the old god). In every locality of Assam one can observe the worshipping places carefully preserved for this omnipotent god, which are identified as Burha Gosair Than, the appeasing place of lord Siva. It is a known fact that Assam is an abode of a good number of tribal communities and most of these communities believe in a pristine tribal god, whose physical features and attributes are akin to those of the lord Siva. As for example, the Bathou of the Boro, Langa of the Rabha, Ublei of the Khasi, Burha, Balia Baba or the Pisadoma of the Deuri are some of the tribal gods resemble closely to the Hindu god Siva. The sanskritised tribal groups of Assam referred such traditional gods as Siva or Mahadeva. Overwhelming majority of the Siva temples of Assam prove the popularity of this god in this remote part of India. Till today the parents of Assam, both tribal and non-tribal, named their offsprings after the names of Lord Siva like Bhairab, Bholanath, Chandrasekhar, Dhurjati, Gangadhar, Gaurisankar, Girindra, Girish, Harendra, Ishan, Mahadeb, Mahesh, Maheswar, Pinakpani, Sailendra, Sankar, Sasankasekhar, Sashadhar, Sashindra, Satish, Siva, Sibasish, *et al.*

In Hinduism, destruction implies reproduction. Lord Siva is also Kameswara, the lord of carnal desire. This epithet clearly relates the deity with reproduction. Due to this character, Siva is generally not appeased in anthropomorphic form, but propitiated in his symbol *linga* (phallus), typical of reproduction. Sometimes a *linga* is worshipped alone or with the combination of *yoni,* the female organ. It is pertinent to note here that in all the temples and shrines of lord Siva, the deity is worshipped with his consort Sati. In different births Sati acquired different names like Gauri, Parvati, Uma, *et al.,* and therefore, in the different Siva temples and shrines lord Siva is appeased with those forms of Sati. In all the Sakti temples also the goddess (Devi) is worshipped with her consort lord Siva. In Vasisthasrama, lord Siva is worshipped with his consort Tara.

Siva is principally propitiated with cow milk, the symbol of sperm or breast milk, wood apple fruit and leaf, which are also symbols of fertility cult. The Monday is believed to be the birthday of Siva, and therefore, auspicious to appease this god, and due to this connection lord Siva acquires the name Somanatha (authority of Monday). It is strongly believed by the Hindus that among the entire gods lord Siva is the best husband, and therefore, the damsels worship this god particularly on Mondays observing some religious taboo to get good husbands and to acquire fortune. It is also believed that this god is very handsome, calm and quite in nature and could be satisfied easily, for which he acquires the name Ashutosa. The Hindus sincerely believe that this coy and amiable god only becomes terrible and turbulent through the vexatious deeds of somebody. His third eye is very destructive, which is located vertically in the middle of his forehead above the two eyes and generally remains close. Lord Siva's wrath is intensified through opening of the third eye, which sight could reduce anything to ashes in splits of a second. In such furry he sometimes perform *tandava,* a kind of vigorous dance, and during that time the whole universe trembles in fear and agony.

III

The mythology says that Vasisthasrama is the hermitage (*ashrama*) of the sage Vasistha, where he meditates to erase a curse cast by the king Nimi. The sage establishes the hermitage in Sandhyachala and lives with his wife Arundhati there. The stone form of Arundhati is lying there in the eastern side of the *ashrama* at a distance. The Ahom king donated 857 *bighas* (1 acre= 3.025 *bigha*) of land to the Vasisthasrama. At present only eight *bighas* of land is with Vasisthasrama and the rest is illegally occupied by the people belonging to different communities including the citizens of Meghalaya, one of the neighbouring states of Assam.

'Polytheism is the pivotal feature of Hinduism. It is also a faith in unity in multiplicity. The faith originated in the initial stage of Hinduism in one of the primary scripture *Rig Veda*, where the concept of one god is conspicuous among innumerable gods and goddesses. In the *Rig Veda* it is described like this: They called it Indra, Mitra, Varuna and Agni. And also heavenly beautiful Kirtiman. The real is one, though sages name it variously.

Although polytheism and heathenism is conspicuous in the *Vedas,* the most dominant tendency of the scriptures is monoism, the realisation of one in many. The philosophical evolution of Hinduism from polytheism through henotheism to monotheism also give rise to a number of sub-religions in Hinduism' (Medhi and Bhuyan, 2015:18).

In the course of evolution of Hinduism, Saivism also originated. The rigid worshippers of lord Siva are known as *Saiva,* who appease the god as the supreme being. In Assam, there is a strong flow of Saivism which is conspicuous by the good number of Siva temples situated in different parts of the state, 'Saivism or the worship of Siva prevailed in Assam from remote period and it was the popular form of religion both among the aboriginals and Aryanised people. In an analysis of the name of sacred places given in the *Kalika Purana* clearly shows that the number of sacred places connected with Siva worship is larger than that of the places associated with Vishnu and Devi worship (Barua, 1951:165). A large number of people in Assam regarded Saivism as an acute expression of their inner feelings to adore some supernatural force controlling the whole universe. The worshipper of lord Siva gives him more than one thousand names. He is also imagined as a combination of male (*purusa*) and female (*prakiti*) and that form is known as Ardhanariswara.

In almost all the temples of Assam lord Siva is propitiated in phallus form. Monier Williams points out that 'Siva is represented as less human and more mythical than that of the incarnated Vishnu. The character in which he is worshipped is that of an omnipotent god, taking the place of Brahma, the creator, granting new life to all created things, but only through death and disintegration. Hence he is not represented by the image of a man and by a mystic symbol, perhaps the best symbol of delegated creative power' (cited in Medhi and Talukdar, 2012:13-15).

IV

It has been already stated that Vasisthasrama is situated in the Sandhyachala hillock in Guwahati, the only city of North East India. The hillock derives it name from two Sanskrit words- '*sandhi'*, means 'joint' and '*achala*', means 'hill', that is 'joint of hills'. It is believed by the Hindus that sage Vasistha was the worshipper of Jogeswara Siva, Jogeswara means 'the great aestic, in whom is centered the highest perfection of austers penance and abstract meditation, by which the most unlimited powers are attained, marvels and miracles are worked, the highest spiritual knowledge is acquired, and union, with the great spirit of the universe is eventually gained' (Dowson, 1987: 298). However, in the Vasisthasrama the principal deity lord Siva is worshipped as Golokeswara Siva. The Vasisthasrama is integral to a good number of legends. According to one of them, Vasistha has acute enmity with Viswamitra, a Kshatriya sage, and on one day Viswamitra killed all the sons of Vasistha. Then Vasistha moved from Gandhara to Kamrupa and built the hermitage at Sandhyachala and appeased Siva with great reverence. Lord Siva was pleased by the penance of the sage and blessed him with three streams from the heavenly Ganga river, and also offered the lives of his deceased sons.

According to the *Kalika Purana* (Neog, 2008:263), Vasistha, the mind son (*manasa-putra*) of the creator god Brahma, had lost his body in the curse of the king Nimi. Vasistha was very angry and due to his wrath the king also lost his physique. Vasistha took shelter in Brahma, who advised him to propitiate lord Vishnu in the Sandhyachala of Kamrupa to regain his body. Vasistha came to the Sandhyachala following the suggestion of Brahma and started worshipping Vishnu there. In his acute reverence the Ganga river came down from heaven to Sandhyachala in the forms of three rivulets. The meeting place of these rivulets is known as Vasistha Ganga, where sage Vasistha used to take his bath regularly. Due to the great penance Vasistha obtained his body. Vasistha appeased lord Vishnu in Sandhyachala to fulfil his desire, but how the Siva temple originated there instead of the Vishnu temple, history is silent about that.

The Vasisthasrama is situated in such a place that the scenic beauty of which can fascinate easily any person. The low green hill with frequent curves makes this corner of Guwahati city an indescribable source of eye-pleasing beauty. This temple is located in a more or less plain area on the lower part of the Sandhayachala, which is principally divided into two parts - the *grabha-griha* (sanctum sanctorum) and the *nata-mandira* (the open hall). Inside the *grabha-griha* lord Siva and Vasistha are located together in a single stone, which is the principal object of revere in Vasisthasrama. In almost all the Siva temples of Assam lord Siva is propitiated in his phallus form. However, in Vasisthasrama and some other Siva temples and shrines of Assam the objects for appeasing the deity are some mythological remnants. It is believed that after the death of sage Vasistha he had mingled with lord Siva and took a stone form, which resembles a lying person. Along with the Siva- Vasistha stone goddess Tara is also worshipped in the *garbha-griha*, which is represented by a comparatively smaller stone. It is pertinent to note that Tara is one of the forms of goddess Durga, the wife and female energy (Sakti) of lord Siva. The *nata-mandira* is a spacious hall and an extension of the main temple where the devotees gathered and the household rituals and community prayers are also arranged.

Outside the *garbha-griha* a phallic form of lord Siva is there. Ganesha, the son of Siva and the remover of obstacles, is worshipped along with devi Saraswati (goddess of knowledge) in another temple situated at a shouting distance from the main temple within the sacred complex. In that temple there is a big stone where meticulously engraved figure of Siddhidata (who fulfils desires) Ganesha is conspicuous. In the same stone engraved figure of Sarasvati is also present. At a short distance from the Ganesha temple there is a statue of sage Vasistha standing in open air. The devotees visit the Ganesha temple to appease the god, but no ritual integral to Ganesha and Saraswati is observed in the Vasisthasrama. There is a tiny Assam Type house within the temple complex known as *dharmasala* for sheltering the devotees of distant areas. Due to the lack of renovation at present devotees could not be kept in that abandoned house. Opposite to the *dharmasala,* in the other side of the main temple, there is another Assam Type house consists of three rooms, which is used as the living house of the priests. On the back side of the *garbha-griha* the Sandhya, the Lalita and the Kanta are flowing gently and at a distance their confluence make the Vasistha Ganga. Adjacent to the Vasisthasrama near the main gate, a few shops are there, which provide articles like clay lamps, incense sticks, flowers and leaves, etc., for propitiating the deity in the temple.

The Ahom King Rajeswar Singha had appointed two sets of persons, the *sevait* and the *paik,* for the maintenance of the temple. The *sevaits* were the Brahmana males coming from the Chamata village of Nalbari district, Assam, engaged in the priestly duties. Till today their decendants are engaged as priests in the Vasisthasrama. The *paiks* are the non-Brahmana male persons, who were entrusted to conduct non-priestly duties integral to the Vasisthasrama. The *paiks* mainly included the Mali (flower supplier), potter and goldsmith, who provided flowers and leaves, earthen wares and gold objects, respectively, required for appeasement of the deity. However, at present there are no *paik* in the Vasisthasrama, and necessary articles used in worshipping the deity are purchased from the market. There are fourteen priests in the temple now, who are referred to as *bar-deuri*. Two persons are appointed there on the basis of monthly salary to keep the temple clean and tidy.

There are two management committees to look after the maintenance of the Vasisthasrama. One of the committee is known as The Management Committee of the Vasisthasrama Devalaya, constituted of eight members from the temple priests and the citizens of Assam headed by the Deputy Commissioner of Guwahati city. The other one is The Vasistha Ganga Seva Samity, constituted by the priests of the temple, which is popularly known as the Purohit Samaj. The Vasisthasrama is somehow maintaining its own existence and surviving only on the money (*arihana*) given by the devotees without any grant-in-aid from the government. Renovation is not done in the temple for a long time due to the dearth of money.

The principal deity in the Vasisthasrama with his consort is appeased through daily, annual and occasional rituals. The daily rituals *(nitya puja)* are performed for three times in a day- at morning, noon time and in the evening. In each morning the deity of the temple is ritually awakened and given ceremonial bath. After that the principal and the subordinate deities are appeased through Vedic norms. At that time the devotees are not allowed in the *grabha-griha*. At the noon time sacred food (*bhoga*) prepared by the *bar-deuris*, consists of rice, pulses and vegetable curry, is ritually offered to the deity. In the evening *sandhyaarati*, i.e., the propitiation of the god through earthen lamps, is performed.

The principal annual rituals (*batsarik puja*) of the Vasisthasrama are Surya Grahana (solar eclipse), Chandra Grahana (lunar eclipse), Sivaratri, literally 'the night of lord Siva', Ashokastami, Ambubachi and Makar Samkranti, which are observed in the temple in accordance to the Hindu almanac with pomp and gaiety. Makar Samkranti is observed in the month of *Puh* (15th December to 14th January), when a luxurious fair (*mela*) is held in the temple campus. The Sivaratri is another cherished ritual of the temple observed in the month of *Magh* (15th January to 14th February), when good number of devotees and tourists visit Vasisthasrama to observe the elaborate rituals. During the Sivaratri also a grand fair is arranged in the temple campus. In the rituals integral to the solar and lunar eclipses, observed in the temple good number of devotees take a dips in the Vasistha Ganga to wreath with the benediction of lord Siva. Along with these pristine rituals performed in the Vasisthasrama a new ritual is added principally percolated from the Hindi speaking Hindu communities of India. This ritual is commonly known as Bol Bom, literally 'utter the name of lord Siva', observed in the month of *Saon* (15th July to 14th August), and a colourful fair is held in the temple complex during the ritual which is known as Saoni Mela. During this time the devotees carry holy water from the Vasistha Ganga and pour it on the Siva *linga* of the Sukreswara temple situated on the hillock Hastachala on the southern bank of the mighty river Brahmaputra in Panbazar area of the Guwahati city. The occasional rituals of the Vasisthasrama principally include some of the crises rite of the Hindus like *Chudakarana*, i.e., tongturing of the male child for the first time, *Annaprasana*, i.e. first solid food giving ceremony to a child, *Upanayana*, i.e., sacred thread giving ceremony to a boy, *Vivah* (marriage), *Sraddha* (mortuary rite), etc.

In the Vasisthasrama, the Assamese women perform nama, i.e., singing of sacred songs as the ode to the lord Siva, particularly on the ritual day. Some of such songs are given below:

(a) *Ai maianedekha-sunanai*
Jatiyabhangura
Gale mundamala
Dum dumdambarubajay.

The broad meaning of the song is: Mother, I have not seen or heard like this; he is with the matted hair, who consumes cannabis regularly, wearing a garland of human skulls encircling the neck, is beating *dambaru* making dum-dum sound.

(b) *Bhang khaipagalaholaheMahadeu*
Aphukhaipagalahola
Kailasare para Gangaknamaiani
Jatatelukuaithola.

Mahadeu, you are becoming mad by consuming cannabis and poppy; you brought (divine river) Ganga from the Kailasa and hid it in (your) matted hair.

V

'Shaivism is one of the oldest belief systems in the world. The remnants as well as existing temples in Thailand, Laos, Champa (Vietnam), Indonesia, China, Korea, Japan, Central Asia and Tibet speak of the spread of the Shaivism in the far corners of the world, from its origin in India. In India, the Shaiva tradition continues uninterruptedly. The twelve Jyotirlinga's situated at different centres from Kashmir to Rameswaram stand to prove its widespread existence. The names of the regions like Telegu region 1, Trissur 2 in Kerela come from names of Shiva, and Shiva temples exist in huge numbers in the map of India which also includes, Nepal, its form and traditions may though differ from region to region' (Sharma, 2015: 85).

From time immemorial there is a strong current of Saivism in Assam which is proved by the innumerable temples and shrines devoted to lord Siva scattered over the hills and plains of the state. Besides the Hindus, many of the sanskritised and animist tribal groups of Assam appease this popular deity through household and community rituals. The Assamese Sikhs made sacred offerings in the village Siva shrines to get their lost cows. In a good number of Assamese folk songs, the appearance, epithets and the virtues of lord Siva have been described in attractive manner. All the villages of Assam are heterogeneous and each of the village is adorned with one or more worshipping centre to adore this lovingly deity, sometimes who is more human than god. Large numbers of the people in Assam have practised the Saivism and Saktism, and due to the close relation of these two ways of worship, it is near to impossible to differentiate the Saiva and the Sakta in this remote part of India.

There are a good number of Siva temples in Guwahati distributed over both the banks of the Brahmaputra River. Most of these temples are mythological integral to the different holy places of India and their mentions are conspicuous in the prime Hindu scriptures. The Vasisthasrama relates this north-east corner of India to the pristine religious canvas of the country. Although due to the flaccid economic condition at present the physical structure of the Vasisthasrama is not praiseworthy, yet this sacred complex attracts a good number of pilgrims and tourists from within and outside the state. Besides the tribals and non-tribals the Vasisthasrama is the meeting place of different language groups of India and abroad, which has created a congenial environment contributing immensely towards peace, amity and acceleration of the country.

References

Barua, B.K., 1951, *A Cultural History of Assam*, Gauhati, Bina Library.

Dowson, John, 1987, *A Classical Dictionary of Hindu Mythology and Religion: Geography, History and Literature*, New Delhi, Rupa and Co.

Medhi, Birinchi K., 2008, 'Concept of Jagannatha among the Assamese Hindus,' in *Jagannatha in Historical Perspectives*, R. N. Dash (ed), Delhi, Pratibha Prakashan: 90-102.

Medhi, Birinchi K. and HimarjyotiTalukdar, 2012-13, 'Ethno-historical and Socio-cultural Dimensions of a Shiva Temple in a Riverine Island of Assam', *Bulletin of the Department of Anthropology*, Gauhati University, Vol. XIV:13-25.

Medhi, Birinchi K. and Monimugdha Bhuyan, 2015, 'Advent of Vaishnavism in an Animistic Environ: The Case of the Deori's, *North Bengal Anthropologist*, Journal of the Department of Anthropology, University of North Bengal, Vol. 3: 17-26.

Neog, Maheswar, 2008, *Pavitra Assam*, 4th ed, Jorhat, Asam Sahitya Sabha.

Sharmah, Nirmala, 2015, 'Lord Siva Across the Northern Land', *Quest:*The Journal of Vivekananda Kendra Institute of Culture, Vol.VIII, No. 2: 85-105.

8

The Kaibartas of Assam: Economy and Society with Reference to Normative Coherence

— *Chandana Sarma*

Introduction

Economic action, specifically the substantive economy, is defined by sets of rules, goals and values which are extrinsic to the economy itself. Though economists are aware, anthropologists sometimes emphasise that man lives by norms alone. In peasant and primitive society the norms and values used to define economic vocabulary—resource, commodity, control over goods and services, the distributive process, standards of economic behaviour—are the norms governing most social behaviour. The economy is not so much differentiated from the rest of the society and culture that one set of values holds there and other values in other contexts. The economic system does not exhibit an ethic counterpoised to the regnant value system (Nash, 1996). This paper attempts to study the relationship between economy and society among the Kaibartas of Assam with reference to normative coherence.

India is composed of numerous villages some of which are segmented by castes. Castes are corporate endogamous units and the caste system resolves into regional variants. Membership comes through kinship and the caste group has a rank vis-à-vis other caste groupings. Castes though discrete, hierarchical, endogamous, and of different ritual purity, are nonetheless interwoven into a complex network of mutual dependencies. Castes are related (and necessary to each other) in terms of ritual interaction, occupational specialisation, and economic exchange (Nash, 1996). A system of individual status or rank is often present in the context of corporate ranking of groups by caste. However, these two systems may or may not be congruent. An individual's position cannot be deduced automatically from his caste membership. There is much interaction and social activity which is highly irrelevant to caste. This gives the impression that castes are not frozen classes based on an unchanging hierarchy and lacking in mobility.

Methodology

The data for the present study have been collected from five Kaibarta villages of Kamrup, Nalbari and Lakhimpur districts of Assam. The data were collected during the years 2004-2007 and 2011-2013. A structured household schedule was used to collect primary data on population pattern including educational status, occupational pattern and others. Data on the economy and social aspects were collected using focused interviews and sampling techniques.

Barpith and Boripara arc situated in Kamrup Districts of Assam and are about 8 kms from Guwahati city. Bornibari of Nalbari District is under North Borkhetri Mouza and is about 18 km from Nalbari town and 88 km from Guwahati city. Koliyoni and Gharmora villages of Lakhimpur District are at a distance of 7 kms from Lakhimpur town and 400 kms from Guwahati city.

The People

The Kaibartas, one of the major Scheduled Caste communities of Assam is mainly found in the plains district of Assam. They are one of the sixteen Scheduled Castes communities of the State as per Constitution (Scheduled Castes) Order, 1950. As they are found all over India including Bengal, social scientists believe that they might have come to Assam at a very early date from the eastern states of Bengal, Bihar or Orissa. Fishing is the primary occupation of the Kaibartas of Assam (Bordoloi and Sarma Thakur, 1994).

The Kaibartas practice endogamy and intersegmental marriages which are regulated by a purificatory ritual. Monogamy is the general rule. The line of descent among the Kaibartas is traced through the father who is the head of the family. All the male members of a family enjoy the coparcenary rights, unless one goes out of the family during the life time of his father. They do not have wider relations with other castes. Fishing as occupation is considered to be polluting and the Kaibartas who practice it, are accorded a low status in the caste hierarchy among the Hindus. The Kaibartas are Hindus who belong to the Sakta sect. In recent years, a large section has become followers of Vaishnavism. The Assamese language of the Indo-Aryan Family is the mother tongue of the Kaibartas and they use the Assamese script.

As regards the etymology of the word Kaibarta it is held that the word Kaibarta is derived from the root *ke* or *ka* meaning water and *vrit* meaning exist. The term Kaibarta thus refers to one who derives their livelihood from water. There are as many as eight internal groups among the Kaibartas namely, *Jalia, Teli, Mali, Halowa, Seoli, Neoli, Katharowa* and *Bhari.* Though each of them is involved in the same traditional occupation of fishing, yet each group has its own distinct traits (Bezbaruah, 2005).

Economy and Society

Fishing is considered to be the only important occupation by the Kaibartas of these five villages even though it is largely a seasonal occupation. There are about 40 to 45 varieties of fish caught by the Kaibartas of the five villages. Generally some of the varieties are available only during the peak fishing season (mid-September to mid-May) while the other varieties are found all the year though in fewer quantities.

A variety of fishing techniques are employed by the Kaibartas, but the techniques vary from village to village. However, there are in general three fishing techniques employed in the study villages. Barpith village do not employ the *katal* technique. The fishing techniques used are (1) Bana fishing technique in which fishes are trapped, forcing them to move along a narrow and long bamboo woven barricade, (2) Katal technique is applied in wetlands (*beels*) by encircling a small, circular area with weeds and bushes (inside a bamboo barricade) and subsequently fishing carried out using drag nets, (3) Filtering technique includes use of fishing gears like dip nets, bag nets, sieve nets and encircling nets in inland fisheries. Though poison is sometimes used to frighten or kill fish, no such method was found to be practiced among the Kaibartas of the study villages. Fishing implements used by the Kaibartas of the five villages are mainly traps and nets.

In addition to the individual family fishing units, joint trips are organised under the leadership of any one villager. Such fishing units are called *thoras* (in Kamrup and Nalbari Districts) and *gut* (in Lakhimpur District). A *thora/ gut* comprises of eight to ten members, who are drawn from a cross-section of the family fishing units of the whole village. They take boats belonging to the Kaibartas and nets and camp on the banks of the wetlands/rivers for three or four days. On the last day they return to the village with all their fishing implements and divide their catch among the members equally. Sometimes they do not camp on the banks but rather visit the *beel* every day for three or four consecutive days. It is with the sheer motive of having a good individual catch that a joint fishing activity is undertaken.

The Kaibartas of Barpith depend on the *beels* and the Khanajan River passing nearby the village for their subsistence. The people do not have any possessory right over these water sources. Some of them, especially women also buy fish from persons owning fisheries or from Maligaon (situated on the southern part of Guwahati city) fish market and sell them in the neighbouring villages. They do not possess individual fisheries except one fisherman. In Boripara also, the Kaibartas do not possess individual fisheries. They catch fish in the fishery (Borhala Beel) owned by fishery co-operative societies which is auctioned by the government for every three years. The working unit, in Boripara, is usually the family (a man, his wife and children) and this unit is frequently self-sustaining. In seasons when fish is found in plenty, each family serves as a small co-operative unit. The man along (husband or father) along with his brothers and sons catch fish in the inland pool and bring home the catch. The women at home remove the fish from the nets. The sons or younger brothers of the fisherman then take the fish to the market to sell.

When fish becomes scarce, it requires the coordinated efforts of several families. Womenfolk would attach baits to hooks and tie these hooks to coconut ropes. Two to three fishermen belonging to different families would then share a boat and carry these ropes and leave them in water either in the inland pool or in paddy fields, which are filled, with water. Later, fish caught is then equally distributed among the different members.

In Bornibari, the Kaibartas unite on the household basis, that is, men from one household have individual fishing business. But during rainy seasons, when more men are needed, fishing is organised on a cooperative basis. These fishermen carry their fishing operations in the Bariabeel and Caplabeel, about three and four kms respectively, from the village. There are 20 individually owned fisheries in Bornibari. Generally, the fishermen start for the beel in the evening so as to reach there in time. On reaching, they fix the nets and sleep. They get up at midnight and haul the nets, mend the holes if necessary and fix it again. When the net is fixed they eat their meals consisting of rice and fish either cooked at home or cooked on the banks itself. In the morning they haul the net and return to the banks with the entire catch.

As soon as they reach the banks, the men go home for bath and meals while the other members of the household or group carry the catch home and hand it over to the women. They spread the used nets for drying and replace them with fresh ones.

The fishermen of Koliyoni and Gharmora villages in Lakhimpur District depend on the inland pools and the Dhol and Gelajan rivers passing nearby the villages. The villagers mainly catch fish and sell it to the fishermen of other villages who sell them in the town market or visit door to door to sell fish. Like the other villages, here also joint trips or gut are organised under the leadership of any one villager to catch fish in the *beels* or rivers. *Beels* are auctioned for one year by the Gaon Panchayat to the highest bidder (Bishaya). Whatever profit the fishermen makes, they need to pay half of the amount to the Bishaya and the other half is distributed equally among the group.

Marketing of Fish

In Barpith, fishermen sell both fish caught by them and purchased from others. As soon as the catch is brought home, it is given in charge of the women of the house. They sort out the saleable fish. Thereafter, either the woman or any male member immediately takes it to the market. The fish is carried to the market by cycle or rickshaw. Some of them, especially women also but fish from persons owning fisheries or from Maligaon fish market and sell in the neighbouring villages (Khanamukh, Dharapur, etc).

In Boripara, marketing of fresh fish is done in two ways. If fish are auctioned by the society as a whole or privately, they are bought by the villagers as well as outside traders. Some villagers buy fish in wholesale and distribute them in small quantities to others by retail, keeping a small quantity for their own retail sale. Others buy small or large amounts of fish directly for retail and also barter fish for vegetables. If the village auction does not take place, fishermen take their produce to the market for retail or sell it to the traders on the banks itself. If they employ rickshaws to lift baskets or carry baskets to markets, they pay them daily wages.

In Bornibari, some of the fishermen sell fish to the wholesalers (both Kaibartas and non-Kaibartas). The wholesalers transport the fish to various centres of fish sale including Guwahati. Sections of the Kaibartas of Bornibari, who are regular sellers, proceed early in the morning, almost at dawn, to the banks of Caplabeel and Bariabeel where fresh fish is auctioned. After buying the fish at the auction, these men proceed to their respective places of sale. They even go to Guwahati.

Those traders who sell fish caught by them have to wait for their own boats to come. As soon as the catch is brought home, it is given in charge of the women folk of the house who then sort out the fish to be sold. The male members then immediately proceed to the market, either by cycle, rickshaw or auto-van (if they take to Guwahati).

Table 8.1: Distribution of the Kaibartas in the three districts, 2004-11

District	*Male*	*Per cent*	*Female*	*Per cent*	*Total*	*Total Number of Household*
Kamrup	304	21.82	259	20.97	563	83
Nalbari	832	59.68	776	62.83	1608	330
Lakhimpur	258	18.50	200	16.20	458	95
Total	**1394**	**100.00**	**1235**	**100.00**	**2629**	**508**

The women sellers, mostly widows, buy fish from wholesalers and sell it in the neighbouring villages (Belsor, Kakaya, etc.) or in the Bornibari bazaar held on Thursdays and Sundays.

The fishermen of Koliyoni and Gharmora generally sell their catch in the town market or to other fishermen of neighbouring villages. Sometimes they visit door to door and sell fish.

Fish traders also advance loans to the fisher folk and as a result the fisher folk are bound to sell the produce at prefixed rates to thc traders. Apart from fish traders finance and credit within the Kaibarta fishing economy are provided by friends and relatives and by professional money lenders from outside the community. Among the fisher folk there is a group of persons who, having accumulated capital by fishing and fish marketing, act as financiers later on.

Income and Expenditure

The savings and expenditure account for a year (Table 8.2) shows an access of expenditure over income. The households dependent exclusively on fishing have deficit family budgets than those who have subsidiary occupations other than fishing. Birth, death, puberty, marriage, illness, etc. are occasions which mostly imbalance the family budgets.

The difference with regards to performance of economic function, division of labour and ownership of assets, find their equivalents in social status, role in political leadership of the community, role in cultural functions, marriage patterns, and standard of living. Labourers not owning any assets live in smaller houses than owners of craft and gear.

Functions performed and rituals are usually connected with economic status. Those with poor income find it hard to perform the various ceremonies associated either with birth, death or marriage in a large scale involving the whole village. Those who can afford to perform these rituals, invite lots of people. The functions again reflect the social status of the person or family who perform the function.

Table 8.2: Annual Savings and Investment by 6 families of Kamrup District, 15 families of Nalbari District and 5 families of Lakhimpur District, 2004-11

Districts	Households	Sources of earning			Investments			Total
		Fishing	Others	Total	Fishing Implements	Miscel-laneous	Food Item	
KAMRUP	S. Das	24000.00	5000.00	29000.00	10000.00	7000.00	12000.00	29000.00
	T. Das	22000.00	4500.00	26500.00	5000.00	10000.00	12000.00	27000.00
	J. Das	30000.00	26000.00	56000.00	12000.00	35000.00	18000.00	65000.00
	B. Das	31000.00	29000.00	60000.00	7000.00	38000.00	30000.00	75000.00
	G. Das	50000.00	15000.00	65000.00	30000.00	3000.00	25000.00	85000.00
	H. Das	55000.00		55000.00	18000.00	15000.00	30000.00	63000.00
Total		**212000.00**	**79500.00**	**291500.00**	**82000.00**	**135000.00**	**127000.00**	**344000.00**
NALBARI	G. Das	8000.00	5000.00	13000.00	3000.00	3000.00	7000.00	12000.00
	G. Das	7000.00	-	7000.00	-	500.00	5000.00	5500.00
	M. Das	21000.00	10000.00	31000.00	5400.00	3000.00	9000.00	17400.00
	M. Das	29000.00	-	29000.00	1000.00	7000.00	8000.00	25000.00
	P. Das	50000.00	2500.00	52500.00	1500.00	5000.00	10000.00	3000.00
	S. Das	15000.00	1500.00	16500.00	5000.00	2000.00	5000.00	12000.00
	S. Das	24000.00	1000.00	34000.00	1000.00	-	1000.00	2000.00
	B. Das	35000.00	5000.00	4000.00	9000.00	4000.00	7000.00	2000.00
	P. Das	31000.00	4000.00	35000.00	9000.00	1000.00	6000.00	16000.00
	R. Das	75000.00	-	75000.00	25000.00	9000.00	10000.00	44000.00
	N. Das	54000.00	-	54000.00	2000.00	5000.00	9000.00	34000.00
	H. Das	24000.00	15000.00	39000.00	7000.00	9000.00	5000.00	21000.00
	K. Das	10000.00	5000.00	15000.00	1000.00	3000.00	7000.00	11000.00
	D. Das	19000.00	3000.00	22000.00	4000.00	-	8000.00	12000.00
	N. Das	30000.00	-	39000.00	9000.00	5000.00	6000.00	20000.00
Total		432000.00	61000.00	502000.00	132400.00	56500.00	112000.00	299900.00

(Contd...)

LAKHIMPUR	S. Das	7000.00	14600.00	21600.00	3000.00	1000.00	9000.00	22000.00
	T. Das	10000.00	-	10000.00	-	2000.00	8000.00	1000.00
	S. Das	11500.00	6000.00	17500.00	5000.00	6000.00	7500.00	18500.00
	P. Das	10000.00	7000.00	17000.00	4000.00	9000.00	6000.00	19000.00
	J. Das	15000.00	10000.00	25000.00	7000.00	1000.00	7000.00	24000.00
Total		**37600.00**	**91100.00**	**19000.00**	**37000.00**	**37500.00**	**93500.00**	**37600.00**

Division of Labour in the Family

With regard to activities related to fishing, men dominate all activities such as fishing, team formation, and procurement of inputs, fish marketing and management of fishery finance. Women, however, help their male counterparts in collecting fish from the nets which they bring home, attaching baits to hooks and attaching floats and sinkers to the nets. Some of the women folk are also involved in fishing, fish marketing and management of finance. Household work including management of family finance is looked after by women with little assistance from male members. In recent days, it is seen that household work is equally shared between husband and wife (in Boripara of Kamrup and Bornibari of Nalbari) as their wives are employed in some institutions (e.g., hospitals, weaving centre, schools, etc.).

Marriage and Family

Caste endogamy is the general rule of marriage in the Kaibarta society. The Kaibartas recognize the hierarchy of the traditional Hindu caste system with its local variation. Marriage with castes like Suri, Jugi, etc., which they consider lower than their own are generally prohibited. But the marriage of a Kaibarta girl with a High caste boy is accepted as a matter of pride. There are cases of inter-caste marriages in all the five villages. In Koliyoni and Gharmora, few cases of marriage with non-Assamese boys have also come to light. In such cases, the caste of the person is not a bar. Generally, the marriage ceremony is preceded by the ring ceremony. But most of the fisher folk of the five villages avoid this ceremony as they cannot afford it. The groom's sister or mother offers the ring to the bride on the *telarbhardiya* occasion (day before the marriage). There is absence of payment of bride price and dowry among the Kaibartas. However, when the bride moves to her husband's house after the marriage, she takes with her certain articles like bronze and bell-metal dishes and bowls and pitchers, clothes and often cash received from the parents as gifts. Poor parents, however, fail to provide most of the items, but well-to-do parents provide their daughters with most of the necessary items.

The number of nuclear families without dependents is the highest in all the five villages. The average size of family in all the five villages is medium (members ranging from 5-10). Reasons for dissolution of extended families as given by respondents of the study villages are quarrels and conflicts between mother-in-law and daughter-in-law, among daughters-in-law and even between daughter-in-law and unmarried sisters due to status conflicts and distribution of work. Quarrels among brothers over contribution to family income and expenditure for consumption are equally important.

Rituals and Fishing

The Kaibartas of Kamrup and Nalbari Districts are Saktas and follow the religious beliefs of the Hindus, while the villagers of Lakhimpur District are followers of the Vaishnavism. However, there are some common fishing rituals in all the villages. These were designed to relieve the fishermen from anxiety and to help them manipulate natural powers. Malinowski (1918) and others have explained the ritual behaviour of fishermen as their attempts to cope with dangers and uncertainties at sea and different water bodies and thus come to terms with nature.

Satyanarayan Puja and Ganga Puja are the two rituals which are directly related to fishing. There is an extricable relation between fishing and these two rituals. Satyanarayan Puja is performed at community level during the month of April by the villagers on the banks of *beel*. However, each household performs this *puja* during different times of the year if they desire so. Ganga *puja* is a ritual performed at the fishing sources by every fishing household of the study villages. It is also known as *Ghot Puja*. This ritual is performed to appease the presiding deity (Ganga or the custodian of the water bodies).

The Kaibartas believe that death or birth as defiling and offensive to the deities and so the fishermen do not undertake any fishing operation for a stipulated period after the birth or death of a relative. They also believe that menstruating women must not touch any kind of fishing gear. Besides these, fishermen avoid from their fishing activities on a new moon day or a full moon day and on such other festive occasions like Viswakarma Puja, Lakshmi Puja and on Bihu (Magh, Bohag and Kati). It has been observed that pollution beliefs reduced fishing efforts considerably by preventing men from fishing during periods of defilement (birth, death, etc.). Although some of this time might have been spent in productive activities such as in mending nets and in preparing other gears, there is no doubt that both religious beliefs and practices reduce fishing operations to a considerable extent. They follow the Hindu religious beliefs and practices like the neighbouring communities.

If a ritual like puberty or mortuary cannot be held for dearth of money etc., Geeta Path (recitation of the Geeta) is taken up as the equivalent alternative at a comparatively low cost. Sometimes for dearth of money they even postpone certain rites. The families, who can afford, however, perform each ritual inviting all the villagers and giving a grand feast on such occasions as a marriage or name-giving ceremony.

Relationship between Education and Occupation

With the rise in the level of education, the percentage of fishing population to the total employed population seems to decline. Table 8.3 shows the relationship between education and occupation.

It is seen from the table that majority of the men engaged in fishing are illiterates. Next, are the men who have had primary education? Those who have studied upto seventh standard form another fishing category. On the other hand, the position is just the opposite so far as the non-fishing occupations are concerned. In the five villages, illiterates are not found to have pursued non-fishing occupations. Persons having secondary education and beyond are found to be engaged in non-fishing professions. Thus, it is seen that with the rise in the level of education, the percentage of fishing population to the total employed population has decreased. The non-fishing occupations are wage earning, business, working as office assistants and working in biscuit factories and so on.

Information gathered about the occupation of a respondent, his/her father's occupation and his/her father's father's occupation revealed that there is a higher rate of occupational mobility among the Kaibartas of Kamrup District than those of the other two districts.

It is evident from the table that the father's (F) and father's father's (FF) of the respondents (R) pursued fishing in the case of the Kaibartas of Nalbari and Lakhimpur Districts. Among the Kaibartas of Kamrup District, 53.85 per cent F and 76.92 per cent F F pursued fishing. Thus, changes in the traditional occupation have occurred among the Kaibartas of Kamrup District, even in the case of F and F F generations. In the case of the Kaibartas of Nalbari and Lakhimpur District, all the F was fishermen like their fathers. In the case of R of Nalbari and Lakhimpur, 72.16 and 43.92 per cent respectively have switched over to various non-traditional occupations.

Conclusion

The above discussion on economic life indicates that the Kaibartas are never self-sufficient. They had to rely on their neighbours not only for the necessities of life like food and clothes but also for the marketing of fish. The Kaibartas who mainly depend upon their traditional calling are experiencing a number of problems like shortage of capital, difficulties in transportation and marketing of their catch, etc. Occupational change has differentiated the Kaibartas from one another in their social as well as economic status. But one thing is clear that occupational mobility never affects the hierarchy of the caste in any way. Even though a person changes his occupation he continues to remain as a member of the caste he is born into.

Table 8.3: Relationship between education and occupation among the Kaibartas of the study villages, 2004-11

Degree of education	*Total Number of Employed Men*	*No. of men employed in*					
		Fishing			*Non-fishing*		
		Kamrup	*Nalbari*	*Lakhimpur*	*Kamrup*	*Nalbari*	*Lakhimpur*
Illiterates	132	45.38	21.26	45.67	-	-	-
Primary (std.1-4)	136	31.94	25.90	44.44	-	5.55	-
Secondary (std. 5-7)	303	22.68	50.25	9.89	51.85	56.94	51.28
Above std.7	136	-	5(2.59)	-	48.15	37.6	48.72
Total	**707**	**119(100)**	**193(100)**	**81(100)**	**54(100)**	**216(100)**	**39(100)**

Table 8.4: Occupations of the Respondents (R), their Fathers (F) and Father's Fathers in the study villages, 2004-11

Occupations	*Kamrup*			*Nalbari*			*Lakhimpur*		
	R (per cent)	*F (per cent)*	*FF (per cent)*	*R (per cent)*	*F (per cent)*	*FF (per cent)*	*R (per cent)*	*F (per cent)*	*FF (per cent)*
Fishing	37.04	53.85	76.92	72.16	100.00	100.00	43.92	100.00	100.00
Wage earning	14.82	15.39	3.85	10.13	—	—	28.34	—	—
Service	16.67	19.23	—	2.55	—	—	8.17	—	—
Driving	9.26	—	—	—	—	—	3.08	—	-
Mechanic	3.70	—	—	1.26	—	—	3.08	—	—
Tailor	5.56	—	—	1.26	—	—	—	—	—
School Teaching	1.85	—	—	—	—	—	—	—	—
Veg. selling	1.85	7.61	—	—	—	—	3.08	—	—
Agriculture	-	3.85	15.38	3.79	—	—	3.08	—	—
Weaver	3.70	—	—	1.26	—	—	—	—	—
Handcart pulling	1.85	—	—	1.26	—	—	—	—	—
Bus conductor	3.70	—	—	1.26	—	—	—	—	—
Factory worker	—	—	—	2.55	—	—	—	—	—
NGO worker	—	—	—	1.26	—	—	—	—	—
Nurse	—	—	—	—	—	—	3.08	—	—
Business	—	—	—	1.26	—	—	4.17	—	—
Total	**100.00**	**100.00**	**100.00**	**100.00**	**100.00**	**100.00**	**100.00**		

There is often a presumption of correspondence between the morphological structure of a society—what exists on the ground and may be observed from outside—and its normative structure, or what is considered by its members as right, proper and desirable, but that correspondence does not hold equally well in every case (Beteille, 1992). Many Kaibartas of the study villages have changed their traditional occupation but continues to be deeply committed to the family. There might be some changes in its morphological form, but the normative basis remains very strong. Other than the size of households, family continues to be the traditional form. The eldest male member is accorded the authority in the family. Kinship ties flow easily across the boundaries of the family. Uncles, aunts, cousins, nephews and nieces continue to figure prominently in the social life of the Kaibartas at all levels of the hierarchy. Even after separation from the joint household, the nuclear units come together for festivals and ceremonies connected with the important crisis of life, birth, marriage and death.

Economy of the Kaibartas also acts as a determinant on the social status of the Kaibartas of the five villages. Most of the fisher folk of the five villages avoid the ring ceremony as they cannot afford it. Poor parents fail to provide their daughters with items like furniture, ornaments, etc. at the time of marriage. Well-to-do parents however provide the daughters with most of the items.

Increased requirements for education among modern professions have led to influx of people from a variety of castes into modern occupations (Sharma, 1999). The educated Kaibartas of the study villages, pursuing non-fishing occupations are often well-off and occupy a high status in the society. Though they have changed their traditional occupation they continue to be committed to the Kaibarta society. Given the occupational underpinnings of the *varna* system and the linkages between occupation and income, it is not difficult to see caste as a system of material inequality (Desai and Dubey, 2011). Except a few cases of inter-caste marriages, most of the Kaibartas prefer endogamy. Caste inequalities seem to be lower in the villages of Kamrup district than the ones situated far away from Guwahati city.

Fishing during peak fishing season or during scarcity of fish requires the coordinated efforts of several families. Marketing of fish also involve the family. Apart from fish traders finance and credit within the Kaibarta fishing economy are provided by friends and relatives and by professional moneylenders from outside the community. A group of Kaibartas who have accumulated capital by fishing and fish marketing, etc. also act as financiers. Thus, the whole fishing economy involves the integrated efforts of both the

Kaibarta as well as non-Kaibarta families. It can never be an individual enterprise. Magico-religious beliefs also play a significant role in their fishing endeavours. Before the start of the peak fishing season or before any individual fishing effort they also perform the Ganga/Ghot Puja on the banks of the rivers or wetlands. The Kaibartas who are followers of Vaishnavism also perform these rituals before they start fishing. Thus, whether they are Saktas or Vaishnavas, the Kaibartas of the five villages are found to practice similar rituals with regard to fishing to appease the presiding deity of the water bodies. The Namghar serves as a local centre of devotional worship for the Kaibartas in the study villages. It is evident as in many other societies that economy and society are not two separate entities for the Kaibartas.

Acknowledgements

Thanks are due to Professor A.N.M. Irshad Ali (Retd.), of Department of Anthropology of Gauhati University, for extending all possible guidance to the author in undertaking the study among the Kaibartas of Kamrup and Nalbari Districts. Thanks are also extended to Mr Debajit Hazarika and Ms Chayanika Boruah of Department of Anthropology, Cotton College, for helping the author in conducting fieldwork in Lakhimpur District.

References

Beteille, Andre.1992. 'Caste and Family' in *Anthropology Today*. Vol. 8. No. 1. Feb. (1992) pp. 13-18. Royal Anthropological Institute of Great Britain and Ireland. http://www.jstor.org/stable/3032808.Accessed on 25-03-2015.

Bezbaruah, Debendra Kumar. 2005. *Socio-economic change and dimension of social mobility*. Project Dalit: Guwahati. Assam.

Bordoloi, B.N. and G.C. Sarma Thakur 1994. *Socio-economic Conditions of the Kaibartas of Assam: a case study*. Guwahati: Assam Institute of Research for Tribals and Scheduled Castes.

Desai, Sonalde and Amaresh Dubey. 2011.'Caste in 21st Century India: Competing Narratives' in *Economic and Political Weekly*, Vol. XLVI, No. 11 (March 12).

Malinowski, B.1918. 'Fishing in the Trobriand Islands'. *Man.* 18:87-92.

Nash, Manning. 1966. *Primitive and Peasant Economic Systems*. California: Chandler Publishing Company.

Sharma, K.L. 1999. *Social Inequality in India: Profiles of Caste, Class and Social Mobility*. Jaipur: Rawat Publications.

9

Religious Practices of Sarania Kachari Population of Kaljhar Village, Baska District, Assam

— *Christene Bora and*
Tiluttoma Baruah

Introduction

Religion is the origin of rites and rituals, which means the system of faith and worship. Rites and rituals are one of the most important institutions of human culture, which relate people to its other on special occasions. It is the expression of the manner, and type of adjustment effected by people with their concept of the supernatural. All societies have some beliefs, which can be grouped under the term religion. According to the 2011 census (Indianexpress.com), 78.35 per cent of the population of India practice Hinduism, Islam (14.2 per cent), Christianity (3.6 per cent), Sikhism (1.9 per cent), Buddhism (0.8 per cent) and Jainism (0.4 per cent) are the other major religions followed by the people of India. There are also numerous minor ethnically-bound faiths, though these have been affected by major religions such as Hinduism, Buddhism, Islam and Christianity.

Frazer (1870) in his book *Golden Bough* says that, by religion it is meant that a propitiation or conciliation of powers superior to man who are believed to bind and controls the course of nature and of human life. Majumdar and Madan (1986:151) in their book "*An Introduction to Social Anthropology*" stated that, the religion is the human response to the apprehension of something or power which is supernatural and super sensory.

In most cases these rites are performed on three occasions, at birth, at marriage and at death. People are not greatly concerned with the spiritual effects of these rites, yet the fact must reflect general feelings that these events ought to be in some way sacral zed (cited in Mair, 1972:232-233). Karsten (1935) stated that, primitive rituals must be essentially an expression of man's instinct of self-preservation, in other words, of his desire to make existence as tolerable as possible. The relation between man and supernatural powers, which he tries to influence by his invocation, prayers and offerings, is not originally an ethical relation.

Methodology

The present study carried out was conducted on Sarania Kachari, a plain tribe inhabiting in Barama town of Baksa District, Assam from 4th November 2012 to 11th November 2012 at Kaljhar village, Baksa district.

Baksa district was carved out of a part of Nalbari, Barpeta, Kamrup and small portion of Darrang district. As a result of historic BTC (Bodoland Territorial Council) accord signed on February 10, 2003, formed BTAD (Bodoland Territorial Autonomous District) with four districts namely, Kokrajhar, Chirang, Baksa and Udalguri. Though the original word 'Baksa' is not above controversy, a good chunk of population prefers to use 'Bagsa' in lieu of 'Baksa'. The popular assumption that 'Baksa' is the misspelt form of 'Bangsa'—a 'Dzonkha' word meaning a farm house and a corridor as it is known that Bhutanese king and subjects used this area for trade and passage to the plains. 'Bangsa' (Bagsa or Baksa) was in fact one of the most important 'Dooars' of Bhutan. Another source says that the name "Bagsa" is originated from Bhutanese language. According to Bhutanese origin, they denoted the area as "Bagsa Duar." "Bagsa" meaning one kind of rice and "Duar" meaning entrance point. As Bhutanese king ruled these areas for a long time in and around first half of the nineteenth century so it might be possible that the name "Bagsa" or "Baksa" had a Bhutanese origin. According to Bodo source the name originated from a kind of rice grain which is known as "Bagsa." The said rice grain is one kind of broken and uncleaned product which is gained after milling the rice. As the name Baksa is itself derived from various sources and antecedents so there exists lots of controversy over the name. But still today no concrete evidence has been found which might determine the final source. Only popular sources and folklores are evident but no historical source has been found. So serious research has also been done in this respect (Official site of Baksa).

Discussion

In this world man is the only cultural being. Religion is a major cultural trait and found to have prevailed amongst all ethnic groups of the world and at all levels of culture – preliterate or literate. Sometimes man gets depressed when he does not get optimum results from his hard labour or becomes unable to solve the problems of life caused by natural calamities, epidemics, diseases of various sorts, poverty, death and so on. In this context he began to think that there is some supernatural power which is responsible for all this happenings. That is why man assumes submissive attitude towards this power and begins to worship it with various paraphernalia to get relief. Thus, religion comes in and plays a great role in every aspect of social life such as birth, initiation, marriage, cremation, economic pursuits, law and government and so on (Das, 1996).

According to the villagers, religion is a part of their living and they are abiding to it. Generally, religion plays an important role in every aspect of life and from children to adult they follow and believe in it. All the inhabitants of this village are Hindus. They are of polytheistic believer and so believe in different Gods and Goddesses. The significance of their religious practices is that they practice the 'Rokto puja'. In this practice they had sacrificed goat, pigeon, fowl, etc for the worship of God. They believe that this practice is similar to the practice of 'Kamakhya Temple'. The people of the village mainly believe in Lord Shiva, as a result of which there is a Shiva Mandir in the village. 'Gopal Mandir' is also there where the people of the village celebrate Janmastami, Lakshmi Puja, etc. They also believe Lord Krishna, Ganesh, Lakshmi and so on. Moreover, almost every house has a private Goshain ghar. Namghar or Goshainghar is the main centre for performing their religious rites and rituals. Like all other communities of Assam Sarania Kachari also observed some religious beliefs and practices. Some of them are as follows:

(a) Baa Gossain Puja

The Baa Gossain is the symbol of Lord Shiva and is celebrated during the month of Bohag (April). In Baa Gossain puja, the rituals are done by Deori priest. First of all, he allowed two of the villagers to cut down a bamboo plant with the help of axe from the village. Along with them the whole villagers and the priest went to the place of bamboo herd and after holy prayer he allows to cut matured bamboo plant and the priest go backs to the Gossainghar. The distinguished villager cut and without dropping the bamboo plant on the ground, took over their shoulder and goes back to the Gossainghar. Again the priest worship the bamboo in front of the temple and sprays holy water to the plant and measures nine hand and finger fingers, again allows them to cut and clean the bamboo according to that measurement. Now, again the priests spray the holy water to the bamboo and the devotees. Then, they enter to the

Gossainghar. Now the priest rubs mustard oil for purification and wore a white cloth to the bamboo. As they believe that this bamboo is a symbol of Lord Shiva, they wore artificial hair, then the devotees at the Gossainghar offer Gamusa, Handkerchief and tie up around the bamboo; and lastly the crown placed over the bamboo. Then they place this bamboo in the Gossainghar and worship communally. From first of Bohag to sixth of Bohag the Lord Baa Gossain used to travel in whole village from one house to another, and the household members takes blessings. All the household members take blessings of Lord Baa Gossain. On the seventh day the Lord Baa Gossain returns back to the Gossainghar and the priest welcome them at the gateway of the Gossainghar. Then they along with the Lord Baa Gossain circulate seven times around the Gossainghar and enter the Gossainghar. After that, a communal naam (prayer) with heartiest worship completes the Baa Gossain puja with distribution of Prasad. Lastly, they immerse their Lord Baa Gossian in water.

(b) Bator Puja

This puja is also celebrated only by the ladies of the village during the Bohag month (at any Tuesday or Saturday). It is performed at any Tiniali (where three roads meet) during daytime. This occasion is performed to relief the villagers from any disaster or any dangerous disease. Here two lady priests perform all the rituals. In this occasion, one pair of pigeon, jackfruit, white and red flower, (dhekia) fern plant, areca nut and betel leaves etc are required. After that they worship communally (Naam). Lastly, they took all the paraphernalia of rituals over a large banana bark and three ladies took that over their head and proceeds towards any water resource. Another lady took the pair of pigeon along with them. After sliding three times over the water, they immerse the bark along with pigeon and never see back. After the distinguished ladies reached the worshipped place, they distribute the prasads.

(c) Bamorpita

It is celebrated at night during Bhada month. In this occasion 10-15 numbers of young youth gather at a courtyard of the village along with one stick and ukhoni (long L-shaped bamboo stick pointed at one side). All the boys sing by making a circle and beating the ukhoni. As at the Bhada month the agricultural works completes, so this occasion symbolise that 'from mud we have to shift to dry'. The household members offer rice to them and take blessings. That completes the Bamorpita occasion.

(d) *Bhakathewa*

This occasion can be performed in any month. Here, two gents' priest and two lady priest perform the occasion. They worship for the wellbeing of the family members. Lastly, the family members offer them cloths, food and rice beer as paraphernalia of rituals. Here, nine pairs of areca nut and betel leaves, a pair of chicken, red and white flowers etc are required.

(e) *Mohkheda festival*

This festival is observed for five days in the month of Aghuon (8th month of Assamese calendar) starting from the full moon day. This festival is also known as 'Bhaluk Nasuwa' festival. As because in this festival a boy is dressed like bear, twisting dry banana leaf. And, a group of boys sings and call up the bear; then the bear comes out and dances in the rhythm of the song.

(f) *Ambubachi*

Ambubachi is known as 'Amati sua' among the people of Sarania Kacharis. It comes in the month of 'Ahar' or June-July month. It is believed that during this time, the mother of earth becomes impure. The farmers are not allowed to cultivate their fields. The village temple remains closed. At the end of the 'Amati sua' the people of the village use to clean each and every corner of their house as they usually do during their menstruation.

Several other pujas are also performed by the Saranias in a year, namely:

(a) Chidra Gossain puja
(b) Jaikuwari puja
(c) Hunkar puja
(d) Sop Bhanga puja.

Rituals Connected to the Life Cycle of a Human Being

Like the rest of the tribal and non-tribal population of Assam, the villagers also perform various ceremonies and festivals related to their life cycle. The ceremonies related to the life cycle of man are birth ceremony, puberty marriage, marriage and death.

(a) Birth ceremony—The villagers of Kaljhar village believe that child is the gift of God. The daughter-in-law goes ahead towards motherhood. Both mother-in-law and father-in-law make their daughter-in-law fit mentally and physically to give birth to the new born baby. While normal delivery, Sarania society has a custom to tie up a new fresh thread to the naval of the new born baby. Then the naval is cut with a new blade or new sharp scraper of bamboo just at the top of the by the new mother. This naval portion is buried just at the gate of the mother's house. The new born baby is washed with warm water. After few days, when the attached naval dried up and falls off, they put it into a cocon and then it is kept in a box or pot. Along with this, the house of the mother cleaned up, cloths are washed; and both the baby and mother worship the sun. An earthen lamp is lighten near the Tulsi tree and water is kept in a metallic cup. The new born baby carried up to the lamp and worship. Then the baby whirled three times over the thorn of plum which implies removal of any hurdles of the road. At the end, the holy water made by any gold ornament and leaves of Tulsi sprinkled all over whole house and campus, to purify.

After one month (in case of baby boy) and twenty one days (in case of baby girl) is born followed by 'Naam-Kirtan' and accordingly feast is solemnised to the villagers.

They also observed the 'Aanaprasan' or 'Mukhot Bhaat Dia' ceremony after seven month (baby girl) and eight month (baby boy). After the ceremony, a baby is allowed to have other staple food other than mother's milk. Here, the maternal uncle plays an important role.

(b) Puberty marriage—Whenever a girl reaches puberty, she is kept inside their neighbour's house so that no man can see her. The girl sleeps on a bed which is made up of straw. Five girls, those does not reached puberty yet, stay with the girl till the day of marriage. On the fifth day, the girl is brought out from the room and got a bath by women. The respective women and the other girl play, sing and dance.

On the first day of reaching puberty, a 'thagi' is offered and it is kept inside the room where the girl is kept. An earthen lamp, areca nut and betel leaf are arranged in a plate and are kept with the 'thagi'. A metal dish containing a cluster of paddy, a metal pot containing water and leaves of mango are kept beside the 'thagi'. In this occasion, an astrologer has an important role. He examines the merit and demerit of the girl on the second day and suggest for the remedy if there is any misfortune or defects. On the third day, in a 'Jhapa' (a box made up of bamboo) is carried to the maternal uncle house. A small knife, three buds of brinjal, two buds of pomegranate, a pair of areca nut and betel leaf are put inside the box binding with a handkerchief. The 'Jhapa' is put in a cover called 'Gajiram'. The home where the 'Jhapa' is kept is considered as the groom's place. The bride's family welcomes the bridegroom's family as they reach the gateway of the bride's house. After that, the bride's family comes to the bridegroom's house along with the 'Jhapa' and welcome them through a thrilling sound called

'Urulee'. Then, the girl got bath with smearing turmeric over whole body below the banana plant. The 'Sakhis' (friends) sprinkle a mixture of water and cowdung over the girl, on the name of purification. This function ended by distributing 'Prasads' and a feast.

(c) Marriage—Various types of marriages are prevalent among the Sarania Kacharis of Kaljhar village, namely: Prajapati Biya, Mala Dia Biya, and Poluwai Niya Biya:

(i) *Prajapti Biya:* This type of marriage is mostly prevalent among the villagers. Since they follow patriarchal family system, the bride goes to the groom's place after marriage. Vedic rituals are followed in this marriage system. A Brahmin priest is invited to perform all the rituals and the holy burning (Hom Jagya) takes place. At the beginning of the marriage the groom's family or the responsible members of the family goes to the bride's home along with areca nut and betel leaf, milk, coconut. All these mentioned materials are offered to the bride's maternal uncle. In this type of marriage, the bride willingly comes and received by the groom's family at the gateway of their house. Both bride and groom enter their house simultaneously by standing side by side of each other. The groom simply touches at the knot of hair of the bride with the little finger; and the bride touches the earthen lamp by her foot that is kept at the veranda of the house. This lamp has to be broken by the groom by his feet. After that, the 'Joran' (a noose between the two sides of a cloth of bride and groom) is tied up inside the house. Then both bride and bridegroom come out to the courtyard to take blessings by the headman as well as the gathering and complete the marriage.

(ii) *Mala Dia Biya:* In this type of marriage, a 'Deori' priest, who is the religious head of the society, performs the religious rituals of this marriage. Here no holy bon fire took place.

Here, it is found that villagers mainly acquire their mates either by negotiation or by elopement method. But they mostly prefer marriage by negotiation since it is socially and religiously accepted.

(d) Death—There are several rituals relating to death too. These are:

(i) *Tilani (a ceremony performed on the third day after death):* The whole family members of the death remain on fast for three days after the death of the person. On the third day, the villagers break their fast via offering them rice flour with milk and banana. This ceremony is known as 'Tilani'.

(ii) *Daha (performed on the tenth day of death):* This ceremony is similar like other Hindu people. In this ceremony 'Pinda' or funeral cake is offered by the family members in the name of deceased person. Banana, rice, ghee, honey, sugar, gur (jaggery), etc are also offered along with the 'Pinda'. After completing the rituals, bones of the deceased member are floated away in river. On the spot, Lord Shiva (Mahadev) is worshipped sitting towards north side. At the end of these above mentioned rituals, the hair of son is totally shaved in the name of purification.

(iii) *Shraaddha (Funeral ceremony):* It is performed on the thirteenth day of the death. The son of the dead, who sits for the rituals of 'Shraaddha' is known as 'Kam Dhora'. He along with the other members of the family remains on fast for three days, and even he himself eats only once in a day from fourth day till 'Shraaddha' without any oil, spices and vegetarian food, which is called 'Habish'. The rituals that are performed by the person at 'Shraaddha' has his meal from the donated rice (Jasaa), wears the same cloth which was worn at the time of putting fire on the face of the deceased till the day of 'Daha'. They do not take milk in the death of mother and banana in the death of father. The whole ceremony is performed at the courtyard of the deceased house. Lastly, a meal consists of meat, fish, vegetable etc are offered to the deceased and the 'Kam Dhora' person takes a communal blessings from the persons gathered at the courtyard.

Thus the SaraniaKacharis have been maintaining their culture.Other than the above mentioned rituals and occasions celebrated by the SaraniaKacharis, they also perform various other festivals similar to other caste peoples, namely, Bihu (Bohagbihu, Maghbihu, Kati bihu); Durga puja; Shiva puja; Janmastami; Biswakarma puja; Laxmi puja; Diwali; Holi; and Saraswati puja.

Conclusion

The present study has been focused on the religious profile of the SaraniaKacharis, their religious belief and traditions, ritualistic patterns. Like other people, SaraniaKacharis are also admirer of festivity. They observe all the rites and rituals with colourful programme. Various types of marriage such as PrajapatiBiya, Mala diaBiya; or PoluwainiaBiya are prevalent among them. Feast either vegetarian or non-vegetarian is compulsory in a marriage ceremony. Like marriage in connection with death ceremony a lot of rites and rituals are observed by the whole village. Therefore, it is important to preserve these invaluable traditions for the coming generation so that they may have the same opportunities to learn about the past and their own roots as we have.

References

- Das, R. C. (1996), *Social and Cultural Anthropology*, Sangam Prakash: Guwahati.
- Frazer, J.G. (1870), *Golden Bough*, New York, Doubleday, Anchor Books.
- Indianexpress.com. http://indianexpress.com/article/india/india-others/census-hindu-share-dips-below-80-muslim-share-grows-but-slower/. Retrieved 2015-01-24.
- Karstern, R. (1935), *Origin of Religion*, London, Kegan Paul.
- Madan, T.N. and D.N. Majumdar (1986), *An Introduction to Social Anthropology*, Mumbai, Asia Publishing House.
- Mair, Lucy (1972), *An Introduction to Social Anthropology*, Delhi, Oxford University Press.

10

Preserving the Cultural Heritage in Contemporary Times: Public Awareness and Involvement

— *Gangotri Bhuyan*

Introduction

Cultural heritage is a wide concept. According to ICOMOS (2002), it is often expressed as intangible and tangible cultural heritage. Cultural heritage is an expression of ways of living developed by a community and passed on from generation to generation, which includes practices, customs, objects, things of artistic values and expressions. Different scholars and organisations have described the term '*cultural heritage*' in various ways. It is unique, irreplaceable and beautiful disseminating knowledge about the past to the future, as such it places a huge responsibility of preservation and conserving on the current generation. Cultural heritage opens up a door to view the past of a society- their social life, economic conditions, their religious beliefs, the flora and fauna present, their value system, customs and practices etc.

Cultural heritage includes tangible, intangible and natural heritage that existed among the community or which formed the unique features of the community. The intangible cultural heritage consists of the non-physical aspect of the society. This includes social values, customs and practices, religious beliefs, artwork, language and other aspects of human activity. The tangible cultural heritage includes anything made by the human hand.

Tangible cultural heritage includes monuments, buildings, bridges, artefacts, works of art like paintings etc, manuscripts, clothes and any other things- moveable or immoveable- which were and are identification markers of the society. Among natural heritage are included the natural landscape, sacred groves and trees, the flora and fauna and the geology of the surrounding area. Cultural heritage was created by the community and for the community. The knowledge that the community had of their past and their present was forwarded to the future through the cultural heritage. As such the cultural heritage had enormous value. The tangible materials of the society could not survive without the intangible materials, both of which survived in the natural surroundings. As such the significance can be interpreted against the background of the socio-economic, political, ethnic, religious and philosophical values. Thus, protection of the cultural heritage for the posterity is much needed.

The act of keeping the cultural heritage- tangible, intangible and natural- safe and protect them from destruction or vandalism is termed the preservation of the cultural heritage. Preservation of cultural heritage is a great responsibility. Preserving heritage means to examine, document, assess, maintain, treat and protect the heritage. It involves protection and restoration. The care of cultural heritage has a long history, one that was primarily aimed at fixing and mending objects for their continued use and aesthetic enjoyment (Pye, 2001). The preservation of the past is necessary as it helps in recognising the things which would tell and validate the story of the past to the future. Lowenthal (1985) observed that objects also validate memories. Although the object of past can be preserved in the form of digitising (through digital media) but the touching the actual object would allow people to feel the past. In contrast, touching the artefacts poses danger of damage to the object by mishandling by the public or the tourist. As a result proper care should be taken in displaying, assessing and maintaining the artefacts. Moreover, the importance and value placed on the past and the artefacts related to the past by different generations may vary (Lowenthal, 1985). Singh *et al* (2001) pointed out that things which are inherited should not be consumed, but should be handed over, enriched, to the successive generations. This was reflected in the fact why Indians attributed importance to the preservation of traditions. Thus, what one generation considered 'cultural heritage', may be rejected by the next generation only to be revived by a subsequent generation. The accessibility of knowledge regarding the heritage, its preservation and conservation is a must for the society. Unless people are not aware of the importance and value of their heritage and what it has in store, generating interest becomes an impossible task. To understand the importance of preserving the Heritage, the heritage cycle diagram (Fig. 10.1) given by Simon Thurley (2005) provided us with the idea how we can make the past, a part of our future.

Heritage Cycle

This paper deals with some of the monuments, structures and artefacts found in and around Guwahati (Fig. 10.2), their preservation conditions and the awareness of the public towards the heritage and its protection and how to make the knowledge accessible for the public.

The methods include both primary and secondary sources. Primary data were collected through questionnaires, interviews and observation. Secondary data were collected from various books, journals, internet sources etc, which were consulted and reviewed from the library.

Interview was conducted among the visitors to the museums and monuments to gather information on their knowledge of the monuments and artefacts displayed in the museums. Data on questionnaires were circulated among the students and the answers were evaluated. Primary data collection also involved observation technique.

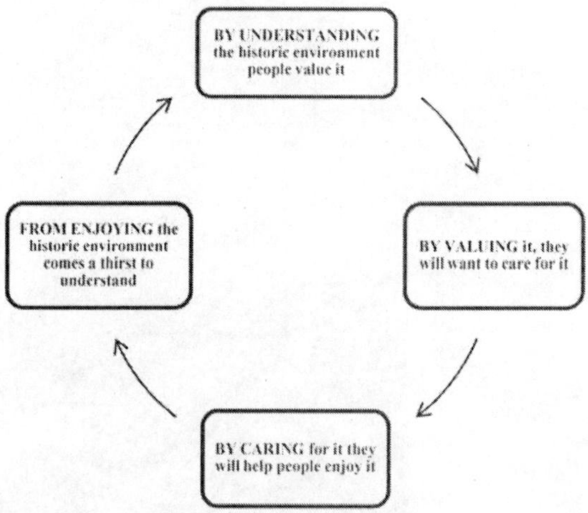

Fig. 10.1: The Heritage Cycle Diagram. Source: Simon Thurley (2005).

Study Area

The region of North-East India comprising of the eight states viz., Arunachal Pradesh, Assam, Manipur, Meghalaya, Mizoram, Nagaland, Sikkim and Tripura lies roughly between 22° N – 30° N latitude and 89° E – 97° E longitude. Assam lies beneath the foothills of the Eastern Himalayas sharing boundaries with all other North-eastern states of India, with the mighty river Brahmaputra flows right through its middle. Assam is situated between 90° E-96° E longitude and 24° N-28° N latitude. Assam is bordered in the north and east by Bhutan and Arunachal Pradesh. Along the south lie Nagaland and Manipur, and to the extreme south is Mizoram. Meghalaya is lies to the south-west and West Bengal to the west of Assam. Assam (Fig. 10.2) occupies a politically strategic position in relation to the rest of India.

The ancient name of Assam was Pragyotishpura – the city of Eastern Light, which later changed to Kamrupa – the land where Kamdeva, the god of love was reborn. The present name 'Asom' an obvious reference to her undulating and uneven landscape is relatively new. During the era of Mahabharata, this land was ruled by Non-Aryans, the first known ruler being Mahiranga Danava of Danava dynasty. Bhagadutta, son of Naraka who participated in the great Kurukshetra war as an ally of the Kauravas, was the most powerful among the Danava Kings. In the mid seventh Century A.D. the most illustrious monarch of Barmana dynasty Kumar Bhaskar

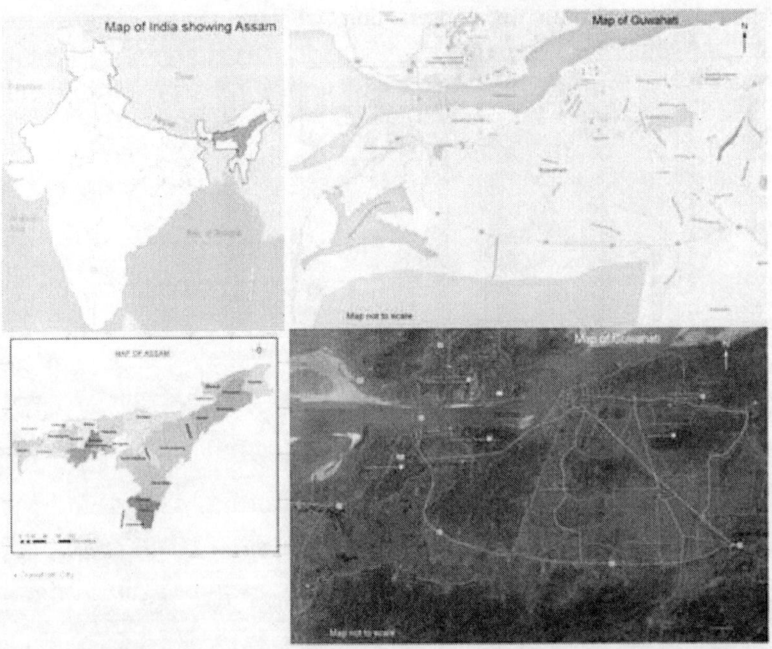

Fig. 10.2: Map of North-east India showing the location of Assam and Guwahati.

Barmana raised ancient Assam from obscurity and placed her in the forefront of Indian politics. Kumar Bhaskar Barmana was a close friend of King Harshavardhana. During this period Hiuen Tsang visited Assam.

Various literary sources, inscriptions and travelogues find the mention of ancient Assam as Pragjyotishpura or Kamrupa and description of the land and people along with the numerous structures on importance like Banabhatta's *Harshacharita*, Hiuen Tsang's writing, Kalika Purana, the Mahabharata etc.

Guwahati (Fig. 10.2) is the link that connects the other North-eastern states. The name Guwahati is derived from two Assamese words '*guwa*' meaning areca nut and '*haat*' meaning market place. Another version states that the name came from two Assamese word '*guha*' meaning cave and '*hati*' meaning elephant. If one views the city from top, the city surrounded by hills portrays the look of a cave and the rivers Brahmaputra and the Bharalu gives it the form of an elephant. Guwahati straddles the valley of the river Bharalu, a small tributary of the river Brahmaputra. It is surrounded by hills except, where the Bharalu discharges into the Brahmaputra. To its west is the Nilachal hills which is the home to the goddess *Kamakhya*. To the north lies the *Navagraha* (nine planets) temple atop the Chitrachal hill. To the south of the city lies the Narakasur hills named after the legendary king of ancient Assam (Baruah, 2013). The importance of Guwahati lies in the fact that it houses the capital of Assam, Dispur, the high court, the Assam Secretariat along with the historical and archaeological site of Ambari, the state museum, the university and several other places of importance and interest. Being well connected by rail, road, air and water, Guwahati saw a constant migration of different populations from time immemorial. Situated on the banks of the river Brahmaputra, the land was fertile enough for cultivation of different crops and vegetables. As a result of which, it became the homeland for several tribes and communities. Thus, at present Guwahati shows a splash of various population streaming in.

Protected Tangible Cultural Heritage in and around Guwahati

Several monuments and structures of historical importance are spread in and around Guwahati. The centrally and state protected monuments, sites and structures in and around Guwahati are as follows-

Sl. No.	*Name of the monument*	*Location*	*District*	*Whether protection under Central (C)/ State (S)*
1.	Ambari Archaeological Site	Ambari	Kamrup	S
2.	Umananda Temple	Urvashi Island	Kamrup	S
3.	Siva Temple	Chatrakar	Kamrup	S
4.	Manikarneswar Temple	Rajaduar, North Guwahati	Kamrup	S
5.	Kanai BoroshiBowa Rock Inscription	North Guwahati	Kamrup	S
6.	Aswaklanta Temple	North Guwahati	Kamrup	S
7.	Dirgheswari Ruins	North Guwahati	Kamrup	S

(Contd...)

8.	Chilating Rock Inscription	North Guwahati	Kamrup	S
9.	Rudreswar Temple	Silsako, North Guwahati	Kamrup	S
10.	Chandrasekhar Temple	Umananda, Urvashi Island	Kamrup	S
11.	Hara Gauri Temple	Umananda, Urvashi Island	Kamrup	S
12.	Na-Math		Kamrup	S
13.	Umachal Rock Inscription		Kamrup	S
14.	Persian Rock Inscription		Kamrup	S
15.	Pingaleswar Ruins		Kamrup	S
16.	Chanda's Merghar/ Chandar Merghar	Chaygaon	Kamrup	S
17.	Siddheswar Temple	Saulkuchi	Kamrup	S
18.	Madan Kamdev	Baihata Chariali	Kamrup	S
19.	Karbi Memorial		Kamrup	S
20.	Basistha Temple	Guwahati	Kamrup	S
21.	Bhairabeswari Temple	Rangia	Kamrup	S
22.	Naziraghat Ruins		Kamrup	S
23.	The carvings, inscriptions and pillar on the Urbashi Island	Guwahati	Kamrup	C
24.	The rock-cut sculptures of Vishnu, Surya, Ganesha, Devi etc locally known as Vishnu Janardan	Guwahati	Kamrup	C
25.	The stone inscription inside 'Poa Mecca Mosque'	Hajo	Kamrup	C
26.	Shri Shri Hayagriva Madhava Temple	Hajo	Kamrup	C
27.	Shri Shri Kedar Temple	Hajo	Kamrup	C
28.	Shri Shri Ganesha Temple	Hajo	Kamrup	C
29.	Shri Shri Kameshwar Temple	Hajo	Kamrup	C
30.	Duargarila Rock Inscription	Foot of the Nilachal hill, Kamakhya	Kamrup	C
31.	Two figures of Ganesha	Foot of the Nilachal hill, Kamakhya	Kamrup	C
32.	Twelve Siva lingas	Foot of the Nilachal hill, Kamakhya	Kamrup	C
33.	One four-handed Bhairavi	Foot of the Nilachal hill, Kamakhya	Kamrup	C
34.	Four miniature sikhara shrines	Foot of the Nilachal hill, Kamakhya	Kamrup	C
35.	One figure of Narakasur	Foot of the Nilachal hill, Kamakhya	Kamrup	C
36.	One figure of two-handed Bhairavi	Foot of the Nilachal hill, Kamakhya	Kamrup	C
37.	One Stone gateway	Foot of the Nilachal hill, Kamakhya	Kamrup	C
38.	Dancing Bhairava engraved on rock locally known as Bala-bhairava	Foot of the Nilachal hill, Kamakhya	Kamrup	C

Source: http://www.asiguwahaticircle.gov.in/assam.html. DOA: 25-03-2015.

There are 57 by central and 96 are State protected monuments under the Archaeology department in Assam. Some of the State and Centrally protected monuments as per the departmental website are mentioned above. But the very important structure of Northbrook gate on the banks of the river Brahmaputra near Sukreswar finds no mention in the lists but is under the Assam Tourism Department. Three known museums in Assam are - the Assam State Museum in Ambari, Science Museum in Kahilipara and the central museum in Srimanta Sankardev Kalakshetra. Apart from these three, the Ambari excavation site has a site museum, Assam State zoo cum Botanical Garden has a museum, Northeast tribal museum and Cultural centre at Nazirakhat near Sonapur both of which are maintained by the State government. Even the Departments of Anthropology in the Gauhati University, Dibrugarh University and Cotton College has a rich collection of artefacts in their department museums.

Brief Outline of Some Tangible Heritage around Guwahati

Some of the tangible heritage i.e., sites, ruins, structures and artefacts have myths and local legends revolving around them. The reason they become famous and acceptable by the community is because of the tales attached to the establishment and origin of the heritage. The folktales, myths and legends prevalent among the community disseminate their history and the material culture complements the authenticity of the heritage and its presence in the community since time immemorial. Mentioned here are few of the tangible heritage found in and around Guwahati and certain myths related to the heritage:

(1) **Ambari Archaeological Site (Ambari, Guwahati):** Lying in the heart of the city of Guwahati, Ambari is one of the archaeologically important sites in Assam (Fig. 10.3). Accidentally discovered while digging for laying foundation of the Reserve Bank of India's

Fig. 10.3: Ambari Archaeological site, Guwahati (Photograph by Gangotri Bhuyan).

building in 1969, the site added to the history of Assam immensely. Various excavations were carried since its discovery till present times revealed two distinct cultural phases – from seventh to twelfth century A.D. and thirteenth to seventeenth century A.D. by the Archaeological Survey of India in collaboration with various other organisations and Gauhati University. The excavations of 2008 revealed evidences of brick steps leading to a tank as well as sculptures belonging to the Sunga-Kushana period (second-first century B.C. to second century A.D.). Salvage operations revealed about 40 stone sculptures (Fig. 10.4) belonging to various Gods and Goddesses like Vishnu, Surya, Mahishasurmardini etc. Pottery included both handmade and wheel made potsherds of kaolin ware, red ware, buff ware and grey ware. Foreign ceramics of arretine ware, roulleted ware, Chinese celadon ware and green glazed ware were also found from the site. Various artefacts included terracotta beads, glass beads, bangles, terracotta figurines etc (IAR 1968-69).

(2) **Ashwaklanta Temple (North Guwahati):** This temple was constructed by King Shiva Singha in 1720. The temple is dedicated to Lord Vishnu and is situated on the banks of the river Brahmaputra in North Guwahati. Various folktales are related to the name of the temple and its existence. One tale mentions that while coming to battle Narakasur, Lord Krishna's horses were tired and rested in this place (Sharma, 2012). As such hooves' marks can be found on the surrounding stones. Hence the name, *Ashwa* meaning horse and *klanta* meaning tired.

Fig. 10.4: Sculptures from the Ambari archaeological site (Photograph by Gangotri Bhuyan).

(3) **Assam State Museum (Guwahati):** The Assam State Museum was established by the Kamrupa Anusandhan Samiti in 1950. The museum represents the whole North-eastern region through the various artefacts and materials displayed (Fig. 10.5). There are various sections of display from Prehistoric period to the modern paintings, sculptures, arms and ammunitions, manuscripts, house types, crafts etc.

Fig. 10.5: Display of artefacts in the Assam State Museum, Guwahati (Photograph by GangotriBhuyan)

(4) **Chanda's Merghar (Chaygaon, Guwahati):** The ruins of the Merghar (a specially built sealed house to prevent entry of any outsider) and replica of Shiva idols are found in the site. The site is attached with the mythological story of a merchant named Chanda Saudagar, his son Lakhindar and daughter-in-law Behula. Chanda Saudagar was an ardent devotee of Lord Shiva, who was cursed by the *Nag Devata* (Snake God) that he will not have any descendants and his son would be killed on his wedding night. Fearing the death of Lakhindar, Chanda built a *Merghar* (a sealed house to prevent the entry of snakes) and confined Lakhindar and Behula inside it. Despite all his efforts, Lakhindar was bitten to death by *Nag Devata* (Snake God). It was the unremitting efforts and prayers of Behula which saved Lakhindar's life later on (Baruah, 2013). As such the ruins are still present in the Chaygaon area of Guwahati. The story also forms a part of the folk songs, sang and danced to during various occasions.

(5) **Dirgheswari Ruins (North Guwahati):** Situated on the north bank of Brahmaputra, North Guwahati, the shrine present is dedicated to Devi Durga. It was built by the Ahom King Pramata Singha around eleventh century A.D. and it consists of several rock-cut images. This shrine is another place where buffalo sacrifice takes place during Durga Puja (Sharma, 2012). Mythology

related to the ruins has it that when Lord Shiva performed *Tandav* and carried the dead body of Goddess Parvati, one of the limbs fell on the hill and hence named Dirgheswari hill.

(6) **Kamakhya Temple (Guwahati):** Located on the south bank of the river Brahmaputra, atop the Nilachal hills, the temple is one of the most famous sacred places in India. It is considered one of the Shakti pithas where the body parts of Sati fell. According to one of the myths, the *yoni* (genital organ) of Sati, the consort of Lord Shiva fell on top of this hillock when Lord Vishnu cut off the self-immolated body of Sati, which was being carried by the grief-striken Lord Shiva with his discus. Another story related to the temple cites that the King Narakasur was mesmerised by the Goddess and proposed to marry her. The Goddess agreed to marry him under one condition- if Narakasur could construct the steps towards the temple from the foothill in one night. Narakasur went ahead with the construction work immediately and was almost going to finish the task, when the cock crowed under the influence of the Goddess. Crowing of the cock indicated arrival of dawn and end of night, furious at the outcome, Narakasur followed the cock and killed it. A little away from Kamakhya is the place where the cock was killed, called '*Kukura kata'* (Bhusan, 2005).

The stone stairway is still present and devotees still walk through the stairway to approach the temple for *darshan*. The Kamakhya temple is the only Shakti pitha which does not have the image of the Goddess. Instead the Goddess is worshipped in the form of yoni (genital organ) circular sculptured on a block of stone in a cave within the temple with water oozing from within the stone block to keep the circular structure moist. Various sculptures and shrines are found in the Nilachal hills surrounding the temple and the temple complex. Some of them are as follows - Duargarila Rock Inscription on the foot of the Nilachal hills, two figures of Ganesha, twelve Siva lingas, one figure four-handed Bhairavi, four miniature shikhara shrines, one figure of Narakasur, one figure of two-handed Bhairavi, one stone gateway, dancing Bhairava engraved on rock locally known as Bala-bhairava and various *yoginis* on the outer wall of the temple.

(7) **Madan Kamdev (BaihataChariali):** It is a rich archaeological site which dates back to eleventh-twelfth century A.D. during the reign of the Pala kings (Sharma, 2012). The first excavation of the site was conducted in 1977 under the Archaeological Directorate of Assam, where plethora of materials was unearthed. This included

a main temple complex, 12 ruins of temples, various sculptures etc. Some of the idols and sculptures found include Bhairav with six heads, four headed Shiva, Kalpavriksha, Sun, various Apsaras, Vishnu with six heads, Saraswati and various other statues of animals. The art in the sculptural panels portray the expressions of erotic acts which can be seen in the famous Khajuraho temples of Madhya Pradesh and the Konark temple of Odisha. There are a few puranic beliefs prevalent regarding Madan Kamdev. According to one, Lord Shiva in a spurt of fury, had burnt Kamdeva or Madan (the God of Love), to cinders and he was reborn and reunited with his wife, Rati in this hillock. The existing portion of Madan Kamdev shows that these were perhaps the finest medieval temples built in the Brahmaputra valley. It still remains an archaeological challenge. There is a small museum established in the site (Baruah, 2013).

(8) Northbrook gate (Guwahati): Located on the bank of the river Brahmaputra, the Northbrook Gate was erected to commemorate the arrival of the then Viceroy of India, Thomas George Baring also known as Lord Northbrook in the year 1874 (Wikipedia, DOA: 09/04/2015).

Fig. 10.6: View of the Northbrooke gate facing the river Brahmaputra (Photograph by Gangotri Bhuyan).

The gate was designed by the British designers resembling the King's College Chapel arches of England. The gate, rectangular in shape was built of brick and lime with 12 arches, five in each of the longer sides and one each on the shorter side (Fig. 10.6). Standing still on the Sukreswarghat, the gate has seen ups and downs of the city of Guwahati from the time it was erected. Recently the tourism department of Assam developed a park surrounding the Northbrook gate as well as conservation work of the gate was carried out which was crumbling down.

(9) **Rudreswar Temple (North Guwahati):** The temple is dedicated to Lord Shiva and is situated on the north bank of the river Brahmaputra. It was built by Ahom King Pramata Singha around 1749 in the memory of his father, Swargadeo Rudra Singha (Baruah, 2013).

(10) **Srimanta Sankardev Kalakshetra (Guwahati):** Established in 1998, the Kalakshetra, one of the largest congregations of culture, is named after the poet, playright and reformer Srimanta Sankardev (Fig. 10.7). It includes an art gallery, children's park, ethnographic museum, library, open air theatre, the Bhupen Hazarika museum, auditoriums, eateries etc. The Kalakshetra displays the artistic excellence of Assam as well as the other states of North-eastern region. Various exhibitions, workshops, ethnic festivals, cultural programmes etc are held in the Srimanta Sankardev Kalakshetra. It reflects the life and culture of the people of North-eastern India.

Fig. 10.7: Entrance to the Srimanta Sankardeva Kalakshetra (Photograph by Gangotri Bhuyan).

(11) **Sukeswar Temple (Guwahati):** It was built in 1744 by King Pramata Singha. The temple complex is famous for the various rock-cut images found facing the mighty river Brahmaputra. These include the sculptures of Vishnu, Surya, Ganesha, Devi etc. which is locally known as Vishnu Janardan. The local tale regarding the shrine point out that the hillock was used by the hermit Sukra to meditate and worship Lord Shiva. In the passing years, he established a hermitage in the hillock which was called as Hastagiri as it resembled an elephant (Baruah, 2013).

(12) **Umananda Temple (Urvasi Island):** Situated in the middle of the mighty river Brahmaputra, the Urvasi island is also known as the Peacock island. As the name suggests the temple is dedicated to Lord Shiva, built by the Ahom King Gadadhar Singha in

1694 A.D. There are various myths related to the island and the hill. According to the Hindu mythology, Lord Shiva created this place for the happiness of his wife *Uma*. Hence the name Umananda, *Uma* means the name of Lord Shiva's wife and *Ananda* means happiness. Another myth narrated in the Kalika Purana mentions that this was the place where Lord Shiva burnt Kamdeva into ashes for disturbing and interrupting in his meditation. Hence the name of the hill Bhasmachal, where *Bhasma* means ashes and *chal* means home in Assamese.

(13) **War Memorial (Guwahati):** The War Cemetery located near Chenikuthi, Guwahati, houses around 500 graves of soldiers who fought the Second World War. These soldiers were not from Assam or North-east India but belonged to various countries like United Kingdom, Russia, India, Australia etc (Kashyap, 2015). Although no battles were fought in and around Guwahati, the soldiers were brought to the military hospitals in the nearby areas and later on were buried in the spot where the Cemetery was built.

Public Review and Findings

Interview was conducted among students, elders, tourists and the monument attendants. Information was gathered using a questionnaire. Due to time constraint the interviews were randomly conducted. Discussion with the visitors to museums and various monuments revealed that people are not aware of most of the above mentioned monuments, sites, museums and structures. They visit some of these places for recreation during weekends to get away from the hustle of the city. The children knew very little about the monuments, sites and other cultural heritage around the city. Students who have personal interest make efforts to know and learn about it. Even in college, students with interest in history get to learn a lot about the History of the World and India but very less about their own states and society. Simple question like the number of museums in the Guwahati left people thinking how many are there in reality. The thought of visiting a museum is not at all amusing for a lot of people especially youngsters. Attending workshops and exhibitions on various occasions celebrating the importance of the heritage was rarely done. Their first reactions are what is there to see; why do we have to see and how will it even help us.

When asked about certain monuments, elders appeared better placed than the youngsters. Knowledge of temples was appealing but as we went into details or specific myths and folktales related to the sites, information blurred out. Most of the elders and monument attendants were aware of the myths and folktales related to the various monuments and sites, whereas the youngsters were not much concerned about the same. The tourists were from different parts of India, visiting the North-eastern region. When enquired about their interest in the heritage, their reply was almost in unison. Most of them came to visit the temples from religious point of view. The other places they visit are either a part of their itinerary or recommended by someone who visited the places earlier. But much background work has been done on the sites, monuments and structures in and around the city before they visit, as they do not want to miss any important and interesting place.

Being a preliminary survey, the replies and interactions although minimum but made us hopeful that some basic steps towards spreading awareness and involving public would be fruitful in future. This in turn would equip the public in preserving the cultural heritage. With changing times, the perspectives of people have also changed. Recognising the importance of preservation and conservation of the heritage especially with developmental activities going around seems to be the need of the hour and the community has to come forward and get involved in preserving the heritage for the future generations.

Conclusion

Cultural heritage is our debt of the past and our promise to the future. Cultural heritage of a community or tribe becomes the identification maker and the story teller of the past. With development and industrialisation, the value for our own heritage is reducing. The want of new technology and developmental projects have led to destruction of many monuments and sites. The initiative from the government to safeguard and preserve them gave rise to the establishment of various organisations and departments since the colonial times. But how far have we succeeded in preserving the cultural heritage. Awareness begins at home. But if people are not aware of the existence of the heritage then how will they preserve or safeguard it for posterity. Public involvement in preserving cultural heritage would help the government initiatives also. The survey was disheartening. Very less students are aware of the heritage around them. Elders are aware of it but no effort is made to spread that knowledge to the younger generation.

Apart from the government departments and organisations carrying out awareness drives, the public can be involved in spreading the awareness about the importance of the heritage and their value. Schools can popularise the knowledge about the history of a place through recommended chapters in the syllabus. Moreover they can arrange visits to museums and monuments with the students and involve them in various activities related to the monuments or sites of visit. The Archaeological Survey of India (Guwahati circle) organises photo exhibitions, essay writing competitions, drawing competitions etc on the occasion of the World Heritage Day celebrated on 18th April every year. Last year saw a wave of youngsters participating in all the events which were held in Hajo, Sibsagar, Joysagar, and Charaideo whereas this year the celebration was held in Bamuni hills Tezpur. They also organised International Museum Day on 18th May, this year at the premises of Archaeological Museum, Sri Suryapahar, Goalpara district with drawing and extempore speech competitions among the students from various nearby schools. This was done basically to spread awareness among the public and spread the knowledge on conserving and preserving the heritage. Similar programmes were also organised by the Assam State Museum this year on the occasion of International Museum Day. Different organisations like other regional circles of the Archaeological Survey of India; Indira Gandhi Rashtriya Manav Sangrahalaya, Bhopal; Indira Gandhi National Centre for the Arts, New Delhi etc organises workshops, seminars, educational programmes, exhibitions, special lectures etc among people from various communities as well as among the school students to spread awareness as well as train the public in preserving the heritage around them.

Similar steps along with quizzes can be organised by the schools and colleges and awareness can be spread among the community. The effects of human and animal vandalism can also be curbed through awareness. Limited information on the importance of the structure makes people care less for its existence. As a result of which, the presence or absence of it makes no difference. But a little effort from the public in spreading awareness among all especially the youngsters and making the knowledge about the heritage accessible to everyone would reduce the humongous task in front of the government agencies. Losing cultural heritage is losing a part of our own culture, so efforts in any form to preserve it would help in keeping safe for the posterity.

References

Baruah, S. K. (2013), *Assam Year Book*, Guwahati: Jyoti Prakashan.

Bhusan, C. (2005), *Assam: Its Heritage and Culture*, Delhi: Kalpaz Publications. http://www.asiguwahaticircle.gov.in/assam.html. DOA: 25-03-2015.

ICOMOS. (2002), *International Cultural Tourism Charter. Principles and Guidelines for Managing Tourism at Places of Cultural and Heritage Significance*. ICOMOS International Cultural Tourism Committee.

Indian Archaeology – A Review. (1968-69), pp. 3-4.

Kashyap, S G. (2015), *Few visitors to World War II cemetery on 70th anniversary of end of war.* In The Indian Express, DOA: 17-06-2015. DOP: 08-05-2015.

Lowenthal, D. (1985), *The Past is a Foreign Country*, New York: Cambridge University Press. DOA: 01-04-2015. https://www.worldcat.org

Pye, E. (2001), *Caring for the Past: Issues in Conservation for Archaeology and Museums*, London: James and James.

Sharma, D. (2012), *Glimpses of Northeast India Archaeology*, Guwahati: Eastern Publishers (India).

Singh, R., P.B. Vrinda Dar and S. Pravin. (2001), *Rationales for including Varanasi as heritage city in the UNESCO World Heritage List*. In National Geographic Journal of India (Varanasi) 47:177200.

Thurley, S. (2005), *Into the future: Our strategy for 2005-2010*. In Conservation Bulletin, English Heritage – The First 21 Years, (49): 26-27.

http://en.wikipedia.org/wiki/Northbrook_Gate. *Northbrook Gate.* DOA: 09-04-2015.

11

The Cultural Tradition of Khatara Satra of Darrang: A Study

— *Gitika Saharia*

Introduction

The institution of Satra is unique features of Vaishnavism in Assam. The Satras are established by Sankardeva, the father of Satriya culture which are like mediaeval monasteries. During those days Assamese societies were facing so many burning problems like superstitions, blind faith, communal fight, human and animal sacrifices in the name of gods and goddesses etc. For uniting the Assamese society Saint Sankardeva went through the Vaisnavite manifastation and established many Satras throughout the state. Even after death of Sankardeva, the tradition of establishing Satras had been continued by his admires. The Satras are not just monasteries, but centres of traditional performing arts like *Borgeet, Bhatima, Satriya dance, Chali dance, Paalnam, Thiyanam, Nagaranam, Ankia Bhaona* etc which were initiated by Sri Sankardeva and his followers. Each residential unit which came to be known as Satra was maintained by his followers for proselytising activities. So, we can say that a new school of art came into being in Assam in the fifteenth century with the adherent of Srimanta Sankardeva. Khatara Satra is one of the blessed sacred institutions having positive influence on religious and cultural aspects of Assam. Khatara Satra has been depicting the triumph of religion and culture since its inception which is undoubtedly an illuminating chapter in the heritage of Darrang as well as of Assam.

The Study Area

The area of the study is limited to Khatara Satra of Darrang District which is situated on the north of the Brahmaputra River. Khatara Satra is located at village Khatara in Dipila Mouza of Darrang District of Assam. Khatara lies at a distance of almost twenty kilometers west of Mangaldai, the headquarters of Darrang District.

Khatara Satra and its past

Khatara Satra, one of the unique and notable Satra of Assam was founded by Lechakonia Govinda Aatoi, a well-known admirer of Saint Madhavdeva in 1568 A.D. Govinda Aatoi was prominent among the twelve *Dharmacharya* of Madhavdeva. Sri Sri Govinda Aatoi was adorned with the title "*Dharmacharya*" by Mahapurush Madhavdeva and Aatoi was sent to Darrang District with the noble objective of preaching Vaisnavism here. Govinda Aatoi, the submissive disciple of Mahapurush Madhavdeva came forward and succeeded in fulfilling his Guṛu's dream. While contemplating to set up a satra in the aforesaid site, Aatoi, caught sight of an unusual scene that a frog was swallowing a big snake. On seeing such a strange scene, Aatoi had regarded this site to be the most sacred and abode of divinity and he determined to build the 'Kirtan Ghar' there although Aatoi faced some problems from the mischievous people used to live there. It is better to mention here that the word KHATARA has derived from the word '*Khot-Hora'*. *Khot* means mischievous person and *Hora* means domination, actually at that time some uncivilised mischievous people lived in aforesaid place situated on the west bank of mighty tributary NONOI. In order to bring the mischievous people towards the religious line, Lechakonia Govinda Aatoi founded Khatara Satra. He was compelled to apply rare strategy in order to dominate the Khats, so that they could realise the perfect way of human life. As the result of Aatoi's strategy idols of Rama, Lakshmana, Sita and Hanuman are found in Khatara Satra which is exceptional in the Vaishnavite movement.

Objectives of the Study

The objectives of the study are as follows-

- To study different traditional cultures performed in Khatara Satra.
- To study different festivals celebrated in Khatara Satra.
- To study the role of culture of Khatara Satra in maintaining communal harmony.

Research Questions

- What are the different traditional cultures performed in Khatara Satra?

- What are the different festivals celebrated in Khatara Satra?
- What is the role played by Khatara satra in maintaining communal harmony?

Data and Methodology

The study is mainly based on secondary sources of data. Data are collected from different secondary sources like books, magazines, souvenirs. The present study has adopted the descriptive method of study.

Discussion on First Objective

Khatarasatra earned reputation as the excellent centre of practicing Satrya and folk culture from the time of Govinda Aatoi. The cultural proficiency of Govinda Aatoi once turned Khatarasatra into a place of amusement. The *Nam-Prasanga, Borgeet, Thiya-Nam, Dadhi- Mathann-ritya, Vyahar Ojah, Kholia Bhaona, Ankia Bhaona, Boka Bhaona, Khol Badan, Natua (dancing boy), Gari Bagar Nritya (dancing by just rounding the body part without touching the floor)* etc of Khatarasatra have a heart-appealing influence on the cultural history of Darrang as well as of Assam.

Kholia Bhaona: The *Kholia Bhaona* (a form of drama) of Khatara Satra is a glorious chapter in the cultural history of Darrang. It is difficult to say about *Kholia Bhaona* of Khatarasatra. But some people believe that *Kholia Bhaona* got immense popularity after the establishment of Khatara Satra. The *Kholia Bhaoria* of Darrang is known as *Kholia Bhaona* in Khatara Satra.The theme concerned to Khatara Satra and contribution of Govinda Aatoi is always deeply related to *Kholia Bhaona* of Satra. Some *Bhaona* (drama) written and performed in Khatara Satra are *Birat Parba, Khatasur Badh, Bhujanga Badh* etc.

Dadhi Mathan (ritual ceremony): Dadhi Mathan is the most attractive culture of Khatara Satra. On the day of the *PaachetiMahotsav, Dadhi Mathan Bhaona* is performed after bringing water from the Borpukhuri. Girls and boys enacting themselves as Krishna, Yashoda, Gopees. With the cooperation of Bhaktas, Gayan, Bayan and Sutradhar *Dadhi Mathan Bhaona* is performed in Kirtanghar.

Nam-Prasanga: Nam-Prasanga is also a common tradition of Khatara Satra. In everyday the Nam-Ghar is resounded with melodious *Ghosa* and *Nam-Prasanga* performed by *Bhakats* and *Mahantas*.

In Thiya Naam

Boka Bhaona: Boka Bhaona is a very interesting culture of Khatara Satra. *Boka Bhaona* is celebrated on the day of '*Nandotsav*'. In *Boka*

Bhaona, a mixture of water, milk, honey, juice of turmeric is made in the floor of Kirtan Ghar. Bhakats start dancing and singing on the floor of Kirtan Ghar and thus they create *Boka*. It is called *Boka Bhaona*.

Fig. 11.1

Gondhar Geet orAdhibas (a ceremony): In the previous night of every festival of Khatara Satra singing 'Gondhar Geet' is considered as an essential tradition. This tradition is related to 'Basudev Puja' or 'Gondh Chaupari Sabha' of Darrang District. Apart from this it is essential to sing on the eve of performing every cultural activity like *Thiya Nam, Nagara Nam, Khulia Bhaona, Dadhi Mathan* etc. This ceremony was introduced by Govinda Aatoi. On the day of Adhibas, an oblation (Sarai) is placed inside the Namghar of Satra after lighting earthen lamps and incense sticks.

Khol Badya: Khol Badya (a musical instrument of Satriya Culture) is one of the most important cultural forms of Khatara Satra. *Khol Badya* is closely related to *Borgeet,* Satriya Dance, *Kholia Bhaona, Gayan Bayan* etc. *Khol Badya* of Khatara Satra bears a unique characteristic. It is well

Fig. 11.2: Dadhi Mathan Nritya Bhortaal Nritya

mentioned that only in Khatara Satra the '*Gari Bagar Nritya*' is practiced. The '*Gari Bagar Nritya*' is a unique contribution of Khatara Satra to Assamese culture.

In Khol Badan

Apart from these unique culture of Khatara Satra, every item of Satriya culture is being practiced here with full of reverence. *Borgeet, Khol Badan*, Satriya Dance etc are taught in the Satra premises.

Fig. 11.3

Discussion on Second Objective

Khatara Satra is also the centre of attraction as the venue of festivals. Various festivals on different occasion have been celebrated decoratively with religious fervour every year in Khatara Satra since time immemorial, amongst them, Paacheti, the Holi festival, Deul Festival, Bor Gopini Sabah, Bar Sabah, the death anniversary of Govinda Aatoi, the founder of Khatara Satra on the fourteenth tithi of dark fortnight, the Janmastami, the Nandotsav, Bihu festival etc are worthy to be mentioned.

The Paacheti Festival: The Paacheti festival is the most popular amongst all the festivals observed in the Satra. The Paacheti festival of Khatara Satra is notable with its own peculiarities among all the 'Pacheti' or 'Paacheti' festivals celebrated in various places of Assam. 'Paacheti' is a ritual associated with the birth circle of Lord Sri Krishna.

Every year, the Paacheti festival has been celebrated on the Sankranti day in between the month of Bhadra and Aswin (fifth and sixth month of

Assamese calendar). It is doubtless that the 'Paacheti' festival would be 430 years old. The main agenda of the Paacheti Mahotsav is Dadhi Mathan, the gondha or adhibas etc. The mela premises of the festival become overcrowded with the rush of people. During the morning hours innumerable coconut seedlings are sold and different kind of articles and goods are sold in the Paacheti. The Bahi Paacheti is celebrated on the following day. The Paacheti festival of Khatara Satra is splendid amongst the Assamese folk festivals like a coloured and scented flower in a lovely garden.

The holy Festival: The holy festival is celebrated in Khatarasatra with full of religious tradition. On the day of *Fakua* or Holy festival, the idol of Laba is brought from Namghar and it is established with Krishna Bhajan song. The whole day is passed with Nam-Kirtan and at the time of evening it is reestablished in the previous place. In the following day the fully decorated idol is surrounded in the nearest villages which is known as '*Sueri Fura*'.

Janmastami: Janmastami is celebrated as Krishna Astami in Khatara Satra. This festival is purely based on religious belief. *Nam-Kirtan, Bor Nagaranam, Bhaona* related to the birth of Lord Krishna are performed in this festival.

Nandotsav: In the next day of Krishna Janmastami, Nandotsav is celebrated in Khatara Satra. Nandotsav is celebrated as a symbol of joy of borning Lord Sri Krishna. *Boka Bhaona* is a special attraction of Nandotsav in Khatara Satra.

Apart from this festivals the death anniversary of Sri Sri Govinda Aatoi, Sri Sri Sankardeva, Sri Sri Madhavdeva is also celebrated in Khatara Satra with full of religious tradition.

Deol Utsav: Deol festival is a unique festival of Darrang District. Deol Utsav of Khatarasatra is based on Bisnu Puja. This Deol Festival is celebrated in Khatara Satra on the day of fifteenth Bohag with different agenda like Nam-Kirtan, Thiya-Nam, Kholia Bhaona etc.

Bor Sabah: In the first week of Jeth Month (the second month of Assamese calendar) of every year, Bor Sabah of Khatara Satra is celebrated. In the previous night of the Sabah singing of 'Gondhar Geet' is a traditional culture of Satra. Byashar Ojapali, an important religious culture of Darrang District is performed at night. People of different villages come to Satra with oblation (Sarai) and want to touch the divinity of the Satra with full of reverence which is the harbinger of good luck and destroyer of misfortune.

Bor Gopini Sabah: Bor Gopini Sabah is celebrated on the tithi of full moon in the month of Bohag. The women folk mainly take part in Nam-Kirtan in this festival. So, it is called Bor Gopini Sabah. People believe that Bor Gopini Sabah helps to create mutual understanding, cooperation, and friendliness and among the women as well as the Nam-Kirtan helps them to develop a feeling of spiritual satisfaction which creates a spiritual environment in their homes also.

Bihu Festival: The traditional Bihu festival is also an inseparable page of the cultural chapter of Khatara Satra. Not only Bohag Bihu, Kati Bihu and Magh Bihu are also celebrated here traditionally. Especially the Bahagbihu is celebrated with full of decoration.

Discussion on Third Objective

Khatara Satra being endearing to all the devotees have been attracting thousands of people since its inception till date irrespective of caste, creeds and colour. The tribal people are seen to come Khatara Satra from different places of Darrang District. Especially in Paacheti Mahotsav, it is very attractive to see the tribal women-folk coming to the Mahotsav putting on their own attire in groups. As a matter of fact people irrespective of caste, creed, colour unite together in the Satra Premises on the day of the Paacheti festival.

The social activities of Khatara Satra which is dazzling with the light of heritage cannot be underestimated. The Daba-Barkah (kettle drum and a gong- an instrument made of metal) of Satra has inspired people all along to work on behalf of the society and integrity. There is mention about uniting people by beating Kettle Drum and Gong of the Satra during the time of 'Patharughat Revolt' in 1894 A.D. It is to be mentioned that the folk songs were also composed relating to Khatara Satra which is related to wedding ceremony and the song is quoted below-

"Ram Krishna Khatara Gosaighar
Ram Krishna dekhotebhayankar
Hari mor oi chakurinahararkhuta
Ram Krishna duphalelekhile
Ram Krishna Ram Lakshamane
Hari mor oi majote Janoki Sita
Ram Krishna Borchorarmukhate
Ram Krishna juriaSinghai
Hari morai ache namgunagai
Ram Krishna Manikutarupare

Ram Krishna sonareKalachi
Hari morai taro j tulanani"

Khatara Temple- looks gigantic -120 pillars of Mesua Ferra, Idol of Sita –placed in between –Ram and Lakshman. This folk song implies image of Khatara Satra in the mind of the common people. Innumerable pilgrims assemble there on the special occasion of New Year especially in the month of Puha, Magha and Bahaga. Non-Hindus have also been seen to show great respect and honour towards Khatara Satra. So, Khatara Satra can not only be said as the centre of Vaishnavite religion but it must be said that Khatara Satra is a centre of communal harmony as it provides the opportunity to pray and worship to all whether they may be Sakta or Vaisnav and this flow of harmony is kept up all along with the unique and attractive cultural heritage of Khatara Satra. Apart from this the divine or supreme power associated with Khatara Satra attracts the devotees of different parts of Assam. So, it can be said that Khatara Satra has been playing a significant role in bridging the gap having in the minds of the people of different caste, creed, and religion.

Summary and Conclusion

From the present study it is found that Khatara Satra is a sacred place having cultural importance. Most of the unique cultural forms are practiced here. The Satra is well known not only for the Satriya cultural, folk culture is of great importance in attracting people of different places of Assam. *Nam-Prasanga, Ghosa, Thiya Nam, Pal Nam, Borgeet, Satriyanritya, Krishna Nritya* are practiced with full of reverence. Especially 'Gari Bagar Nritya', Kholia Bhaona, Boka Bhaona, Dadhi Mathan Nritya etc are unique and attractive cultural practice of Khatara Satra.

Regarding festival it can be said that Khatara Satra is a place of festivals and joy. *Paacheti, Deol Utsav, Janmastami, Bor Sabah, Bor Gopiuni Sabah, Nandotsav*, Death anniversary of Govinda Aatoi, Sankardeva and Madhavdeva etc are celebrated with full of traditional decoration.

Khatara Satra earned reputation as the excellent centre of practicing Satriya and folk culture from the times of Govinda Aatoi. The cultural Excellency, divinity and democratic administrative system makes Khatara Satra one of the most popular and unique Satra of Assam. At present, Khatara Satra has become the centre of attraction for religious tourists. Though the government has not yet declared Khatarasatra as 'religious tourist centre', the day is so near to announce it in the list of tourist centre of Assam shortly after getting the required infrastructural facilities. The cooperation of both government and public along with the strong effort of the Satra managing committee, Khatara Satra, the sacred place would be prominent by becoming charming and attractive one among all the Satras in Assam. The cultural resources of Khatara Satra mainly the 'Gari Bagar Nritya' which is not practiced in any other Satra of Assam except Khatara Satra, popularity of Paacheti Mohotsav, Kholia Bhaona, Boka Bhaona and the unique rituals associated with all the religious activities and festivals make Khatara Satra very unique and special which is the positive aspect of attracting the tourists irrespective of caste, creed and religion. Apart from these regarding literary activities Khatara Satra has been occupying a special and important position. The ancient '*Barkakat*' preserved in Khatara Satra is a valuable document which is written on the bark of sanchi tree is six feet seven inches by length and nine and half inches by breadth. There have been writings in the three feet ten inches space of the '*Barkakat*' and remaining ten feet nine inches of the same has remained unwritten. It is almost one hundred and seventy years old. To get the government recognition and come under the scheme like 'Dharmajyoti', the managing committee of Khatara Satra and regional-public, well-wishers should come forward and make some contemporary steps in a planned manner. Attempt should be made to utilise science and technology to develop the buildings, museum, library etc without hurting people's religious beliefs. In real sense, Khatara Satra is a glided historical institute of Assam's religio-cultural sphere. Khatara Satra with its own glory will always be glittering amidst us.

References

Barua, Birinchi Kumar, "Sankardeva Vaisnava Saint of Assam", published by Chandan Dey, College Hostel Road, Guwahati, Assam.

Bhatta, Akhil Ranjan, "Khatara Satra", an article published in 'Setubandha', 2010 (pp. 87-95).

Das, Sri Kailash (chief Editor) (2004), "Panchajanya", a souvenir published on the occasion of the 73rd annual conference of Srimanta Sankardeva Sangha, Ganeshguri, Ghy-5.

Deka, Kamalakanta (2010) (Editor), "Setubandha", a souvenir published by Sri Boloram Baishya on the occasion of the Assam Satra Mahasabha, Pahileser prints, Mangaldai.

Deka, Kamalakanta (Editor) (2006), "Asamar Satra Sanskritiaru Khatara Satra", a collection of articles published by Bangshi Kumar Baruah on behalf of celebration committee, the 438th anniversary, Pahileser prints, Mangaldai.

Nath, Lokeswar and Deka Navajyoti (compiler and Editor) (2014), "Khatara Satrar Paacheti" published by Khatarasatra Managing Committee, Navaneeta Printers, Bamunimaidam, Ghy-21.

12

Nutritional Status of the Preschool Sonowal Kachari Children of Lakhimpur District, Assam

— *Gulrukh Begum, Pankaja Dutta*

Impact of Cultural Heritage on Health among the Sonowal Kacharis of Lakhimpur District, Assam

Cultural heritage is that which exists intellectually in a culture. It is often defined as a legacy from our past on to future generations to learn from, marvel at and enjoy (UNESCO, 2004). Today an anthropological approach to heritage leads us to consider it as a social ensemble of many different, complex and interdependent manifestations. Culture influences diet, choices of food and food preparation and traditions, beliefs and values are among the main factors influencing preference, methodology of food preparation and nutritional status.

Food habits, in general are culture specific but in the last few decades dynamic changes have occurred due to the fast growing economy, changing technologies, globalisation, evolving tastes and increased demands for "fast" and processed foods throughout our country. Due to the fast paced life, parents are too busy to prepare home-cooked foods. Fast food chains have been the solution to that problem.

Social and cultural practices have a great influence on what people eat, or how they prepare food and on the foods they prefer. On one hand it is said that cultural food practices are very rarely the main or even an important cause of malnutrition (FAO, 2014). On the other hand many practices in every culture are specifically designed to protect and promote health.

Culture has a profound effect on the way nutrition and health is defined and experienced. It is here equally important to recognise that most of the members of a cultural or ethnic group share the same values, beliefs and food choices. To Hochbaum (1981) and Crockett and Sims (1995) nutrition-related attitudes and behaviour usually are established early in life and are primarily determined by cultural, psychosocial and socio-economic factors.

The process of change occurs naturally over time and cultural heritage has always played an important role in nutrient needs of a community. It is with this notion; the present study has been done to study the effect of cultural values on the nutritional status of the Sonowal Kachari pre-school children. The cultural values sometimes may conflict with optimum nutrition. The food consumed by the people determines their nutritional status and it is considered as a powerful tool for determining health and well being of a population. Different studies in India provide a preview on the significant extent of nutritional shortfalls in tribal children and adults, mostly explained to be caused by insufficient diet, improper knowledge and seasonal episodes of food scarcity (Rao *et al.,* 1994, 2006; Rao and Rao, 1994; Mukhopadhyay *et al*., 2010; Laxmaiah *et al*., 2007; Chakma et al., 2009; Parimalavalli, 2012).

Materials and Method

The Sonowal Kacharis are one of the Bodo tribes which are predominantly concentrated in the districts of Dhemaji, Lakhimpur, and Dibrugarh. They are also scattered in the districts of Tinsukia, Jorhat and Golaghat. It is said that during the reign of the Ahom kings, some Kacharis were engaged in washing the gold particles from the sand of the rivers and therefore the prefix 'Sonowal' (gold washer) was added to signify them. (Bordoloi and Thakur, 1988). According to 2011 census, the Sonowal Kacharis constitute 7.1 per cent of the total Scheduled Tribes population in Assam with a population of 2,35,881.

Agriculture is the sole means of livelihood and rice is the staple food of the Sonowal Kachari people. The typical dress includes the '*Dhoti-Kurta'* and '*Phulam Gamocha'*. The Sonowal Kachari women are expert weaver. Both male and female member of the society are equally laborious and cooperation is seen among them (Bordoloi and Thakur, 1988).

The sample for the study is composed of 282 children of which 155 are boys and 127 are girls of age ranging between three-six years. The data are arranged in eight (8) different groups with an interval of six months. The age of the children were collected from the written records with the parents, from the pre-primary educational institutions known as 'Anganbadi

Schools', from the mothers of the children etc. The data was collected from nine villages of Lakhimpur district.

The somatometric measurements selected for the study were stature and weight which are essential for the detection of under nutrition with the help of anthropometric indices. Stature was measured with the help of an anthropometer and weight with the help of a portable weighing machine. For the nutritional status assessment the following indices have been considered. These are:

(a) Weight-for-age, (b) Height-for-age and (c) Weight-for-height

Weight-for-age: As prescribed by WHO (1986) children with more than 80 per cent of the expected weight-for-age i.e. 50th percentile of the reference population defined by US National Centre for Health Statistics (NCHS, 1974) taken as 100 per cent of the expected weight-for-age and were termed as normal. Children weighing between 71-80 per cent were taken as suffering from malnutrition (Grade I), between 61-70 per cent as moderate malnutrition (Grade II) and less than 60 per cent as severe malnutrition (Grade III).

Height-for-age: Children with more than 90 per cent of the expected height-for-age (50 per cent of the reference population defined by US National Centre for Health Statistics (NCHS, 1974) taken as 100 per cent of the expected height-for-age) were taken as normal; between 89-80 per cent were termed as Grade I malnutrition, also termed as stunted; 79-70 per cent as Grade II and less than 70 per cent were Grade III.

Height and weight measurements of the children, taking age and sex into consideration, were converted into Z-scores based on the National Centre for Health Statistics (NCHS) reference population recommended by the World Health Organisation (WHO). Children whose measurements fall below -2 Z- scores of the reference population median are considered undernourished, i.e. have stunting, wasting or underweight. Those children with measurements below - 3 Z-scores are considered to be severely undernourished. Prevalence of moderate under nutrition was defined as Z- score $\geq$ - 3.0 — $\leq$ -2.0 (WHO, 1995).

Since in many studies it has been seen that all these indices estimate different proportion of under nutrition in a single populations which Svedberg (2000) suggests that if children with wasting, stunting or who are underweight are all considered undernourished or to be in a state of "anthropometric failure" a new aggregate could be used called as composite index of anthropometric failure (CIAF). Therefore, this particular composite index has also been applied for the present study.

χ^2-square test was performed to look into the variation between the number of affected boys and girls being statistically significant.

Results and Discussions

The different anthropometric measurements are presented with reference to their mean values, standard deviation and co-efficient of variation. Table 12.1, table 12.2, table 12.3 and table 12.4 shows the statistical constants for stature and weight for both boys and girls. In case of stature it is seen that up to 4.5 years the boys are taller than the girls, but after five years the girls are taller than the boys. Again in case of weight, it is seen that at 3.0 and 3.5 years the girls are heavier than the boys. But at four years the boys have superseded the girls but again to be overtaken by the girls from five years. But at six years both the sexes show exactly the same weight.

Table 12.1: Statistical constants of stature (cm) of Sonowal Kachari boys

Age Group (yrs)	*No. of boys*	*X±S.E.(cm)*	*S.D.±S.E.*	*C.V.±S.E.*
3.0	14	99.2±1.13	4.23±0.79	4.26±0.81
3.5	11	100.62±1.07	3.56±0.76	3.54±0.75
4.0	23	102.6±0.38	1.80±0.26	1.75±0.26
4.5	25	102.8±0.49	2.46±0.35	2.40±0.34
5.0	22	110.2±0.94	4.39±0.66	3.99±0.60
5.5	21	112.3±1.26	5.79±0.89	5.36±0.83
6.0	21	114.0±0.41	1.89±0.29	1.67±0.26
6.5	18	114.5±0.26	2.65±0.44	2.31±0.39

Table 12.2: Statistical constants of stature (cm) of Sonowal Kachari girls

Age Group (yrs)	*No.of girls*	*X±S.E. (cm)*	*S.D.±S.E.*	*C.V.±S.E.*
3.0	9	94.86±0.88	2.63±0.62	2.77±0.65
3.5	8	90.2±0.86	2.42±0.61	2.68±0.67
4.0	26	100.0±0.60	3.07±0.43	3.07±0.43
4.5	25	100.84±0.64	3.19±0.45	3.23±0.46
5.0	15	113.92±0.54	2.07±0.38	1.82±0.33
5.5	14	115.02±0.76	2.86±0.54	2.49±0.47
6.0	16	117.19±0.47	1.87±0.33	1.65±0.29
6.5	14	117.27±0.30	1.17±0.21	2.97±0.18

Table 12.3: Statistical constants of weight (kg) of Sonowal Kachari boys

Age Group (yrs)	*No. of boys*	*X± S.E. (kg)*	*S.D.±S.E.*	*C.V.±S.E.*
3.0	14	14.75±0.50	1.88±0.36	12.75±2.41
3.5	11	15.13±0.58	1.93±0.41	12.76±2.72
4.0	23	18.0±0.44	2.11±0.31	11.71±1.73
4.5	25	18.4±0.64	3.20±0.45	17.40±2.46
5.0	22	18.6±0.46	2.18±0.33	11.98±1.81
5.5	21	18.95±0.47	2.15±0.33	12.80±1.98
6.0	21	19.30±0.21	0.95±0.15	5.14±0.79
6.5	18	19.95±0.42	1.79±0.42	9.46±1.58

Table 12.4: Statistical constants of body weight (kg) of Sonowal Kachari girls.

Age Groups (yrs)	*No. of girls*	*X±S.E. (kg)*	*S.D.±S.E.*	*C.V.±S.E.*
3.0	9	15.45±0.64	1.92±0.45	12.43±2.93
3.5	8	15.33±0.59	1.67±0.42	10.89±2.72
4.0	26	14.64±0.32	1.64±0.23	11.28±1.56
4.5	25	14.98±0.37	1.85±0.26	12.36±1.75
5.0	15	18.87±0.45	1.73±0.31	9.21±1.68
5.5	14	18.99±0.53	1.99±0.38	10.92±2.06
6.0	16	19.30±0.30	1.20±0.21	6.52±1.15
6.5	14	19.55±0.25	0.92±0.17	4.70±1.26

Table 12.5: Distribution of malnutrition as per weight-for-age

Age groups	*No. of*		*Normal*		*Malnourished*	
	Boys	*Girls*	*Boys*	*Girls*	*Boys*	*Girls*
3.0	14	9	13 (86.67 per cent)	9 (100 per cent)	1(7.14 per cent)	0
3.5	11	8	10(90.90 per cent)	7(87.5 per cent)	1(9.09 per cent)	1(12.5 per cent)
4.0	23	26	23(100 per cent)	25(96.15 per cent)	0	1(3.85 per cent)
4.5	25	25	22(88 per cent)	19(76 per cent)	3(12.08 per cent)	6(24 per cent)
5.0	22	15	21(95.45 per cent)	15(100 per cent)	1(4.54 per cent)	0

(Contd...)

5.5	21	14	15(71.43 per cent)	13(92.86 per cent)	6(28.57 per cent)	1(7.14 per cent)
6.0	21	16	21(100 per cent)	16(100 per cent)	0	0
6.5	18	14	15(83.33 per cent)	14(100 per cent)	3(16.66 per cent)	0
Total	**155**	**127**	**140(90.32 per cent)**	**118(92.91 per cent)**	**15(9.68 per cent)**	**9(7.09 per cent)**

Table 12.6: Distribution of malnutrition as per height-for-age

Age groups	*Number of*		*Normal*		*Malnourished*	
	Boys	*Girls*	*Boys*	*Girls*	*Boys*	*Girls*
3.0	14	9	14(100 per cent)	9(100 per cent)	0	0
3.5	11	8	11(100 per cent)	8(100 per cent)	0	0
4.0	23	26	23(100 per cent)	26(100 per cent)	0	0
4.5	25	25	25(100 per cent)	21(84 per cent)	0	4(16 per cent)
5.0	22	15	22(100 per cent)	15(100 per cent)	0	0
5.5	21	14	17(80.95 per cent)	14(100 per cent)	4(19.04 per cent)	0
6.0	21	16	21(100 per cent)	16(100 per cent)	0	0
6.5	18	14	18(100 per cent)	14(100 per cent)	0	0
Total	**155**	**127**	**151(97.42 per cent)**	**123(96.85 per cent)**	**4(2.58 per cent)**	**4(3.15 per cent)**

Table 12.7: Age wise distribution of under nutrition as per weight-for-height among the pre School Sonowal Kachari children

Age groups	*Number of*		*Normal*		*Malnourished*	
	Boys	*Girls*	*Boys*	*Girls*	*Boys*	*Girls*
3.0	14	9	12(85.71 per cent)	9(100 per cent)	2(14.28 per cent)	0
3.5	11	8	10(90.91 per cent)	8(100 per cent)	1(9.09 per cent)	0
4.0	23	26	22(95.65 per cent)	26(100 per cent)	1(4.34 per cent)	0
4.5	25	25	25(100 per cent)	24(96 per cent)	0	1(4.0 per cent)

(Contd...)

5.0	22	15	21(95.45 per cent)	15(100 per cent)	1(4.54 per cent)	0
5.5	21	14	20(95.24 per cent)	14(100 per cent)	1(4.76 per cent)	0
6.0	21	16	21(100 per cent)	16(100 per cent)	0	0
6.5	18	14	17(94.44 per cent)	14(100 per cent)	1(5.56 per cent)	0
Total	**155**	**127**	**148(95.48 per cent)**	**126(99.21 per cent)**	**7(5.56 per cent)**	**1(0.79 per cent)**

In the detection of under nutrition as per weight-for-age and height-for-age, it could be seen from Tables 12.5 and 12.6 that maximum percentage (28.57 per cent and 19.04 per cent) of under nutrition is present in the age group of 5.5 years among the boys and in 4.5 years age group among the girls (24 per cent and 16 per cent). Table : 12.7 shows 100 per cent of boys as normal at 4.5 years among the boys whereas for the girls at all ages they are 100 per cent normal except at 4.5 years when only 1 (4 per cent) girl has been found to be malnourished as per the index weight-for-height.

The analysis of the result also reveals that according to the three parameters that have been considered, the percentage of under nutrition as detected is very less (Table: 12.14). Moreover it is also seen that both the sexes do not differ in a large extent from each other (1.94 per cent among the boys and 1.57 per cent among the girls) in their current nutritional status as detected by weight-for-age. The sexual difference is significant ($\chi^2 = 4.313$) in the detection of malnutrition as per height-for-age. Height is assumed to be affected by malnutrition of long duration (Rao, 1980). On the other hand the percentage of occurrence of malnutrition among both the sexes is also very less, so any conclusive explanation could not be given based on this index.

Classification of body weight deficit has been considered as good indicator for an evaluation of community nutritional status (Rao *et al.*, 1981). This parameter is also considered to be more sensitive and is most frequently used and direct assessment of growth expressions and inadequate nutritional condition could be obtained through it (WHO, 1986). The insignificant sexual difference in the current nutritional status among the Sonowal Kachari people may be because of the fact that discrimination is not maintained between boys and girls in respect of food, education and other social conditions affecting the final nutritional status. It is also to be noted that since the primary occupation of the people is agriculture therefore they live on food produced on their own and food scarcity is not present among them. This could be a contributing factor of a better level of nutritional status.

Development economist Peter Svedberg argues that the conventional indices are not sufficient for measuring the overall prevalence of under-nutrition among young children. Since being underweight (having low weight-for-age) is a product of stunting and wasting and not the sum, it misses some children who are considered undernourished by the other indices, so producing an underestimate. Svedberg suggests that if children with wasting, stunting or who are underweight are all considered undernourished, or to be in a state of "anthropometric failure", a new aggregate indicator is needed, one that incorporates all undernourished underweight. Constructing a "Composite Index of Anthropometric Failure" could help solving the problem (Svedberg, 2000).

Seven groups of children have been identified (Table : 12.13). These groups include children with height and weight appropriate for their age (i.e. who are not in anthropometric failure) and also children whose height and weight for their age are below the norm and thus experiencing one or more forms of anthropometric failure. The CIAF excludes those children not in anthropometric failure (i.e. group A) and counts all children who have wasting, stunting or are underweight (i.e. group B to F) therefore providing a single measure with which to estimate the overall prevalence of undernutrition.

Table 12.12 presents the number of children who are stunted, wasted and underweight as well as it shows the number of children as measured by CIAF. From the table it could be seen that 2.84 per cent are stunted, 2.84 per cent are wasted and 8.51 per cent are underweight and the CIAF shows the prevalence of under nutritionas 12.77 per cent children suffering from anthropometric failure. Stunting is a well-established child health indicator for chronic malnutrition-related to environmental and socio-economic circumstances (WHO, 1995). It can be due to a low weight-for-height (wasting) or a low height-for-age (stunting) or to a combination of both.The anthropometric index weight-for-age represents body mass relative to age. Weight-for-age is influenced by the height and weight of a child and is thus a composite of stunting and wasting.

In Table 12.13 of the sub-groups with undernourished children, group Y (underweight only) accounts for highest percentage of undernourished children (6.38 per cent). No child is found in the group D (simultaneously having stunting, wasting and underweight).

The prevalence of percentage of undernutrition among the Sonowal Kacharis in the present study is very less as compared to the other populations

Table 12.8: Level of undernutrition as per different anthropometric indices

Indices	*Total no. of children*		*Percentage normal children*	*Percentage Under-nourished children*
Weight-for-age	Boys	155	140(90.32 per cent)	15(9.68 per cent)
	Girls	127	118(92.91 per cent)	9(7.09 per cent)
Height-for-age	Boys	155	151(97.42 per cent)	4(2.58 per cent)
	Girls	127	123(96.85 per cent)	4(3.15 per cent)
Weight-for-height	Boys	155	148(95.48 per cent)	7(4.52 per cent)
	Girls	127	126(99.21 per cent)	1(0.79 per cent)
Body Mass Index	Boys	155	123(79.35 per cent)	32(20.65 per cent)
	Girls	127	100(78.74 per cent)	27(21.26 per cent)

Table 12.9: Age-wise distribution of malnutrition as per Z score of weight among the Pre-School Sonowal Kachari children

Age groups	*No. of children*		*Normal*		*Malnourished*	
	Boys	*Girls*	*Boys*	*Girls*	*Boys*	*Girls*
3.0	14	9	14(100 per cent)	9(100 per cent)	0	0
3.5	11	8	10(90.91 per cent)	8(100 per cent)	1(9.09 per cent)	0
4.0	23	26	23(100 per cent)	26(100 per cent)	0	0
4.5	25	25	25(100 per cent)	25(100 per cent)	0	0
5.0	22	15	21(95.45 per cent)	15(100 per cent)	1(4.54 per cent)	0
5.5	21	14	21(100 per cent)	14(100 per cent)	0	0
6.0	21	16	21(100 per cent)	15(93.75 per cent)	0	1(6.25 per cent)
6.5	18	14	17(94.44 per cent)	13(92.86 per cent)	1(5.56 per cent)	1(7.14 per cent)
Total	**155**	**127**	**152(98.06 per cent)**	**125(98.43 per cent)**	**3(1.94 per cent)**	**2(1.57 per cent)**

Table 12.10: Age-wise distribution of malnutrition as per Z score of height among the pre-School Sonowal Kachari children

Age groups	*No. of children*		*Normal*		*Malnourished*	
	Boys	*Girls*	*Boys*	*Girls*	*Boys*	*Girls*
3.0	14	9	12 (85.71 per cent)	9(100 per cent)	2(14.29 per cent)	0
3.5	11	8	10(90.91 per cent)	8(100 per cent)	1(9.09 per cent)	0

(Contd...)

4.0	23	26	23(100 per cent)	26(100 per cent)	0	0
4.5	25	25	25(100 per cent)	24(96 per cent)	0	1(4 per cent)
5.0	22	15	19(86.36 per cent)	15(100 per cent)	3(13.64 per cent)	0
5.5	21	14	20(95.24 per cent)	14(100 per cent)	1(4.76 per cent)	0
6.0	21	16	21(100 per cent)	16(100 per cent)	0	0
6.5	18	14	17(94.44 per cent)	14(100 per cent)	1(5.56 per cent)	0
Total	**155**	**127**	**147(94.84 per cent)**	**126(99.21 per cent)**	**8(5.16 per cent)**	**1(0.79 per cent)**

Table 12.11: Age-wise distribution of malnutrition as per Z score of weight-for-height among the pre-School Sonowal Kachari children

Age groups	*Number of children*		*Normal*		*Malnourished*	
	Boys	*Girls*	*Boys*	*Girls*	*Boys*	*Girls*
3.0	14	9	12(85.71 per cent)	9(100 per cent)	2(14.28 per cent)	0
3.5	11	8	10(90.91 per cent)	8(100 per cent)	1(9.09 per cent)	0
4.0	23	26	22(95.65 per cent)	26(100 per cent)	1(4.34 per cent)	0
4.5	25	25	25(100 per cent)	24(96 per cent)	0	1(4 per cent)
5.0	22	15	21(95.45 per cent)	15(100 per cent)	1(4.54 per cent)	0
5.5	21	14	20(95.24 per cent)	14(100 per cent)	1(4.76 per cent)	0
6.0	21	16	21(100 per cent)	16(100 per cent)	0	0
6.5	18	14	17(94.44 per cent)	14(100 per cent)	1(5.56 per cent)	0
Total	**155**	**127**	**148(95.48 per cent)**	**126(99.21 per cent)**	**7(4.52 per cent)**	**1(5.56 per cent)**

Table 12.12: Prevalence of undernutrition among the Pre-school Sonowal Kachari children

Group	*No. of children*
Stunted	8(2.84 per cent)
Wasted	8(2.84 per cent)
Underweight	24(8.51 per cent)
CIAF	36(12.77 per cent)

Table 12.13: Sub-groups of anthropometric failure among the pre-school Sonowal Kachari children

Group	*No. of children*
A (no failure)	246 (87.23 per cent)
B (wasting only)	4 (1.42 per cent)
C (wasting and underweight)	6 (2.13 per cent)
D (wasting, stunting and underweight)	0
E (stunting and underweight)	3 (1.06 per cent)
F (stunting only)	5 (1.77 per cent)
Y (underweight only)	18 (6.38 per cent)
Total	**282**

Table 12.14: Prevalence of undernutrition of the pre-school Sonowal Kachari children as per Z-score

	Boys	*Girls*	*Total no. of children*
Stunted	8 (5.16 per cent)	1 (0.79 per cent)	9(3.19 per cent)
Wasted	7 (4.52 per cent)	1 (5.56 per cent)	8(2.84 per cent)
Under weight	3 (1.94 per cent)	2 (1.57 per cent)	5(1.77 per cent)

studied in Assam (Choudhury and Begum, 1995, Medhi, 2014). Diet determines the nutritional status. The diet of the Kachari people of Lakhimpur is very simple and is in harmony with the environment. Fishing is a favourite past time for both the sexes and they consume fishes in plenty. They consume meat of water and land fowls, eggs and insects. Their diet seems to have a high nutritional value, dietary diversity and good nutrient balance and a diet survey may supplement the present findings. The diet of the tribal people in Assam is always known to contain no denatured food or additives and colourings. One of the characteristics of traditional diets given by Price is that traditional diet is extremely nutrient dense. It has much higher levels of vitamins and minerals than we get in our diets today. So on one hand, the diet among the tribal of rest of India falls much below the recommended dietary allowances (RDA) as laid down by the Indian Council of Medical Research particularly involving deficiencies in proteins and other micronutrients (NNMB, 2000; 2009), the diet among the Sonowal Kacharis could not be compared with the rest of India. Their ethnic food carries a lot of importance to them. Social factors and cultural practices have a great influence on what we eat and on how food is prepared and the foods preferred. The same food could be cooked in different ways, thereby altering its nutritive value. In a study done by Choudhury and Begum (1995), it was found that the children of three communities differed in their nutritional status even when they came from the families with similar economic status.

Social factors influence food choices as well as a person's ability to deal with health and nutrition problems e.g. cultural heritage can affect food preferences. Many aspects like food preparation and eating are culturally defined and individuals may consciously or unconsciously participate in these activities to preserve traditions. Attitudes and beliefs regarding food and values placed on food needs to be studied further among the Sonowal Kacharis.

So in the present population, their food ways is important as well. Ethnic food has already gained a status of heritage.The cultivation, preparation, and consumption of food are used to create identity claims of "cultural heritage." If the Kachari food ways is helping them to enjoy a good nutritional status then it is a matter of pride for them and they could expect a heritage status.

References

Bordoloi, B. N. and G. C. Sharma Thakur 1988. *Tribes of Assam,* Part II, Guwahati, Assam Institute of Research for Tribal and Scheduled Castes.

Chakma, T, Meshram, P K, Rao, P V, Singh, S B, Kavishwar, A 2009. Nutritional status of Baiga – A primitive tribe of Madhya Pradesh. *Anthropologist*, 11 : 39-43.

Choudhury, B and Begum G 1995. Anthropometry in the identification of malnutrition among the children of Guwahati city. *The Ind J Nutr Dietet*, 32 : 51-59.

Crockett, S. J. and Sims, L. S. 1995. Environmental influences of children's eating, *Journal of Nutrition Education*, 27 (5) : 235-249.

FAO Corporate Document Repository 2014. Causes of malnutrition Part I . Food and Agriculture Organisation.www.fao.org/docrep/(Retrieved on 24th April 2015).

Hochbaum, G M 1981. Strategies and their rationale for changing people's eating habits, *Journal of Nutrition Education*, 13(1), suppl. : S59-S65.

Rao, K V 1980. Efficiency of anthropometric indices for the diagnosis of malnutrition. *The Courier,* 30 : 113-121.

Rao, K V, Radhaiah, G, Raju, SVS and Swaminathan, M C 1981. Relative importance of various anthropometric measurements and indices for an evaluation of nutritional status. *Indian Pediatrics,* 18 : 223-231.

Rao, DH, Rao, KM, Radhaiah, G and Rao, NP 1994. Nutritional status of tribal preschool children in three ecological zones of Madhya Pradesh. *Indian Pediatr.*, 31 : 635-640.

Rao, KM, Balakrishna, N, Laxmaiah, A, Venkaiah, K, Brahmam, GNV 2006. Diet and nutritional status of adolescent tribal population in nine states of India. *Asia Pac. J. Clin.Nutr.*, 15 : 64-71.

Laxmaiah, A. K Mallikharjuna Rao, R Hari Kumar, N Arlappa, K Venkaiah and G N V Brahmam 2007. Diet and nutritional status of tribal population in ITDA project areas of khammam district, Andhra Pradesh. *J Hum Ecol*, 21 (2) : 79-86.

Medhi, D 2014, *Growth and Nutritional Status among the Muslims of Barpeta District, Assam.* Unpublished Ph D Thesis of Gauhati University.

Mukhopadhyay, DK, Mukhopadhyay, S, Biswas, A B 2010. Enduring starvation in silent population : a study on prevalence and factors contributing to household food security in tribal population in Bankura, West Bengal. *Ind J Pub Health* ; 54 (2): 92-96.

National Nutrition Monitoring Bureau 2000. Diet and nutritional status of tribal population, Report on First Repeat Survey *NNMB Technical Report* No. 19, National Institute of Nutrition, Hyderabad.

National Nutrition Monitoring Bureau 2009. Diet and nutritional status of tribal population and prevalence of hypertension among adults, Report on second repeat survey. *NNMB Technical Report* No. 25. National Institute of Nutrition, Hyderabad (ICMR).

Parimalavalli, R 2012. A study of socio-economic and nutritional status of the tribal children. *Stud Tribes Tribals*, 10(2) : 183-187.

Rao, Hanumantha D and Mallikharjuna Rao, K 1994. Levels of malnutrition and socio-economic conditions among Maria Gonds. *J Hum Ecol*, 5 : 185-190.

Rao, Mallikharjuna K, R Hari Kumar, K Venkaiah and GNV Brahmam 2006. Nutritional Status of Saharia – A Primitive tribe of Rajasthan. *J Hum Ecol*, 19(2): 117-123.

Svedberg, P 2000. *Poverty and undernutrition: theory, measurement and policy.* New Delhi, Oxford India Paperbacks.

World Health Organisation 1986. Use and interpretation of anthropometric Indicators of nutritional status. *Bulletin WHO*, 64(6) : 929-941.

World Health Organisation 1995. Expert Committee on Nutrition and Physical Status: uses and interpretation of anthropometry. Geneva : WHO.

13

Bamboo Traditional Craft and Its Importance in Assamese Culture

— Lipika Sarmah

Introduction

The making of bamboo and cane products is perhaps the most universal of all the crafts practiced by a large number of artisans scattered throughout the state. It is practiced generally as a household industry and no mechanical device is used. Cane and bamboo products are used for a wide range of purposes and extensively used in every household. No definite records are available to establish the antiquity, history and origin of this craft in Assam. However, it can be safely assumed that the craft was practiced since the misty past with the very dawn of civilisation. In the early period in Assam, bamboo was held with special reference and is forbidden to cut in "auspicious days." It is a general belief that bamboo possesses auspicious character and is of religious significance.

An idea about the flourishing state of cane and bamboo products of Assam was found even during the time of Bhaskara Varman (early part of the seventh century A.D.), the king of Assam, may be from the following extract. (An extract from "The History of Civilisation of the People of Assam" by Dr P.C. Choudhury). It is observed that there is no particular caste or community in the Assam valley who are exclusively connected with this traditional craft. It is generally carried on by all, particularly the peasants irrespective of caste, community or creed. Without the use of bamboo the great Assamese culture cannot be complete. Bamboo cannot be used only in agricultural, fishing, keeping and storing purposes, it can also be used in as a musical instrument. Bamboo can also widely used as a folk medicine in rural Assam. As a source of livelihood through Bamboo works if we want to study then have to discuss, the role and importance of it in our Assamese culture. The approach of developing cluster study is essential here to clear the idea. The approach of developing livelihoods through cluster development method having a holistic doctrine of enriching livelihoods through need based capacity development, technology up-gradation, product development along with market promotion has been found to be an effective way out. (United Nations Industrial Development Organisation, Department for International Development, Food and Agriculture Organisation). The main aim of the study is to reduce poverty by enabling the poor households to access gainful self-employment and skilled wage employment opportunities, resulting in appreciable increase in their incomes, on a sustainable basis through building strong grass roots institutions of the poor. The State Rural Livelihoods Mission, Assam has been designed to address rural poverty with the aims to enhance social and economic empowerment of rural poor by creating self-managed community institutions of the participating households and enhancing income through promoting sustainable livelihoods (Sipajhar Bamboo Cluster, 2012).The programme will be effective only when it is driven by the poor themselves. To be driven by the poor themselves, SRLM needs to develop social capital of the poor. The programme also involves huge preparatory activities at the state and district level. It is important to ensure that the quality and effectiveness of the interventions is not diluted. Therefore, to ensure the quality, it is proposed to adopt phased approach for implementing the State Rural Livelihood Mission in Assam (Promoting livelihoods in North Eastern India: The cane and bamboo networking project, 2014).

The Study Area: The area of the study is called Rajakhat. It is under Janigog village, Block: Pub Nalbari, Gram Panchayat: 8 No. Uttar Bahjani, District: Nalbari, Assam. The total population of the village is 693 and out of it 399 are male and 294 are female. 203 numbers of people of this village are busy in doing bamboo works as a main occupation. Second largest occupation of this village is agriculture.

Methodology: The present study has been carried out by covering 519 populations. To fulfill the objective, both primary and secondary data have been used and analysed in the study. Observation, case study, interview methods have been used extensively to collect qualitative data and Schedule method has been used for collecting quantitative data.

Scope of the Study: The study carried out would aid in:

1. Ultimate development of the cluster.
2. Developing the standard of living of its principal stakeholders.
3. Identifying stakeholders, leaders and suitable counterparts who can contribute to the process of growth and development of the cluster.

Strengthening of local democracy through strong and transparent Gram Panchayats and active Gram Sabhas and facilitating good governance is an important factor to promoting the rural entrepreneurship through livelihood study. Mahatma Gandhi's vision of creating a model village is also based on promoting better livelihood opportunities (SAGY, 2014).

Bamboo, a fast growing, versatile woody grass is found across the country. It is an economic resource having immense potential for improving the quality of life of rural and urban communities with environment regeneration qualities like carbon sequestering (Dristee, 2012). Bamboos has versatile uses as building material, paper pulp resource, scaffolding, food, agriculture implements, fishing rods, weaving material, substitute for rattan, plywood and particle board manufacture. Pickled or stewed bamboo shoots are regarded as delicacies in many parts of the country. The major user of bamboo in India is paper industry, which consumes sizeable proportion of the total annual bamboo production. Today bamboo adorns the homes of the rich and elite and mud-houses alike. Many useful as well as decorative items are made out of them. Baskets and mats are the most popular items in this category. Fishing contraptions are prepared of bamboo and cane, each with a distinct shape. One of the most interesting and colourful item is bamboo and leaf-headgear for tea garden workers and farmers. Umbrella handles made of bamboo are a specialty of the northeast. A number of designs like leaves, plants and creepers are etched on them. A variety of furniture items are made to suit the modern homes. Bamboos are good soil binders owing to their peculiar clump formation and fibrous root system and hence also play an important role in soil and water conservation (Bairabi Bamboo Cluster, 2012).

Major Findings

Total population in Rajakhat is 693 within 152 households. Out of that 519 populations are under Muslim minority community. For this present paper, researcher only selected Muslim people as her area of study.

From the analysis it has been cleared that it's a Muslim dominated area.

Table 13.1: Total Population

693	Hindu	174	25.10 per cent
	Muslim	519	74.89 per cent

From the analysis it has been cleared that it's a Muslim dominated area.

Table 13.2: Male-female distribution of Muslim community

Male	289	55.68 per cent
Female	230	44.31 per cent

Number of female population is comparatively11.37 per cent less than the male population.

Table 13.3: Literacy rate

Category	*Literate*	*Illiterate*	*Not applicable*
Male	242(46.62 per cent)	24(4.62 per cent)	23(4.43 per cent)
Female	172(33.14 per cent)	30(5.78 per cent)	28(5.39 per cent)

Though literacy rate is found quite a bit satisfactory but the level of education is very poor. (For maintaining the norms of this paper, the researcher yet not discussing briefly about the level of education here). Female literacy rate is lower than the male.

By observation and collecting data, it was found that bamboo works are recognised as the main occupation of the said hamlet.

Table 13.4: Main occupation of the people

Occupation	Male	132	91.66 per cent
Bamboo works (144)	Female	12	8.33 per cent

Both male and female are busy in bamboo works. Mode of work is different for both the sexes. Male are exclusively busy in bamboo works. Female are also doing it as a profession but after completing their household responsibility. In most cases we found place of occupation is always home. A community work place centre called CBTC is physically there but due to lack of expertise facility they prefer home as their main work place.

Result

From the study it is cleared that they are expert artisan by birth. Economically they are poor. But if they get chance, definitely they want to do something better for the society in this field. As we all know that, poor have a strong desire to come out of poverty and they have innate capabilities to do so. Technically they are not well sound but instead of that they prove themselves that they are expert and they can do anything related to cane and bamboo works. Raw material is easily available. Male are expert in making *dola, kula, pachi, duni* etc. These are recognised as the agricultural products. For keeping and storing purpose these kinds of implements can be used.

Photograph 13.1: The researcher with local artisan during data collection.

Photographs 13.2, 13.3: Agricultural products ready for selling.

Female are busy in making some light works. Mostly they are busy in making decorative items.

Photographs 13.4, 13.5, 13.6: Ornamental and home decorative items.

Male can also makes excellent furniture and decorative items if they get any chance. Some of the photographs prove it clearly.

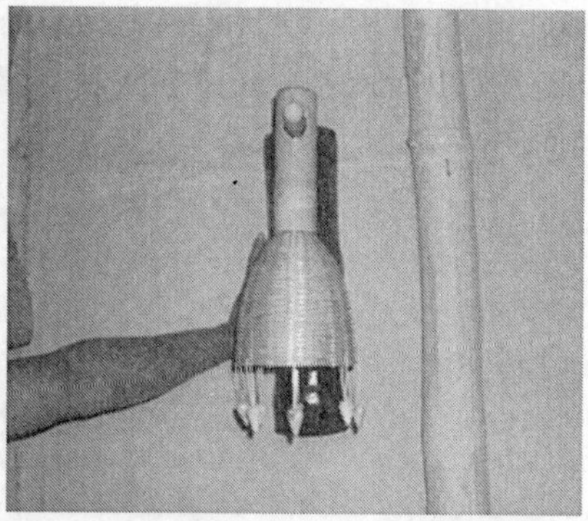

Photographs 13.7, 13.8, 13.9, 13.10, 13.11, 13.12: Decorative lamp set.

From the above discussion it is cleared that, to increase household income through sustainable livelihood, people should give importance on vulnerability reduction and livelihood enhancement by creating new opportunities. Generate employment building skills through bamboo works.

Conclusion

Though raw material is available in this village but economic condition negatively affect the people of this area. They did not get any satisfactory skill development training. From the government sector they did not get any financial help. If government gives importance of their hidden potentialities in right way, the area can be considered as an industrial place as well as model village in near future. According to Model Village Plan envisages sustainability of a village community by supporting all the pillars of sustainability namely, livelihood, infrastructure and services (SAGY, 2014) and after research as a conclusion we can say that, the entire area is fit for model village concept. The concept of creating Model village helps to identify new business models for rural micro-enterprises as well as low-cost technology solutions that can help deliver more efficiency. As a researcher my humble request to the policy-maker that the area should be adopted as a Model Village in near future.

References

Bairabi Bamboo Cluster, 2012. NAS Report for DCS-MSME. Research and Documented by EMOTOME, NDBI, National Institute of Design, Ahmedabad, Gujarat- 380007.http:// www.emotome.in

Choudhury, P.C. 1996. "The History of Civilisation of the People of Assam".

Dristee (Connecting India Village by Village), 2012. Model Village Plan.

Promoting livelihoods in North Eastern India: The cane and bamboo networking project, 2014. UNIDO project numbers: SF/IND/08/004, US/IND/08/002, XP/IND/12/006, United Nations Industrial Development, Organisation, Vienna.

Saansad Adarsh Gram Yojana (SAGY) Guideline, 2014. Department of Rural Development, Ministry of Rural Development Government of India.

Sheikh Moidun Nilufar, 2012. *Sipajhar Bamboo Cluster,* Interactive Design StudyCluster Level Report.

14

Cultural Assimilation and Integration of the Partition-Displaced

— *Moushumi Dutta Pathak*

Partition-Displaced Bengali Hindus are a distinct category of Bengali Hindu migrants into Assam. They came in the wake of the Partition of India, 1947 that had drawn a line of demarcation between territories on grounds of religion. This led to the division of territories and the emergence of two states of India and Pakistan. Sylhet that was an integral part of East Bengal initially had been amalgamated as a district of Assam in some portions of history by reasons of political contestations. This led to much argument, dispute and confusion over the years and therefore accompanying the Partition of 1947 took place the Sylhet Referendum over the question of the identity of Sylhet. With the Referendum it was ultimately decided to incorporate Sylhet as a part of East Pakistan. What now remained important was the migration of a large group of migrant-population identified as the Partition-Displaced from Sylhet and other districts of East Pakistan to various parts of India. Assam was once such province wherein a majority of such migrants came in. This group of migrants who filtered into Assam were in majority Bengali Hindus. They came to be looked upon as a part of the larger Bengali community who had migrated here into this region since the colonial period as *baboos.* But this particular group of migrants who came into Assam in the midst of the Partition phase reflected a distinct cultural process.

Several disciplines have tried to theorise migration and its relative comprehensive experiences of daily living. Beyond the historical understanding and interpretation of the same, this paper is an attempt to look into the matters of adaptation and culture change both of the Partition migrants and the host society. In contextualising this aspect of the study, we may move on the same plane as American historian Hasia R. Diner whose study of migration is based on set of questions that beside 'who moves' and 'why moves' looks onto the experience on a cultural level the act of leaving one place and relocating elsewhere? (Diner, 2000:9). To construct the degree of cultural adaptation, the paper explores to the 'historical past' and looks to the colonial Bengali migration too.

The study which looks onto the migrants and the host in the context of assimilation and integration needs to conceptualise these terms. The Encyclopaedia of the Social Sciences (Seligman, Vol. 1, 1930: 281) popularly defines Assimilation as a political rather than a cultural concept. It is the name given to the process or processes whereby people of diverse racial origins and cultural heritages, occupying a common territory, achieve a cultural solidarity sufficient at least to sustain a national existence. Integration, according to the *Oxford Reference Dictionary* (2001) means the mixing of people or groups previously kept apart. Integration into the country of first refuge is considered by the UNHCR as one of the three possible durable solutions to refugee problems (Kuhlman, 1991: 2). The UNHCR defines integration as 'the process by which the refugee is assimilated into the social and economic life of a new national community' (UNHCR undated B: 5). Few scholars have grappled with defining refugee-integration (Wijbrandi, 1973; Bernard, 1973; Bulcha, 1988). Among them, Harrell-Bond suggests that it refers to 'a situation in which host and refugee communities are able to co-exist, sharing the same resources —— both economic and social —— with no greater mutual conflict than that which exists within the host community, (Harrell-Bond, 1986:7).

The Question of Assimilation and Integration

Migrants pass through three stages in the process of their assimilation in the country of settlement————re-settlement, re-establishment and integration. 'Re-settlement' first of all means finding the first job and accommodation, which associates with certainty and security for the refugees, 're-establishment' is the acquisition of more permanent accommodation, a more satisfying job, advanced technical or linguistic training if required, family re-union and a reasonable satisfactory social life; 'integration' is the stage following successful re-establishment when a migrant becomes so identified with his new country that he decides to become naturalised (Benyei, 1960 :83).

Anindita Dasgupta in the introduction to her Ph.D. thesis "Emergence of a Community: The Muslims of East Bengal Origin in Assam in Colonial and Post-Colonial period", (Dasgupta, 2000) refers to *Assamisation* and *Asamiyasation* as two analytical categories used by social scientist Amalendu Guha to conceptualise the different stages of assimilation experienced by the migrants in Assam especially the Brahmaputra Valley. Guha in personal communication to the researcher had made a conceptual difference between the two. According to him, the first takes place when the migrants shift their homes to new area and acclimatised to the environment of the place. Gradually changes seem to appear in their habits like in the aspect of food, dress, social attitudes etc. But at this stage however they do not adopt the language of the dominant group of the receiving society. Only their dialect undergoes some changes. The second takes place when the migrant makes a conscious attempt to adopt the *'Asamiya'* language as mother tongue and adopt the *'Asamiya'* culture as such.

Assimilation would mean that the migrants as a group eventually become more or less indistinguishable from other members of their adopted society. Integration finally means that the migrants maintain their own identity, yet become part of the host society to the extent that host population and the displaced can live together in an acceptable way (Kuhlman, 1991:6). The degree of assimilation and integration depends upon the law and policy of the concerned state, the attitude of the locals in providing a congenial environment to the displaced for easy integration and finally the ability and desire of the displaced to integrate into the new environment (Chhangani, 1995:480).

Colonial Bengali Migration and their Cultural Influence: The Background

The Bengali Hindus who migrated in the colonial period were an important segment of population flow to Assam. They were brought into the region to man the administrative bureaucratic structure of the incipient colonial economy. Historically, however the Bengali Hindu migration could date back to pre-colonial times when groups of people came to satisfy the need of the King and the state in accordance to the skill and labour they rendered. By way of being the first recipient of western education, the Bengali society experienced substantial transformation, until the time Assam was colonised and in the cultural realm it took the form of a 'Bengali Renaissance'. As a consequence, Bengali culture came to be considered at that particular point of time as the most 'advanced' among the native cultures in India. Institutes of higher education began to be established in Bengal to groom up a section of the colonial administrative staff. The state administrative apparatus in Assam, with the introduction of the British rule consequently replaced the Ahom official aristocracy to be manned with the

Bengali *baboos* educated in these colonial schools of Bengal. (Misra, 1961; Seal, 1968; Hussain, 1993) The Bengali language too for administrative convenience was introduced as a medium in revenue administration and education in schools since1836, as a measure to cut down the expenses of the colonial regime (Chowdhury, 1994:72; Barpujari, 1998:34). In the process, this relegated the local language and brought in the predominance of the Bengali language, being recognised as the language of schools, administration and the law courts in Assam (Baruah and Bhattacharjee, 1983:72). Prosenjit Chowdhury speaks of a process of 'Bengalisation' to have set into the Assamese society in the initial years of the British rule, wherein the tendency to regard the Bengali intelligentsia as a model of imitation in the spheres of language, literature, political ideas, reformative ideals became prominent (Chowdhury, 1994:71). Gunabhiram Barua in his *Asam Bandhu* writes about the introduction of Bengali delicacies and dresses with the coming in of the Bengali Hindu migrants (Barua, 1885:84). Even Lakshminath Bezbarooah spoke of the Assamese looking for upward social mobility towards the Bengalis and imitating their language, Bengali songs, Bengali hair-cut, considering them to be 'positive reference' group. (Hazarika ed.1988: 19). The gradual cultural influence of the Bengalis began to reflect upon the Assamese mind. However, with the introduction of English education, development of the communication network and the impact of the Bengali Renaissance there gradually evolved an Assamese middle class or intelligentsia who successfully instilled in a reasonable linguistic and cultural awareness in the Assamese mind. From a 'positive reference group' the Bengalis came to be considered a 'negative reference' group. With the essence of job-centred conflicts, and apprehension of the linguistic and cultural superiority of the Bengalis that pervaded the Assamese mind, "the de-Bengalisation process came to be welcomed and encouraged by the colonial intellectuals of Assam" (Chowdhury,1994:76). The theory of holding the Bengali clerks or *baboos* responsible for the conspiracy of dislodgement of the Assamese language largely influenced the process *(ibid)*.

The Partition-Displaced Bengali Hindus: Their Cultural 'Ghettoisation'

The Bengali Hindus who came into Assam as Partition-displaced in the wake of partition riots were an unwanted community for the receiving society. The economic challenges of an incipient nation state and apprehension of a larger Bengali dominance were issues to combat for the local populace. The Assam Tribune in its editorial columns around that time reflected the attitude of the Assamese middle class who looked upon the Bengali Hindu migrants to be "apparently wanting to create a

Bengal in this province" (Goswami, 1997:28). The Assamese middle class apprehended that since the Bengali population had already constituted a sizeable section in the province with the *baboo* migration, the new entry of the Partition-displaced Bengalis would strengthen the cause of the Bengalis posing a severe threat to the Assamese language and culture (*ibid.* 1997:28). These migrants came and settled down in already specified residential localities demarcated to be 'safe havens' by the colonial migrants and that was how areas like Babupara, Amolapatty, Railway colonies emerged (Nag, 1990:75). These were the areas where the Bengali residents lived in isolation cornered in Bengali 'ghettoes' or enclaves establishing their own schools and clubs and celebrating their own festival.

Assamese intellcctuals passionately points out to the 'liberal outlook' of the Assamese people and their capacity to take within their fold people of varying cultural and linguistic hues and the most common example of the region's 'accommodative power' is referred by scholars is that of the 'Asamiyisation' of the Ahoms who came from Upper Burma, bringing with them a culture and religion that was distinctively their own (Misra, 2014:162). Therefore, the question is raised then as why the power of assimilation failed as regard to the displaced Bengali migrant. The Partition displaced Bengali Hindu too led a cloistered life confining them in 'pockets' within the geographical topography of Assam. Perhaps, it was in their bid to search for security against Assamese sub-nationalism that they were unable to associate within the mainstream social sphere. The displaced Bengali Hindu was a much later entry in this region when the threat of Bengali dominance to Assamese identity, language and culture was already looming large over the head of the locals. The flow of the Bengali Hindu refugees or displaced further added to the identity fears of the Assamese middle class (*ibid:* 58) The post-partition years witnessed large degree of animosity of the Assamese nationalist against the Bengali Hindus who in their bid of 'cultural expansionism' were unwilling to give up their linguistic identity and their right to education in their mother-tongue (op.cit:58). Their reluctance to assimilate within the Assamese fold gets reflected through contemporary news report of the regional press (See Assam Tribune, 1948 and 1949). But in recent years however, empirical reality indicates to an increase of a generation of Bengalis being educated under an Assamese medium of instruction in the Brahmaputra Valley. But that was mainly among those group who were under economic constraints and for whom schooling in English was a far-off thought.

Within the parameters of conflicts of interest, the debate gets underway as to whether the displaced Bengali Hindu 'could not' or 'did not' assimilate in the socio-cultural life of the 'host or receiving' society. The blame game continues. Either they were insular and did not want to adapt to the host society or perhaps it was the attitude of the receiving society that did not allow them to amalgamate. This long drawn vice of the history of Partition continues to haunt even after so many years of independence.

References

Barua, Gunabhiram, 1885. *Asam Bandhu* re-edited and compiled by Nagen Saikia, Publication Board, Assam (in Assamese).

Barua, Sandhya and J. B. Bhattacharjee, 1983. Middle Class and Language Politics in Assam during the Colonial Period in B. Datta Ray ed. *The Emergence and Role of Middle Class in North-East India,* Uppal Publishing House, New Delhi.

Barpujari, H.K 1998. *North-East India: Problems, Policies and Prospects*, Spectrum Publications, Guwahati.

Benyei, L 1960. Greek and South Slav immigrants in Melbourne, in C.A. Price ed. *The Study of Immigrants in Australia,* Canberra.

Bernard, W. S. 1973. Indices of Integration in the American Community, *International Migration* 11.3 The Hague: Intergovernmental Committee for European Migration.

Bulcha, M. 1988. *Flight and Integration: Causes of Mass Exodus from Ethiopia and Problems of Integration in the Sudan,* Uppsala, Scandinavian Institute of African Studies.

Chhangani, R. C. 1995. Local Integration of Refugees in Nigeria in *Journal of the Indian Law Institute*, Vol. XXXVII, No. 4 October-December.

Chowdhury, Prosenjit 1994 *Socio-Cultural Aspects of Assam in the 19th Century,* Vikas Publishing House Pvt. Ltd., New Delhi.

Diner, Hasia R. 2000, History and the Study of Immigration: Narratives of the particular in Caroline B.Brettel and James F. Hollifield (eds.) *Migration Theory: Talking across Disciplines*, New York and London; Routledge.

Goswami, Sandhya 1997. *Language Politics in Assam*, Ajanta Publications, New Delhi.

Hazarika, A. ed. 1988. *Bezbaroa Granthavalee*, Vol. I, Sahitya (reprint) Prakash, Tribune Buildings, Guwahati (in Assamese).

Hussain, Monirul 1993. *The Assam Movement, Class, Ideology and Identity*, Manak Publications, New Delhi.

Kuhlman, T 1991. The Economic Integration of Refugees in Developing Countries: A Research Model, *Journal of Refugee Studies,* Vol. 4, No.1.

Misra, Udayon 2014. India's North-East-Identity Movements, State and Civil Society, OUP, New Delhi.

Nag, Sajal 1990. *Roots of Ethnic Conflict:Nationality Question in North-East India*, Manohar, New Delhi.

Wijbrandi, J. B. 1986. *Organised and Spontaneous Settlement in Eastern Sudan: Two Case Studies on Integration of Rural Refugees,* Department of Development Studies, Faculty of Economics, Free University, Amsterdam.

15

Livelihood Change of Two Village Communities of a Flood Prone Area: A Cultural Ecological Perspective

— *Mondira Boruah*

Introduction

Steward developed the theory of cultural ecology as early as in 1930's in his classic book namely, *Theory of Culture Change: the Methodology of Multilinear Evolution* (1955). The concept of cultural ecology in relation to human beings can be considered as an attempt of adaptation to their respective environment with the knowledge of culture. It is the relationship among a given society, its natural environment, the life forms and ecosystems. MacMillon Dictionary of Anthropology defines "cultural ecology" (1986:62-63), "As an area of anthropological enquiry, also called ecological anthropology, which focuses on the relationship between human population and their environment, and attempts to provide a materialistic explanation of human society and culture as products of adaptation to given environmental conditions."

Salzman and Attwood (1996:169) said that "Human populations have ongoing contact with and impact upon the land, climate, plant and animal species in their vicinities and these elements of their environments has reciprocal impacts on humans." With this viewpoint he focused upon the complex relation between people and their environment. Environment is the reason which is responsible for the change of habitation and livelihood of a group of people.

Cultural ecology usually shows the creative processes involved in the adaptation of culture to its environment. Cultural ecology is an adaptive process that explains culture and its productive knowledge. The culture area is a construct of behavioural uniformities which occur within an area of environmental uniformities. It is assumed that cultural and natural areas are generally co-terminus because the culture represents an adjustment to the particular environment.

Vadya and Rappaport (1968) studied from the Steward's approach to show first how a cultural and an environmental feature co-vary in their functional inter-relationship. Secondly, Steward has treated the cultural core as if it included only technology. Several studies show that ritual and ideology also interact with nature. Finally his approach does not include the study of interaction between culture and biology, while studies shows that culture and biology go by hand in hand in several areas such as nutrition and that one cannot understand without the other (Vadakumchery 2003:40).

Harris (1966), Vidyarthi (1963) have studied about the cultural ecology of multiple ecological conditions and focuses upon the complex relation between people and their environment. In Indian context the studies are done on the human and nature contexts. North East Indian studies are mainly concentrated on the disaster of different ecological aspects and impacts.

Cultural ecology defines livelihood pattern of various communities of various environmental situations. The main aspect of the cultural ecological theory is to describe or study about the relationship between man and their surrounding environment. That is how the people try to live in their available environment with the help of the cultural knowledge. People genuinely have a characteristic of adaptation in any given environment.

Livelihood of the people is change from time to time due to the ecological and environmental situations. It is purely depend on time and place. Environment is more or less responsible for the different livelihood patterns. Cultural ecology is the theory which studies about the natural resources and the technology used to extract by the various populations. To adapt to a respective situation people used to apply the knowledge of culture to the utmost extent. The livelihood patterns are never same to a respective population. When the ecology changed the culture of livelihood changed automatically. So it can be said that for the changing livelihoods of the people the changing ecological situations are responsible. This situations made people knowledgeable and experienced on the various types of adaptations on the various ecological setups. Julian Steward studied about the cultural ecology of the various populations of various ecological situations to study the pattern of livelihood management. He tried to study about peoples various patterns of livelihood and change of livelihood according to the changing ecological setups.

With the help of knowledge of culture and utilisation of technology to the utmost extent people used to adapt to any kind of ecological system. Generally people try to find out the livelihood patterns to live with the environment or cope with the situation.

The mode of subsistence generally depends upon mostly on the availability of the natural resources. Basically common and available natural resources are different kinds of lands such as wet land, forest land, marshy land etc. Forests and rivers are two most important sources of natural resources. With the ultimate use of technology and knowledge people try to find out the probable mode of subsistence in any ecological setup. They know how to change their livelihood according to the ecology. Some of the basic livelihood patterns are agriculture, hunting, fishing, cultivation, pastoralism, crafting, sericulture etc other than the modern industrial technologies. People use to select one of the convenient subsistence patterns according to the response of the available ecological and environmental situations. But sometimes the drastic change in ecology made change to the livelihood patterns totally. Instead the pattern of livelihood changed from time to time according to the changing ecology and time from one to the other.

Objectives, Methods and Micro-field

The objective of the study is to describe the changing livelihood patterns due to the chronic flood situation by the two communities.

Both primary and secondary data are collected, the methods used are observation, interview, case-study; case history method etc. In-depth interviews were conducted. The secondary data are collected from the various documents, journals, newspaper etc.

For the study purpose two chronically flood affected villages are selected. The villages are namely, Chamarajan village and Ujoni Kekuri village inhabited by Chutiya and Mishing communities of Chamarajan Panchayat and Jiadhal Panchayat respectively of Dhemaji district. Demographically there are a total of 95 and 76 households in the village Chamarajan and Ujoni Kekuri respectively. Total 214 males and 220 females are found in Ujoni Kekuri. Total 226 male and 228 females are found in Chamarajan. Total number of joint family is 22 and 48 in the village Chamarajan and Ujoni Kekuri. Chamarajan has only one and Ujoni Kekuri has total nineteen numbers of extended family. Total number of nuclear family is 72 and 9 in Chamarajan and Ujoni Kekuri respectively.

The Flood Condition and the River Jiadhal-Kumotia

Flood is a very complicated term to define. Ward said that it is related to incorporation of damage and inundation and a body of water which rises to overflow land which is not normally submerged (1978: 5). Assam is one of the states of India which is facing the damages of flood every year. The chronically flood prone areas are submerged during monsoon period and its effect lasts for a long period during the year. The areas are casually affected by flood and are terminated as occasional flood prone areas. Dhemaji district comes under the chronically flood affected areas of Assam.

The river Jiadhal is one of the main rivers of Dhemaji and known as the sorrow of the district. This river flows down from the mountains of Arunachal Pradesh. It becomes very active during the summer season (starting from April to July). Generally erosion takes place, causing disintegration of roads and bridges in every year and disrupts the communication linkage with other parts of the state. The district experiences usually heavy rainfall and the rain bring a lot of misery to the people. Roads and bridges are frequently washed away, crops are affected and livestock are lost. Flood of the river affects in the areas like Jiadhal, Chamrajan, Batghoria, Naruwathan, and Ghuguha under Dhemaji block.

Results and Findings

Livelihood patterns change due to the changing ecological situation of the present studied population. The populations are living in a flooded condition since 1983. The conditions of these people are very distressful and depressing because they have been suffering from flood and temporary displacement. The changes come to their life due to flood in all aspects of life, such as socio-economic and religion.

These three parameters will be discussed in this paper on the changing patterns of livelihood due to flood.

The flood ecology of both the villages is not same though the villages are found in the same ecological situation. The village Chamarajan is situated in both the sides of the National Highway 52 and it is situated at a distance of 11 km from the nearby town Dhemaji. It is situated at the bank of the river Jiadhal Kumotia. The village Ujoni Kekuri is situated at a distance of 3 kms from the river Jiadhal-Kumotia and about 16 kms from the nearby town. The river is generally full of water for six months and empty for rest of the months. People used to face continuous temporary displacement due to the flood in every calendar year. The village Chamarajan faces a devastating flood current during the time of monsoon, which generally caused temporary displacement for three to four months, and the village Ujoni Kekuri suffers from rain water logging ecology along with high devastating kind of flood for half of the year. It is worth mentioning that the two villages are facing two different kinds of environmental conditions.

The socio-economic life of these people is change through the whole year according to the flood condition. Due to flood most of the families are getting small amount of production from agriculture, so they are searching for other better options. The economic life of the people mainly depends on agriculture and animal husbandry. There are various kinds of changes on every aspects of their livelihood. Sometimes things are added and omitted from their lives due to the flooded condition.

Transformation of land is one of the reasons of changing livelihood among the people of the villages. The cultivable productive lands of the village populations have changed to unproductive barren lands. This is one of the reasons of fewer cultivators found in the villages. There are lots of silt deposition takes place in the village Chamarajan. There is no land for a single kitchen garden in their homestead lands. The land is totally unproductive and the lands which were cultivable before are situated to the both sides of the river Jiadhal Kumotia. As the river is changing its path every year the cultivable lands of the village are coming under the river and become waste land. This situation is very common in the village Chamarajan and their nearby places. There are also natural vegetation is less due to the land transformations. It is one of the reasons that they are also unable to engage in animal husbandry.

This situation is a bit different in Ujoni Kekuri. There is also no land available for a kitchen garden because for six months the whole village situated under water. Both the villages have different ecological set ups and it is the result of devastating flood. In Ujoni Kekuri it is observed that more people are engaged in agricultural activities than Chamarajan. The people of Chamarajan have been facing the problem of siltation in the productive homestead land as well as cultivable lands. On the other hand though the people of Ujoni Kekuri is suffering from water logging for six months; only their homestead land is effected but not their paddy fields. So it is observed that between the villages agriculture is basically observed by the Mishings of Ujoni Kekuri. This is one of the most important changes in their livelihood due to the ecological conditions present at their places. Land provides people the way of livelihood and so the pattern of livelihood changed to a drastic way in the villages.

As cultivation is the primary occupation, their main wealth and assets of every household are the bullocks, cows, buffaloes, wet lands, seeds, granary, etc. Due to flood people lost their properties every year, those are lands, houses, household materials, livestocks, stored seeds and planted paddies. After losing the main asset of cultivation the people face a very difficult situation. So they take wet lands, cows, and seeds, paddy seedlings on lease for one or two years from some rich people of the village or from other villages. This process is known as *roina lua.* So, for each cow an amount have to pay by the borrower per month. The mode of payment is of three types; they pay money per month or work in the owner's field or give paddy of that amount at end of harvesting. They use the cows for both the seasonal cultivation and give the cows back after completion of harvesting season. Taking of loan is one of the common things happen to every household. It is observed that the people are habituated with the situation of loan payment and repayment with interest; whether it is in the form of money, animal or seeds. This is one of the change has taken place to their lives after the continuous flood had occurred since 1983. Before that the people were very wealthy enough and they were living a good and prosperous lifestyle.

Due to this reason the village population of Chamarajan has not shown any interest on the agricultural activities and that is why the people are less wealthy in comparison to the village Ujoni Kekuri. On this point another point can be added that the ecology of the village Ujoni Kekuri is also providing an opportunity of occupation by their ecological situation. There are ample amount of grass land is present to the nearby high lands and this is helping them to earn their livelihood from agriculture to animal husbandry. Nowadays, animal husbandry is one of the most important livelihood patterns in Ujoni Kekuri. The both villages were before highly wealthy on production of agriculture and fishing. But now-a-days unwanted problem such as temporary displacement made them less interested in the traditional occupations. This is how ecological conditions effecting their life and livelihood patterns. Again in Chamarajan people are engaged in wage labour, private jobs (driving cars), agricultural labour etc. They are engaging on other services rather than the agricultural works. Some of them are also engaged on farming of domesticated birds and animals such as duck, chicken, pig, cow etc.

On the other hand the wetlands posses by the people of Ujoni Kekuri has situated near to their village on the southern direction of the village. The land is in middle of the village and the embankment of Jiadhal. The land is affected only near to the river by flood but the other part is not affected much. People are interested in agriculture and animal husbandry rather than other occupations. This is the way the people are managing their subsistence in a flood prone area.

The rich families higher some of the groups of men and women as agricultural labour during the cultivation season, who are paid in the mode of money or paddy. This is a common practice among the people of the village. The pattern of economy is changed in few years because a few years back these people were very rich but they are poor and below poverty level nowadays. This drastic change on socio-economic life is observed among them due to flood and displacement.

Transportation is one of the most important problems faced by the village population of Ujoni Kekuri. This village is facing the problem of transportation due to water logging for six months. They have no options of transportation other than using the traditional techniques such as bamboo bridges, boats made of wood, bamboo and plantain tree trunks. The students, the working population and the household workers all are facing the problem of transportation. Their houses and main village road are under water for long period and that is the reason every single people including the children and women know how to ride a boat. This is an adaptation to the flooded ecology as well as a change to their common livelihood.

Communication and transportation has a huge impact on the education system of both the villages. In Chamarajan the Lower Primary School along with the High School comes under water for about three to four months. On the other hand in Ujoni Kekuri the nearby all schools and the households comes under water which made the schools closed for a longer period. They are sending their children along with one elder member of the house to stay outside of the villages for study purposes.

The flood ecology has changed their social life to a great aspect. Because of the prevailing ecology, the social institutions and social life of the studied villages have affected to a larger extent. Such as family, kinship and marriage are three important social institutions which have been changed in due course of flood to large extent. Family is breaking down from joint to nuclear and the reason is meager production from agriculture. Marriage ceremonies are not observed properly because of their poor economic conditions. They cannot afford the kind of lavish marriage ceremony organised the general Assamese society. So they prefer to marry by the process of elopement. The marriage distance is also significant. The area is famous for flood situation so most of the people do not prefer to hand over their girls to the boys of the villages. So, most people are married at a distance of only one km to half km. They are married in their own villages only. Kinship ties are unable to perform by the people due to constant flood situations.

Two villages have their own cultural activities which were performed before very elaborately. But nowadays these people are unable to perform some of the rituals as well as regular festivals due to the flood ecology. They are minimising their social activities which are related to unity and co-operation of the populations. Such as annual festivals are not observed or less observed in both the villages. For example, Bihu is not observed among them due to flood problems. This festival is observed in the months of April, October and January. Due to flood and its havoc the people are unable to observe the festivals. On the other hand the Mishings are unable to perform their most important festival Ali aye ligang due to the ecological conditions.

Level of income is also low and their lifestyle is very slow and steady. This is a change to their livelihood. People are trying to meet the needs on that flooded ecology. They are trying their hands on many types of occupations.

Cooperation is one of the scenery seen during the flood situation among the people. There are a cooperatives society which is helping the people on production of paddy and other crops. People have lots of waste land but they do not posses productive lands. So the co-operative society helps them. They take lands on lease from the villagers and provide the production on interest bais. It also helps in community building process. The collective labour is very strong among them. The villages have a custom of doing labour on groups in agricultural fields known as *hariya mota*, such as groups of male (10-15) are higher for toiling the soil, and a group of females (8-9) for plantation of the paddy seedlings. Generally 400-500 is paid to the both male and female per *bighas* of land. Nowadays tractor is also used for toiling the soil and pay per hour.

The division of labour is one of the issues which have been changed in due course of time. Earlier the people have a kind of traditional pattern of livelihood but now due to loss of traditional knowledge system and less population in the villages the working pattern has been changed to lots of ways. The changing situations have changed the division of labour from man to women. The men and women both are engaged in the agricultural process. The men are engaged in selecting seeds, toiling the soil, sawing the seeds, threshing the paddies and look after the farms of buffaloes etc. The young boys are engaged in look after the cows and buffaloes in the highlands situated at a distance of four to five km from the village mainly in Ujoni Kekuri.

Regarding household duties the women members have their voice on selection of land for cultivation and type of seeds. The women used to perform duties such as cooking of food, weaving, looking after the household works. The agricultural activities performed by them such as withdrawing of seedlings, paddy plantation, harvesting of paddies and making rice out of the paddies. Both the sexes are engaged in fishing. The male members are also not interested in the agricultural labour due to the meager production and engaged in different occupations. There are a few people found in the villages because of the flood situation. Most of the family prefers to have a house in the non-flooded town area where they send their children for study purposes. Also one of the mature male members of the house is sent there to take care of their children.

Regarding religion it is seen that, it is one of the parameters which has mostly affected due to flooded ecology. The ecology of the area has a broader impact on the religious aspects, aspirations and nature of rituals. Religion of the people is Hinduism in both the villages. They adapted to the Vaishnavism (*Ek naam dharma* introduced by *Srimanta Sankardeva*) later on. According to Vaishnavism, they only believe in one God. But they also believe in a Goddess Dholeswari (impersonation of the Goddess of Water current). They are performing rituals for the Goddess in every household as well as publicly in a place named Jiadhalmukh by performing a Bhaona (a kind of drama introduced by *Srimanta Sankardeva*) yearly for the sake of their lives from flood. They are performing Vaishnavism and also worshipping the Goddess. Ecological conditions have great impact on the socio-religious life of the people. The condition of believing in both the religious thoughts is not common to the general Assamese villages. So it is the ecology of flood which has a great impact on their religious life. Though they are not able to perform *Shaktism* by rules but to escape from havoc of flood they are accepting the *Shaktism* (sacrificing of animals) along with Vaishnavism (Bhaona).

There are a significance change in occupational pattern is observed. For the convenience of the study classifications of occupations are made on the basis of primary and secondary occupation. There are mainly three types of occupation is found in the villages such as traditional, seasonal and other occupations. Traditional occupation is that occupation done by the people with the age old knowledge of culture and environment. These occupations mainly depend upon the available natural resources. The available natural resource of the area is land; homestead land, wet land, forest land, waste land and marshy lands. The river is also an important part of the natural resource. These resources are utilised to the utmost extent by the people with their productive knowledge of culture. The modes of subsistence depend upon the environmental condition. According to the nature of resources available to the environment the livelihood patterns exists in a particular situation. Some of the common traditional occupations of the villages are cultivation, animal husbandry, farming of poultry, weaving, collection of wood and bamboo from the nearby forests. This is a kind of adaptation to that kind of flood situation.

Probable Adjustments and Government's Role

The floodplain dwellers have overcome the disadvantages and problems through adjustment, abatement and control. Some of the basic modes of adjustment are discussed below.

Emergency action system is a kind of adjustment through evacuations and protection whenever the warning is received. Government is generally unable to provide information before hand but the people are much more experienced so they try to get the information before hand through various sources. They use to collect immediate necessary things and properties before flood. They take rapid steps to evacuate men, properties and cattle to safer and raised platforms free from flood. They are good swimmers and they try to help other persons as well as their belongings. This is one of the impacts of ecology. They use small country boats, *bhur* (made of trunk of banana) to escape from flood. Every village is provided with a speed boat by the disaster management department but both the villages are not getting the facilities.

Flood proofing is another adjustment process in the areas. The Mishings are pile dwellers and to a certain extent they can save their belongings. But the Chutiyas of Chamarajan are plain dwellers and nowadays most of the household is constructing their homes with raised platforms. But this is very costly and not easy task for every household because of their poor economic conditions. They use to make a *borsang* (a raised flat platform at a height of 15 feet) inside every household to keep produced items for future use as well as to use during the time of flood in Chamarajan. They use to construct the granaries to a raised platform and keep belongings over there during flood.

To make a better living people utilise the available natural resources and use indigenous knowledge. They are trying to do eco-friendly cultivation in the available lands. As such, they use to saw *koni bao* seeds in the damaged wet lands and use various ploughs for various lands types. Waste land is also used as grazing lands for the cattle. Selection of species of high yielding crops and use of right type of implement is very necessary for good production in those flood affected areas. Government should study about the soil with the local experts of the respective area. Then it will be easier

Fig. 15.1: Water logging in the village.
Village-Ujoni Kekuri, Photographer-Author.

Fig. 15.2: An old man is passing by a bamboo bridge.
Village-Ujoni Kekuri, Photographer-Author.

to select seeds for high yielding and flood resistant species for the silt deposited lands. The species should be provided to the needy people on time.

The government provides paddy seedlings, animals and bird for domestication, loans and implements for the cultivators. They have provided items such as warm cloths, plastic cloth and plastic bucket etc. Relief items provided to the flood affected families are rice, lentils and salt. They should be given rehabilitation fees through a proper channel. Government should make a proper scheme for the welfare and better livelihood of the people of flooded area. The government must provide loan for cottage industry or small scale industry particularly in agriculture, farming of buffalo and weaving etc.

Conclusion

There are many changes observed in social and economic life of both the villages. The condition of flood is a kind of threat to their livelihood and culture. To cope with the situation people are trying their hands on various adaptive measures. They are using the available natural resources to the optimum to sustain in a flooded ecology. The traditional occupations are unable to maintain by them due to the ecological problems. They have been changing their occupations according to time and situation. Animal husbandry, weaving and fishing are becoming important means of livelihoods among them. Impacts of hazardous flood can be seen in all aspects of their life. These people are losing their culture, family, the kinship ties, land, animals, plants and paddy fields due to flood. Though changes occurred to a greater extent to their lives they have been trying the best to adapt to the flood ecology with the knowledge of culture.

Acknowledgements

Active guidance and constant instructions of my guide Professor Nitul Gogoi help me to complete the field work and writing the seminar paper. I extend my sincere thanks to the people of both the villages for co-operation and help during the field visit.

References

Harris, M. 1968. *The Rise at Anthropological Theory*. London: Routledge and Kegan Paul.

Salzman, P.C. and Donald W. Attwood. 1996. Ecological Anthropology. *Encyclopedia of Social and Cultural Anthropology.* Alan Bernard and Jonathan Spencer (Ed.). London, Routledge.

Seymour-Smith, C. 1986. *Mac Millan Dictionary of Anthropology*. London: Mac Millan Press Ltd.

Steward, J.H. 1955.*Theory of Culture Change: The Methodology of Multilinear Evolution*. Urbana: University of Illinois Press.

Vedakumchery, J. 2003. *Tribes and Cultural Ecology in Central India*. New Delhi: Mittal Publications.

Vayda, A.R. and R.A. Rappaport. 1968. Ecology culture and non-cultural. *Introduction to Cultural Anthropology*. J.A. Clifton (Ed.). Boston: Houghton Miffin.

Ward, R. 1978. *Floods-A Geographical Perspective*. London: The Mac Millan Press Ltd.

16

Dimensions of *Namghar* in a Tribal Village of Assam

— ***Monimugdha Bhuyan***

Introduction

Animism is one of the oldest form of religion, which is professed by almost all the tribes of the world. 'The foundation of the theory of *animism* is the work of Sir E.B. Tylor and may be found in his *Primitive Culture*, 1971. The notion was a part of theory of primitive religion which endeavoured to account for the attribution by some people of a spiritual existence to animals, plants, and even on occasion to inanimate objects' (Mitchell, 1970: 6). Most of the tribes of North East India, both in the hills and plains, professed animism from time immemorial. Gradually different religions were originated and due to various reasons many a societies have adopted alien religions abandoning their pristine system of faith, and due to that universal process a good number of societies have adopted Hinduism. Hinduism is not only a religion, but it can be called as a way of life. The pivotal pedestals of Hinduism are *dharma* (religion), *karma* (duty), *gyan* (knowledge) and *bhakti* (unflinching devotion). Although initially *varna* system was integral to Hinduism, at present caste system is the basis of the Hindu society. The Hindus also believe in *punarjanma* (rebirth), i.e., a man has to take innumerable births, assuming innumerable bodies according to the status of his consciousness and finally culminates into *moksha* (salvation) when he is free from all desires for being embodied.

One important 'sub-religion' of Hinduism based on monism is Vaishnavism. According to this religion there is only one God and He is Vishnu. 'Vishnu is the Supreme Being for the Vaishnavas, His worshippers, and they believe that all things emanates from the deity. Vishnu, the preserver and restorer, has enormous popularity in India....... Vishnu has been manifested to the world in ten incarnations (*avatara*) taking a variety of forms like fish (*matchya*), tortoise (*kurma*), man-lion (*nara-simha*), etc. In course of time the numbers of these incarnations have been increases to twenty four. Lord Vishnu took those forms to end some evils in the world. While all these incarnations are revered by the Hindus, Rama and Krishna, especially Krishna is greatly honoured as the full incarnation (*purna avarata*) of Lord Vishnu. He is the most cherished mythological hero of India and believed to be direct manifestation of Vishnu himself' (Medhi, 2008: 90-91). The followers of Vaishnavism are known as Vaishnava.

'Sankaradeva propagated a form of Vaishnavism in Assam which was simpler and more accessible than the ritualistic Hinduism of that time. The doctrine propounded by Sankaradeva proved to be a great unifying force in Assam and initiated the concept of oneness among the people irrespective of caste and creed in this part of the land. The caste Hindus, different tribal groups, even the Muslims were brought in the universe of neo-Vaishnavism and had accelerated the process of integration among the diverse groups of Assam' (Medhi, 2008: 92-93). In the noteworthy book entitled *The Place of Assam in the History and Civilisation of India,* S.K. Chatterjee writes: He 'gave to Assam a new discipline of faith and helped Assam to break away with a past with its complicated esoteric doctrine and its unmeaning practices and gave to the people something simple and straight forward devoted of all questionable associations or implications. He was the greatest builder of Assam bringing in a proper spiritual life, and although circumstances prevented his influence from being spread into other parts of India, as a religious leader he is unquestionably one of the greatest India has produced and he deserved to be mentioned with Sankaracharya, Ramanujacharya, Basavappa, Ramananda, Kabir, Chaitanya, Mira Bai, Guru Nanak and Tulsidasa. He was truly the medium through whom the spiritual light of medieval India as a whole shone upon the life of Assam' (cited in Neog, 1988: 1). In Vaishnavism of Assam, idolatry is strictly tabooed. There is no division of high and low among the Vaishnava. For the appeasement of the God, no complicated rituals are required, and, therefore, Vishnu is propitiated only through *nama-kirtana*, i.e., uttering of the God's name again and again. To propagate the faith Sankaradeva adopted various means, among which mention may be made about two religious institutions: the *namghar*, i.e., the village prayer house, and the *satra*, broadly the Vaishnavite monastery, which proved to be very effective. Assamese Vaishnavism is institutionalised in *namghar* at the village context. At present there are 650 *satras* in Assam (Cantlie, 1984: 152).

The area of present study is Majar Chapari Village of Lakhimpur District, Assam. The village is located about 60 km away from the district headquarters North Lakhimpur. It falls under Narayanpur Revenue Circle, Narayanpur Development Block and Panbari Gaon Panchayat. The village is four km away from Narayanpur town. It is a homogenous village inhabited by Deori population having 629 souls distributed through 118 households. The Deoris, an aboriginal community of Assam have been maintaining their distinct identity in social, religious, cultural and traditional practices from the long past. The Deoris are one of the four divisions of the Chutiyas. These divisions are Hindu Chutia, Ahom Chutia, Borahi Chutia, and Deori (Bodoloi *et al.,* 1987:22). About the Deoris Dalton (1872) writes, 'An isolated colony on the river Dikrong in Lakhimpur calling themselves Deori Chutiya who had a peculiar language which they called Chutiya and they were styled Deoris'. It has been stated in the available documents that the Deoris are ethnically affiliated to the great Tibeto-Burman tribes of North-East India (Deori, 2002:11). The Deoris are distributed in different parts of Assam. Mainly their present habitations are spread in the riverine areas of Lakhimpur, Dhemaji, Dibrugarh, Sibasagar, Jorhat and Sonitpur districts of Assam. According to Brown (1895), the original seat of the Deoris was in the region beyond Sadiya.The whole Deori community is divided in to four broad divisions (*khel*) - Dibangia, Tengapania, Bargaya and Patargaya. The Deoris are patrilineal tribe and their descent, inheritance, succession, authority and residence after marriage are traced in male line.

Assam, the gateway of North East India is mosaicked by both non-tribal and tribal including various religious groups. These groups belong to different racial stocks, speak different languages and have varied socio-cultural traditions. In Assam most of the villages are heterogeneous and people from different castes and religion live in a village in peace and amity. The tribal groups of Assam live in close contact of the Assamese Hindus and a good number of Assamese Hindu culture percolated to the cultures of different tribal groups. The Deoris are also not exceptional to this. Many animist Deoris of Majar Chapari Village had adopted Vaishnavism and start propitiating the new faith in their village. In this present paper a modest attempt has been made to examine the dimensions of the village level Vaishnavite prayer house *namghar* in the midst of animist Deori Village.

Methodology

The primary data for the present paper is collected from Majar Chapari Village of Lakhimpur District, Assam. The data were collected by applying various anthropological methods. Prior to fieldwork, intensive library work has been undertaken for collecting secondary data.

Results and Discussion

The villagers of Majar Chapari Village professed their age old traditional religious faith. There is a well-established *deoshal*, religious institution of the Deoris, in the village. But few years back there was some changes in the religious environ of the village. So of the villagers had abandoned their traditional animist religion and adopted the faith of Vaishnavism. One Deori boy of the village married a Assamese Hindu girl from a Vaishnavite family. Few years after marriage she wished to profess Vaishnavism by getting difficult to mix up with the animist religion. After getting permission from the village elders and religious experts of the village, she established a small Vaishnavite prayer house, *namghar*, in her own household. Every morning after taking bath she used to clean and wipe the floor of the prayer house with clay and cow dung mixed up with required amount of water. After that she lit an earthen lamp in front of the pedestal and burnt incense sticks and incense powder there. Both in dawn and dusk she used to pray there singing different Vaishnavite verses. The scent emitted by incense sticks and incense powder burnt in the prayer house had created a holy environment in her household as well as in the neighbourhood. Such an environment in that tribal village was a rare exception. Day by day some other villagers were also inclined towards the new faith and started professing it. Among the total 118 families of Majar Chapari village, at present there are 32 (27.12 per cent) families which had adopted Vaishnavism.

In the year 1973, the Vaishnavite Deoris of the village established a big *namghar* towards the east side of the village. The *namghar* is the centre for devotional activities of a village, neighbourhood or of a social group. It is a village prayer house where the devotees, present as the congregation, sings the names of God. In the Assamese language, *'Nam'* means prayer and *'Ghar'* means house and hence *namghar* means a prayer house. In every *namghar,* besides devotees (*bhaktas*), there are choir singers, principal singer *(gayan)*, drum players (*bayan*), etc. All the devotees take part in the religious assemblies held in *namghar*. In addition to religious activities, judicial, social and recreational activities of a local group are organised through a *namghar.*

The shape of the *namghar* is a rectangular building with a gablet roof. It is established from east to west. In the central part of a *namghar* where the sacred scripture is kept is known as *manikut.* The *manikut* is taken as the head of the *namghar*. The *manikut* is build towards the eastern side of the *namghar*. There are three rooms in the *manikut*. The middle room is the place of worship. In that room *thapana* or *ashana* is installed. The *ashana* of the *namghar* is called *singhashana* or sometimes it is called as *Guru ashana.* The main body of the *namghar* consists of a big hall with two attached verandas. This space is used for offering prayers and *nam kritan*.

This part of the *namghar* is also used as an assembly hall. Different kinds of gathering are made in this part of the *namghar.* Meetings, discussions etc are done here. Beside these the religious activities, *bhaona* (one act Vaishnavite play), *gayan bayan* etc are done in this part of the *namghar*. In the left side of the *namghar* there is a hall. This hall is called *Cho-ghar* which is used as a dressing room by the artists of a ritual play. This hall is mainly used in the case of *bhaona.* The *bhaona* artists change their costumes in this room. The makeup of the *bhaona* artists is also done in this room. Another important part of the *namghar* is the *Alahi ghar* (guest house). It is a big house with some rooms for the guests coming to attend the religious functions held in a *namghar*. The *Alahi ghar* is situated in the left side of the *namghar* and there is about ten feet gap between it and the *Cho-ghar.*

The *namghar* is managed by the *Namghar* Management Committee which is formed by the general members of the *namghar*. All the head persons of the village households under the *namghar* are the general members of the *Namghar* Management Committee. From the general members of the village, an executive committee is formed. The executive committee is formed sometimes by election and sometimes by selection. There is one president, one secretary, one assistant secretary, two cultural secretaries, and one treasurer in the executive committee. Besides them there are five executive members in the committee. The term of executive committee is two years. The main function of the *Namghar* Management Committee is development and construction of the *namghar*. The other functions are to raise funds, maintain the *namghar*, to observe various annual and occasional rituals, performance of cultural affairs and to maintain social solidarity. An important function of the *Namghar* Management Committee is to maintain congenial relations with the members.

The *namghar* is the nerve centre of the village. On the last day of every month they assembled in the *namghar* and perform *nam kritan* there. All members of the *namghar*, from minor to adults take part in the functions like Bisu, Janmastami, Sankara Utsav, Bar-sabah etc. Besides these, all members take part in the social and cultural functions of the *namghar*. *Namghar* is a common place for the villagers of meeting and to exchange and discuss different thoughts and ideas. Again any disputes among the villagers are settled in the *namghar*. One important part of the *namghar* is the *bhoana* (ritualistic one act play), in which the villagers participate. After all, there is a strong and conspicuous relationship between the *namghar* and the villagers.

The daily rituals of the *namghar* are performed by the Namgharia of the *namghar*. The Namgharia daily cleans the *namghar* twice. Every morning the Namgharia comes to the *namghar* in the early morning. First of all he cleans the *namghar*. The floor of the *namghar* is cleaned with a cloth instead of a broom. The floor is wiped out with a wet cloth. After cleaning the *namghar* he lit the *chaki* (earthen lamps) and incense sticks (*dhup*) in front of the *thapana* where the sacred scriptures are installed. One important part of the daily ritual is the beating the *daba*. Every morning and evening the Namgharia beats the *daba* and at that time the villagers takes the name of the almighty by facing towards the *namghar*. Like morning the Namgharia again cleans the *namghar* in the evening. After that he lit the earthen lamps and incense sticks before the *thapana*. Every evening he prays to the God by reading the Holy Scriptures. All other Vaishnavite rituals like Bar Sabha, Janmastami, Bhaona are also performed in the village *namghar.*

Conclusion

Vaishnavism is a great force which has developed literature and culture conspicuously in India. It is one of the main factors to create unity, amidst, diversity of the people in this great country. A section of the Deoris of Assam also adopted Vaishnavism abandoning their pristine animistic religion. The simplicity of Vaishnavism without complicated rituals and power exercise by the Brahmins made Vaishnavism acceptable to all irrespective of caste and creed. Although Vaishnavism has no long history among the Deoris of Majar Chapari village, it is one of the main pedestal of their society which has act as a powerful catalyst in balancing and acceleration of the society. *Namghar* is the nerve centre of the village where after prayer villagers chats on different topics integral to agriculture, conflict, resolution, marriage, house buildings and so on. The Vaishnavites of the village rigidly observe the rituals integral to the faith and also discuss on the mundane problems and prospects. The *namghar* united the people and helps to develop peace and amity among them.

References

Bordoloi, B.N., G.C. Sharma Thakur and M.C. Saikia, 1987, *Tribes of Assam* (Part-I). Guwahati. Tribal Research Institute, p. 22.

Brown, W.A., 1895, *An Outline Grammar of the Deori Chutiya,* Shillong, Assam Secretariat Printing Press.

Cantlie, A., 1984, *The Assamese.* London and Dublin. Curzon Press Ltd, p. 152.

Dalton, E.T., 1872, Descriptive Ethnology of Bengal. Kolkata. Office of the Superintendent of Government Printing Press, p. 5.

Deori, Saranan, 2002, *Religious Practices of the Deoris,* Guwahati, Bina Library.

Medhi, Birinchi K., 2008, Concept of Jagannath among the Assamese Hindus. *Jagannatha in Historical Perspectives,* R.N. Dash (Ed.). Bhopal. Indira Gandhi *Rastriya Manav Sangrahalaya.* pp. 90-91.

Neog, Maheswar., 1988, *The contribution of the Sankaradeva Movement to the Culture and Civilisation of India.* Guwahati 781001. Lawer's Book Stall.

17

A Cultural Study of Myths and Performing Arts with Reference to Kherai Worship and Kherai Dance of the Bodos of Assam

— *Mridul Das*

Introduction

The study of folklore touches on every dimension of human experience and artistic expression. It has grown out of the study of literature, has roots in anthropology, and contains elements of psychology and sociology. In many ways, it is the study of culture, visual and performing arts, sculpture, architecture, music, theater, literature, linguistics, and history rolled into one. The discipline of folklore has evolved into a way of thinking about how people learn, share knowledge, and forms their identity. Studying folklore is a way of learning about people, of thinking about how we communicate and make meaning. It is different from its related disciplines in its approach and focus. (Sims and Stephens, 2005: 3)

The arguments cited above are really apposite as far as the folk cultural heritage of the Bodos, an aboriginal ethnic community of the state of Assam, is concerned. The contribution of the Bodos and their traditional festivals in the uplift of the cultural heritage of the greater Assamese society has indeed been undeniable. The wide varieties of folklore materials of the Bodos which have really enriched the community with glorious culture are of extreme importance in the formation and development of cultural heritage of the state of Assam. The grandeur and magnificence of the tradition, custom, art, culture, literature, folk life and the heartwarming splendor of the folk mind and imagination of the folk society of the Bodo community of Assam are indeed admirable. It has been found that the Bodo community follows a good number of traditional festivals which bear the emblem of their rich cultural practice. These have tremendous social as well as cultural values since these are found not only to transmit the traditional materials towards the future generations, but also to endow the present society with multifaceted plinth for sustaining socio-cultural harmony among the people in larger but intricate society of the present century. As far as the festivals of the community are concerned, basically one finds the practices of Religious, Seasonal, and Agricultural festivals in among the Bodo tribe. These festivals are indeed significant as far as the folk life and social context of the Bodos is concerned. The festivals are found to observe a wide number of rites and rituals that reflect the folk tradition of the people of the community. The Bodo society in general is found to be agriculture-based society. They bear a good number of traditional and enlightening materials associated with their usual life. Thus, Kherai Puja is one of the prime religious festivals of the Bodos. Kherai worship is organised for the welfare of both the private life and social or larger public life of the community. Traditionally the Bodos observe four types of Kherai worship during different seasons of every year. While the first type being— *Dwrswn Kherai* also familiar as *Lwkhi Kherai*, or *Sali Kherai* held in the month of *Kati* (September/October), the second one is *Umrau Kherai*, observed in the month of *Asar* or *Ahar* (June/July) in the interests of crops. It is held immediately after *Amthisua* or *Ambubasi* is over. The third type recognised as *Phalw Kherai* is observed in the month of *Magh* (January) specifically on *Maghi Purnima*, while the fourth one called *Noauni Kherai* is observed by each family for the welfare of their respective family members, at their convenient time. Though related to religion, Kherai Puja has also relationship with agriculture and other household activities of the folk life of the community. Kherai puja, as a result is found to play a very pivotal role in enriching the storehouse of the folklore and heritage of the Bodo tribe, particularly of Assam

Methods and Objectives

The primary focus of the present paper is to assess the oral narratives and performing arts of the traditional culture of the Bodos associated specifically with the grand Kherai festival. Relying both on primary and secondary source data the present paper makes an endeavour to deliver certain aspects of the origin myths of Kherai worship and the types of dances and religious rites performed in the process of practicing the festival stated. Secondly, the present study would also try to through a glimpse on the supernatural elements in the myths, along with some scope of glance on the performing arts such as—Kherai dances, playing of musical instruments etc. in the stated festival of the community. Primary data through personal interviews with few Bodo people of Baksa district of Assam are collected to prepare this paper. Further, a good number of books and journals have also been used as secondary source for data collection and reference. The methodology applied here is descriptive and analytical one.

Why Study Myths

Existing from the beginning of human life and society, although with variations in concept, culture or the knowledge of culture has been playing a pivotal role in regulating the lives of people from birth to death by certain norms or acceptable forms of behaviour. Thus, here arises the concept of Folklore which may be regarded as the traditional and incessant practice of culture, heritage and performances etc. that cover all forms of traditional narratives, including customs, manners, rites, rituals, materials, prohibitions and so on and so forth, of all individuals residing in a society. Accordingly, here lies the importance of studying myths of any community to explore their rich culture and heritage, since myths are the indispensable part of tradition, culture and legacy. Hence, studying of myths of the ethnic community has been considered to have significant implications in the present research paper.

Kherai Festival and the Bodo Myths

It is in fact pertinent to have a glance on the concept of myth before making any deliberations on the myths related to the origin of Kherai worship among the Bodos. Myth could be defined as, "a story presented as having occurred in a previous age explaining the cosmological and supernatural traditions of a people, their gods, heroes, cultural traits, religious beliefs etc." (Leach, 1949: 778). According to W.R. Bascom, "Myths are prose narratives which, in the society, in which they are told are considered to be truthful account to be what happened in remote past. They are accepted on faith; they are taught to be believed; and they can be cited as authority in answer to ignorance, doubt or disbelief." (Bascom, 1981: 98). Thus, myths could really be accepted as the essential part of the tradition and culture of a group of people or community. Keeping pace with the same tone, it could safely be stated that the Bodos also possess traditional myths relating to the origin of Kherai worship, including the traditional Kherai dance. According to one such narrative, in the distant past there was a Bodo old man called Zara Phagla who had five sons and five daughters-in-law. People ironically called him Phagla (insane) though he was really not so. Owing to the expansion of family when the granary of the old man exhausted, he sent his sons in search of a fertile land for more cultivation. Thus, the old man remained in his house taking care of the family i.e. - the daughters-in-law. As a guardian he loved all five of his daughters-in-law; however, he loved one among them called Mongli the best, because she was not only beautiful but she had also possessed more remarkable human qualities compared to the other four. So he took a bit more or absolute care regarding Mongli's food, work etc. and often wanted her to stay near him. But Mongli developed a misapprehension regarding the intention of her father-in-law, and thus, under misconception and out of fear she fled away from home on an early dawn. The old man went on searching for her but could not find. Thus, losing the most loving daughter-in-law, day by day the old man became reluctant to his food and even forgot to pay heed to his own dress and cloths too. Hence, people identified him as Phagla. After several days he had a dream, where an old man appeared and advised him to perform the Kherai puja observing all necessary rituals, with the accompaniment of the musical instruments such as—Kham, Cerza, Siphung, and Jotha/Tal. So, the Zara Phagla brought back home all his sons and performed Kherai worship in a full moon night. During worship when the musical instruments were being played, a lady appeared suddenly and started dancing as Doudini *(a lady with unbelievable power)* and this woman was found to be none other than Mongli who fled away. This is how the Kherai worship and Kherai dance originated. The old man performing the Kherai worship was Moncing Brai *(the first Bodo human),* and the old man in the dream was Bathwu Borai *(Lord Siva)*. This mythical narrative is quite significant in the sense that it recounts the tale of the early fore-father of the Bodo community faithfully supposed to be true. It is indeed an indispensable part of Bodo traditional narratives that illustrates the culture of the Bodos. Further, one may notice that supernatural elements are also available in the account, for instance—the magical dream, sudden emergence of Mongli through Kherai dance and the appearance of god Bathwu Brai in dream etc. along with other religious contour. A few folk songs are also found to be prevalent in among the tradition bearer of the community relating to the account of Zara Phagla, as pursued in the field work.

There prevails another mythical narrative among the Bodos recounting the origin of the term Kherai. It is found that sacrifice of birds and animals is necessary for the Kherai worship. It is said that when a goat or a pig is sacrificed in front of the alter of Bathwu by slashing the animal's neck with a big sword-like weapon called *Dao,* then out of pain the animal utters the sound *Khe*. So the followers of Bathwu believe that the term Kherai originated from the sound *Khe* in combination with *Rai* which means the formula of charms chanted in front of the prime god Bathwu also known as

Kherai Bwrai. In this account also supernatural implications are often found with religious overtone, for instance—the belief of sacrificing animal, the charms to satisfy god etc. Although mention has been made about supernatural elements in the cited religious festival and its process, it is however, indeed very difficult to state about the concept of supernatural objects and elements in the arena of religious faith. Therefore, it is better to mention here that this paper discusses the part of religion with due regard and honest sincerity; however, at the same time it attempts to investigate certain phenomena concerned with the process of the festival with scrupulous note to have a glimpse on possible supernatural elements inherent in that corpus. Further, the religious rites of worshipping to their God, the rites and customs of sacrificing animals and other offerings are indeed noticeable as far as Kherai worship and its rites and rituals are concerned. These really remind people of a very integrated folk society of the community.

Performing Arts in *Kherai*

Assam has got a very rich and colourful tradition of folk performance. The ethnic and cultural diversity of the land has really multiplied the forms of these traditions and has made them further lively and enchanting. The potential of traditional folk performance of the Bodos are also indeed praiseworthy. As far as the performing arts of the Bodos in the festival of Kherai are concerned, the dance of the Doudini, the application of different rites and rituals, the devotional and tonal reciting of various charms (folk songs) by the medicine man or Ojha or the priest, and the entire procedure of Kherai worship festival and Kherai dance with divergent types etc. could be mentioned. The different types of dance of the Doudini such as—*Bathwugidingnai, Chotrali, KhapriChipnai, KhoijamaPhonai, GondulaBannai, NaoBonai*etc magnificently demonstrate the divergent performance of superb traditional folk arts of the community. In the book *The Flute and the Harp*, the author Dr. Anil Boro states: the shamanic dance of the Doudini keeps the pious congregations enthralled and deeply engrossed. The dance of the Doudini during the Kherai festival has given birth to specific art forms. It is worth mentioning that not less than eighteen dance forms have been sprouted from the dance of the Doudini. (Boro 2004: 40)

All the rites and rituals of the puja are traditionally followed under proper religious supervision to satisfy the sacred Bathwu Borai and other gods and goddesses. However, in a few of these procedures, a touch of supernatural elements may possibly be felt. For instance, the three-fold activities of the Doudini—first, the Doudini being enchanted by the spells of Ojha, secondly, the Doudini transforming to an abstract trance stage, and lastly, the Doudini being converted to the spiritual or divine state and uttering the tales of the gods and goddesses etc. Further, the soothsaying of the Doudini about people's fate, drinking the blood of the sacrificed hen by the Doudini, and the Ojha declaring at the end of the puja that the Doudini has owned the state of *Mainao* goddess may also be noticed from the similar angle of magical influence.

Next, there is the use of a wide variety of materials of performing art during the three day long programme of Kherai worship and dance festival. These are the materials of traditional nature indispensable for the religious rites but at the same time these materials reflect the folk tradition of the Bodo society from primitive to the present times. These materials include the musical instruments such as –the *Khum, Jotha, Siphung* including the weapons like— the *Thungri*, *Dhal*, and other objects essential for arranging the Kherai worship. It is to be noted here that these materials have also possessed a number of myths of their origin or creation which have really enriched the storehouse of folk literature of the Bodos. Apart from these; the materials are also the inevitable parts of the performing arts of the Bodos. The musical instruments for instance, exemplify a superb performance of art of traditional cultural heritage with artistic exuberance. Further, the sword and other objects also exhibit the additional input of vibrant performing arts of the customary socio-cultural mores of the ethnic community.

Summing up

The wide variety of materials and resources of folklore probe into the fields of cultural heritage of the region and disseminate knowledge to the divergent fields of the folk society in order to define multifaceted aspects. Hence, the prominent role playing by folk festivals and rituals in the study, research, and uplift of the folk-cultural heritage of the globe can ever never be ruled out. In this respect the Bodo community has also not been lagging behind. Their rich traditional zeal and cultural diversity is indeed praiseworthy. These have enriched the storehouse of the culture and heritage of the state of Assam. Plenty of philosophical insights could be perceived from these, if enquired with a meticulous and analytical mind. However, in the contemporary time modern trends and popular culture have posed serious threats in the preservation of the traditional resources, materials, culture and heritage of the folk-society. There prevail number of problems and challenges— like the managing of the festival and its rituals, its actual implications and penetrative insights etc. in the modern century; it might be owing to the developments in information and technology, impact of globalisation, urbanisation etc.

Finally, the massive waves of modernisation have been bringing sweeping changes in traditional life, both tribal and non-tribal at a pace unprecedented in any period of history before, and have been striking at the very roots of traditional group identity. This is, of course, not an isolated phenomenon witnessed here in India. The process is all too familiar in all parts of the world where tradition-bound small societies have been hit by the onslaught of modernisation (Datta, 1999: 59). Be what it may, prospects are also emerging day by day; and in order to retain and develop the positive aspects and prospect of their culture, the present generation of the community has to do a lot more so that transmission of traditions as indispensable part of the culture keep moving on vigorously to endow the community with culture specific glory and magnificence.

Thus, in conclusion it could safely be commented that the Bodo tribe has possessed very rich folk literature and strong culture with heterogeneous performing arts, traditions, customs, rituals, along with astounding traditional material culture. Therefore, it is the moral obligation of the present generation to preserve the traditional culture and heritage, and transmit towards their subsequent generation successfully in order to equip the future society with well-established cultural heritage of their rich folk history and lore. Last but not the least, it is indeed mention worthy that more and more extensive study and further serious research on the divergent cultural aspects of the Bodos is really the prominent need of the hour.

References

Anderson, J.D. 1895, *Kachari Folktales and Rhymes*, Shillong.

Bascom, W. R. 1981, *Contributions to Folkloristics*. Meerut, India: Folklore Institute Archana Publications, p. 98.

Baishya, Dinesh 2009, *Traditional Science and Material Culture of Early Assam*, Guwahati, Eastern Book House.

Boro, Anil, 2004, *The Flute and the Harp*, GBD, Kolkata, p. 40.

Boro, Anil, 2010, *A History of Bodo Literature,* Sahitya Akademi, Kolkata.

Brahma, Kameswar, 2009, *A study in Cultural Heritage of the Boros*, Bina Library.

Dorson, R.M., 1972, *Folklore and Folk-life: An Introduction*, Chicago, UCP.

Dutta, Birendranath, 1999; *Folkloric Foragings in India's North East* Guwahati: ABILAC, p. 59.

Goswami, P. 1960, *Ballads and Tales of Assam*, Guwahati, Lawyer's Book Stall. 1982, *Essays on the Culture and Folklore of North-East India*, Guwahati.

Leach, Maria (ed.), *Standard Dictionary of Folklore Mythology and Legend*. New york: Funk and Wagnalls Ltd. 1949, p. 778.

Narzi, B., 1966, *Boro Kacharir Samaj Aru Sanskriti*, Bina Library, Guwahati *(Assamese).*

Sims, Martha C, and Stephens, Martine 2005, *Living Folklore: An Introduction to the Study of People and Their Traditions*, Utah State University Press, Logan, Utah, (e-book) p. 3.

Sarma, N.C. 1995, *Status of Women in the Traditional Performing Art Forms of the Tribals of Assam with special reference to the Bodos,* in the Bulletin of the department of Folklore Research, G.U., No. 3, 1994-95.

Informants

(i) Sri Sarat Ramchiary, 59 yrs, Karemura, Baksa, Assam.

(ii) Rama Boro, 72 yrs, Barimukh, Baksa, Assam.

18

Silk Culture in Colonial Assam

—*Mridutpal Goswami*

Discussion

Assam with its geographical setting possesses a suitable natural environment for rearing a variety of silkworms on a commercial scale. But the practice of rearing silkworm and of weaving of silk has probably entered Assam from China at a remote period of its continuing history. Today, no doubt it is indigenous and traditional thereby occupying a sacred place in the Assamese cultural heritage.

The *Kiratas* (people of Mongolian origin) are believed to have introduced the cultivation of silk of different varieties in Assam in those ancient times. As such, all the hill tribes of Assam are expert weavers of silk of some form or other.[1] In his famous work *Arthasastra* written sometime between 321 B.C. and 300 B.C., Kautilya referred to one of the principalities or chieftainship of ancient Kamarupa (early name of Assam), *Suvarnakundya* where he stated to have produced the best quality of *patrona* (*pat* cloth) and *dukula* (*muga* cloth).[2]

From that time onwards till coming of the British, the silk culture has a free flourishing condition. Most vital importance of the silk was that with its three varieties, it could provide the basic need of clothing to every section of the Assamese society. The *pat* and *muga* silk garment used to be in general standard dress of the upper and middle classes of both the sexes. While, lower classes used to at least wrap themselves in winter with a piece of *eri* cloth.[3]

The royal houses used to provide due honour to the silk culture. The Kings of ancient Assam were patrons of local arts and crafts. The manufacture of silk was economically gainful and cloth was accepted in the royal treasury as payment of revenue since circulation of coins was not widespread.[4] The Varman dynasty (350 A.D.-650 A.D.) was the earliest historical ruling dynasty of Assam. A king of this dynasty, Bhaskaravarman (600 A.D.-650A.D.) offered *ksaumani* and *dukula* as royal presents to King Harshavardhana of Thaneswar. Banabhatta in his 'Harshacharita' too mentions that the *abhoga* umbrella sent to King Harshavardhana by King Bhaskaravarman was wrapped in *dukula*.[5] *Ksaumani* is probably the *Khauma* identified as *eri* silk by P. C. Choudhury while referring to 'Harshacharita'.[6]

By the ninth century A.D. silk became a popular product among the tribals and lower castes of the Aryan Hindu Communities of Assam and it began to find mention in the royal inscriptions.[7] Sualkuchi as we all know today is regarded as the 'Manchester of the East' for its silk culture. It was during the eleventh century A.D. that the tradition of silk weaving started there. The Pala dynasty ruled over Assam in ancient times from 900 A.D. to 1100 A.D. A ruler of this dynasty, Dharmapala (1035 A.D. -1060 A.D.) patronised greatly the silk culture and brought 26 weaving families from Tantikuchi to Sualkuchi which was then known as 'Siyalkuchi'.[8] Tantikuchi was probably another village of weavers in Kamrup where later on during sixteenth century A.D. SrimantaSankardeva himself acted as the headman of a professional weavers' guild being appointed by the Koch King Naranarayan (1540 A.D.-1587 A.D.).[9]

However, the most developing period for silk culture in pre-colonial times was the Ahom period from 1228 A.D. to 1824 A.D. In ancient Assam, the silk culture was considered as degraded one by the upper castes of the Aryan Hindu Communities. But, the Ahoms rulers in medieval Assam extended the manufacture of silk cloth to all sections including those of the upper castes.[10] Sericulture as a profession on the basis of caste grew in Assam in the medieval period.[11] Momai Tamuli Barbarua, an official of the Ahom King Pratap Singha (1603 A.D.-1641 A.D.) made it compulsory for every women of Assam to spin at least two bundles of silk thread per head each night before going to bed. For execution of this order weekly and bi-weekly vigilance was enforced.[12]

A 'Department of Weaving' was established by the Ahom kings and silk weavers were maintained to supply clothes to the royal wardrobe. The weavers received rent-free lands and other favours in return for their services.[13] Elaborate arrangements were made for keeping in the Ahom Royal store sufficient quantity of clothes of different varieties of presentation to foreign courts and dignitaries.[14] The different varieties of clothes in the

Ahom Royal store definitely included silk clothes as Assam enjoyed a high reputation for producing silk of fine texture.[15] The Mohammedan Wars during the Ahom period turned the Assam silk into a commercial commodity. The Ahom King Suhungmung (1497 A.D.-1539 A.D.) provided the first facilities to the artisans for rearing and manufacturing of silk in order to solve an economic deadlock in the Ahom kingdom. Then Pratap Singha (1603 A.D.-1641 A.D.) played an instrumental role in raising the commercial value of the *pat*, *muga*, and *eri* silk transforming it into a commodity of trade.[16] Walter Hamilton in the last decade of the Ahom rule in Assam noticed that silk cloth formed a significant part of the clothings of the natives and a part of it was also exported.[17]

Since the time of the Mohammedan Wars, the Assam silk has become a costly commercial commodity. The English East India Company after establishing its capital in Fort William at Calcutta at once realised the immense commercial value of Assam silk and found it as an exportable commodity to Europe. They visualised a good future for the industry, because Assamese silk cloth had reputation for consistent quality and competitive price. The Court of Directors in London repeatedly investigated the affairs of indigenous silk trade in India through the authorities at Fort William. Their aim was to manufacture silk in Assam through their own agencies. But it was difficult since manufacture of silk was carried out within homesteads by women.[18]

However, a French company was successful to open a factory at Goalpara by permission of the Ahom King Rajeswar Singha (1751A.D.-1769 A.D.).[19] But in 1769, the British authorities objected the French traders trading in silk for export which compelled the Ahom Government to stop the trading rights of the French in Assam and their factory at Goalpara was closed.[20] In 1786, the English East India Company resolved to open trade with Assam. Actually even before the Company assumed power in Bengal in 1757 the British traders had commercial contact with Assam.[21] The commercial potential of the *pat*, *muga*, and *eri* silk as was well known to the British, they were looking for the earliest opportunity to extend their trade beyond the borders of Bengal to Assam. The Ahom power in Assam started tottering from the last quarter of the eighteenth century because of internal troubles. This provided the opportunity to the British to enter Assam as a saviour of the Ahom kingdom and then to occupy it by misinterpreting the treaty of Yandaboo.[22]

The silk industry during the colonial period had to pass through several phases of prosperity and depression. As such there are different opinions among scholars regarding the conditions of the silk industry in the colonial period and the efforts of the Government towards it.[23]Actually, the British entered Assam at a period when the British manufacturer stood against the East India Company's trade monopoly. As such, the policy of British administration under the guidance of David Scott (1825 A.D. - 1832 A.D.) and Francis Jenkins (1834 A.D. - 1866 A.D.) were directed towards making the economy of Assam a producer of commercial-cum-industrial crops like sericulture.[24] In fact, to the material well-being of the people Scott found no other industry more suitable than sericulture and because the soil of Assam and the genius of her people both favoured the production of the silk and silk manufactures.[25]

Despite of being a British official, David Scott at personal level favoured the silk products of Assam for its consistent quality and competitive price. Along with sericulture, he too wanted to lay emphasis on the weaving of the produced silk. Hence, he in order to produce quality goods out of the Assam silk on a commercial scale put forward an elaborate scheme before the Government of Bengal which was turned down by the authorities in Calcutta as a doubtful experiment. Still, privately Scott continued with his scheme in 1831 at Darrang, but his premature death towards the close of the same year and utter indifference showed by his immediate successors affected the success of the scheme. Finally, in December, 1832, when the Board of Trade expressed an unfavourable opinion of the market value of the Assam silk, Robertson brought the experiment of Scott to a close.[26]

Amongst the three prominent varieties of silk produced in Assam, namely, *muga* (antheraeaassamensis), *pat* or mulberry silk (bombyxmoril) and *eri* (philosamiaricini), the *eri* happens to be the most promising because of being cheaper, more abundant, and reared entirely indoors.[27] C.H. Lepper had made the earliest attempt at growing *eri* silk on a commercial scale in 1873. He was an agent of 'Messrs. Lister and Company' of Brad Ford. His first experiment for growing *eri* worm was significant but due to scarcity of labour the experiment was closed.[28] According to B.C. Basu, between the years 1884 and 1889, many experiments were made for growing the *eri* silk on a commercial scale but none of these were successful.[29] No attempt seems ever to have been made to develop the cultivation of *muga* for the English market.[30] In 1877, Colonel Keatinge viewed that the *pat* silk industry need not be seriously discussed and the industry has perhaps undergone a decline since then.[31]

The failure of efforts to set up silk industry on a commercial scale by the British and other European entrepreneurs convinced the colonial government of the necessity of viewing the silk trade from a different perspective. They made no further attempt to manufacture silk on a commercial scale. Rather, keeping in tune with the general policy of deindustrialisation, the trade in silk was now conceived of in two forms: the export of thread and the export of cocoons. Further, the export of cocoons was preferred as indigenous reeling was considered as "unfit for employment for any purpose" by English manufacturers. Hence, it was believed that instead of investing in machinery in Assam for the manufacture of silk pieces, it would be more profitable to export the cocoons.[32]A profitable trade of exporting cocoons already existed in China as manufacture of silk fabrics out of waste cocoons was a flourishing industry in England. China was then the principal source of supply of waste cocoons to England, which meant that the English manufacturers were largely dependent on Chinese suppliers. But when they discovered that the Brahmaputra Valley of Assam was abundant with silk cocoons, the British traders pounced at the opportunity. The Trade Report of the Provincc for 1906-07 shows an export of 643 mounds of raw silk from the Brahmaputra Valley. Significantly, the Report does not mention any export in silk piece goods.[33]

G. N. Gupta in his survey report on the industries and resources of the newly created province of 'Eastern Bengal and Assam' conducted in 1907-1908 saw that in the silk industry of Assam a decrease of export and the increase of import was there in terms of manufactured silk. Even the report reveals the entry of the Marwari Mahajans known as *Kayans* in the silk industry of Assam which provided further setback to the already depressing condition of the silk industry. Majority of the silk weavers lost their direct touch with the actual consumers. The cocoons required were acquired from different areas of Assam by the *Kayans* and they used to sell it to the weavers at higher rates. Even the cocoons were given as advance or wages for weaving which shows that *Kayans* used to take the finished silk products for selling from the weavers. Almost the entire export business in raw silk and piece goods gradually passed away into the hands of the *Kayans* who had no interest in the welfare of the silk weavers or in the introduction of any improvement in the silk industry.[34]

However, after the First World War, the Colonial Government realised the importance of the indigenous industries in the economy of the province as these traditional industries, apart from serving as a source of livelihood to many families, provided additional employment to the otherwise seasonally employed cultivators. The government therefore, set forth to arrest the further decline of industries like silk and sericulture, cotton, gold washing, metal work etc. and to regenerate these industries if possible. Attempts were made by the government to lead local enterprises into these industries as well as to attract the Indian capitalist with whose collaboration the English merchants could set up a profitable trade in these products.[35]

According to the new policy of giving positive support for the promotion and growth of indigenous industries, a separate 'Department of Industries' was created in Assam in the year 1918.

The activities of the Department of Industries were however confined mainly to the fostering of handloom weaving and sericulture and to the administration of technical and industrial education.[36] Silk weaving was a special part of the handloom weaving and training was imparted as part of technical and industrial education for training of demonstrators in silk weaving on improved looms and in the use of time and labour saving appliances such as jacquards and dobbies. A government weaving institution was set up at Gauhati. There was other technical school at Kohima, Industrial School at Tura, Government School of Handicrafts at Sylhet, etc. Factories were established like the Daklangia Weaving Factory, Kharupatia Weaving Factory, etc for manufacturing of silk products. Towards the end of the year 1919, for assisting the silk weavers in marketing their goods without involving the *Kayans*, a Co-operative Society called the 'Assam Co-operative Home Industries Society' was organised at Gauhati (presently Guwahati) with initial jurisdiction over the districts of Kamrup and Darrang. For promoting sericulture, *pat*, *muga*, and *eri* seeds were distributed from the Titabor station. Demonstrations on sericulture were organised in Cachar, Sylhet, Dibrugarh, Sibsagar, Darrang and Kamrup. All these governmental measures resulted in substantial progress of silk culture in colonial Assam. The silk industry came out of its stagnant condition and survived.

Apart from the governmental efforts, the silk culture being an invariable part of Assamese life successfully survived in colonial Assam. As a heritage skill, people belonging to any caste or faith in Assam were more or less involved in sericulture as well as silk weaving. The silk items had a great internal or local demand as rich or poor every Assamese cannot think of any socio-religious occasion without it. Being an indigenous industry, traditionally for producing silk or silk items, there was hardly any need of extra labour. Most importantly, in a single process of the loom many diverse wears like *chador*, *mekhela*, *gamocha*; etc can be produced out of the silk.

Findings of the Work

- The silk industry existed in Assam from the ancient period of its existence.
- In the pre-colonial period it was in a flourishing condition.
- The colonial officials in Assam favoured the silk products of Assam for its consistent quality and competitive price.

- Still, more than manufacturing of silk products, the colonial officers encouraged production of raw silk as part of their colonial policy to provide impetus to the sale of manufactured or produced goods of their mother country in Indian market.
- This to an extent affected badly the condition of silk industry in Assam. But the industry survived as manufactured silk products of Assam had an extensive local consumption because of being an integral part of Assamese peoples day-to-day life.

Conclusion

To conclude, the silk culture in colonial Assam underwent through different ups and downs. Despite of facing severe odds, it ultimately survived. This was because it existed in Assam from ancient times and had developed in a free flourishing manner during the pre-colonial period. Even the colonial officials had appreciation for silk culture though as part of their colonial governmental policies tried to partially destroy it retaining only the sericulture part to an extent. But later on they tried to revive the silk culture to its pristine glory which was successful not only because of their governmental measures but also as silk culture is an integral part of the cultural heritage of Assam.

References

1. Nath, R. M. (1948), *The Background of Assamese Culture*, Dutta Baruah and Co., Guwahati, p.15.
2. Baishya, P. (2005), *The Silk Industry of Assam*, Spectrum Publications, Guwahati, pp. 38-39.
3. Barpujari, H. K. (1980), *Assam in the Days of the Company (1826-1858)*, Spectrum Publications, Guwahati, p. 258.
4. Sen, D. (1984), *Ethnic Elements in the Silk Industry of Assam*, NEIHA Proceeding Volume, 5th session, Aizwal, p.72.
5. Bhattacharjee, M. (2009), *Gender in Silk Industry: A Study of Women Silk Weavers in Sualkuchi, Assam*, Department of History, NEHU, p.79.
6. Choudhury, P. C. (1966), *History of Civilisation of the People of Assam*, Historical and Antiquarian Studies, Guwahati, p. 342.
7. Sen, D. (1984), op. cit. p. 72.
8. Kalita, R. (2013), *The Sericulture Industry of Assam*, PeeGee India, Guwahati, pp. 21-22.
9. Barua, B.K. (1969), *A Cultural History of Assam* (*Early Period*) *Volume-I*, Lawyers Book Stall, Guwahati, p.108.
10. Bhattacharjee, M. (2009), op. cit. p. 83.
11. Gogoi (Nath), J. (1993), *Sericulture and Cotton Manufactures in Assam in Medieval Times*, NEIHA Proceeding Volume, 14th session, Jorhat, p.173.

12. Bhuyan, S.K. (1975), *Swargadeo Rajeswar Singha*, Publication Board Assam, Guwahati, p. 262.
13. Barua, B.K. (1969), op. cit. p.105.
14. Gait, E. (2003), *A History of Assam*, Surjeet Publications, Delhi, p. 272.
15. *Ibid.*, p. 271.
16. Sen, D. (1984), op. cit. pp. 74-75.
17. Gogoi (Nath), J. (1993), op.cit. p. 174.
18. Sen, D. (1984), op. cit. pp.72-73.
19. Bhuyan, S.K. (1975), op. cit. p. 83.
20. Sen, S. N. (edited), (1949), *Fort William India House Correspondence, 1767-1769 A.D., Volume-V*, National Archives of India, Delhi, p. 236.
21. Bhattacharjee, M. (2009), op. cit. p. 87.
22. The treaty of Yandaboo was signed on 24th February, 1826 between the Burmese and the English East India Company to end the First Anglo-Burmese War which broke out in Assam in 1824.
23. Kalita, R. (2013), op. cit. p. 3.
24. Baishya, P. (1989), *Small and Cottage Industries: A Study in Assam*, Manas Publications, Delhi, p. 86.
25. Barpujari, H. K. (1980), op. cit. p. 257.
26. *Ibid.*, pp. 257-258.
27. *Report on the Administration of the Province of Assam, 1911-1912*, 1913, Assam Secretariat Printing Office, Shillong, p. 17.
28. Stack, E. (1896), *Silk in Assam*, in 'Noteson Some Industries of Assam (1884-1895)', Assam Secretariat Printing Office, Shillong, p. 4.
29. Basu, B.C. (1915), *The Silk Industry of Assam*, Assam Secretariat Printing Office, Shillong, p. 25.
30. Stack, E. (1896), op. cit. p. 4.
31. Basu, B.C. (1915), op. cit. p. 35.
32. Goswami, P. (2005), *Indigenous Industries of Assam Retrospect and Prospect*, Anshah Publishing House, Delhi, p. 29.
33. Goswami, P. (2012), *The History of Assam From Yandabo to Partition, 1826-1947*, Orient Blackswan Private Limited, Kolkata, p. 165.
34. Sarma, B. (2007), *The Marwaris and the Economy of the Brahmaputra Valley in the Early Twentieth Century*, in Goswami, P. (edited), 'Changing Patterns of Economy and Society', Department of History, Gauhati University, p. 128.
35. Goswami, P. (1999), *Assam in the Nineteenth Century: Industrialisation and Colonial Penetration*, Spectrum Publications, Guwahati, pp.168-183.
36. *Report on the Administration of the Province of Assam, 1924-1925*, 1926, Assam Secretariat Printing Office, Shillong, p. 23.

19

Festivals of the Kuki in Assam

— *Nancy C Malsawmtluangi*
Mini Bhattacharyya Thakur

Introduction

Festivals are cultural celebrations and have always occupied a special place in societies. Their celebratory roles, and many cultural and social implications of ritual and festivity, have long attracted the interest of sociologists and anthropologist. 'Festivals have importance and multiple meaning within societies and cultures that transcend individual experiences. To fully understand and create knowledge about festivals it is also necessary to consider who produces them and why, how they are planned and managed, why people attend (or do not), their outcomes on multiple levels, and the dynamic forces shaping individual festivals and festival populations'. (Getz, 2010). Festivals have been defined by Falassi (1987, p. 2), in the classical cultural-anthropological perspective as a sacred or profane time of celebration, marked by special observances. Festivals celebrate community values, ideologies, identity and continuity. Perhaps more reflective of the modern approach to naming events as festivals, (Getz, 2005, p. 21), defined them as 'themed, public celebrations'. Pieper (1965) believed only religious rituals and celebrations could be called festivals.

The Kuki society rich in cultural heritage have been blessed with different types of festivals. The kinds of festival found in their society are-harvesting festival, hunters festival, and religious festivals (based on Christianity). The Kuki people are music lovers and it calls for a sure feast and dance and music to mark their glory over a hunt or war. Merri making and singing together drinking *zu* (local rice beer) was a predominant feature of feasting or celebration. Whether it be an animist worshipper or being

Christian the Kuki people never forgets to give thanks giving to god for bountiful harvest, or victory over hunt or warfare. Though a great shift may be found in the rituals and culture of the Kuki after a mass conversion into Christianity we cannot deny the fact that the Kuki people are still socially and mentally intact to their age old customs and traditions. A beautiful statement made by A.R. Radcliffe-Brown in his ethnography 'The Andaman Islanders' that 'A tribe that dance together stays together'. This predominant feature is still found in Kuki society today. The importance of this study is that the Kuki society which is very much alive and rich in cultural heritage has not been able to come into lime light in anthropological field. The reason well known is due to the identity crisis, with no state or autonomous council of its own. This tribe with immense unexplored area deserves a special notice where we find social solidarity, Pre-Christian rites and rituals, the changes that has taken place after coming of Christianity, the sacred and profane part of festivals etc.

This paper is an attempt to throw light on the beautiful yet unnoticed festivals of the Kuki people in Assam. And to do so some methodologies were adopted. They are- selecting key informant, interview method, case study method, participation method and observation method. Not only that some information was collected with the help of secondary sources like- books, articles and internet.

The first part of the paper is introducing the problem and the second part of the paper will highlight the different festivals of the Kuki people which are - harvesting festival, hunters festival and victory over war celebrations. The third part of the paper will discuss about '*Chavang Kut'*, which is still followed today with a blend of traditional touch and Christianity. And the last part of the paper is the conclusion.

Festivals of the Kukis

The Kuki people have several festivals celebrated since the time of their ancestors. Things were much different before the advent of Christianity. Society was more secular and profane than that of today. The highest authority next to God was of *thempu* (priest) and chieftain and the festivals and celebrations were led by them. The *thempu* does all the rituals of sacrificing or thanksgiving to God and the festivals begins with drinking *zu* (local rice beer) followed by singing and dancing and merry making. This was the criteria generally followed then. But today in Kuki Christian life the position of *thempu* (priest) has been taken over by church pastors. And drinking of *zu* (local rice beer) has been completely abolished and replaced by tea.

The different festivals of the Kuki are- *chaangai, lomkivah, somkivah, gal-ai, sa-ai, chon and mimkut.*

Chang-Ai

Chang-Ai is a feast celebrated by the entire village in honour of the womenfolk. It is significantly a celebration of bountiful harvest of paddy '*chang*' at the end of the season. It signifies success and accomplishment by the women, of their hard work and labour in the *jhum* all throughout the year. This festival is equivalent to the *SA-AI*, which is performed in honour of the great hunters. This festival reflects the status and prestige of the women in the Kuki society, which they hold with pride and dignity. *Chang-Ai* festival is usually hosted as a symbol of status and pride only by the wives of the Chiefs or of a very wealthy man as it is an expensive affair. On the day of '*Chang-Ai'*, women who have performed this feast are permitted to wear the dark blue cloth or shawl with intricate embroidery at the two ends in red and white cotton, which is the *'Thang-nangpuon'*.

Chang-Ai festival begins with invitation sent to kith and kin. In the evening, prior to the day of '*Chang-Ai*, announcement is made by the *'khosunglhang-va'* regarding the celebration of the festival. It is repeated early in the morning on the big day and the entire village then proceeds towards the field from where begins the '*Chang-Ai'* festival. A priest called *'Thempu'* leads the community. He performs the rituals by reciting mantras to invoke the 'god of paddy' called *'Chang-lhakoupathen'*. The priest then puts bowls of paddy into the bamboo basket/bowl or bags of each individual and as he does this, he remains silent and undisturbed. Once the priest finish performing the rituals, the entire villagers proceed back to the village to the house of the person performing *'Chang-Ai'*. As they proceed, the villagers broadcast and throw the paddy on all sides along the way and shout *'heijam'* a victory cry, accompanied by the sounds of *'pheiphit'*, which is a traditional flute. This is necessarily done in order to please the *'Chang lhapou Pathen'* for his blessings.

The women performing the '*Chang-Ai'* then feed the entire village. A yak *'sel'* or a buffalo *"mithun"* is sacrificed for the grand feast. She puts up a platform about six inches above the ground level. Small upright stones representing the numbers of the women's '*beng*', basket of paddy are placed on the platform, which are consumed on that day. On the centre of the platform two stones are placed upright, one larger than the other which is known as '*shong-muol'* (Spirit stone). This stone does not represent the spirit of the woman performing the '*Chang-Ai'* or of her husband, rather it is placed for the '*Pathen*' or Supreme God to know where '*Chang-ai'* has been performed before he selects a good place at '*mithi-kho'* (Village of the death) for the one performing the '*Chang-ai'*.

The '*Chang-ai'* feast can be performed only three times by a person. Singing of folk songs, dancing to the tune of different traditional musical instruments and drinking of '*Ju*' goes on for the whole day and night in the house of the person performing the *'Chang-Ai'*. Apart from these, traditional sports such as '*sieltuoldel'* (catching of let loose '*mithun*'), *'sielkal'* (high jump or jumping over the yak), '*bonkho*' (wrestling) and '*lhochil* dances' are also performed on the day. The entire village celebrated this festival with great enthusiasm, with great pomp and valour.

Lom-Kivah

This is another ritual practiced by the member of a *lom* (youth corpse of the village). The 'mithun' is to be slaughtered in this feast of *Lom-kivah.* On the first day an exciting event takes place where every boy tries to demonstrate his individual prowess and grapples with the tied 'mithun'. While wrestling takes place, old and young, men and women drink *'Ju'* (local rice beer) and the night is spent in singing and dancing.

The second day of *Lom-kivah* the boys and girls have to sing and dance in the courtyard of well-to-do persons in the village. For the successful running of this celebration, the services of *Lom-Becha, Lom-Tucha, Lom-lhangva,* Female *Lom-upa* is required. During this ritual the *Lom-Upanu* serves a special wine of honour called *Lal-Ju*. The wine prepared by the girls is called *Jutep*. A special meat called *sapang* is served to the *Semang – Pachong* and *hausa* of the village, *selju* wine is also served and distributed in three rounds. In a spirit of mirth and hilarity wine is poured into the mouth of dancing partners. Inspite of the participation of young and old alike in the ceremony there is no clash of opinions between them. This is because there is in the traditional Kuki custom, a reverence towards those in authority a tradition consecrated by the society. The ceremonies performed and rituals observed are considered most sacred by the members of the Kuki society. The members of the *'Lom'* sing in the house of the person who is celebrating *Lom-Kivah* rituals. A feast is then laid out for them in this house. After the feast, the *'lom'* members go to spend the night in the house of '*Hausa'*. The next night the '*Lom'* members take leave of the house owner and departs bidding farewell, while the house owner pleads with them to stay on. In this way the '*Lom'* members sing and gradually depart bringing the '*Lom-kivah'* ritual to a close.

Som-Kivah

This feast is quite similar to *Lom-kivah.* This festival is observed by the '*som-gie*' group, the permission of the '*Hausa*' is first sought, and when it has been granted, the *'Thempu'* offers a sacrifice of a few chunks of heart meat and a little of greasy meat to appease the evil spirits and makes an incantation. Thus, propitiation of evil spirits takes place before the feast begins. Following this, the villagers' part takes the feast served by the '*Som-gie*'. Dancing, singing and drinking of '*JU*' continue the whole night, till the early hours in the morning. The first day is called '*Som-kivahpini*'. The second days functions are called '*Som-kivah Sapang, Ju-choini.* Here pitchers of wine with measuring sticks called *'Leng'* and sipping pipes are given. All are supposed to sip from a set of Jars. This sipping of wine is called *'ju-tuiluon'*. The third day function is called *'In-nei-Ju-buhni'*. Drinking of wine and merriment continues in the midst of singing and dancing. The last days function is called '*Ju-chih-don-ni*'. Where the best quality of wine preserved is drank in a Mug. The owner of the house also offers wine called '*Som-lhah-Ju*'. Early the next morning the guests leave the house and the *Tucha and Becha* clean the house, drink the remaining wine and the '*Som-kivah*' ritual comes to a close. In any social or religious celebration, the rituals performed are mostly for the propitiation of evil spirit. There is always excessive drinking of wine which often leads to intoxication of the villagers in the Kuki society.

Mim-Kut

The mimkut festival is a post-harvest festival of the Kukis. This festival is celebrated in Nagaland and Manipur but not in Assam. The festival is recognised by the government of Nagaland and the Kukis of Nagaland celebrated this festival on the 17th Kuki month of *Tolb*ol (January) every year.

The Mimkut is essentially a wrap-up for more abundant harvest in the coming years. It is marked by feasting and drinking of *"ju"* (rice beer). The youths engaged themselves in various types of merrymaking and fetching of water and firewood. Traditional sports like wrestling and other games continue throughout the day and night. The older people sit by the fire-side singing traditional songs and more enthusiastic ones dance and crack jokes from time to time. But due to the advent of Christianity wine is not used any more but the festival is celebrated with much pomp and gaiety. Varieties of folk dances are performed by different villages, traditional games and sports and traditional trap makings are exhibited. Music competition and misskut contest are also held to give platform to young talents.

But after the majority of the Kukis have embraced Christianity, some of the traditional practices, such as the incarnation of *Thempu* or priest are no longer in practiced. Instead, today the *Thempu* is rather named as '*Kut*

Pa' or father of the *Kut* who takes the position of the priest or *Thempu* to invoke the blessing of the Almighty God for bountiful blessings in the coming year.

Chon

This is the most highly prized feast and can only be performed by those who have performed the *Sa-ai* three times. In this ritual everything has to be done seven times. Seven *"mithun's"* are to be killed and everything else must be in multiples of seven. This has not been done for a very long time and so the exact rites are not clearly known. A person is supposed to have achieved a high social status only when he entertains the community with a grand feast. Thus, it becomes significant that one puts on as much show and sacrifice in the form of many *"mithun's"* as far as possible. Even the songs and genealogical trees had to be repeated seven times. The whole ceremony takes days to complete and the expense incurred being fabulous. A person who has performed the Chon ceremony, after his death his body had to be carried round seven times and everything pertaining to burial rites had to be done seven times. For that they resorted to smoking the bodies of such persons to avoid decomposition before the entire rites are completed.

The *Chon* ritual gives the soul of a person a paramount seat in *Mithikho* (the village of death) which ensures eternal happiness. *Chon* was basically a feast where the performers show off the wealth of his family. Thanksgiving ceremony is performed in honour of his ancestor whose blessings have brought him wealth and prosperity. It takes several days to perform this feast. Villagers and neighbouring folks congregate for this celebration, feasting, dancing, drinking of *'Ju'* (rice beer) and merry making marked this auspicious occasion.

SA-AI: The Great Hunters' Ritual

The *Sa-ai* ritual is performed by a great hunter to gain complete dominance over the spirit of the killed animals. The sheer act of the killing of the animals, as is believe, is not effective enough for the hunter to have total dominance over the killed animals. According to legends, if the spirits of the killed animals are left unsaddled and are not brought under the hunter's control they may afflict the hunters spirit during his life time and even after his death. By performing the ritual of *Sa-ai* during his lifetime the hunters gains absolute control over the spirits of the killed animals.

Sa-ai is performed only by hunter of great eminence who have the distinction of killing large numbers of animals, particularly elephant and tigers, besides other small and big animals.

Gal-Ai

Gal means war and *ai* means feast. The feast which is performed after gaining victory from the war is called *gal-ai*. Nothing much is known about this ritual. But it sure reveals of the fact that the Kuki people were brave and courageous. Before any war every man was made to enter a quest wherein they had to prove to be borne warrior through a ritualistic dance called 'Suhta-lam'. "Suhta" is an instrument to trash the paddy. This dance is actually not a merry-making dance. Many have tried it and failed to survive the test it holds. This dance comprises of woods, held and struck by four sworn warriors or 'Lom' leaders. They form a sequence of a foot-trap like rows and columns with the wood and these warrior strikes their wood together while the competitor dances at the intensely harmonic as well a very dangerous game of the four warrior. The competitor has to jump across each and every gap formed in the process of the dance without his legs getting trapped. And in doing so, if he succeeds to complete the test/ quest, he is called a real warrior. And that he is worthy to take part in the war fares, to protect their people and the village from the attack of the enemies.

Chavang Kut

Chavang means autumn and '*Kut*' means festivals. So, *Chavangkut* means autumn festival. It is usually celebrated in the month of November or December after harvesting season is over. The primitive Kuki social life is encircled with numerous feasts, rituals and festivals. Most of the festivals revolved round agriculture as it is their chief occupation. Close observation of such festivals undoubtedly bears the testimony that it is thanksgiving and propitiation to the '*Nunjai Pathen/ Chung pathen'* (The God high on the sky) and '*Noimangpathen / Noipathen* (The God below the earth who ruled under world) whom they believed is the source of bountiful crops harvested. Merriments and enjoyments from 'ju' their home made rice beer, singing and dancing are parts of the festivities. Aged-old people and women folk, the youths alike enjoy the festivities with their hearts content. Autumn, the third season of the year, has always been regarded as a season of mirth and festive just as the poet Keats has remarked autumn to be a season of mellow fruitfulness, it sure brings the fruits of the yearlong labour. Unlike the other feats, the *Chavang Kut* is regarded as the only festival of everyone, like the sweet autumn season shine for everyone. The way of celebration and arrangement is also simple in nature. Feasting marks the celebration. The youths arrange for *mithun* to be slaughtered. The arrangement is called *selpanglap*. The *mithun* before being slaughtered is tied to a strong pole where *selkan*, meaning jumping over the *mithun*, the most daring and enjoyable event is executed. Each young man displays his strength and valour by jumping (also to impress their heart throbs). Only male mithuns are used for this event singing and dancing traditional songs and dances in traditional gear is one exciting part of the *Kut*. Both young and old dance and sing hand in hand. Most of the songs are like ballads and *qawalis*. It is in this *Kut* one can exhibits his skill by participating in the competition of the sports like - long jump, high jump, wrestling, javelin throw, etc. at right the cultural and traditional items like dancing, singing, competitions, by the coming of civilisation and modernisation and to suit our taste and times, fashion shows and selection of Miss *Kut* items has been added in a pretty graceful way. The *Kut* last for days together. *Chavangkut* is therefore a time where group of people and individual communicate without hesitation, malice, in a brotherly manner. It is a time, as the pleasant weather, where all cares, anxieties, misunderstandings are totally shed and prayers offered with thanks, giving to the creator of all the *Kuts*, *Chavang kut* is the only widely celebrated and the only prevalent festival of the *Kukis*, which is celebrated with much pomp and gaiety every year. Since 1992, the Autonomous District Council of North Cachar Hills has also declared 1st November as *Chavang Kut* festival holiday.

Chavangkut is the only existing festival of the Kuki today. All the festivals have lost its importance today in Kuki society. The reason being, they are no more head hunters or warriors or just an agriculturist. It is not possible for the Kuki people to celebrate each festivals so to keep their festive heritage alive all the festivals have minimised itself to one single festival, 'Chavang Kut'.

Conclusion

From the above findings and discussions it has been proved that the Kuki are rich in cultural heritage. With different kinds of festivals they have variety of folk dance and songs. Singing together to the tone of traditional music and drinking of *zu* was outstandingly beautiful. It showed their identity and love for one another. Technology, modernisation and other outer forces was not present to pollute the ethnicity of the Kuki people then. They practiced head hunting and it was believed that it would give them place in *mithikho* (place of death where the soul rests) and also held a high position in the society. Not only that the Kuki people were also good hunters. They come home with a big kill and proclaim their victory by playing the mouth organ call *pheiphit* inviting the whole village which calls for a sure feast with dancing, merry making and drinking of *zu.* To the hardworking animist Kuki each day gave them a new reason to celebrate over a big kill, or bountiful harvest. Each festivals and celebrations was celebrated in a common ways like, drinking of *zu* (local rice beer), feast, merry making, games and sports, singing and dancing together. The festivals lasted a week or so and kept them going on and on forgetting all the stress and toiling throughout the year.

But, a huge dimensional shift has taken place in Kuki society today. They are no more head hunters or hunters, nor are they warriors. They are neither animist worshipper anymore. They have accepted Christianity today and all the festivals which are related to hunting, wars, or other ritualistic festivals are no more celebrated today except *chavangkut* (an autumn festival or post-harvest festival). The rituals that the Kuki once followed had a contradictions with Christianity as such they had to give away some of their age old customs and traditions which they inherited from their ancestors. Drinking of *zu* (local rice beer) which was once the part and parcel of every occasion and festivals has been abolished and replaced by tea. And *thempu* (priest) has been replaced by pastors.

Though these traditional festivals are not celebrated any more they have not been forgotten completely. The tradition of drinking *zu* (local rice beer), wrestling, festivals which lasted for weeks or so, singing and dancing together etc has still been fresh in the minds of the people and some of this traits has been incorporated in the only existing festival *Chavang Kut* which is known as Autumn Festival or Post Harvest Festival. This festival today acts as a medium to keep integrity and unity amongst the people. It fills the people with happiness and love for one another. More than just reproducing the sacredness of society, preventing it from falling apart these practices emphasise on what Marshall Sahlins calls 'The mutuality of being' where he says that 'festival is of people who live each other's lives and die each other's death'.

References

Gangte, T.S. (2012), The Kukis of Manipur, A Historical Analysis.

Gangte, M. Priyadarshni and Aheibam Koireng Singh (2010), Understanding Kuki Since Primordial times, Essay by late Dr T.S. Gangte.

Goswami Tarun (2008), Kuki life and lore.

Haokip, P.S. (2008), Zale'n-Gam The Kuki Nation.

Haolai Thangkim (2006), Kuki Culture in North Cachar Hills Before And After The Advent of Christianity.

KhupZa go (2008), Zo Chronicles, A documentary study of History and Culture of The Kuki-Chin-Lushai Tribe.

Rizvi S.H.M. and Shibani Roy (2006), Kuki-Chin Tribes of Mizoram and Manipur.

Suantak Joseph (2012), Chin + Kuki + Zo Genesis and Exodus.

20

Rhyme and Reason: Intersections of Oral Heritage and Vernacular Architecture in Assam

— *Paramita Kakati*

Introduction

Architecture is an important aspect of managing the human-environment relationship as a codified 'scientific' practice. In this paper, I examine the intersection of oral traditions, vernacular architecture and environment. I argue that the 'folkloric' tradition uses a notion similar to that of *orientation,* a technical concept used in modern architecture to manage space. What is unique about using 'orientation' to achieve climatic control is that it can be *done so without major disruption to the environment*, which has the potential to disrupt conventional notions about human-environment relations.

The lessons learnt from this study can be possibly valuable in trying to develop alternative modes of managing space and the environment, and particularly the human-environment relations. Moreover, this paper also shows how the historically constructed binaries between tangible and intangible can be disrupted through examining the relationship between the folkloric tradition and the built environment. The dominant epistemic modes of knowledge can be disturbed through examining these interactions. In the Northeast, this is of particular relevance has colonial discourses have historically worked towards producing strong binaries of 'othering'.

Oral traditions form an integral part of Assam's 'intangible' heritage. The oral traditions, as this paper suggests can find possibility of being textualised not just in written form, but in a material manifestation found in the built heritage. The use of metaphors and rhythmic mnemonics in some of these oral traditions offer simplified codes for using strategies of orientation of built environment in order to master the micro-climatic conditions. Unlike, *Vaastu Shastra*, which can still claim the status of being a 'scientific' tradition and borrowing legitimacy from a 'grand' narrative of 'Indian' tradition and 'high culture' and perhaps unintelligible to the common rural populace.The folkloric tradition on the other hand offered a more simplified alternative. The concepts inscribed in the oral tradition seem to show great sensitivity to the ecology, and combined form, function and an aesthetic manipulation by the use of orientation techniques that *did not even necessitate changing the built materials.*

The vernacular architecture of any region is usually dependent on two factors, locally available building materials and the macro climate. The latter often dictates the former in addition to the built form and structures. The micro climate on the other hand can be manipulated so a comfortable living environment can be achieved within the built form. In architectural studies, the placement of built form on a site with respect to the cardinal directions is called 'orientation'. Using my background in architecture and planning, in this paper, I seek to demonstrate how strategies of orientation were inscribed in the folkloric tradition of Assam by bringing together architectural knowledge and vernacular oral heritage. It is a work in progress and the following are summarised notes on the project in this short paper.

Reasoning the Rhyme

A brief discussion on the climatic terrain of the region is important in order to contextualise the matrix of human-environment relations. Assam can be typically zoned into the 'tropical monsoon rainfall' type, with high levels of humidity and heavy rainfall. People here enjoy a moderate climate all throughout the year, with warm summers and mild winters. In the monsoon season, the whole state comes to life with the beauty of nature. Climatic variations can be seen regionally. The summer season in Assam starts from the month of March and extends till the end of June. The season is characterised by extreme humidity and frequent showers.

The average temperature during this time of the year is between 35 and 38 degree Celsius, usually not exceeding 38 degrees, even in the hottest month of the year. The monsoons season brings relief from the scorching heat of summer. In winter, Assam is basically characterised by scanty rainfall and misty mornings and evenings. The season starts in November and continues till the month of February. The mercury reading at this time of the year is around 6 to 8 degree Celsius or 43- 46 degree Fahrenheit. Spring (March-April) and Autumn (September-October) in Assam, are usually pleasant seasons, with moderate temperature and rainfall.

The climatic terrain is outlined above in general terms. It is these in particular climatic conditions (with margin for error given the diverse types of geographic terrain found in the region) that the application of the folkloric knowledge as well as practice of vernacular architecture can be contextualised. More particularly, rather than an overarching generalisation, these conditions, as well as the material and folkloric methods of managing space are also more applicable to the plains of Assam than the hills regions. The latter form a distinct micro-climatic economy.

In the section below, I shall briefly examine the traditional mode of achieving climatic control, which is through the mode of using vernacular architecture rooted in the tangible built structures. In trying to describe the various scales of human-environment interaction in space, I shall classify it as *macro* and *micro* modes of achieving climatic control.

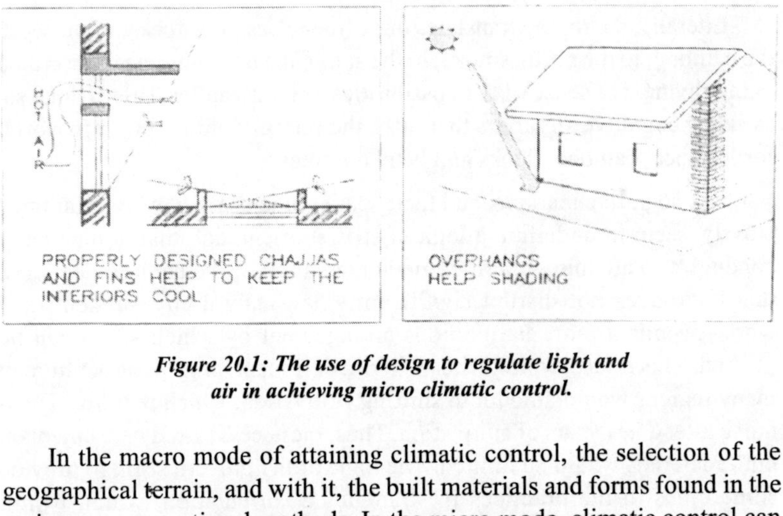

Figure 20.1: The use of design to regulate light and air in achieving micro climatic control.

In the macro mode of attaining climatic control, the selection of the geographical terrain, and with it, the built materials and forms found in the region are conventional methods. In the micro mode, climatic control can be understood in more complex and specific terms, for instance, in the design of spaces, selection of plots and orientation. In this paper, I shall for obvious reasons of understanding the spatial dynamic of climate control, focus on the micro-climatic mode, and more particularly, the use of orientation. Orientation, in very simplified and non-technical jargon, signifies the *placement* of a built form on a particular site, with respect to the four cardinal directions.

So far, we have dealt with the 'tangible' built tradition in the vernacular mode of architecture. *Phakarajojana* or proverb/rhyme has been a mode of literary transmission in Assam. Of significance within this tradition in Assam is *Dakar Boson,* translation roughly, to the 'sayings of Dak', an imaginary figure embodying wisdom in the oral literary mode of transmission of knowledge. This has predominantly been part of the oral tradition in the Assamese language and rural landscape. The proverbs employ a mnemonic mode used to remember words and phrases. In the proverbs I examine, the mnemonic code is meant to help remember, and thus materialise, the correct orientation of a built habitat. In the absence of other mechanical means of controlling climate, the built structure was oriented in a particular manner so that the climatic factors could be regulated to an advantage. In modern day parlance, this would be called 'landscaping', used to create a micro climate which in turn ensures a comfortable living environment within the built form.

Here is a relevant proverb in the *Dakor Boson* tradition:

Pubehans, paschimebaah, Uttaredhuwa, dakhinegua

Literally, the rhyme translates thus, 'to the east, the ducks; to the west, the bamboo; to the north, smoke; to the south, the betel nut trees'. Inscribed in the rhyme, is a sense of the possibilities of landscaping. This is done so, by using cognitive signifiers that mark the imagery of the rural life world, for instance, bamboo, ducks and betel nut trees.

The cognitive markers, and their spatial organisation, when examined closely, seem to underline a logic if spatial orientation that is inherently conducive to attaining micro-climatic regulation of the environment. Yet, this logic does not disrupt significantly, the natural environment, and work towards a more harmonious arrangement by which space can be utilised. This is also useful, when where a dominant mode of agriculture in many regions would amount to shifting cultivation, which requires one to move after a few years of cultivation. Thus, the access to and investment on built materials would be limited. The logic of the proverb seem to provide some clues in the practices in strategies of orientation, which would provide an economical as well as an ecological tool to regulate the environment.

The following logic of spatial orientation can be identified in this rhyme. The smoke to the north signifies the location of the hearth. The space to the north if left free would allow for flow of moderated sunlight, without the sharp glare. This light is ideal for all activities which require softer light, like cooking, winnowing rice and weaving on the loom.

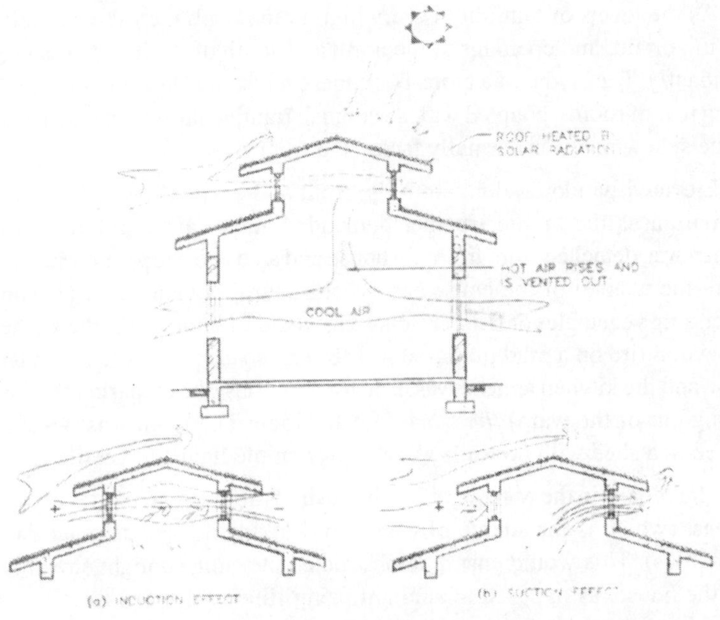

Figure 20.2: Roof design to regulate air and temperature control.

Moreover, the predominant wind direction is on a south-north axis in the region. This passage must be kept free which is ensured by placing the shelter in a manner where the northern section is devoid of big trees and the spaces between the thin betel trees in the south allows for a smooth passage of the south-north wind. A moderate amount of alteration of the environment is possibly entailed in the clearing of trees or planting of betel nuts.

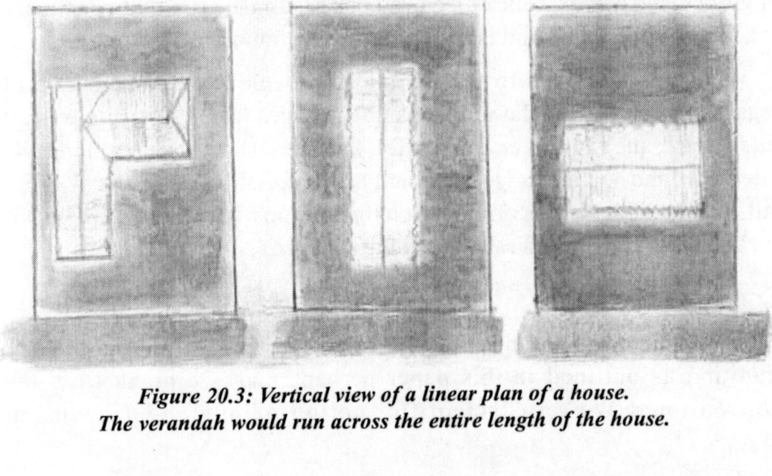

Figure 20.3: Vertical view of a linear plan of a house.
The verandah would run across the entire length of the house.

As the levels of humidity is very high in the region, cross-ventilation was important, and openings to the north and south of the house was used abundantly. The layout of a typicalAssamese house was linear in plan, with a long row of rooms, coupled with a verandah running throughout the length of one side which was normally facing the front.

Elevated windows along both the front and back, allowed for cross-ventilation as the humid weather demanded ample air circulation. The kitchen was detached from the main house and also had a separate verandah where the women of the house carried out their daily chores of cleaning and cutting vegetables or fish. The cooking would be done inside the kitchen over wood fire on a mud plastered hearth. The space in between the main house and the kitchen annexe was used for activities like preparing the yarn (laying out of the warp) /*batikarha* for the loom.The loom was typically housed in a shed with no walls allowing for ample light and ventilation.

The 'ducks in the east' signifies the desired presence of a water body to the east (which is the source of water for drinking as well as other daily necessities). This would ensure unobstructed morning sunlight streaming into the house, as opposed to sunlight being filtered through trees which would have grown in the eastern space place had there been no pond. The infra-red rays of the morning sun also purifies and energises the water. Small ponds and fisheries in every household is a common feature of the village organisation of rural Assam.

The presence of a bamboo grove to the west is meant to obstruct the sunlight coming in from the west. The afternoon sun in the west is very strong and probably the hottest, and using a screen of bamboo plants to block this is a fine way to tackle the heat and glaze of the afternoon sun. Bamboo, is essentially a form of grass, which grows very fast into tall clumps or groves, and acts as a thick green veil obstructing the sunlight effectively. It is found abundantly and is easy to grow very quickly.

The betel nut trees to the south also provide a similar function of regulating light. When the sun 'sposition changes from the east to west, it tilts towards the south at an angle of 22.4 degrees. Hence, at noon and early afternoon, the south sun is strong and uncomfortable. Betel nut trees are tall, slender with clumps of foliage on the tree tops.The angle of sunlight is such that the foliage serves to block the sunlight.

Conclusion

The potential logic of orientation that can be identified in the oral tradition as outlined in this paper perhaps marks a break from the conventional Western 'scientific' notion of human-environment relationships. These relationships are predominantly understood within the prism of 'transformation' of natural environment. Here we see an inherent concept of managing spaces, without entailing downright disruptive transformations, but rather by using a mode of managing space and environment through practices of orientation.

Whether such practices were actually materialised is another question. But the presence of an inherent logic of orientation in an 'intangible' mode of knowledge transmission leaves potential to spatialise, and at least derive an understanding of cognitive modes of regulating space to achieve human agency over the environment. Moreover, the intersection of an 'oral' form with the more 'tangible' built forms of vernacular architecture allow possibility of inscribing the oral beyond the realm of intangibility. Thus, the binaries can become fuzzy.

In examining these processes, I am wary of the dangers of projecting present day concepts such as 'orientation' into the past, or of glorifying one form of knowledge over another. It is perhaps at best, an attempt to visualise interactions in alternate modes of understanding space, knowledge, folkloric tradition and cognitive maps. The paper indirectly seeks to question assumptions on the politics of epistemic practices in historical literature on 'science' and 'reason', and ultimately suggests that there may be more 'reason' to the rhyme.

References

Baruah, Manjeet. (2013), *Mapping Literature: Culture and Region Formation in the Brahmaputra Valley*. New Dehli: Museum.

Bremner, G. Alex. (2005), "Nation and Empire in the Government Architecture of Mid-Victorian London: The Foreign and India Office Reconsidered." *The Historical Journal* 48 (3): 703-42.

Cohn, Bernard S. (1984), *The Census, Social Structure and Objectification in South Asia*. Soertryk.

Crowley, Daniel J. (1997), "The Assam Dragon: Folklore and Folkloristics in India's Long-Closed Northeast Frontier." *The Journal of American Folklore* 110 (435): 68.

Dalby, Simon (August 11, 2015), 'Anthropocene Formations: Environmental Security, Geopolitics and Disaster', *Theory, Culture and Society*, (published online before print). doi:10.1177/0263276415598629

Datta, Birendranath. (2012), *Cultural Contours of North-East India*. Oxford: Oxford University Press.

Kenny, Judith T. (1995), "Climate, Race, and Imperial Authority: The Symbolic Landscape of the British Hill Station in India." *Annals of the Association of American Geographers* 85 (4): 694-714.

Kumar, Deepak. (2004), "Emergence of 'Scientocracy': Snippets from Colonial India." *Economic and Political Weekly* 39 (35): 3893-98.

Lowenthal, David. (1975), "Past Time, Present Place: Landscape and Memory." *Geographical Review* 65 (1): 1. doi:10.2307/213831.

Metcalf, Thomas R. (1984), "Architecture and the Representation of Empire: India, 1860-1910." *Representations*, no. 6 (April): 37–65. doi:10.2307/2928537.

Mitter, Partha.(1986), "The Early British Port Cities of India: Their Planning and Architecture Circa 1640-1757." *Journal of the Society of Architectural Historians* 45 (2): 95-114.

Nath, Sanjeev Kumar. (2011) *The World of Assamese Folktales: A Study of the Tales of Lakshminath Bezbaroa and Troilokyeswari Devi Baruani*. Guwahati: Bhabani Print & Publications.

Robb, Peter. (1997), "The Colonial State and Constructions of Indian Identity: An Example on the Northeast Frontier in the 1880s." *Modern Asian Studies* 31 (2): 245-83. doi:10.2307/313030.

Sarma, Madan M., and Parasmoni Dutta.(2009), "Baresahariya Bhaona: Community Drama Festival of Assam: A Living Tradition." *Asian Theatre Journal* 26 (2): 303-19.

Scott, James C. (1998), *Seeing like a State: How Certain Schemes to Improve the Human Condition Have Failed*. Yale Agrarian Studies. New Haven: Yale University Press.

Tickell, Alex. (2004), "Negotiating the Landscape: Travel, Transaction, and the Mapping of Colonial India." *The Yearbook of English Studies* 34 (January): 18-30. doi:10.2307/3509481.

21

Traditional Food Practices among the Misings of Majuli

— *Parismita Saikia*

Introduction

Food is the most visible and frequently encountered cultural manifestation of a community. Though not strictly artifact in the sense that it is the most luminal of categories and continuously responds to cultural realities, food provides an idea about the values and mode of life of a community (Dutta, 2008).

Food habit of a community is influenced by geographical as well as social environment. Food procurement and its preservation are conditioned by the climate, varying seasons, community size, economic condition, infrastructure and technological knowledge. Traditional norms, religious belief and societal values also influence consumption pattern (Saikia, 2013). The study of food ways is very important to shape community, personality and family. Thus, study of food ways fills the gap to understand the culture and historical periods. The food culture of any community reflects its culture and tradition of its own. Anthropologists study food from different perspectives. Some look at eating and drinking in connection with other aspects of social life. Others are concerned with dietary matters and how food-related practices and beliefs affect physical wellbeing. These two points of view referred to respectively as, "the *Anthropology of food*" and "*Nutritional Anthropology*", need to be considered together if one wants a complete picture of a food culture (Kumari and Dutta, 2012).

Materials and Method

To study the traditional food practices of Misings, the investigator selected three villages of Majuli, these are- Borpomua, Lakhimi Borpomua and Kumarbari village. Borpomua and Lakhimi Borpomua falls under the Jengraimukh Gaon Panchayat and Kumarbari village falls under the Cherpai Gaon Panchayat of Majuli subdivision of the Jorhat district. Majuli is famous as one of the greatest river Island in the world. At present Majuli is an administrative subdivision of the Jorhat district of Assam with its headquarter in Garamur. Misings are the largest plain tribes and the largest tribal community of Majuli.

Mising is a distinct tribe inhabiting the areas north of the Brahmaputra River in upper Assam. They are the second largest plain tribes of Assam. As per the Census of India, 2001 the population of the Misings in the state of Assam at the time of enumeration was 587,310 (Male 299,790 and female 287,520) which constitute 17.3 per cent of the total scheduled tribes population of Assam. The Misings in general belong to the Tibeto-Burman family of the great Mongoloid race. In the long back they used to live in the hilly areas in between the Siang and Subansiri districts of present day Arunachal Pradesh and came down the plains of Assam around 14th-15th century. Since then they used to settle on the riverside areas of the Brahmaputra and the Subansiri rivers of Assam. They are mostly found in the districts of Dhemaji, Lakhimpur, Jorhat, Sibsagar, Golaghat, Sonitpur and Tinsukia. They are also sparsely found to inhabit in the Koliabar area of Nagoan and Goalpara district (Pegu, 2013).

The Misings comprise of several loosely knit 27 and apparently indistinguishable groups namely, Pag-ro, Delu, Shayang, Dambuk, Oyan, Moying, Samuguria, Tamar and Somua." (Pegu, 2011). The Misings women are expert in handloom and weaving art. Traditionally the Misings dwell in stilted houses. A grand stilted house, its pillars made of wood or bamboo and roof of straw, a porch in the front part of the house and a wooden Jakhala (ladder) attached with the house is common in a Mising house. Now-a-days concrete pillars and metal sheets have substituted these but the traditional architecture is remaining unchanged.

Method

The present study is a descriptive study based on both primary and secondary data. The primary data sources include interview with some kitchen women, who regularly prepare the food items and some elderly persons of the Mising community of Majuli subdivision and the secondary data is collected from various books, journals, magazines etc.

The main objective of the study is to highlight the traditional food items and their method of preparation among the Mising community of Majuli. The investigator will also try to highlight the medicinal value of the food items. For the present study the traditional food habits of the Misings of Majuli are categorised into two heads- food items prepared for day-to-day consumption and food items prepared for some special occasion.

Traditional Food Items

The Misings are agriculturists by tradition and their livelihood is essentially based on agricultural productions. In the study areas the main agricultural products are rice, mustard, black pulse, potatoes and some other vegetables. According to the informants originally they used to produce these crops only for consumption but now-a-days they also produce mustard, black pulses and potatoes for commercial purpose.

Mising have created a unique local identity in food habits, style of preparation and for its delicacy. Similar to other people of Assam rice is the staple food of the Misings. They are basically non-vegetarian and they know how to prepare delicious items from meat and fishes. Their great delicacies are fowl and pork for which flock of fowls and herd of pigs reared by many families (Pegu, 2011). The traditional food habit of the Mising people consisted mainly boil items of fish and meat with wild leafy vegetables, such as, *Ombe* or *mesaki* (Debregeasia wallichiana wedd), *Pakkom* or *nephaphu* (clerodendron colebrookianuan walpers), *Dermi (Meliosma pinnata Rox), okang, takuk, takpiyang, tajik or dimoru* (Ficus scandium), etc. Apong is also essential in every meal. Dried meat and fish are very popular among them. Most of the rural peoples of Mising used more wild green vegetables than the cultivated (Gam and Gam, 2010).

Traditional Food Items Prepared for day-to-day Consumption

The Mising women have good knowledge of preparing different types of delicious traditional curry for day-to-day consumption. Some special types of curry are prepared only on some ritual occasions to serve important invited guests (Pegu, 2010).

They are one of the culturally rich ethnic tribe of Assam, mostly dependent on nature for their livelihood. They rear pigs and poultry in every household which is a part of their custom. Fishing in rivers and beels is another important practice of these people. Besides, they use plenty of wild plants as vegetables in their daily food items from time immemorial.Their food items have hardly any fried items among the Mising people. They prepared food items with minimum edible oil and spices. The Mising community of Majuli has presented unique local identity of traditional food preparation. Their cuisines are reputed for their extra flavour. Some traditional cuisines of the missing Community are:

Ba:nam: *Ba:nam* (roasted) meat or fish is their hot favourite. They prepare roasted meat and fish in different traditional manner. In this technique meat and fishes are fixed in a bamboo stick and roasted in naked fire and sometimes in side of the fire until it is ready to take. Besides the meat and fishes, they also used to eat roasted garlic, potatoes with rice in traditional manner.

Pam:nam: It is also a favourite dish of Mising community. In this process meat, fishes and different leafy vegetables are wrapped in banana leaves or wild cardamom (tarapat) and steamed. Meats and fishes are sliced into small pieces and mixed properly with spices like salt, ginger, garlic, turmeric powder etc and put under the fire and keep tossing it to boil properly. With meat or fish other green leafy vegetables can also be steamed. The steamed 'moa fish' (a small river fish) is good dish for health. Fish can be steamed in swamp also. Pam:num can have with fish, meat or rice beer.

Purang: Another tasteful item of the Mising community is '*purang'*, a rice cake wrapped in wild variety of flavourful leaf called '*Tarapat'* (wild cardamom), which is somewhat sticky. On the festive occasion, specially in the *Ali-Aye- Ligangpurang* is a compulsory item. *Purang* is traditionally served with meat or fish, but one can taste it with milk or card also.

La:sar: La:sar is a favourite boiled vegetable recipe of the Mising community. It is prepared without slicing the vegetables. Leafy vegetables such as, *Lai sak* (wild mustard), *Lapha sak* (Lapha), *Mula sak* (Raphanus Sativels), *Sariyah Sak* (Mustard Leaf), *Dimoru* (Ficus scandium), *Mesaki* (Debregeasia wallichiana wedd), *Dermi, okang, takuk,* etc are consumed as La:sar. It may be served with rice and *apong* as well.

Ra:sor Oying: This is a type of boiled leafy vegetables without putting extra ingredients into it. It can be consumed with salt and chilli powder. Usually the following vegetables are prepared as Ra:sor oying such as, *pakkom* or *nephaphu (clerodendron colebrookianuan walpers), Begenang* (brinjal), jute, bean, *Bangko* (*Solonum indicum* Lin.), *Iki-oying*, *tapaanne* etc.

Jabor Oying: Jabor Oying or Ka:pa oying is another favourite food items of Mising community. This is a type of mixed curry of either fish or chicken or pork with different leafy vegetables such as *pakkom* or *nephaphu (clerodendron colebrookianuan walpers),* ombe or *mesaki (Debregeasia wallichiana wedd)*, *okang*, *bilongoni (Polypodium* spp.Lin.*)*, *tajig* (a variety of tall fig tree), *nekung*, *sampa (Dillenia indica* Lin.), *I:kung* (a shoot of bamboo) etc.

Pe:red Oying: Pe:red oying is another very delicious food items of Mising.This is a type of curry prepared with black pulses and pork. For the better taste khar, an alkaline solution can be mixed with this. Pe:red oying can also be prepared with chicken, fish etc mixing with some vegetables like Sompa *(Dillenia indica* Lin.), ombe or *mesaki (Debregeasia wallichiana wedd)*, Tajig *or dimoru* (Ficus scandium) etc. They prepared this for day-to-day consumption and also for different festivals, rituals etc.

Jaal: This is one of the most important food items of Misings. This is a curry consist of colocasia leaf with sheath, black pepper, sour and meat of hen. The spices used for jaal curry are, chilly, ginger, garlic, salt, black paper etc in a large quantity. Generally jaal curry is offered to mothers of new born baby.

I:kung Oying: I-Kung means a shoot of bamboo. To cook I-kung oying first step is the boiling water and after boiling water add I-kung with sompa (*Dillenia indica* Lin.) and pork. After that add spices like ginger, garlic, turmeric etc and boil these until ready to eat.

Ku:ne Oying: This is a type of curry having acidic taste prepared using dry fish, chicken, pork etc with different vegetables. Pork or chicken with nekung, dry fish with I:kung etc are some combination for a tasteful curry. (Kuli, 2003)

Pasalang Oying: Pasalang oying is one of the special traditional food items of Mising community. This item can be prepared with chicken and pork. To cook this item firstly fry the meat in sufficient oil and then add finely chopped *pasala* (a young shoot of the plaintain tree used for curry) and cook until ready to eat. This can be served with *apong* and rice.

Num:sing: Nam:sing is another popular item among the Misings of Majuli. It is a special type of preserved dry fish in a bamboo tube. The dry fishes are first grinded, mixing with arum petiols etc and kept in a bamboo tube called *otung*, the mouth of which is closed tightly to prevent air entering into it. The sealed bamboo tube are then hung about two to three feet above the mud oven in the kitchen or fireplace where upon the Mising people cook food as outdoor kitchen. It is the preserved fish which can be used after a long period of time even after a year. Nam:sing is consumed after steam cooking or after preparing curry along with vegetables. For steam cooking required amount of nam:sing is taken out from the bamboo container and mixed with chilly and some spices like ginger, garlic, onion, turmeric.

After mixing properly, wrapped with a fresh tara pat (wild cardamom) and cook in steam along with rice. The mixture is then ground to a paste or chutney and eaten with rice.

A num:sing curry is also prepared by Mising people with vegetables such as ridge gourd and leafy vegetables i.e., spinach, mustard leaves, pumpkin leaves, arum leaves etc. The product is mixed with the ingredients of curry and cooked in a curry pan with sufficient amount of gravy. It gives a sweet flavour and characteristic odour to the curry.

Again fish boiled with *Sompā* (*Dillenia indica* Lin.), meat boiled with either *om:be* or *tākuk* or *tākpiyāng* (all wild leaves) are some other tasty and popular curry of Mising community. Sometimes only boiled leaves, plain rice, grinded chilly and salt make a popular item. These were known as *tu:le rā:nām, om:be rā:nām, tākukrā:nām* etc. in which the former is the name of different leaves and the latter means 'boil' (Kuli, 2003).

Though they prepared different delicious curry with leafy vegetables, fish and meat, but they do not mixed some vegetables with other, e.g. they never mixed tomato with sompa (*Dillenia indica* Lin.) ; Dhekiya sak *(Diplaziumesculentum)* with pork and chicken; bitter with sour etc. They eat only seasonal vegetables. They are generous in using pepper, ginger and turmeric which they used to cultivate themselves, but spices available in the market are sparingly added to their dishes. Traditionally after having meal they do not eat any type of sweets but they eat bettlenut, korpur etc. for mouth freshening. Traditionally they drink water in less quantity and instead of water they use apong for drink. Fried items are not unknown to them but the roasted, steamed and smoked items prefer more.

Traditional Beverages of the Misings

The Misings have unique process of procuring flavoured liquor, called '*Apong*'. The *Apong* is of two varieties differing in taste, colour and the method of preparation. *Nogin Apong* is creamy white and fermented from the boil rice, but '*Poro Apong*' has a dark greenish colour due to addition of ashes of straw rice and paddy husk. But on both the preparation, an extract of various medicinal plants called *'eppop'* is in right proportion." (Pegu, 2011). Fermentation starts in '*Nogin*' within four days and is generally ready for extraction within seven days. It is extracted by adding hot or cold water, squeezing through a bamboo sieve (Korai) and served immediately. *Po:ro Apong* takes longer time to ferment and is extracted through a funnel shaped bamboo cone (Taasuk). Fermented *Nogin Apong* cannot be preserved for more than two weeks, but *Po:ro Apong* can be preserved for several month.

Traditional Food Items Prepared for Rituals and Festivals

Since earlier the Misings as a whole had a common traditional belief and practices and no any religious divisions among them therefore, there were no any restrictions or boycott of the food items on religious grounds. *Āpong* is an integral part of *Mising* beliefs and practices. Right from rituals, ceremonies to festivals no any instance is found in which the use of *Āpong* is prohibited. They consider this drink as auspicious. *Apong, purang Apin,* fish curry are some delicious food items are cooked for *Ali-aye-ligang. Pasalang oying, Jabor oying, Pe:red oying, ye:ktak oying* etc are prepared in different traditional rituals and festivals like *Po:rāg* (a post-harvest festiva), *Āli Ā:ye Lígāng* (national festival of the *Misings*), *Dodgang* (funeral ceremony), *Midang* (marriage ceremony), *okum gisang* (entry into as new house) etc. *Purang Apin* and *Ngeregoying* is specially prepared in *Ali-aye-ligang*. They can consume these in day-to-day life also. What domestic fowl to be scarify in what custom and ritual practices, were determine and fixed by the priest (Mibu), and these practices transmitted generation to generation. To some extent, the wild greens are also fixed to cook with certain meat in certain traditional religious customs, ritual practices and festivals.

Food preparation and food service is an art. Mising women have to obey some rules while preparing and serving food. The main lady of the family or the eldest daughter-in-law has responsibly to cook food. After cooking they have to serve food for each and every member of the family. The head or eldest person of the family is to be served first.

Medicinal Value of Traditional Food Items of the Misings

There are some medicinal values almost in all the food items of Mising community. *Apong* is used also as medicines in times of various diseases. If a person is detected of symptoms of Jaundice, then the first extraction of *Po:ro Apong* is made to drink. It is also taken as energetic drink if taken within limit. In case of urinal problems, *Po:ro Apong, manimuni (Centilla asiatica) duportenga (Bryophyllum pinnatum)* etc is useful and in case of stomach problem *Nogin Apong* and boiled *Mesekisak* with *Takuk* is very useful. While describing about the advantages of *Nogin Āpong* B.S. Guha has written, "We have analysed many samples of their fermented drinks *Nogin Āpong* and found that it alcoholic content does not exceed four per cent; but its nutritive value mostly in vitamins is of highest importance. It supplies 10 per cent calories, 5.5 per cent of protein, 5.3 per cent of calcium, 11 per cent phosphorus, 29 per cent iron, and 8 per cent of niacin." Similarly the *Po:ro Āpong* also have its own advantage and medicinal value if consumed within limit. Leafy vegetables like *Manimuni (Centilla asiatica), bhedailata (Pacderia foctida), pipli (Piper longum), mosondori (Houttuynia cordata), black peper* etc help to cure cough, fever etc. Khar (an alkalin item) help in digestion. Though some leafy vegetables have this type of medicinal value, some other vegetables may be harmful for human body, e.g. Star fruit with Barali fish and if pregnant women eat *the keratenga* and spices in large quantity then it may harm the health of the women. *Bilongoni (Polygonum hydropiper)* is cooked with chicken for enhance milk of the newborn baby's mother.

Conclusion

In 2010, food made its first appearance on UNESCO World Heritage lists with the inscription of three diverse cuisines and one type of culinary product: the Mediterranean Diet, the French Gastronomic Meal, Mexican/ Michoacán Cuisine, and Croatian gingerbread. How we eat, and what we eat, and when we eat, and with whom we eat, all uniquely vary from place to place, group to group, time to time. Food is often a primary marker of individual and group identity. Food is therefore extremely affective; its taste on our individual tongues often incites strong emotions, while the communal, commensal experience of such sensations binds people together, not only through space but time as well, as individuals collectively remember past experiences with certain meals and imagine their ancestors having similar experiences. When this occurs, food is transformed into heritage. (Giovine and Brulotte, 2014). The present investigation indicates that Mising culture is a agro-based culture. Rice is their staple food and Apong is essential in every meal.

Every food items of Mising community have some special features, which separated them from other communities of Assam. Every food items are related to their culture and festival. Pigs and fowls provide an important source of protein to their diet. Moreover, sacrifice of pigs and fowls is an essential part of different rituals, marriage ceremony, ancestor worship, funeral ceremony, worship of any other spirits. Thus, there is a great demand of pigs and fowls in Mising household. Now-a-days some changes are taken place among the Mising society. This may be due to modernisation or demand of time. Now-a-days uses of milk, egg, oil are included in their food habits which is very recent trend, whereas they never prefer these items in the past days. In some villages they offer betel nut (tamul-pan) to the guests instead of Apong now-a-days. This shows that Mising people have accepted the regional Assamese culture.

References

Almerico, G. M. (2014), Food and identity: Food studies, cultural, and personal identity, *Journal of International Business and Cultural Studies* 8, 1-7.

Census of India, (2001), Directorate of Census Operation, Assam.

Dutta, P. (2008), *Indian Folk Life* 31, 20-21.

Das, A. (2012), *Axamar Janagosthiya Lokakhadya,* Ank-Baak 3 publication, Natun Saraniya, Gandhibasti, Guwahati-781003.

Giovine, Michael A. Di. and R. L. Brulotte, (2014), *Edible Identities:Food as Cultural Heritage,* 1-25.

Gam, N. K. and J. Gam (2013), Ethno Medical Claims Existing among Mising Tribes of Assam, *International Journal of Science Invention Today* 2, 284-291.

Kuli, J. J. (2009), *Mising Sanskriti*, Dibrugarh Kaustubh Prakashan, New Market, Dibrugarh-1.

Kuli, J. J. (2012), *The Misings : their History and Culture*, Kaustubh Prakashan, New Market, Dibrugarh-1.

Kumari, P. (2012), Kitchen and Dining Space: As A Way of Eating Manner in Mising Community, *IOSR Journal of Humanities and Social Science (JHSS)* 4, 23-28.

Kittler, P.G; K.P. Sucher and M.N. Nelms (2012), *Food and culture (6th ed.)*. Belmont, CA: Wadsworth.

Pegu, N.C. (2005), *The Mishings of the Brahmaputra Valley*, Milan Nagar, Dibrugarh-3.

Pegu, I. (2013), *Religious beliefs and practices of the Misings of Assam: A case study of Majuli,* unpublished thesis, department of History, Gauhati University.

Saikia, S. K. (2010), *Asomiyar paramparagata khaidya*, Banalata publication, New Market, Dibrugarh-1.

Saikia, A., Food-Habits in Pre-Colonial Assam *International Journal of Humanities and Social Science Invention,* 2319-7714.

References

22

Archaeological Remains of Guwahati City

—*Paromita Das*

Introduction

According to UNESCO, "Cultural heritage is the legacy of physical artefacts and intangible attributes of a group or society that are inherited from past generations, maintained in the present and bestowed for the benefit of future generations." The term cultural heritage thus encompasses several main categories of heritage both tangible and intangible.

Tangible heritage includes buildings and historic places, monuments, artefacts, etc., which are considered worthy of preservation for the future. These include objects significant to the archaeology, architecture, science or technology of a specific culture. Tangible heritage can again be divided into movable cultural heritage that includes paintings, sculptures, coins, manuscripts, etc. and immovable cultural heritage like monuments and archaeological sites both terrestrial as well as underwater; like submerged cities, ruins shipwrecks. Intangible cultural heritage on the other hand includes oral traditions, performing arts, rites and rituals, etc. The archaeological remains of Guwahati fall within the UNESCO definition of tangible cultural heritage.

The city of Guwahati dates back to the remote past. In the *Ramayana* and *Mahabharata* it was known as Pragjyotisapura. In the historic period it was also the seat of the Varman and Pala rulers. During the reign of the Koch king Raghudev North Guwahati was the seat of his government and during Ahom rule Guwahati was the headquarters of the Bar Phukan. From the beginning of the thirteenth century up to the end of the seventeenth century C.E., it was a major theatre of war and witnessed conflicts between the rulers of Assam and the Turko-Afghans and Mughals. In the colonial period too Guwahati was the headquarters of the Agent to the Governor General of the English East India Company. As such the city has a rich tradition of archaeological remains that stand mute witness to its history and culture.

Objectives: It is proposed to examine the nature of the archaeological remains of Guwahati, their state of preservation and interpret their historical significance.

Methodology: A field study was carried out to identify and document the archaeological remains in the pre-colonial period. Literature, both primary and secondary was utilised to situate the remains in time and space. The remains were first identified, documented and then tabulated chronologically to gain insights into the history of the city.

Discussion

The archaeological remains of Guwahati are in the form of pottery, terracotta plaques, sculptures, icons, cannons, cannon balls, step wells, ramparts, mud wells, standing temples and temple components, etc. These remains help us to reconstruct the history of the city, especially for those periods where we have very little literary sources to help us. To understand their importance we shall now discuss a few of these components of archaeological heritage.

Inscriptions: More than sixty inscriptions have been discovered within the limits of the modern city of Guwahati. These inscriptions can be found engraved on rocks and boulders, stone slabs, temple walls as well as copper-plates. The earliest of them belongs to the fifth century C.E. This is the **Umachal Rock Inscription** of *Maharajadhiraja* Surendravarman. It records the excavation of a cave temple to the Vaisnavite deity Balabhadrasvamin.[1] The language of this inscription is Sanskrit and the script is Eastern Indian Gupta Brahmi. This inscription is the first surviving inscription of the Varman dynasty that had their headquarters in the Guwahati region. It proves that Surendravarman, identified with Mahendravarman, an ancestor of the famous Bhaskarvarman, was a great king and had adopted Sanskrit as the official language of his court.

At Ambari, in the heart of Guwahati city was discovered an inscription belonging to the early part of the thirteenth century C.E. In this **Ambari Stone Slab Inscription**[2] it is stated that in the kingdom of Samudrapala who was equal to Aditya (the Sun God) a *sattra* was established at Yogihati, i.e. residential quarters were established for the Yogis. This inscription dated in the Saka Era corresponding to 1232 C.E. proves that the rule of the Pala dynasty of Kamarupa continued well into the third decade of the thirteenth century.

At North Guwahati near the ABILAC centre we find three inscriptions, two on a big boulder with the image of a rock-cut Ganesa sculpture and the third on a rocky surface facing the river. The latter, popularly known as the **Kanai Barasi Bowa Rock Inscription** contains the first evidence of the Assamese script. It states that on the 13th day of the month of Chaitra, in the Saka Era 1127, corresponding to 1205 C.E., the Turuska (i.e. Turks) coming into Kamarupa were totally destroyed.[3] This is a reference to the failed expedition of Muhammad Bin Bakhtiyar Khalji that finds mention in Minhaj-ul-Siraj's *Tabaqat-i-Nasiri.* It records that the "Rae of Kamrud" (Raja or king of Kamrup) caused the destruction of the entire army of Muhammad Ibn Bakhtiyar in the year 1205 CE.[4] The other two inscriptions, also dated in the Saka Era, corresponding to 1667 C.E. refers to the recovery of Guwahati by the Ahoms after killing the Mughal Thanedars Syed Sana and Syed Piroz (Firoz) and the erection of defensive ramparts in the area.[5] It mentions the names of different Ahom officials, but not Lachit Bar Phukan. The latter finds mention in the Fatasil Ambari Pillar Inscription where he is called the Namjani Bar Phukan or Governor of Lower Assam, i.e. Ahom territories west of Kaliabor.[6] These three inscriptions at North Guwahati are very important to reconstruct the sequence of events in the conflict between the Ahom kingdom of the Brahmaputra Valley and the mighty Mughul Empire. In 1662, the Mughul general Mir Jumla had conquered Assam and occupied the Ahom capital Garhgaon. Thereafter a treaty had been concluded whereby the region of Lower Assam up to Guwahati remained under Mughul occupation. In 1667, after Lachit was appointed the Bar Phukan under his leadership the Ahoms were able to recover their lost territories. Following this the Mughul Emperor Aurangzeb had dispatched Ram Singh to punish the Ahoms but the latter won a decisive naval victory at Saraighat which is recorded in the Fatasil Ambari Pillar Inscription.

A majority of the inscriptions record the construction of temples in Guwahati on both banks of the River Brahmaputra. The reconstruction of the famous Kamakhya Temple on the Nilachala Hill by Sukladhvaj, the brother and General of the Koch ruler Naranarayana in 1565 CE is recorded in two identical inscriptions on the *antarala* (ante-chamber) of the main temple of Kamakhya.[7] The dancing hall of the temple also has two life sized images of the Koch king and his brother. The Pandunath Hari Temple Inscription dated 1585 CE records the construction of this Vaishnavite shrine by the Koch king Raghudeva Narayana.[8] A stone inscription dated 1694 CE records the construction of the Umananda Temple at Bhasmachala Island in mid-Brahmaputra by the Ahom king Gadadhara Simha.[9] However, a land deed in the possession of the *Doloi* (priest) of the temple states that it was issued in 1667 CE by the Mughul Emperor Aurangzeb (1657-1707 CE) reconfirming a grant of land to the temple priest.[10] This land grant is significant for two reasons. It proves that the Mughuls who had conquered Guwahati honoured the land grants of their predecessor. Secondly, a Brahmanical temple must have existed at Bhasmachala prior to the construction of the present temple by the Ahom king. The temple enshrines a huge Sivalinga and also contains a number of Saivite sculptures. Successive Ahom monarchs constructed or reconstructed a number of temples on the remains of earlier shrines (that had fallen into ruins) which are recorded in stone inscriptions on the temple walls.[11]

Inscriptions also refer to the excavation of ponds and the copper plates record Land and Servitor grants to temples. In 1695 CE, Gadadhar Simha issued a copper-plate assigning land and twenty-six *paiks* (servitors) to the temple at Umananda. This is the earliest reference of an Ahom monarch granting land to a Brahmanical temple. In 1697 CE, the next ruler Rudra Simha also granted land and servitors to the same temple.[12] Rudra Simha also commissioned the compilation of a list of existing *tirthas* (holy places) of Guwahati and the adjoining region[13] which would serve as a reference point for the construction of structural temples by successive Ahom rulers right down to the beginning of the nineteenth century. They erected numerous temples in Guwahati most of which have survived to the present time. They also issued copper plate inscriptions granting land for their maintenance together with servitors, as well as land to the Brahman priests attached to the temples.[14]

Structures: Structural remains are of two types – religious and secular. To the former category belong rock-cut shrines and temples. These are more than thirty in number, the most famous being the Kamakhya Temple on the Nilachala. The oldest shrine is a cave on the eastern side of the Nilachala known as Umachala where a cave shrine was excavated in circa fifth century CE for the worship of Balabhadrasvami a Vaishnavite deity[15] as discussed earlier. Archaeological evidence of twenty-nine temples exists in the Guwahati region. However, many of these shrines have been abandoned or fallen into ruin. In the period sixteenth to nineteenth century the Koch and Ahom rulers constructed temples on the foundations of these former temples and the majority of them are at present living shrines. A great many of these reconstructed shrines that exist today on the Nilachala (like the Kamakhya Temple) are dedicated to ten different forms of Shakti or the Mother Goddess, known as the Dasamahavidya. Other Saktipithas are Dirghesvari in North Guwahati and Ugratara in Jor Pukhuri area. Besides, we also find temples of their Bhairavas on the Nilachala and also on the island of Umananda in mid-Brahmaputra. On the Chitrachala Hill in the centre of Guwahati city is the Navagraha Temple enshrining aniconic forms of the nine planets as well as their anthropomorphic representations. On the rocky island of Urvashi we find the impression of a *yonipitha* along with other remains. In Bhasmachala Island there are three Siva temples, namely Umananda, Hara Gauri and Chandrasekhara. Other Siva temples are those of Banesvara, Sukresvar and Vasisthasram on the south bank of the Brahmaputra and Manikarnesvara in North Guwahati. Pandunath Hari, Janardana and Asvaklanta are dedicated to different forms of Vishnu. The Saivaite shrines have no images, only the aniconic *linga.*

Secular structures primarily belong to the Ahom period, in the form of ramparts. We also have old roads like the Rajgarh road whose foundations date to the pre-Ahom period. Other secular remains consist of mud wells, some of which have been discovered while excavating in the area of present Ambari and Cotton College Indoor Stadium. At Ambari we also find remains of a step-well, a semi-circular foot path and narrow cells with brick walls. At Cotton College was found the remains of a temple and a bow shaped courtyard. A list of the different categories of structural remains can be found in Appendix B.

Sculptures: By far the greatest number of archaeological objects comprise of sculptures of varying sizes. The earliest is a portion of a terracotta figure of a female with a beaded head-dress recovered from Ambari assigned to the Sunga period (second-first century BCE) on stylistic grounds. The largest group has been recovered from Ambari. These are mainly of stone. More than two hundred small sculptures have been recovered from the site of the Ambari excavations. The majority of them are of Mahisamardini Durga. The rest are of Siva and Vishnu. Moreover, terracotta sculptures have also been recovered from the region of Ambari, Cotton College, Kukurmuta (Hedayatpur) and Uzanbazar. These depict divine figures as well as secular themes like dancing girls and apsaras. Metal sculptures have been recovered from the Narakasur region of Odalbakra in Kahilipara area. The majority of the sculptures recovered from Guwahati are of religious figures like Surya, Visnu, Nataraja, Mahisasuramardini, Indra, Brahma, Sarasvati, Uma Mahesvara, etc. We also find a lot of animal sculptures, especially the *gajasimha* motif. For a list of sculptures see Appendix D.

The sculptures are executed according to canonical norms and exhibit similarity with eastern Indian art idioms. As some of the sculptures are made of black basalt, a stone not available in the region, it indicates that a rich clientele must have existed to commission such sculpture the material for which must have been procured from the Rajmahal Hills of Bihar, the nearest quarry. That the artisans and craftsmen were cognizant of canonical norms indicate the spread of Brahmanical culture in the region.

Artefacts: These consist mainly of pottery, terracotta balls, terracotta toys, religious objects like *linga* and *yonipith,* inkpot, clay boats and coins. All of them are housed in local museums, namely the Ambari site museum, Assam State Museum and the museums of the Anthropology departments of Cotton College and Gauhati University. For details see Appendix C.

Findings

1. The archaeological remains of Guwahati are in the form of pottery, terracotta plaques, sculptures, icons, cannons, cannon balls, step wells, ramparts, mud wells, standing temples and temple components, etc. Detailed lists of the remains are appended at the end of this paper.
2. The remains date from the 1st century C.E./B.C.E. up to the beginning of the twentieth century.
3. The remains are mostly concentrated along the river side, i.e. Brahmaputra and on the range of hills surrounding Guwahati on both banks of the river Brahmaputra as well as on the rocky islands of Urvasi and Umananda. Thus, we find remains on the hills of Nilachala, Pandu, Fatasil, Kahilipara, Kalapahar, Sukresvar, Sarania, Chatrachal, Chitrachala and Sarania on the south bank; Dirghesvari, Asvaklanta and Manikarnesvara hills on the north bank. Other areas include Fancy Bazar, Latasil, Uzanbazar, Chenikuthi, Cotton College campus, Ambari, Hedayatpur and Chandmari on the south bank and the Rudresvara and Sil sako area on the north bank.
4. As many of the temples are living shrines, constant exposure to ritual worship like smoke, incense, vermillion and oil have damaged many structures. Secondly, as the needs of the community of worshippers increase there has been wanton destruction of existing structures in the plea for "modernisation" and so called "development."
5. Pressure of population has led to encroachment of archaeological sites, especially ramparts, often considered a "safe place", free from floods, to construct schools and houses and even new motorways.

6. Ignorance of the necessity to preserve archaeological remains that constitute our common heritage besides providing a tangible record of our past is very often at the root of the slow destruction of many artefacts and archaeological sites. Fear is another factor. Apprehension that "the government" will dispossess people of their land and property to protect heritage sites is very often at the root of many problems.
7. Thus, while many of these remains have been preserved in the Assam State Museum and at designated protected sites by the Archaeological Survey of India and the Directorate of Archaeology, Government of Assam, others have been partially or wholly destroyed by the actions of time, nature and man.

Observations: The archaeological remains discovered in the city till date, clearly indicate continuous human habitation. Beginning with the prehistoric age, as evidenced by stray finds of neolithic tools and pottery[16] the area under review has been occupied till the present day. The pottery remains at Āmbāri, within the heart of the city includes specimens of Chinese Celadon ware datable to the early years of the Christian era.[17] The earliest structural remains at Āmbāri in the form of a step well, have been assigned to the first century C.E./B.C.E.

The structural remains at Nilāchala go back to the fifth century C.E. The Umāchal Rock Inscription[18] recording the excavation of a cave temple by *Mahārājādhirāja* Srī Surendravarman, points to the existence of an organised form of government in the vicinity of the modern city. The imperial title "king of kings" (*Mahārājādhirāja*) enjoyed by this ruler indicates the existence of subordinate ruling authorities. The Guwāhatī area was thus under the jurisdiction of an imperial monarch. Our sources however are silent about these other rulers.

The majority of the remains discovered in the modern city belong to the period nineth-thirteenth century C.E. Except for the stray finds at Kāhilipārā, no remains are datable to the period of seven and eighth century C.E. There is again a dearth of remains during thirteenth- 1st half of the seventeenth century C.E. This suggests the decline in the importance of Guwāhatī immediately after the death of Bhāskarvarman in the middle of the seventh century CE. Epigraphic evidence[19] of the Sālastambha rulers tells us that their capital was at Hadappeúvara, located near the modern town of Tezpur in Assam. The evidence of *Life*[20] in conjunction with that of the Nidhānpur grant[21] suggests that already Bhāskarvarman, towards the later part of his reign, abandoned his old capital Prāgjyotisapura (probably Guwāhatī) and established a new capital at Karnasuvarna in Bengal.

According to *Life,* the Kāmarûpa monarch proceeded to meet Harsavardhana, the king of Kanauj, with an army of 20,000 elephants, and he sailed down the Brahmaputra River and up the Gangā in 30,000 ships to Kajangala. It appears that the king deserted his kingdom with his forces. Hiuen-Tsang tells us that after reaching Kajangala Bhāskarvarman accompanied Harsa to Kanauj and Prayāga (Allahabad) to attend the latter's religious assemblies.[22] He was thus absent from his kingdom for nearly a period of one year. The Nidhānpur grant[23] was issued from Karnasuvarna wherein resided the king himself as well as the admiralty, elephant corps, cavalry and infantry:

Bhāskaravarman may have shifted his capital to Karnasuvarna. His successor Sālastambha probably had his own support base in Tezpur area and therefore the Sālastambha dynasty abandoned Guwāhātī. The paucity of remains reflects the declining political importance of the city. However, when the Pāla rulers established the new capitals of Durjjayā, and later Kāmrûpnagara in the Guwāhātī area, the site witnessed resurgence. This is reflected in the profusion of remains that belong to the period nineth-thirteenth century C.E.

Prāgjyotisapura, the capital city of legendary Naraka, as described in the *Rāmāyana* and the *Mahābhārata,* and in the inscriptions issued by the ancient kings of Assam, tally to a large extent with the topography of the modern city of Guwāhātī. The Brahmaputra River was the *Lauhitya Sāgara of* ancient inscriptions. Descriptions of Prāgjyotisapura as found in the land grants of king Balavarman and the Aphsad Inscription of Adityasena lend credence to the claim that the capital city of Naraka was identical with the modern city of Guwāhatī.[24] This city has always been referred to as Prāgjyotisapura in inscriptions of the rulers of Assam. The tradition continued down to the middle of the seventeenth century C.E. An inscribed canon seized by Gadādhara Simha from the Mughuls in the seventeenth century C.E. refers to the city of Guwāhātī as "*guvākahattyā.*"[25]

Due to its topography and proximity to the river Brahmaputra, Guwāhātī was found eminently suitable to be an administrative centre. If its identification with the ancient city of Prāgjyotisapura is accepted it was the capital city of the legendary Naraka. It also enjoyed this position during the reign of the Varmans and the Pālas. Guwāhātī witnessed a long drawn conflict for its occupation by the Muslim rulers from the west, and local and regional ruling houses. The existence of epigraphs, moats and ramparts scattered around the modern city testify to the fact that the city was a theatre of war from the early thirteenth century C.E. till the end of the seventeenth century C.E. During this period it witnessed a series of invasions from the west as well as the east. First the Sultans of Bengal, and later the Mughuls attempted to occupy the city. During the interlude when it was part of the Koch kingdom king Raghudeva had his capital at North Guwāhātī near the Aúvakrānta Hill.

Due to its topography it was also found to be the ideal location for defensive warfare. During the period of Āhom -Mughul conflict in the seventeenth century C.E. the Āhom general Lāchit Bar Phukan aptly remarked: "We could fight as if we were sitting in our own homes."[26] Montgomery Martin in his description of the city in the nineteenth century C.E. writes, "Goahawtee occupies an extent of hilly country on both banks of the great stream; the hills on each side form a specious amphitheatre which have been equally well fortified by nature and art."[27] The Āhoms, who occupied Guwāhātī, made it the headquarters of their Governor styled Bar Phukan. As it functioned as the seat of the Āhom Viceroy it also enjoyed political importance, for this officer conducted and maintained the relations with Bengal in the west as well as with the neighbouring chieftains in the area under his jurisdiction. Thus, in the period of Ahom supremacy Guwāhātī, due to its strategic location, was both a military base and an administrative headquarters.

The river Brahmaputra that divided the ancient settlement into two parts viz. north and south was the lifeline of the city. It facilitated transportation of men and material during times of peace and war. Moreover, the earliest remains discovered in the city are all near the riverside. All the land grants of the period indicate the riverine nature of the settlements. As agriculture was the basis of the economy the river and its tributaries sustained life in the state. Almost all the lands grants of Assam refer to streams on the boundary of the lands granted.

The religious nature of the remains discovered in Guwāhātī is a significant feature. All the existing shrines of Guwāhātī were built under royal patronage as indicated by the inscriptions.The nature of the remains indicates that the city was an important religious centre down the ages and still enjoys that position. Saivism was the dominant religion, followed by Vaisnavism. The worship of Śakti was also popular. Buddhism was not very popular as indicated by the scanty remains and the testimony of Hieun Tsang.

The sculptures and inscriptions discovered in the city are seen to be the best pointer of its inhabitants. A community well acquainted with what is generally accepted to be the culture of the Indo-Aryans lived in the city. All divine figures are depicted according to iconographical norms prevalent in the rest of India. At the same time the physiognomic type indicates the presence of people with Mongoloid features. From the sixteenth century onwards, one notices Islamic influences in the temple architecture. This is evident in the *sikhāra* of the Kāmākhyā temple where a dome is placed over the typical *pancharatha bada* when the Koch king Naranārāyana rebuilt it. This spire was taken as the prototype for the temples built by their successors the Āhoms. Thus, the people of the city had intercourse with the west as well as the east. They were also engaged in a variety of professions to sustain themselves. However, agriculture remained the primary occupation of the people who lived outside the city limits.

In the period fifth-eighth century C.E. the material remains are primarily confined to the area around Nilāchala and Āmbāri. These areas were under the jurisdiction of a ruler with imperial affectation. The growth of this urban settlement probably began from the end of the eighth or beginning of the nineth century onwards when the areas along the riverside near Sukreúvar, and the Uzānbazār area were occupied. The remains indicate that the centre expanded southwards and also to the islands of the Brahmaputra and across the river to the North Bank by the tenth century C.E. Nilāchala and Āmbāri continued in importance. By the thirteenth century the area under habitation had spread further a field on both banks of the river. The hills in the midst of modern Guwāhatī were by now adorned with magnificent temples. The hills on the North Bank were likewise utilised to build temples. The remains indicate that the city had extended up to Kālāpāhār in the south, and the present Chāndmāri region bound by the Rājgarh Road formed its eastern boundary. The Nilāchala and Pāndu marked its western boundary on the South Bank. The Agiathuti range formed its western boundary on the North Bank. The modern town of North Guwāhatī bounded by the Chilāting range and *Momai Kota Garh* up to Dirgheúvarī in the east marks the boundary of the ancient settlement on the North Bank. However, only stray remains in the form of architectural components and rock-cut sculptures mark the location of the important sites in the pre-Ahom period.

In the succeeding centuries the city did not expand much beyond these early boundaries. The paucity of remains in the period thirteenth-mid sixteenth century makes it difficult to determine the extent of the city during this time. The seventeenth century witnessed the construction of defensive ramparts on an extensive scale, which encircled the city on both banks.[28] Some of these ramparts survive to this day.

Inscriptions on stone and rock discovered in the city mark the entry points called *duārs,* during this period. They were five such *duārs* or *chowkis* on either side of the Brahmaputra as corroborated by contemporary literature of the time. The western entrance on the South Bank, called *Duār Garila*, was at the southern foot of the Nilāchala Hill. The eastern entrance called *Jai Duār* was located near Chāndmari. The northern entrance was through the *Pānī Duār* at Latāsil. It was accessible by the river. Another entry point near the river was at Pāndu, to the west of the Nilāchala Hill. The southern entrance to the city called *Dharam Duār* was at Fatāsil Āmbārī. On the North Bank of the river the town "occupies the space within the following passes through the fortified hill, viz. *Kanaibarasibowa, Sillar Chowki, Sindurighopa, Pat Duār* and *Pānī Chowki* or *Korai Chowki.*"[29] Thus, Guwāhātī was a fortified city in the pre-colonial period.

References

1. D. Sharma ed., *Kamarupasasanavali,* 1981, Published by Publication Board of Assam, Guwahati, p. 2.
2. *Ibid.,* p. 227.
3. *Ibid.,* p. 226.
4. *Cited in* K.L. Barua, *Early History of Kamarupa,* 1988 (1933), 3rd Edition, Published by Lawyer's Book Stall, Guwahati, p. 129.
5. M. Neog ed., *Prachya-Sasanavali,* 2008 (1974) 3rd Edition, Published by Publication Board of Assam, Guwahati, Introduction, pp. 145-146.
6. *Ibid.,* p. 146.
7. *Ibid.,* pp. 15-16.
8. *Ibid.,* p.16.
9. *Ibid.,* pp. 7, 22 and 147
10. S.C. Goswami, "Land Grant to the Temple of Umananda at Gauhati by Badshah Ghazi Aurangzeb Salar Khan, 1667 March" in *Readings in the History and Culture of Assam,* 1984, Published by Kamarupa Anusandhan Samiti, Guwahati, pp. 151-155.
11. For details, refer to the Appendix A.
12. M. Neog, *op.cit.* p. 8.
13. S.K.Bhuyan, ed., *Kamrupar Buranji,* 1987 (1930) 3rd Edition, Published by Department of Historical and Antiquarian Studies, Guwahati, pp.108-110.
14. For details see Appendix B.
15. D. Sharma ed., *Kamarupasasanavali,* 1981, Published by Publication Board of Assam, Guwahati, p. 2.
16. *Indian Archaeology – A Review,* 1965-66 (1973), p. 6; 1977-78, p. 77.
17. *Ibid.,* 1968-69 (published in 1971), p. 3.
18. D. Sharma edited, *Kamarupa Sasanavai,* p. 2.
19. D. Sharma edited, *Kamarupa Sasanavali*, pp. 56 ff, H.K. Barpujari edited *Comprehensive History of Assam*, Volume I, p. 130ff.
20. S. Beal, translation, *The Life of Hiuen- Tsiang by Shaman Hwuii Li, Book V,* pp. 172ff.
21. D. Sharma edited *Kamarupa Sasanavali*, p. 20ff.

22. S. Beal trans, *Si-Yu-Ki (Buddhist Records of the Western World),* p. 406.
23. D. Sharma edited *Kamarupa Sasanavali*, p. 20.
24. P. Das, *History and Archaeology of Northeast India,* p. 27.
25. M. Neog edited *Prachya Sasanavali,* p. 108.
26. S.K. Bhuyan edited *Assam Buranji*, p. 93.
27. M. Martin, *The History Antiquities Topography and Statistics of Eastern India,* Vol. V, p. 631.
28. S.K. Bhuyan edited, *Assam Buranji,* pp. 92-94; *Kàmrupar Buranji,* p. 92, v: 161.
29. M. Martin, *The History Antiquities Topography and Statistics of Eastern India,* Vol. V, p. 631.

APPENDICE *for Paper of Paromita Das*

List of Archaeological Remains of Guwahati

APPENDIX A: INSCRIPTIONS

1. Umāchala Rock Inscription of King Surendravarman, 5th century C.E., Nilāchala Hill.
2. Copper Bell Inscription of Śri Kumāra, c.8th century C.E., Narakāsur Hill.
3. Pushpabhadra Copper-Plate Inscription of King Dharmapāla, 12th century C.E., dry bed of the Pushpabhadra River, North Guwāhātī.
4. Kānāi Bārāsi Bowā Rock Inscription, 1206 C.E., North Guwāhātī.
5. Āmbāri Stone Inscription of King Sāmudrapāla, 1232 C.E., Āmbāri.
6. Chandrabhārati Mandap Rock Inscription, c.15th-16th century C.E., North Guwāhātī.
7. Kāmākhyā Temple Stone Inscription of King Naranārāyana, 1565 C.E., Nilāchala Hill.
8. Ganeúvara Pushkārini Stone Inscription of King Herambadhipati Dhununtrarāi, 1577 C.E., Ganeshguri.
9. Pāndunātha (Hari) Temple Rock Inscription of King Raghudevanārāyana, 1585 C.E., Pāndunath Hill.
10. Land Grant with priest of Ūmānanda Temple reaffirming gift of land by Mughul Emperor Aurangzeb. (1667 C.E.)
11. Kānāi Bārāsi Bowā Rock Inscription of Atan Bānhgarhiyā Burhāgohain, Rājmantrin, 1667 C.E., North Guwāhātī-I.
12. Kānāi Bārāsi Bowā Inscription of Atan Bānhgarhiyā Burhāgohain, Rājmantrin, 1667 C.E., North Guwāhātī-II.
13. Pillar Inscription of the Nāmjāni Barphukan, 1667C.E., Fatāsil Āmbāri.(A.S.M.)

14. Ūmānanda Temple Rock Inscription of King Gadādhar Simha, 1694 C.E., Bhasmāchala, in mid Brahmaputra.
15. Ūmānanda Temple Land and Servitor (Paik) Copper-Plate grant of King Gadādhar Simha, 1695 C.E., Bhasmāchala.
16. Ūmānanda Temple Land and Servitor Copper-Plate grant of King Rudra Simha, 1697 C.E., Bhasmāchala.
17. Copper-Plate Land grant of King Śiva Simha, 1715 C.E. (granting land to Brahmans of Kāmākhyā, Pāndunāth and Ugratārā temples).
18. Kāmeúvar Śiva Temple Stone Inscription of King Śiva Simha, 1718 C.E., Nilāchala Hill.*
19. Siddheúvar Temple Rock Inscription of King Śiva Simha, 1718 C.E., Nilāchala Hill.*
20. Inscription on Ūmānanda Vigraha, of King Śiva Simha, 1719 C.E., Bhasmāchala.
21. Asvakrānta Temple Rock Inscription of King Śiva Simha, 1720 C.E., North Guwāhātī.
22. Kurma Janardhana Phalgutsava Temple Rock Inscription of King Śiva Simha, 1721 C.E., Asvakranta, North Guwāhātī.
23. Mandākatā Rampart Rock Inscription of King Śiva Simha, 1723 C.E., near Chandragiri, North Guwāhātī.
24. Kamaleœvara Temple Rock Inscription of King Śiva Simha and Queen Phulesvari, 1728 C.E., Nilachala Hill.
25. Rang Mahal moat Rock Inscription of King Śiva Simha, 1732 C.E., Rang Mahal, North Guwāhātī.
26. Duār Garilā (western gateway) Rock Inscription of King Śiva Simha, 1732 C.E. foothill of Nilāchala Hill.
27. Vijaya Duār (Southern gateway) Rock Inscription of King Śiva Simha, C.E., Sarbāchala, Fatāsil (Kālāpāhār area).
28. Dirgheúvarī Temple Rock Inscription of King Śiva Simha, 1735 C.E., Dirgheúvarī Hill, Rang Mahal, North Guwāhātī.
29. Dirgheúvarī Temple Rock Inscription of King Śiva Simha, 1738 C.E., Dirgheúvarī Hill, Rang Mahal, North Guwāhātī. (II)
30. Dakshin Vijay Duār (Barphukan's *Durbar Mandir*) Rock Inscription, (southern gateway) of King Śiva Simha, 1738 C.E., found in the grounds of Guwāhātī Circuit House.(ASM)
31. Jaya Duār (Barphukan's mantra bhawan) Rock Inscription (northern gateway), of King Siva Simha, 1738 C.E., found near Latāsil. (ASM)

32. Copper-Plate Inscription of *Devottara* grant towards daily puja (worship) at the Ūmānanda Temple, of King Śiva Simha, 1739 C.E., Bhasmachala.
33. Rock Inscription above mouth of a cave, 1685 (Saka or C.E.?), (reign of King Śiva Simha?), Bhasmāchal.
34. Copper-Plate Land grant of Asvakrānta Temple, of King Śiva Simha, 1719 C.E., North Guwāhātī.
35. Copper-Plate Inscription of Ūmānanda Temple, of King Śiva Simha, 1741 C.E., Bhasmāchal.
36. Copper-Plate Inscription of Dharmottara Land grant of Janardana (Visnu) Temple, of King Śiva Simha, 1742 C.E., Sukreœvar.
37. Stone Inscription of Janardana (Visnu) Temple, of King Pramatta Simha, 1744 C.E., embedded in the wall of the reconstructed temple, Sukreœvar(?).
38. Rock Inscription of Amratākesvara (Śiva) Temple, of King Pramatta Simha, 1744 C.E., northern side of Nilāchal Hill at Amrājuri.
39. Sukreúvar Temple Rock Inscription, of King Pramatta Simha, 1744 C.E., Sukreúvar Hill, Pānbazār.
40. Rock Inscription of Durgā Sarovar, of King Pramatta Simha, 1744 C.E., near Nilāchala, to the south of the motorable road to Kāmākhyā. (it is now a swamp, parts of which have been filled up and is under human habitation).
41. Stone Inscription of the Rudreúvar Temple, of King Pramatta Simha, 1749 C.E., Rang Mahal, North Guwāhātī. (ASM).
42. Stone Inscription of Janardana's Phālgutsava Temple*, of King Pramatta Simha, 1750 C.E., found at Sukreœvar. (ASM).
43. Stone Inscription of Phālgutsava Temple*, of King Pramatta Simha, 1750 C.E., found at Nilchāla. (The inscription is now in the office of the temple management).
44. Rock Inscription of Kedāra Temple, of King Rājesvar Simha, 1751 C.E., Nilāchala.
45. Rock Inscription of the Western Ajita Duār of Barphukan's *Sabha Mandir* (audience hall) or *Dopdar* (daftar?), of King Rājesvar Simha, 1752 C.E., Guwāhātī.
46. Stone Inscription on the wall around Rudreœvar Temple, 1752 C.E., Rang Mahal, North Guwāhātī. (King Pramatta Simha initiated the construction of the wall, but it was completed three years later under King Rājesvar Simha. (ASM)

47. Stone Inscription of Navagraha Temple, of Rājesvar Simha, 1752 C.E., Chitrāchala.
48. Stone Inscription on the Navagraha Puskārini, of Rājesvar Simha, 1753 C.E., Silpukhurī. (ASM)
49. Rock Inscription of Manikarneúvar Temple, of King Rājesvar Simha, Rang Mahal, North Guwāhātī.
50. Inscription on silver umbrella covering the Devī-pitha of the Dirgheúvari Temple, of King Rājesvar Simha, North Guwāhātī.
51. Stone Inscription of the Nāt Mandir (utsav-mandir/rang-ghar) of the Kāmākhyā Temple, of King Rājesvar Simha, 1759 C.E., Nilachala.
52. Copper-Plate grant towards daily *puja* (worship) at Sukreúvar Temple, of King Rājesvar Simha, 1761 C.E., Sukreœvar.
53. Rock Inscription of the Vasisthāsrama Temple, of King Rājesvar Simha, 1764 C.E., Vasistha, Guwāhātī.
54. Copper-Plate Inscription of Bhuvaneúvarī Temple, of King Gaurināth Simha. (the date cannot be read as it is in a damaged condition).
55. Two Stone Inscriptions embedded on the walls of the *batsoura* (entrance gateway) of the Chatrāchala Devi Temple complex, of King Kamaleúvara Simha, 1799 C.E., Chatrāchala Hill, Uzānbazār riverside.
56. Copper-Plate Inscription (land grant) of King Mādhava of Kāmarûpa's 25th regnal year, 3rd day of Asvina, Nilāchala Hill.

The following are in the Assam State Museum (ASM)

57. Copper-Plate Inscription of King Gaurinath Simha, 1792 C.E., recording appointment of Katakis at Guwāhātī, as well as donation of lands at Beltolā.
58. Copper-Plate Inscription of King Lakshmi Simha, 1771 C.E., reconfirming *devottara* and *brahmottara* grants made by King Śiva Simha to Siddheúvari Temple; also a plot of land and homestead in Pāndu was granted.
59. Copper-Plate Inscription of King Kamaleœvara Simha, 1800 C.E., recording donation of *paiks* (servitors) to make the *gosain* and *gosani* (icons) of Chatrakāra.
60. Copper-Plate Inscription of King Brajanath Simha, 1818 C.E., donating land to a priest (Bordoloi) in Japorigog village of Beltolā. (It is a forged copper-plate)

61. Canon Inscription of King Udayāditya Simha, 1672 C.E., Curzon Hall (Nabin Chandra Bordoloi Hall).
62. Canon Inscription of King Gaddhar Simha, 1682 C.E., Curzon Hall. (Bilingual)
63. An inscribed copper disc belonging to Rāni royal family, dedicated to a Govinda icon by Smti Dhāritri Rāimātā in 1767 (Saka ?)

APPENDIX B: STRUCTURES

Temples

1. Kāmākhyā (yoni of Devī Sati), Nilāchala Hill.
2. Ghantākarna, to the west of Kāmākhyā.
3. Kedār Kshetra (Siva linga).
4. Amratakesava (Siva).
5. Bhuvaneúvarī (Devī Mahāgaurī), Brahmaparvat.
6. Kāmeúvara (Śiva).
7. Phālgutsava.*
8. Siddheœvara (Śiva).
9. Kamaleœvara.
10. Pāndunātha (Visnu), foot of Visnu Varāha Hill, to the west of Nilāchala.
11. Janardana (Visnu), Sukreœvar Hill.
12. Sukreúvar (Śiva), Sukreúvar Hill. (Hasti Parvat or Hastāchala?)
13. Baneœvara (Śiva), opposite 11 & 12.
14. Ugratārā (Devī's navimandala), near Jorpukhuri, Uzānbazār.
15. Ūmānanda (Śiva), Bhasmāchala.
16. Chandrasekhara (Śiva), Bhasmāchala.
17. Haragauri (Saivite), Bhasmāchala.
18. Urvasi* (Śiva?), Urvashi island near Bhasmāchala.
19. Karmanāsā* (Jalpeúvara Śiva), Karmanāsā island near Urvasi.
20. Chatrākāra (Mangalachāndi), Chatrākāra Hill, Uzānbazār riverside.
21. Navagraha (aniconic nine planets), Chitrāchala Hill.
22. Ganesguri (rock-cut Ganesa), Ganesguri.
23. Lāl Ganesh (Ganesa), Dhirenpārā.
24. Vasisthāsrama (Jogeúvara Śiva), Sandhyāchala, Vasistha.
25. Manikarneúvara (Śiva), North Guwāhātī.
26. Rudreúvar (Śiva), Rajaduar, North Guwāhātī.

27. Dirgheúvari (Devī Durga), Rang Mahal, North Guwāhāti.
28. Asvakrānta (Anantasāyi Visnu), Majgaon, North Guwāhātī.
29. Kurma Janardana (Visnu), North Guwāhātī.

*These temples are no longer in existence.

Other Structures

At Ambari Excavation Site

1. A step well
2. A semicircular footpath
3. Rectangular enclosures with brick walls
4. Two mud wells

At Cotton College Campus

1. Two brick structures
2. A slightly concave courtyard floor with broken potsherds
3. Two mud wells

On the Nilachala

1. A flight of rock-cut steps on the western face of the hill
2. Rock-cut sikharas enshrining lingas
3. An excavated cave on the northeastern face of the hill with an inscription

Ramparts

North Guwahati

1. Narakasur garh from the river to the Dirghesvari Temple
2. Rangmahal garh from Agiathuri Hill to Narakasr garh along with Rangmahal Moat
3. Momaikota garh from Saraighat Hill (Chillar Chowki) to Agiathuri Hill

Guwahati city

4. Jalukbari garh from the Jalukbari Hills up to the Rangali garh
5. Rangali garh from Jalukbari to Nilachala
6. Arjikhowa garh from Nilachala to Bharalumukh*
7. Garhchuk Garh from Jalukbari hills to Fatasil Hill
8. Fatasil garh from the Fatasil Hill to Kalapahar Hill
9. Rajgarh along with Rajgarh moat* from Kalapahar Hill upto Jai Duar Chowki (with a gap at Bhanga garh due to the Bharalu River)

APPENDIX C: ARTEFACTS

Coins

5 undeciphered circular silver coins in the Assam State Museum, North Guwāhātī.

1 circular silver coin of Ghiyāsuddin Iwāz-I-Husain, first Sultan of Bengal, dated A.H. 620.

3 circular silver coins of Sultan Mālik Ikhtiyāruddin Yuzbak Tughril Khān.

Pottery

Toys

Cannon balls

Canons

APPENDIX D: SCULTPTURES

1.	Ganeśa	38
2.	Śiva (icons and lingas)	70
3.	Visnu	63 big and 32 small
4.	Brahmā	4
5.	Devī (including yonipithas)	163
6.	Surya	12 big and 21 small
7.	Miscellaneous deities (Indra, Kubera, Agni, Manasa, Avalokitesvara, Buddha, Tara, etc	57
8.	Other sculptural remains	74

(Including terracotta plaques, animals and other architectural and sculptural motifs).

N.B. The figures take into account only those identified during field study and in published sources.

23

Ojā-Pāli: An Intangible Cultural Heritage of Assam (A Case Study)

— *Purabi Baruah Talukdar*

Cultural heritage refers all type of physical and non-physical object inherited from past to bestow the future generation for many purpose. The cultural heritage whether tangible or intangible has close connection to society. The purpose of keeping the cultural heritage from the past to future is called preservation. Various aspects of intangible culture such as folklore, oral history, language etc. can be understood the best way by traditional art and practices. The intangible cultural heritage is constantly recreated by communities in response to their environment and provides a sense of identity and continuity, thus enhancing the scope of human creativity. Hence, Intangible Cultural Heritage (ICH) or a cultural legacy inherited by means of Folklore too. Besides Folklore, the other aspects of ICH include tradition, customs, language that have a communication from present to future by means of orality. In that sense, ICH basically connected by performance of social customs - the ways and means of behaviours.

The concerned scheme and the project on Preservation was undertaken.This research paper is a part of the project titled '*Māre-gān*: An epic singing performance of Assam' undertaken by UNESCO in the framework of Sangeet Natak Akademy of India under the scheme of 'Safeguarding Intangible Cultural Heritage of Diverse Tradition of India'. The preservation had been taken interested and initiated by various reputed international body such as UNESCO to cherish the identity for future generation. Prior to the UNESCO Convention, efforts had been made by a number of other countries such as Japan, South Korea, the Philippines, the United States, Thailand, France, Romania, the Czech Republic, and Poland to safeguard their intangible heritage have since created similar programmes.[1]

In 2003, UNESCO adopted the Convention for the Safeguarding of the Intangible Cultural Heritage. UNESCO has also created other intangible culture programmes, such as a list called Proclamation of Masterpieces of the Oral and Intangible Heritage of Humanity.[2] The **Lists of Intangible Cultural Heritage** are established by UNESCO aiming to ensure the better protection of important intangible cultural heritages worldwide and the awareness of their significance. Indian cultural heritage included by them in the lists can be cited as Kutiyattam, the Tradition of Vedic Chanting, Ramlila, Ramman, Mudiyett, Kalbelia, Chhau dance, Buddhist chanting of Ladakh etc. The programme currently compiles two lists. The longer Representative List of the Intangible Cultural Heritage of Humanity comprises cultural "practices and expressions that help to demonstrate the diversity of this heritage and raise awareness about its importance." The shorter list of Intangible Cultural Heritage in need of urgent safeguarding is composed of those cultural elements that concerned communities and countries consider require urgent measures to keep them alive.

Ojā-pāli

Ojā-pāli, an orally handed down traditional art form of Assam is significant to her intangible culture. This is a traditional choral singing accompanied by rhythmic body movement along with small cymbals at their hands. The choir comprises of a master (Ojā) and his assistants (pāli). Ojā, the chief of the choir recite as well as perform the traditional verse (*pada/geet*) to the accompaniment of body language and the pālis follow him by playing cymbals at their right hands and taking rhythm on their feet in a certain pace. The performance of the *Ojā-pāli* is kept alive in the memory and handed down from generation to generation with reworking. So, the tradition of *Ojā-pāli* performance is orally transmitted. This is important to mention here that cultural heritage is very much concerned about community creation rather than individual composition.

Ojā-pāli bears the tradition of epic singing in Assam based on written manuscripts as well as oral traditions. Besides the Ramayana and Mahabharata, a number of local epic and their performance are very much handy in various areas of Assam. One of such dominant micro or local epic is *Manasā*. It is a long narrative about the legendry power of snake deity widespread among various groups and sub-groups of Assamese community.[3] Few previous studies reveal that the spirit possession and religious integration of tribal belief system perceives *Manasā* worship in the villages of West Assam. Today Manasa *pujā* is become a community celebration to bring fortune and wellbeing to the society of Tribal and Animist Hindus. The indigenous people of Assam believe in the legendary power of the snake deity and worship her to get protection from the poisonous snake bites.[4] The narratives about *Manasā* are a combined form of different stories added to it in different periods from long past.There have also been observed different style of performing *Manasā* singing[5] in other parts of Assam which has almost similar version of narratives in relation to goddess power and superiority. Different manifestations of this epic singing at various performance level are-

(a) *Suknānni Ojā-pāli*, follows the composition by the poet Sukabi Narayandev.
(b) *Bixaharigān* follows the composition by Durgabar and Mankar.
(c) *Paddā-puranargān* follows Sukabi Narayandev performs during marriage ceremony.
(d) *Māregān* follows the traditional songs of *Manasā.*
(e) *Tukuriā Ojā-pāli* follows traditional *tukuriā* song.
(f) *Gitālugeet* follows traditional songs of *Manasā.*
(g) *Manasā* geet follows traditional songs of *Manasā.*

(Sharma, 1996: 68-86)

Among these, orally practiced *Māre-gān* of Pati-Rabhas has been contended songs in local dialect along with body movement, distinctive rhythm and tune.

Māre-gān: *The case study*

Although there are found a number of variants of *Ojā-pāli* in Assam, this paper will discuss about the case of Rabha tribe. The *Ojā-pāli* form popular among the Pati-Rabhas of West Kamrup and East Goalpara is known as *Māre-gān* or *Māregua Ojā-pāli*. The performing group has one leader called Ojā and his assistants generally may be counted from 8 to 12 members are called as Pāli. The performers sing the traditional verse *paddapuranar geet* or *may awantibisahari* songs of the oral epic about the goddess of serpent on the auspicious occasion of *Bisahari Puja* during the Assamese calendric months Chot-Bhada (March-August). The songs mainly describe the *lilas* or *maya* of the serpent goddess *Bisahari*. The *Māreguā Ojā-Pāli* and an embodied performance called *Deodhani* are the key feature of Bisahari ritual worship.[6] The project has been carried out taking the village 'Mandalgram' and 'Bornamjuli' of Goalpara (East and Middle) as the empirical sites to witness the contextual performance and to conduct preservation process.

The Community

Rabhas are the one of the nine Scheduled Tribes in the plains districts of Assam mostly scattered in the undivided districts of Goalpara, Kamrup and Darrang. Besides Assam, their distribution spreads over Meghalaya, Bangladesh, Nepal, West Bengal and Manipur. As per 1971 census, they constitute 8.63 per cent of the total plains tribal population of Assam and 0.63 per cent of the State population. Dr Grierson held the view that the Rabha was a Hindu name of the Kacharis[7] (cited by Bordoloi *et al,* 1987: 128). However, the Rabhas has certain groups and subgroups amongst which Pati-Rabhas are the most advanced section of the tribe had adopted Hindu customs for all intents and purpose and due to loss of their mother tongue had taken to speak a pato is of the Assamese language. The Pati-Rabhas are quite numerous in the southern bank in the belt stretching from Guwahati to Dudhnoi. Previous scholars found them as animists in their religious outlook although influenced by Hindu culture and used to celebrate pan-Indian festival such as Durga Puja, Ganesh Puja etc. They are the followers of both saktism and saivism along with the traditional faith in animism. The Rabhas and its different groups celebrate their ritualistic festivals which relate more or less to their own religious concepts and beliefs. The Pati Rabhas of South-East Goalpara and South-West of Kāmrûp institute '*Mārepujā* or *Mārāipujā*' to propitiate *Bishahari* regarded as the most important festive occasion of much socio-cultural importance. Goalpara is the westernmost district of Assam in the Brahmaputra Valley, spread over both the banks of the mighty river Brahmaputra.[8] The people are *Rājbansi, Bodo, Rabha, Garo, Hazong, Jugi, Kalita, Doms, Bhuimālis, Hirās and Kumārs, Nāpits, Phulmālis.* The heaviest concentration of the Rabhas is in the south bank of the Brahmaputra in the present Goalpara district, among whom there are both the Assamese-speaking semi-Hinduised groups and those retaining their old tribal ways.

The Oral Tradition and Expression in Māre-gān

Oral tradition is basically orally transmitted the lore by means of folk tales or narratives over generation after generation without knowing the authorship. Most of the oral forms incorporate performances or some activities to get more communication. *Ojā-pāli* might be such an example of performance of the then community culture to reach to the public. *Māre-gān* is the traditional *Manasā* songs performed in a form of group singing called *Māreguā Ojā-pāli* contains four to eight persons where *Ojā* is the leading singer and *Pālis* are the assistants. These songs are expressed in a form of folk theatre, customs and rites, sacrifices, art and an embodied practice *Deodhani*. The dramatic performance featuring verse songs, dance and acting which is also considered as the part of ritual. The ritual ensues the Assamese calendric month *Chot* (March-April) during when rainfall is started. The ritual is performed as a series of events that can be observed as *adhivās* (pre-phase of worshipping), *gham burani* (plummeting of pottery and settle), *sakudān* (vision of the divine), *deohākura (*welcome/calling of deities), *dak* (a state of trance), *bali (*Sacrifies), *thagi* (remnant of blessings or grace), *rangilā* (amusement). The ritual endures interesting folk art of image making and painting on pith/paper. The paintings are the various episodes of songs mostly the story of *Beula*.

Methodology

The performance of verbal art is more than words.[9] It's not easy to make a clear distinction between the boundaries of music and speech. Singers and narrators employ similar vocal devices.

The study of text and contextual approach is the main focus of Folklore. The text is the performed narratives (verbal and non-verbal) that retain in singing, body movement and dramatic interplay. The lore derives from the text of singing i.e., oral literature and orality handed down in support of performance. The singing and dancing during the performance of the narrative help them to recollect the synchronise steps of body movements and the narratives. This also signifies about how they recollect the epic. The stages of Folklore research included collection, classification and analysis. To textualise the folklore text with the help of translation and match the text with gesture, other features of performance, expression etc. help to understand setting of the ritual.

Contextual convention which is different from everyday speaking set up expectations for aesthetic performance. Performance as a cultural behaviour for which a person assumes responsibility for presentation to an audience, not merely culture, nor behaviour but something creative, realised, achieved, even transcendent of the ordinary course of events. A cluster of interacting variables characterises a performance event. Because of the aesthetic mode of communication, the text allows the audience to perceive the performance. The text is always to be read or interpreted. In case of performance as a text it may be a live performance or may be a textual record/report.

Hence, the folklore text and performance text both are interrelated to understand the orality or the transmission.

The entire *Māre-gān* performance is very long and completed in three nights and four days in the auspicious occasion of *Manasā* puja. What's artistic about the performance is that the performers create and recreate the ritual objects including the deity's welcome to the seat of induced altar (temporary). The usage of language/text of singing yet another important dimension of its aesthetic transaction. The religious faith and the convention of the social wellbeing encourage public to patron the performance musically.

Māre-gān *Performance: A field based report*

The report has been written on the basis of observing the ritual more than three times by the different singing group in a same temple of Mandalgram village.

- **Setting:** *Mareguā Ojā-pāli* is hired to any temple of shakti worship including serpent goddess. Because of the folklore text, the performance is limited to only rites and ritual context. The epic performance reflects that the deity Paddā comes every year and takes seat at the temporary altar of *Maju* of the ritual space. The ritual is held annually (April-August) and continues for several days with the help of divine possession. Empirical experience of *Māre-gān* performance at Mandalgram Paddya Mandir during stipulated season is known as *Bisahari puja*. *Māre-Gān* that is documented at this temple is situated at the Dudhnoi village of Goalpara area. During this festival, the space is decorated which has cultural significance. Various offerings such as rice powder, fruits, grains, milk, flowers, herbs etc. are given to the deity to receive her good will and propitiate the destructive urges. *Māre-gān* as a ritual progression as well as a folk ensemble is hired with a Deodhanito this village. *Māre-gānguā Ojā-pāli* helps the Deodhani, the ritual specialist to call upon the deity into her/his body and disseminate the blessings. Musically, possession is marked at a distinct point of the epic singing. The moment of possession and goes into the trance by the Deodhani is ritually very important. The using of temple space, water body at a particular time schedule on the ritual days are however, do not forbid the freedom of musical creativity/flexibility by the Ojā-pāli singers.
- **Tradition:** The tradition of performing *Māre-gān* can be viewed under the following events. The songs are like the processor to lead the ritual until the end of the *pujā*. The events perform at a specific time to bring the actual mood for the stories are to be narrated. These events are considered under emic point of view given by the traditional bearer.

1. Pre-phase of worshipping-*gusanigagua* (awakening deity).
2. Plummeting of Pottery and settle-*gham burani.*
3. Making divine flower garden *Malanchkamani.*
4. Vision of the divine-*Sakudān.*
5. Welcome/calling of deities-*DeoHākura.*
6. State of trance *bhardak.*
7. Sacrifies-*Bali*

Besides, the dramatic interplay plays a crucial role to establish a communicative mode between the audience and the performing artists. The amusement part to create the laughing atmosphere during the epic singing is performed in accompaniment of drum beats only. One of the palis dressed up like a clown and use to entertain the audience with their simple steps.

The sung version of the epic

It is important to mention here that the epic singing comprises creation songs, origin of gods-goddesses, rituals, the story of 'Beula' and '*Jhunageet*'.

Māre-gān begins with the **invocation** as the initial phase of *Mārepujā.* The invocations are termed as *Bahanisirasti* which invite the gods and goddesses to take seat at the altar. *Bahani* indicates the style of performance i.e., to invocate in sitting position while *sirasti* indicates the creating. The singers invite them to take seat at the place of performance. This phase is known as *gusānijaguā* or *gusāijàgani* begins in the evening time of the previous day. It might be resembled with the concept of *Adhivās* of Sanskrit vocabulary and understood as the preliminary ceremony to solemn a rite which is propitiated generally the previous day. The purpose is to awaken the deity concerned in the temple. There are two kinds of *Maraipujā-Phoolmarai* and *Bharmarai*. The *Bharmarai* last for four days and four nights whereas the *Phoolmarai* for three days and two nights.

The initial invocation depicts the 'seat of singing' inviting the goddess of music/learning. This is the prayer songs of Saraswati *(saraswati vandana).* She is described as the daughter of □ *isi* Brahma and wife of Bishnu. She is invited to situate at the throat of the singers so that the presence of Saraswati enables them to sing.

***Pada*/verse *and* translation**

Aainebulemaosaraswatiāminābalangāi
(Others say 'ma' to you Saraswati, we don't say 'ai')
Amar kanthatmaosaraswatibasiyāloibathāi
(O mother Saraswati take seat at our voice)

Amar kanthacharimaosaraswatiaainarkanthatjābi
(O mother Saraswati, if you go from our voice to another)
Duhāilāge dharma ānadimāthākhābi
(kindly think at least Dharma Anandi)
Madhyegitālarmastakcharhimaosaraswatilāharikhelāba
(You play *lāhari* and depart from the Gital who sits in the middle)
Karna nālexumābimaosaraswatimukhnālebāir hoi jābi
(O Saraswati, you enter through the hole of ears and goes out through the mouth)
Duhāilāgemaosaraswatiānandirmāthākhābi
(Kindly think at least Dharma Anandi)
Dinatfuribimaosaraswatiswetanākauwahoiyā
(O Saraswati, you travel as a white or black bird in the morning)
Gadhulāāhibimaosaraswatigitalxungariyā
(In the evening, mother Sarasawti, you come back to the Gital players)
Hātenajānangmoi e tālmandirāmukhenajānangmoigeet
(I don't know how to play *mandirā* by hand and sing songs by mouth)
Saragatesirajilebiyālākhitārāmunisatexirajilegeet
(The sky creates stars, and human creates *geet*…)

(Summary: Goddess Saraswati, please come and take rest at our voice and our hands, so that we can sing and play cymbals and blessed by you. Like the sky creates stars, we create songs, if you go somewhere in the morning as a bird kindly come back to us in the evening and so blessed by Anandi Gohai)

Next invocation is the 'installation of seats'. The form consists of invitation of *Barmani* to the temporary altar, creation of ritual objects, cymbals cast in the same pattern of lines which makes the prayer sounds repetitive. The link to the Manasā epic is inserted between the list of the owner (Mareyā) of the ritual and the group performers (gital-pāli-dedhani).

The most important accompanying musical instruments i.e., the cymbals as well as the ornamental anklet of the Ojā are all washed and placed over a banana leaf together beforehand in front of their sitting arrangement. After the second invocatory piece the 'creation of cymbals' are sung and the pālis take cymbals in their hands to proceed the next songs. This is a ceremonial way to a rhythmic begin of the ritual playing the cymbals by the pālis. This part describes how the cymbal makers *(kahār)* dreamt by the goddess Barmani after her installation in the space to make cymbals and anklets and give them to the Ojā-pāli.

The next invocation is performed in the standing stance known as *uthasirasti*. This is the prayer to goddess (*deviiswar*), main gods (Brahma, Bishnu, Maheswar) and various other gods of *Indrapuri* (court of various omnipotent gods in heaven under the king Indra). They all are awaken towards the seat of installation. An outline in praise of goddess Bisahari is also complementary.

Thus, in invocations, the choir Māreguā Ojāpāli pray the homage to various gods and goddesses. All the other gods that are deemed important are then invited to the altar one after another such as Saraswati, Brahma, Bishnu, Maheswar, Indrupuri gods and goddesses, Krishna, Narayan, Lakshmi, Gohain, Basumati, Nag-nagini, Risiajagar etc. Later, when other gods are invited, the formula addressing Barmani is regularly repeated with different other epithets of her such as *padma, mainarbisahari, bengkhaowakani, kanibeti, padmamala* etc.

The gist of performance on invocatory piece is to awaken various gods and goddesses at the point of ritual by means of possession. This is significant during the next phase of singing i.e., during the songs of creation *(sirastipātan)*.The singers are dressed informal while in sitting point and the standing part is performed with proper costume of significant uniform colours.

The songs of creation (*sirastipātan*) actually start with the creation songs of cymbals *(tālsirasti)* at the sitting position immediately after first invocation. The *sirasti* indicates here is the world/universe and *pātan* indicates the beginning. The third invocation leads to the songs of creating the universe and the stories on Creator of the universe or *ānandigohāi* as well as a couple of birds *(pakhu-pakhiyani)*. *Pujā* begins informally with the mix up sounds of the beating of the traditional drums *nāgārā* and *dhol*[10] in the late evening. The *nāgārā* is already a permanent ritual object of the temple placed up at the right side of the goddess idol. *Dhols* are carried by the *Ojā-pāli* performers during this pujā.

Songs of origin of gods and goddesses begin with the narrative of Durga *(Durga Janam)* and continue until the epic proper i.e., the birth of snake deity (*padmājanamgeet*). The story of Beula is yet another important narrative of the *Māre* songs. According to the story, Beula is victimised and become a widow on her wedding night because of the discord between the snake deity Manasā and the merchant Chandosadagar. Beula's husband Lakhindhar, the youngest son of Chandosadagar is bitten by snakes and she promises Chando to bring her husband's life back for no reason. Manasa wishes to be worshipped by Chando, who declines her wishes. Chando finally admits to do so as Beula able to keep her promise. Beula brings her husband Lakhindhar's life back after she has overcome the tricks and mishap created by Manasa. This narrative is ritually performed.

The **rituals** adhere to the *Māre-gān* are Deodhani and settlement of *Maju* performance. The ritual objects such as banana leaves *(kalpāt)*, brass pot *(ghati)*, the fan *(bisan)*, the stick *(don-dāli)*, the lighting arrangement *(sāki-bāti)*, iron sword *(dā)*, rice *(sāul)* etc. are used by the *Deodhani* performer. *Deodhani* is the shamanistic performer (female) who possesses divine power.

Jhunageet are the inclusion to the *Māre-gān* as a part of the folk life. These songs have no direct connection to the faith or the context of the performance. In fact, these are mostly composed in satirical way to represent a contemporary social livelihood. These are mainly the colloquial speech performed on request from the audience.

There has been collected three *Tāl*-rhythmic variety of *Māre-gān* viz., *khartāl, ekktāl, dui tāl.*The naming is based on the concept of the rhythm.

- ***The style:*** The style of the *Māre-gān* performance is lead by the Ojā. He initiates the singing part that has been observed as a formal beginning of the each of the verse. The Ojā recites the lines and repetition is customary by the *palis*. The pālis assist him to repeat the lines and continue the pace. They take the rhythm with the help of cymbals playing and spontaneous foot works. The language, tone and composing style of the songs is very much inherited to local/Rabha culture. The Ojā wears a traditional anklet at his feet, traditional garment *dhoti-chola* and scarf *fali* with a white cotton turban. The pālis also use to wear uniform garments such as *jāmā* (long scart with number of plates on waist) and *fāli*. They call their shirts as *jersi*. There are no such dancing postures but the pālis perform in circle behind the Ojā and often take turn to frontage and back. They perform facing the seat of the altar until the end of the ritual. The entire scenario of the performance can be considered as ritual theatre. The discord with *Chandoadāgar* with the snake goddess *Padda* is more popular because of its dramatic routine. The performer is mainly the female who possesses spirit. The pālis (one pāli at a time) take part in the scene by changing the appearance (applying make-up on face or wearing coloured dress code) during ritual interlude. The *Maleyā*, the local artisan who makes the *Maju* is ceremonially remunerated during performance events.

- ***Lore:*** The lore or the knowledge handed down from past generation refers to the knowledge system embedded in cultural traditions of the local communities. Traditional knowledge is found in various skills, know-how, practices maintained by the people. This is also included the ecological knowledge, local architecture, climate etc. *Māre-gān* is so much close to the Pati Rabha tribe that the reflection has been seen in their daily life-in the sect of social customs and beliefs. The concerned believe narrative on *Bisahari* and her discord with a merchant has achieved a religious faith among the devotees for whom every act in the performance is sacred. Few belief and customs derived from *Māre-gān* closer to Rabha society may be cited here as:

1. Belief on goddess Bisahari is that she comes every year to receive the offerings and provide power and prosperity.
2. Custom of keeping the altar of *lakhardeo* at east side of cow poultry.
3. Custom of keeping a hole at the south corner of every house.
4. Sitting custom of bride and groom on marriage.
5. Belief derives from marriage of Birds.
6. Belief on the poisonless cobra etc.

Findings, Analysis and Preservation

The following model[11] (Fig. 23.1) shows the elements, factors and an interrelationship involved in artistic verbal performance, and in addition, distinguishes verbal art performance from other speech communication. According to this model and further discussion given by E. Fine, that Performance is not only perception of communicative process, but an aesthetic mode of communication (Fine, 1994:87). The record and report of the text are represented by the text maker highly depends on the hermeneutic act of translation. The text maker must decode an aesthetic transaction (manifested through observable behaviours) and re-encode that transaction in another medium, for another audience, so that they participate vicariously in the original performance (*ibid:* 88).

Māre-gān is an admixture of verbal and non-verbal art may follow the basic concepts of Performance approach[12]:

(a) An Aesthetic mode of communication.

(b) Integrally related to a particular event.

(c) Culture specific and cross-culturally variable.

Although there is a number of stories and knowledge inherited into them is the subject of *Māre-gān*, there are few such stories such as *Beula*

Lakhindhar which is very closer to the community. For them, this narrative is sacred. The folklore text is the verbal art used by the performers to communicate and express the tradition. The performance has a close connection to Serpent goddess and integral towards spirit possession and exorcism. This can be found mostly in the tribal belief system.

- ***Performance text:*** The live performance witnessed at the villages has been recorded. The performance has been observed more than three times and found hardly any changes. The songs have invocation part in the beginning of the performance viz., 'seat of singing' and 'installation of seat' where the performers perform in sitting position. The tone and the gesture show a bowing nature to the deity. The anklets and the cymbals to be used are placed in front of them considering them as sacred.

  There is refrain and verse. The last part of the refrain repeatedly performed by the pālis. In many places of the songs, the pālis surround the Deodhani and perform clockwise and anticlockwise motion. One emphasised rhythm on feet in support of the fluidity of the verse yet another significant of the performance tradition. There is also rhythmic variation playing cymbals and foot works to control the flow of the performance.

- ***Folklore text:*** The oral literature of the performance has been textualised and then translated. This is important to mention here that the songs are expressed by the Deodhani in very many symbolic ways. Usage of vermillion (sindur) and fan, stick etc. are remarkable in this regard.

  As the language of text is the local Rabha dialect, the communication is plausible to the audience. The poetics nature of the texting has given the singing version an aesthetic mode of communication and attention.

  The audience has no high expectation from this ritual performance but curious about the traditional route of performance and outcome. There has been observed a change in the ritual reducing the duration of the ritual days from seven to three.The requirement of preserving the traditional singing is not only preserving the form but also the content which is the reflection of a mass creative process with natural environment. The performing genre of this region is undoubtedly attached with the tradition of *Katha* or narration along with rhythmic dance. This became a source of knowledge which was disseminated by the male folk. The condition of traditional

Māre-gān singing is very downward today as performers are not able to find out their security of daily livelihood out of this practice.

- ***An interview with a traditional bearer:*** Pradip Rabha, a practitioner of *Māre-gān*, of age 42-43 years, has been practicing the form since his early age. Besides a seasonal performer of *Māre* songs, Pradip Rabha is a farmer and his livelihood depends mainly on agriculture. The members of his troupe live nearby and they practice almost every evening at his (he is the leading singer or the *Ojā*) place of residence. His locality Barnamjuli is 6-7 km away from the centre Dhupdhara of Goalpara region. This village has a mixed population of Rabha clan.

  Pradip Rabha started his professional singing career as *Pāli* and later got promotion to sing as *Ojā,* the leading singer. He has been practicing *Māre-gān* since last 28 years. He has altogether 16 persons in his group who used to travel in the villages as professional Māre-gān singers. Among them, there are two Ojās, one *deodhani* dancer and rests are pālis. There is a good harmony among the Ojas, pālis and deodhani performers. The entire sung version and practice is orally transmitted till date with the presence and guidance of the *gor*[13] *Ojā.* The active performers' in the group are-

  (i) Pradip Rabha (*gor* Ojā).

  (ii) Haricharan Rabha (*gor* Ojā).

  (iii) Thaneswar Rabha (*aag*[14] pāli).

  (iv) Kanu Rabha (*aag* pāli).

  (v) Octob Rabha (*pās*[15] pāli).

  (vi) John Rabha (*aag* pāli).

  (vii) Brajen Rabha (*aag* pāli).

  (viii) Bhubneswar Rabha (*aag* pāli).

  (ix) Yadav Rabha (*pās* pāli).

  (x) Anima Rabha (deodhani)

The transmissions of the songs are orally handed by the previous singers and this is experienced as really a harsh by P. Rabha. He sings from memory which is the only way to learn *Māre-gān*. In his words,

My guru was Jugeswar Boro. It was very difficult to recollect the lines in the beginning. I used to see the book[16] *and try to remember. I could not gather the courage to sing and performed many years as pāli. I had*

> *no confidence to sing but later I could do it due to the support of my seniors and my own dedication and faith on the goddess Manasā. Each time, I practiced 35 lines of one paragraph in the paddy field where nobody was present and nobody could see me singing the lines. Because it is very difficult to perform in public. I believe that if I could sing at least 35 lines, it might help the other singer to take little relax/rest. This thought helps me to get into the practice more deep and finally the leadership. It took a long time to acquire the practical knowledge of Māregeet...I guess there are about 300 paragraphs in the Māre-gān and there are also some innumerable additional songs. We sing the songs on the occasion of Durga puja, Kali puja, Kamakhya puja, Thakurani puja, Padda puja, Banabasi puja...*
>
> *...But if these songs are so important even today, why are we not properly hosted? We need changes of their (Villagers) hosting customs and this is, I guess, a distance hope. I am intended to go outside or to towns to attain income and secure my livelihood. Oja-pali given me depression in these villages in my daily livelihood and I can see deterioration of my health because of spontaneous elongated performance. I am willing to give up this profession.*

In this circumstances where the performer has no longer hope to continue it neither transmitting the profession, then who will continue the form? This is the threat for the tradition.

The idea of preservation has been designed in order to focus the dignity of the performer as well as to preserve the singing approach are as follows:

- The form has been encouraged to preserve the bodily practices by means of traditional ritual or other.[17]
- The singing has been recorded to bring it into the mass with the help of digital medium.
- A new context has been created to redefine the space of the form.

The measures of preservations are taken on the basis of usage of body and space. The dissemination, on the other hand, was central to promote and encourage the form and practices. The third point has been visualised to look at the form as a scheduled Art performance. The data has been collected such as various kinds of *tal* and content of the songs.

Data has been created by organising a training workshop of *Māre-gān* taking the rhythmic movements as a focus. It has been tried to preserve and work out on the dance and movements. The workshop was held at

Barnamjuli, Goalpara from 2nd-14th December, 2014. The venue of the workshop is at the residence of the collaborator while a presentation had occurred at the yard of the temple of their village. In this temple, the villagers also organise the ritual for one day and perform *Māre-gān*. The workshop has been given by Pradip Rabha who is also a collaborator of the project. There were another two participants of new generation of the respected tribe joined the workshop to begin their basic steps of the dance.

The workshop, however, could not cover the songs related to *Maju, Jhunageet* and *Deodhani* dance. It is believed that once they start their singing about a particular verse, they by hook or crook have to complete the story within it. The workshop was successful as it has tried to encourage and uplift the traditional singers along with two newcomers into the tradition. Data has been collccted on invocation part and few circular movements frequently use in between the performance. A new space has been created to present the form. This transportation will help to transform and minimise a desired area within the limitation of performance. Besides, a VCD has been made on contextual performance of the ritual (April 2014) and transporting performance (December 2014).

In many places of the singing, the singers are unwilling to come out the periphery of the ritual. The *Māre-gān guaoja-pali* performance has been decontexualised from religious moorings in the workshop and a final presentation was organised at the premise of village temple.

Proper preservation may serve to raise awareness of intangible heritage and provide recognition to communities' traditions and know-how that reflect their cultural diversity. The preservation is required to reveal the traditional way of understanding creation and natural contacts. The important is to preserve the belief and so the form. This preservation will help us to understand who we are and enable us to become who we want to be. Despite of accepting the fact that Folklore has its own seed of deconstruction, this is wiser to preserve the past and regenerate the positive force in our lives. I conclude by what Mark E. Workman stated that if we look at the viewpoint of the dynamics of Folklore, it can be said that by preserving the past, however dynamically, folklore does not simply provide a reservoir of traditional troupes for the definition of self. Instead, the bequest of tradition is as much a gesture of negative repression as it is an endowment or legacy that makes the future possible. As such it guarantees that, sooner or later, successive generations will reject that repression in order to experience, however tenuously, their own freedom (Workman, 1996:35-40). Thus, preservation will help to create and recreate the folklore.

Notes

1. Taken from Wikipedia. in
2. This list began in 2001 with 19 items and a further 28 were listed in 2003 and another 43 in 2005 (ibid).
3. It has been debated if *Manasā*, which is closely connected with the worship of the snake goddess *Manasā*, can be considered as an epic or a cycle of epic songs but according to L. Honko's definition.
4. It has all the qualities of an oral epic.
5. Different epithets has been found on *Manasā* at various level or sub-level of West Assam such as *Bishahari* (one who heals poisonous pot), *Padmāwati* (one who bears lotus, the flower), *Paddā* (which may signify 'of lotus'), *Barmāni*, *Mārai* (goddess of pestilence), *Kāni* (blind of one eye), *Totalā* (stammerer), *Bāhurā* (separated or lonely).
6. *Manasā* songs have been found composed by three poets, viz., Mankar, Durgabar and Narayanadev. Sukabi Narayandev was the most prominent among the three who lived in between the 16th and the 17th centuries. *Suknnani Oja-pali* follows Narayandeva's version of *Manasā songs* in Sipajhar of Darrang district.
7. *Manasā*, the Hindu serpent goddess is told as the wife of *Anadi Guhai* (godhead) in the oral epic among the Pati-Rabhas. Instead, more appropriately, Bisahari is the term used for the serpent goddess which means inhalator of poison.
8. The Bodo-Kacharis of Assam are the original autochthones of Assam as has been pointed out by Rev. S. Endle in his renowned work the 'Kacharis'. In Upper Assam they are identified as Sonowal and Thengal Kachari, while in the western Assam they are popularly Boro or Boro-kachari. They are belong to the great Boro group of the Indo-Mongoloid family within the Assam-Burmese linguistic section.
9. 'Goalpara, however, never formed part of the Ahom Kingdom and though it is one of the districts of Assam valley, it belongs more to Northern Bengal than to Assam proper' (cited by B. Dutta, pg 2).
10. E.C. Fine (1994, pg no.1).
11. Traditional drums of Assam.
12. The model is taken from the analytical essays on performance by E. Fine.
13. *Ibid.*
14. *Gor* means initial or main. Hence *gorojā* means the main leader.
15. Aag means beginning or front. Hence the aagpāli means the pālis in the first row.
16. Pās means backside. Hence the pāspāli means the pāli singers in the second row.
17. He might have indicated some personal notes or records by himself or by the other learners.
18. There had been conducted a training-cum-workshop to implement the idea of preservation of body movements of *Māre-gān*. This was worked out in the area of Goalpara (Bornamjuli-Dhupdhara) with the help of the collaborator.

References

Baruah, B.K. (2003), *A Cultural History of Assam,* Guwahati: Bina Library.

Baruah, L.K. (1999), *Oral Tradition and Folk Heritage of North-east India,* Delhi: Spectrum Publication.

Bhattacharjee, Kishore. (2006), *Constructing Community, Gender and Kinship through Epic Singing,* Indian Folklore Research Journal (ed.) M.D. Muthukumaraswamy, Vol. 3 (6):1-12.

Bordoloi, B.N., G.C. Sharma Thakur and M.C. Saikia (1987), *Tribes of Assam Part-I.* Guwahati: Tribal Research Institute.

Dutta, Birendranath. (1995), *A Study of the Folk Culture of the Goalpara Region of Assam,* Guwahati:University Publication Department.

Fine, Elizabeth C. (1994), *The Folklore Text*, Bloomington: Indiana University Press.

Goswami, P.D. (1995), *Festivals of Assam,* Guwahati: ABILAC.

Honko, Lauri. (1998), *Textualising Siri Epic,* Helsinki: S. T. A. S. Fennica.

Kaeppler, Adrienne L. (2000), *Dance Ethnology and the Anthropology of Dance*, Dance Research Journal, Vol. 32(1): 116-125.

Rabha, Praneswar (ed.). (1987), *Mayavanti Bisahàri* or *Dakhin Goalpara Mare Geet Sangraha.* Guwahati: Published by editor with the financial assistance of The Tribal Research Institute, Assam.

Rangacarya, A. (1986), *The Nàm yaúàstra,* New Delhi: Munshiram Manoharlal Publication.

Sharma, Nabin (ed.). (1993), *Padma Purana,* Guwahati: Bani Prakash.

(1996), *Asamar parivesya kala Ojà-Pàli.* Guwahati: Bani Prakash.

(2012), *Manasà Kàvya*. Guwahati: Bani Prakash.

Vatsyayana, K. (1980), *Traditional Indian Theatre,* New Delhi: NBT.

(1981), *A study of Some Traditions of Performing Arts in Eastern India Margi and Desi Polarities,* Guwahati: Gauhati University.

(1987), *Traditions of Indian Folk Dance,* New Delhi: Clarion Books.

Workman, Mark, E. (1996), *Folklore and Freedom*, Journal of Folklore Research, Vol. 33(1): 35-40.

24

Eating Habits and Indigenous Cuisines of the Karbi Tribe of Kamrup District, Assam

— Ritu Geu Goswami, Mini Bhattacharyya Thakur

Introduction

Eating habits and the methods of preparation of foods is a distinct identity of Karbi culture and form an intrinsic part of their heritage. The present paper reveals the indigenous food cuisines and the method of preparation and eating habits among the Karbi of Assam. Assam is well-known as a land of varied socio-cultural elements with many tribes and non-tribes staying together maintaining their own identity in terms of food, eating habits and indigenous methods of preparing foods. The tribal population presently living in the state of Assam are the Chakma, Dimasa, Garo, Hajong, Hmar, Karbi, Khasi, Naga, Bodo, Barman, Deori, Mech, Mising, Rabha, Sonowal, Tiwa, etc. The other inhabitants are the Hindus, Christians, Sikhs, Buddhists and Muslims. Beypi and Biswas (2012) in a study of the Karbi tribe mentioned that Karbi tribe is culturally very rich and unique with some of the cultural markers such as dress, food, festivals, myths and language.

Eating habits and the methods of preparation of food among the Karbi is unique as the Karbi of Kamrup district is able to conserve the cultural heritage in terms of food. The indigenous preparations of cuisines which were very traditional and have come down from generations are still prevalent among the Karbi. The food cuisines are prepared by using foods available in and around them and also by using simple methods of cooking. The food cuisines were very nutritious. The food habits and method of preparation helps to preserve the nutrients which indirectly help to maintain good health and nutritional status among children, adolescents, adults and in old age.

In-depth research is required to analyse the nutrient content of the foods used by the Karbi as the method of preparation of foods and use of indigenous herbs and plants are blessings in disguise for maintaining good health among them. In the present research paper, an attempt has been made to know the eating habits and indigenous cuisines of Karbi of Kamrup district of Assam.

Research Methodology

The present study was undertaken among Karbi women of Kamrup district of Assam. The objective of the study is to understand the eating habits and inclusion of indigenous cuisines of Karbi tribe. The data was collected from 15 villages and 400 women respondents where Karbi population was densely populated. Focus group discussion was conducted in every village to collect data on eating habits and method of preparation of cuisines included in their day-to-day life and during festive and special occasions. It was analysed thematically. Two blocks of Kamrup district i.e. Chandrapur and Dimoria were selected as these two blocks were densely populated by Karbi population. Chandrapur which is a semi-urban area is located approximately 15 km from Dispur, the capital of Kamrup district. Due to its hilly terrain Karbi tribe were found densely populated along with other non-tribes. Dimoria is in outskirt of Guwahati city and has several communities including Karbi, Tiwa, Boro, Rabha, Garo, Tea Tribes and some others living together.

Results

Food habits, eating and cooking practices were found to be integral part among Karbi community. Eating habit means the way by which the people select the food they want to eat. It also depends on the food available in the nature or market. Making the food appealing and appetising to one and all in a family depends on the knowledge of the food and its preparation.

Eating Practices among the Karbi Women

Eating practices varies region wise, state, religion, caste, tribe, etc. and depends on socio-economic condition of the family. It may be mentioned that eating main meals i.e. breakfast, lunch and dinner were considered in the study. Taking little snacks and tea were not considered as main meals. Maximum (62 per cent) of Karbi women population of the studied area ate main meals three times a day (Table 24.1). First meal is taken in the morning at 7 am to 8 am followed by lunch at 12 noon. The last meal for the day was taken in between 8 pm to 9 pm. Women who ate meals two times a day was 22.25 per cent. Marak (2007) reported the Garo tribe of Meghalaya consumed three meals a day consisting of rice and a dish. It was observed that the families who had two time meals were not present during noon. Male members goes either to office, business or field and female members engage themselves either in household work or field. The children go to school or colleges. The Karbi women who had two times main meals mentioned that as they take a heavy breakfast in morning, they prefer to take tea with puffed rice laddu or biscuits if they feel hungry during lunch time. Very few (15.75 per cent) takes meals more than three times per day as they prefer to take an additional meal at 3 pm to 4 pm. Lyall (1997) in a study among Karbi tribe mentioned that Karbi take first meal at around 7 am to 8 am which consists of rice and the evening meal is cooked after the day's field work.

Table 24.1: Eating practices of Karbi women (15 years – 49 years)

Eating practices	*Total*	*(Per cent)*
2 times	89	22.25
3 times	248	62.0
More than 3 times	63	15.75
Total	**400**	**100**

Foods most commonly eaten during meals: All tribal groups residing in India as well as in Assam prefer non-vegetarian foods. Mittal and Srivastava (2006) found that all Oraons tribe of West Bengal were non-vegetarian. They consumed pork, rat, meat, beef and various birds. Another study conducted by Saikia (2012) on food pattern of tea tribes found majority of people prefer non-vegetarian food.

Karbi tribes of Kamrup district were non-vegetarians. Foods which are commonly eaten at meal times were rice, green leafy vegetables, fresh fish, dry fish powder (*hukoti*), dry fish (*oakreng)* and meat. The frequency of consuming most preferred food of the Karbi women is present in Table 24.2.

Table 24.2: Frequency of consumption (per week)

Days/week	*Rice*	*Green leafy vegetable*	*Fish (fresh/dry)*	*Meat*
1-2 days	-	24 (6)	-	90 (22.5)
3-5 days	-	153 (38.25)	72 (18)	85 (21.25)
6-7 days	400 (100)	223 (55.75)	328 (82)	225 (56.25)
Total	**400 (100)**	**400 (100)**	**400 (100)**	**400 (100)**

Rice: The staple food of Karbi is rice. All the three meals viz. breakfast, lunch and dinner Karbi tribe prefer to take rice. In some of the indigenous cuisines, rice powder (*pithaguri*) was used as a key ingredient. Cereals are one of the most important sources of energy and carbohydrates. A study conducted by Marak (2007) reported that staple food of Garos, a tribe of Meghalaya was rice.

Green leafy vegetables: Karbi include one or the other type of green leafy vegetable in every day meals. Green leafy vegetables are rich sources of micronutrients i.e. vitamins and minerals. The preference for indigenous green leafy vegetables such as *kasiduria* (Fig. 24.1), *silpat* (Fig. 24.2), *panjari* (Fig. 24.3), *mayongsak* (Fig. 24.4), *bahekatita* (Fig. 24.5), *mandhania* (Fig. 24.6), *gunkochu* (Fig. 24.7), *bihdhekia* (Fig. 24.8), *Kosu* (Fig. 24.9), etc. were more than other vegetables like cabbage, brinjal, ladies finger, etc. Karbi use herbs like coriander (*dhania*), herb of grace (*brahmi*), asiatic pennywort (*manimuni*), shunkvine (*vedailota*), mint (*pudina*), lemon leaves (*nemotenga pat*), curry leaves (*narahingo pat*), etc. for flavour and taste. Herbs are very nutritious and their inclusion in regular diet among Karbi gives them immunity to body.

Figure 24.1

Figure 24.2

Figure 24.3

Figure 24.4

Figure 24.5

Figure 24.6

Figure 24.7

Figure 24.8

Figure 24.9

Fish (fresh/dry):Karbi like fresh as well as dry fish. They prepare fish with bamboo shoot and green leafy vegetables. Dry fish is prepared with chillies, onion, garlic and tomato. Another delicacy mentioned was dry fish prepared with alkali called *khar/phelo*. The Karbi prepare dry fish by putting it in boiling water with white gourd, garlic and ginger and adding *khar* to it. They do not use turmeric when in the delicacies prepared with *khar*. A traditional recipe is prepared with dry fish by roasting the dry fish and making it into paste with red chillies, ginger and garlic. The chutney is very hot and it is liked by one and all.

Dry fish is stored in bamboo tubes for around one year and this dry fish is called *hukati*. The Karbi women mentioned that as non-tribal Assamese people use oil in their special recipies, Karbi put *hukati* in each and every item like vegetables, green leafy vegetables, etc. The Karbi people mentioned that during rainy season when the ponds and rivers are flooded, all men and women go together for fishing and collect fish in plenty. They dry the fish by putting them in the above bamboo shelves (*bhanglang*) of the kitchen where lit the firewood (*Chullah)*. The fish gets dried and the dried fish is filled up in the bamboo tubes and kept in dry place. The dry fish becomes like powder and they put the dry fish powder while cooking any kind of vegetables. *Hukati* have a strong flavour but when it is cooked it gives a pleasant aroma.

The liking for non-vegetarian food is found among tribes of other districts. Moitra and Choudhury (1991) stated about 4.3 per cent of Mals, 2.9 per cent of Kumarbhags and 1.8 per cent of Saurias and 7.2 per cent of Santhals ate fish/meat regularly. Dry fish is relished by all the tribal population of northeastern region. *Jaguanakam* is the dry fish which is liked by Garo tribe of Meghalaya and prepared by roasting, boiling, steaming, in alkali and in mustard oil. Marak (2010) in a study of *jaguanakam* (dry fish) mentioned that inclusion of the dry fish lies in gastronomic appreciation and habitual consumption. Jonsson *et. al*. (2007) revealed that dried fish was very rich source of proteins, containing 80-85 per cent of protein. A study conducted by Muzaddadi *et. al*. (2013) mentioned in a study of ethnic fish product prepared by Mishing tribe that food processing techniques like drying, smoking and fermentation are compatible means of preserving fish for scare fish seasons and a partial solution to protein malnutrition.

Meat: Among meat Karbi prefer pork and mutton more than other meats. They mentioned irrespective of the quantity, even a small piece of non-vegetarian food satisfies their satiety level and they can have enough rice without any other curries or vegetable. They cook non-vegetarian with spices and oil like the modern delicacies but prefer boil meat prepared with vegetables like colocasia tubers, potatoes and green leafy vegetables. Boil meat is prepared by marinating the meat (mutton/pork/chicken) with ginger-garlic paste and adding to boil water. It is cooked till the meat is tender and before serving lot of chilli is added to give a hot taste. Qamra (2006) mentioned in a study of Bhil tribe of Madhya Pradesh that although all Bhils are non-vegetarian and extremely fond of consuming fleshes of animals and birds, yet its consumption was limited to only ceremonial and festival days. Mittal and Srivastava (2006) also mentioned that the use of non-vegetarian items among Oraon tribes was limited to two to three times a month usually on days when they are paid for their work. The consumption of non-vegetarian items among Karbi seems to be more and it was observed despite of the income level of the respondents, they prefer non-vegetarian items most frequently. Basumatary (2012) studied traditional food habits of Bodos and mentioned meat especially pork is highly prised means of diet and an essential item in the Bodo society.

Method of Cooking Indigenous Food Cuisines of Karbi Tribe

Tribal cooking methods are little bit different from non-tribal people. Tribal prefer cooking with less oil whereas non-tribal prefer oil. Present study among the Karbi found that the most common methods used for cooking were *kanthu* (wrapped in banana leaves), *kemang* (cooked in bamboo pipes), *kangdang* (roasting), *keok* (boil in salt and spices/steam), *hang-lanthung* (boil with salt), *ka-bhaji* (frying with oil), *kephi* (smoking in stick). All Karbi irrespective of their financial status prefer foods cooking without oil. Teronpi *et. al.* (2013) studied indigenous knowledge of management of fish resources and revealed that hill Karbi cook fish by *kangthu* and *kemang* method. Another study by Saikia (2013) on food habits in pre-colonial Assam mentioned common modes of cooking were boiling, steaming, frying, grilling and baking in banana leaf and minimum use of oil.

Kanthu: In *kangthu* method, the food is wrapped in banana leaf and smoked in red hot burning charcoal (*angotha*)/ hot iron pad (*tawa*). Fresh fish and vegetables are prepared with this method. Fresh fish is mixed with salt, turmeric, ginger, garlic, red chilli, *mandhania* and marinated in a banana leaf. Then the banana leaf is wrapped and tied tightly. The wrapped banana bundle is put in hot charcoal/ hot iron pan till it is cooked properly (Fig. 24.10).

Kemang: In *kemang* method, dry fish and green leafy vegetables such as colocasia, lettuce leaves, etc are cooked in bamboo tubes with one closed end. The colocasia (*kola kasu*) leaves and stem are cleaned and mixed with dry small fish, turmeric, spices and salt. Mixed ingredients are filled up in

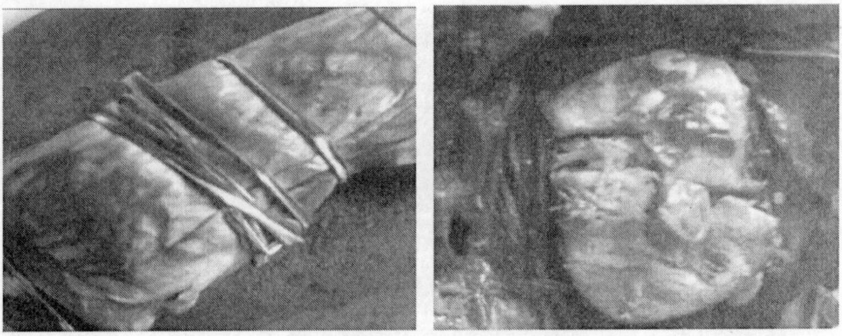

Figure 24.10: Fish in banana leaf* (kanthuaoak) *by* Kanthu *Method.

fresh bamboo tube with mouth covered with banana leaf. Then the bamboo tube is burnt in firewood till the food is cooked (Fig. 24.11). In between the vegetable is stirred in bamboo tube with a stick. The fish prepared by *kemang* method is a delicacy among Karbi irrespective of any age group.

Figure 24.11: Colocasia and dry fish in bamboo tube (*Hendukimungaahaan*) by* Kemang *Method.

Kangdang: Grilling especially non-vegetarian foods like fish and meat over hot charcoal on an open fire or by using wire mesh in direct heat or heated charcoal is known as *kangdang*. Fresh fish is marinated with salt, turmeric and spices and are grilled in wire mesh over hot charcoal (Fig. 24.12).

Keok: The method of cooking food by boiling with spices and steaming in Karbi is known as *keok*. Method of steaming is nutritious as the foods do not come in contact with water directly and food is cooked in steam. So the water soluble vitamins are retained in the foods. Steam cooked foods are light, fluffy and easily digestible. Yuan *et. al*. (2009) revealed that steaming method of cooking is best in retention of the nutrients in cooking broccoli.

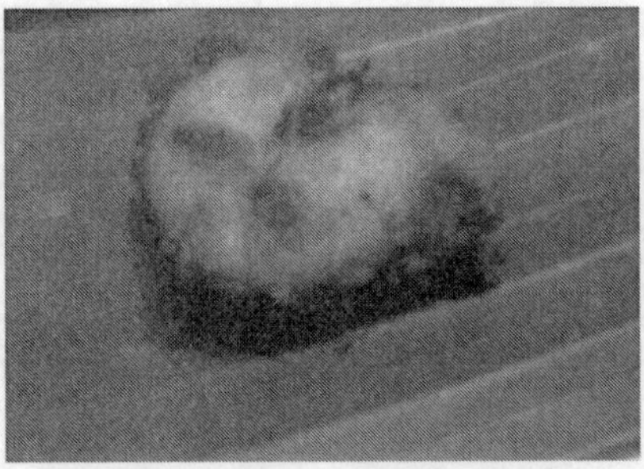

Figure 24.12: Fresh fish grilled in wire mesh by* Kangdang *Method.

The Karbi tribe mentioned that usually vegetables and local chicken is prepared with this method and is a remedy for persons suffering from cough and cold. Spices like turmeric, onion, ginger, garlic and pepper is added along with salt. The use of pepper gives relief from cough and cold. Fig. 24.13 shows local chicken prepared by *keok* method.

Figure 24.13: Local chicken with spices by* keok *method.

Hang-lanthung: Cooking food by boiling with salt is known as hang-lanthung. Usually vegetables, pulses and meat are prepared with this method. Fig. 24.14 shows red gram dal (*masur dal*) cooked with wild plaintain flower (*paharikaldil*) with salt.

***Ka-bhaji**:* Frying method of cooking uses fat or oil as a medium of cooking. Shallow fat frying uses fat as well as water to cook the food. In Karbi frying with oil is known as *ka-bhaji* but this method of cooking is not so frequent. Mutton, fish and vegetables are cooked by this method. Fiddlehead fern (*dhekia*) is fried with potatoes, salt and turmeric (Fig. 24.15).

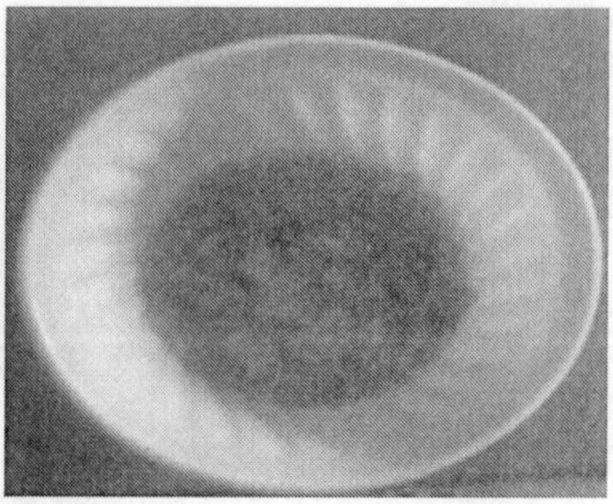

Figure 24.14: Boil dal with plaintain flower* (angdungpihuk) *by* hang-lanthung *method.

Figure 24.15: Fiddlehead fern* (dhekia) *by* ka-bhaji *method.

***Kephi**:* Cooking fish in stick by method of roasting in direct heat is known as *kephi* among Karbi tribe (Fig. 24.16). The heat seals the outside part of the food and the juice inside the food cooks the food. Roasting is mainly used when cooking fleshy food like fish, meat or chicken. When heat is applied to the outer covering of the food, it seals it up thereby trapping all the juices inside the food. The action of direct heating, heats up the juices inside the food, which then cooks the food. In this method of cooking nutrient loss is minimum and the flavour of the food is retained. Idah *et. al.* (2013) reported nutrient content like protein, fibre, lipid and ash content of smoke dried fish increased from the initial values and moisture level decreased. The smoked (*puramaas*) fish mashed with salt, chilli, ginger and garlic and taken as chutney (Fig 24.16).

Medium used for cooking indigenous cuisines: Most cuisines were prepared using alkali (*khar/phelo)*, sour foods (*hanthor*) and oil. The cuisines prepared by using alkali and acid as a medium of cooking is known as *kangmoi* and *hanthor* respectively.

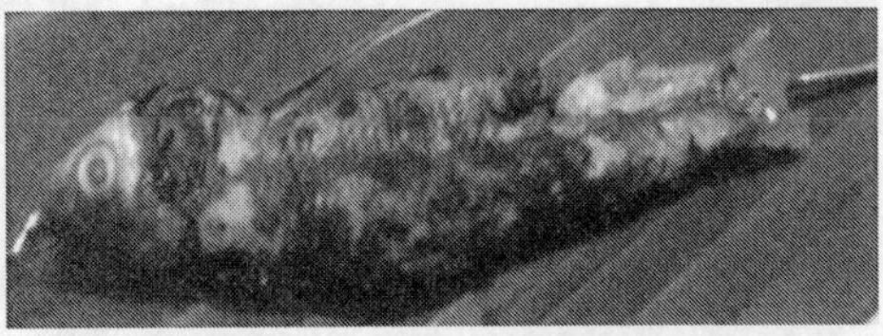

Figure 24.16: Small fish is roasted in direct fire (*kephi *method).

Kangmoi: The alkali used is known as *khar/phelo* which is prepared by burning stem of banana plant and peel (*athiakal/bhimkal*). All alkaline preparations are known as *kang-moi*. Fig. 24.17 and 24.18 below gives two indegeneous cuisines prepared by using alkali (*khar*). Colocasia (*Kola kasu*) leaves and steam is cleaned, skin removed and cut into small pieces. Chilli, garlic and ginger are grinded in the traditional Indian stone grinder. A pan is heated and the colocasia with grounded chilli-garlic paste is added. Then alkali is added and boiled till the colocasia is cooked properly. Dry fish powder and salt is added before the colocasia is finally cooked (Fig. 24.17).

Ingredients: Colocasia leaves (*Kola kasu*), chilli, ginger, garlic, dry fish powder (*Hukati*), alkali (*Khar*), salt to taste

Macronutrients: Carbohydrate, protein, fat

Micronutrients: Iron, calcium, potassium, magnesium, Vitamin A, C, K

Figure 24.17: Colocasia with dry fish powder using alkali (Hendru Fule Along Kitoon Aahan).

Curry leaves is cleaned and made into paste with chili, garlic and ginger in traditional Indian stone grinder. A pan is heated and the curry paste with spices is added. Dry fish and alkali is added till medium thick consistency is maintained. Salt is added for taste (Fig 24.18).

Han-thor: Karbi like sour cuisines also. Most sour cuisines are prepared by using bamboo shoot (*upthor/ hanguk*) which is prepared by method of fermentation. All sour cuisines are known as *han-thor* and predominate

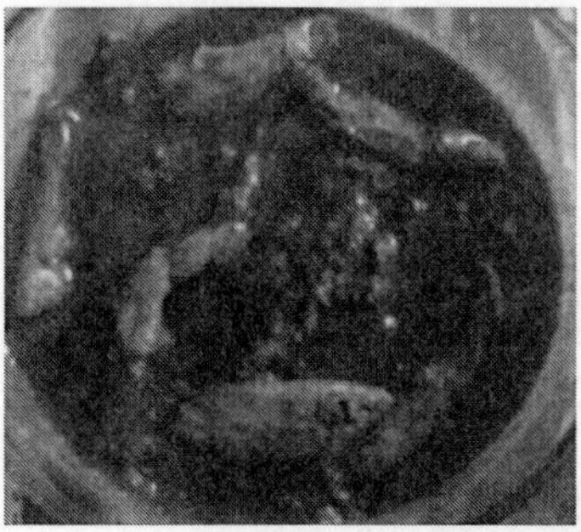

Ingredients: Curry leaves, chilli, ginger, garlic, dry small fish, alkali (*Khar*), salt to taste

Macronutrients: Carbohydrate, protein, fat

Micronutrients: Iron, calcium, vitamin A, C

Figure 24.18: Curry leaf curry with dry fish using alkali (Norosinghoarusukanmaas).

among Karbi traditional cooking. Bamboo shoot is also an integral part of Karbi community. Both tribal and non-tribal population of north-eastern region consume bamboo shoot either fresh at the time of harvesting, dried, fermented and picked which is taken around the year. Bamboo shoot contains valuable nutrients. Nongdam and Leimapokpam (2014) studied the nutritional facts of bamboo shoot and found that shoot contains high content of useful proteins, amino acids, carbohydrates, and many important vitamins and minerals and low in fat. Goswami (2012) mentioned that each 100 g of young bamboo shoots contains 3.28 g of proteins, 4.47 g carbohydrates, 22 mg calcium, 56 mg phosphorus, 0.1 mg of iron. They are low in fat (0.13 g) and sugar.

Ingredients: Small fresh fish, ginger, garlic, bamboo shoot, oil, coriander leaves, rice flour, salt to taste

Macronutrients: Carbohydrate, protein, fat

Micronutrients: Iron, calcium, phosphorus, vitamin C

Figure 24.19: Small fish prepared with fermented bamboo shoot (hanthor).

Oil: Although use of oil is less among the Karbi tribe yet in some indigenous cuisines oil is used. Chicken, fresh fish, vegetables, etc are prepared with oil. Karbi respondents mentioned that bottle gourd is an indispensible part of Karbi culture and used in many cuisine and also during marriage and worships. Teron (2005) in a study among Karbi tribe mentioned that the seeds of bottle gourd are believed to have been gifted by a Karbi God, *SongsarRecho*, the creator to the ancestor of the Karbi and till today gourd seeds are considered as one of the assets of the tribe. Fig. 24.20 depicts a cuisine prepared with bottle gourd and oil which is relished by all people of Karbi community.

Ingredients: Bottlegourd, potato, onion, ginger, garlic, chilli, onion stalks, oil, salt to taste
Macronutrients: Fat
Micronutrients: Calcium, phosphorus

Figure 24.20: Bottle gourd prepared with oil.

Special foods: Two indispensible cuisines i.e. pork cooked in fig leaves (*dimoruapa*) and fish prepared with bamboo shoot (*hanthor oak mas*) are relished by Karbi and a must during marriage and special occasions.

Dimoruapa: Pork with fig leaves is the most special cuisine among all Karbi tribe. In every special occasion like marriage, engagement, name giving ceremony, arrival of guest, etc. the cuisine is prepared with love and care. This cuisine is part and parcel of their life. The preparation is very simple. Pork is cooked with fig leaves, alkali, garlic, ginger, chilli, spices, salt, etc. When the meat is cooked properly, raw rice powder is added. Special dish is liked by all age groups.

Ingredients: Pork, fig leaves, ginger, garlic, chilli, rice powder, alkali (*khar*), salt to taste
Macronutrients: Protein, fat
Micronutrients: Iron, calcium, phosphorus, vitamin B and C

Figure 24.21: Pork with fig leaves (dimoruapa).

Hanthor oak mas: Sour cuisine is also a special food cooked during marriage and other occasions. Karbi include dry fish in every meal and in the usual cuisines oil is not added. But this special cuisine is sour prepared with bamboo shoot and oil. Fresh fish is fried in oil and kept aside. Then fermented sour bamboo shot is fried in oil with ginger, garlic and chilli. Water is added and when it starts boiling fried fish is put and cooked till the fish becomes soft. Before finishing raw rice powder, salt and a spice mixture containing 12 indigenous spices is added for flavour and taste. The fish dish is a liked by all.

Ingredients: Fresh fish, bamboo shoot, rice powder, oil, ginger, garlic, chilli, local spices, salt to taste
Macronutrients: Protein, fat
Micronutrients: Iron, calcium, phosphorus, Vitamin C

Figure 24.22: Fish with bamboo shoot (hanthor oak mas).

Hor: The Karbi of Kamrup district is still following the age old tradition of preparing *hor* (home-made rice beer) by fermentation method. Teron (2006) in a study mentioned use of *horlank* in marriage and worship is customary and mandatory among Karbi people. Highly concentrated rice beer in small quantities is used among rural masses to cure dysentery, pharyngitis and cholera. The preparation of *hor* may be differ from region to region among Karbi for availability of resources. Lyall (1997) also mentioned the preparation of *hor* among Karbi of Karbi Anglong. In Kamrup district, *hor* is prepared in every Karbi household. The preparation was found to be very simple. First the rice (any variety) was cooked properly and cooled. Then *bakorguri* (a substrate) which is bought from the market is mixed to the rice and kept for one to two hours. In the meantime, big colocasia leaves are spread in the floor evenly so that no floor is seen. In the colocasia leaves the rice is spread evenly and the rice is covered with colocasia leaves and the covered rice is kept for 24 hours. Care was taken to keep the room free from any disturbance of people. After 24 hours it was mentioned that a sweet smell of the beer comes out and water oozes out from the rice. The rice with the water is poured into a clean container or big drum according to the quantity of the rice beer prepared. More water is added to the rice and this is kept as such for another two more days. After two days, the rice with the water is strained which is kept in the bottle. It was reported that the rice beer can be kept for around one year and with time the rice beer becomes very clear and with ageing the colour and taste increases. Das *et. al.* 2012 in a study on methodology of rice beer preparation in some tribal communities of North East India found that the fermentation process is carried out in earthen pots and starter cultures are locally procured and the method of preparation of almost same which are followed by the *Boro*, *Karbi*, *Ahom*, *Mising*, *Deori*, *Dimasa*, *Kachari* and *Angami* tribes. *Apong* an alcoholic beverage of Mishing community is an indispensable part during festivals and rituals and in social life (Pegu *et. al.* 2013). Traditional home made rice beer of the tribal is nutritious.

Ingredients: Rice, substrate.
Macronutrients: Carbohydrate, protein, fat
Micronutrients: Calcium, sodium, potassium, iron, phosphorus

Figure 24.23: Home-made rice beer (hor).

Festive foods: Different types of *pitha* (dumplings), *lobong-han* (special non-vegetarian foods), *hangbangchuk* (green leafy vegetable), etc. are prepared during festivals like *Dehal rongkher* and *nangte.*

Dehal rongkher: This festival is celebrated in first Tuesday of *Phagun* month (coincides with February and March). All Karbi people pray in Karbinamghar. They take *prasad* with soaked whole bengal gram (*boot*), soaked whole/ split green gram (*magu*), fruits, roasted dry rice powder (*sangsirik*). All Karbi people lit lamp (*chaki*), *incense* sticks (*dhoop*), etc. and pray to God for blessing of well being of the family members. After prayer, *prasad* and fruits are distributed. In the evening, a goat is sacrifice and the meat is distributed to one and all. The meat (*prasad*) is prepared with banana stem (*posola*) in a nearby shelter (not in the *namghar*). At night after *naam* the *prasad* known as *lobong-tan beokhan* is distributed to all. Sometimes, if the people feel they prepare rice to be taken with the *prasad* but otherwise the Karbi people mentioned that rice is not compulsory.

Nangte: *Bihu* of Assam is celebrated by all tribal and non-tribal people. Among Karbi, in all the three types of *Bihu* they pray to family God in their home. After praying in the morning, they have breakfast at around 7 am consisting of dry rice powder (*sandahguri*), jaggery, dumplings (*pitha*), rice cakes, etc. with tea. Dry rice powder and jaggery is a must among the Karbi tribe which is taken in dry form. After the morning meal the male member go to out to with the cattle to a water source like a pond, river or deep open non-plugged cultivation field etc. The elderly girls and married adult women go to the hills to collect green leafy vegetables. It is a tradition to collect green leafy vegetables (108 varieties) and distribute among all the Karbi families. The 108 varieties of green leafy vegetables are known as *hangbangchuk**. The Karbi people mentioned that due to urbanisation if they are unable to collect 108 varieties, they at least try to collect 44 varieties. A chicken is given on sacrifice to family God. The sacrificed chicken is cooked with the collected green leafy vegetable. So, the lunch consists of rice and local chicken cooked in 108 types of green leafy vegetables. In

Bihu all men and women take home made rice beer (*hor*). In dinner, the Karbi tribe prepare the sacrifice local chicken prepared with oil, spices and dry rice powder.

*(*Hangbangchuk:* Consists of local leafy vegetables and herbs such as *dhekia, panikasu, sengmora, bihdhekia, mayong, gun kasu, suwat pat, mani muni, demoru, narahingo, silpat, mesta, sarat pat, germini bon, motmotitenga, alongabur pat, bedailota, arpisanmsra, gorloti pat, sanmah saw, kasiduria, hannehrang, behuritita, satna, kasi pat, dhoriada, gomarish, oakengsak, belurisak, rupesuwat, sungsung, kumu, hanmekimi, mesenga, rikundu, pipali, tululuwang, katiribhul, kothal pat,* etc.*)*

Conclusion

Karbi indigenous cuisines and its method of preparation were unique. It was happy to note that the Karbi tribes of Kamrup district are able to preserve the intangible cultural heritage till today. The cuisines were rich in macronutrients i.e. carbohydrates, protein and fat. The cuisines were also rich in micronutrients (vitamins and minerals). It can be concluded that the indigenous methods of food preparations and the type of food consumed in day-to-day life, special occasions and festivals among the Karbi should be encouraged and conserved as the indigenous cuisines were nutritious and balanced in macro and micro nutrients.

References

Basumatary (2012)
Beypi and Biswas (2012)
Das *et. al.* 2012
Idah *et. al.* (2013)
Jonsson *et. al.* (2007)
Lyall, 1997
Marak (2010)
Marak N.R. 2007
Mittal and Srivastava (2006)
Moitra and Choudhury (1991)
Muzaddadi *et. al.* (2013)
Nongdam and Leimapokpam (2014)
Pegu *et. al.* (2013).
Qamra (2006)
Saikia (2012)
Teron (2005)
Teronpi *et. al.* (2013)
Yuan *et. al.* (2009)

25

Matrimonial Laws of the Bodos of Assam: Impact on Women

— R.P. Athparia

The Bodos

The Bodos are numerically and anthropologically one of the most important tribes of North East India.The generic name Bodo was first applied by Hodgson (1880:1). The first ethnographic account on the Bodos of Assam was published by Rev. Endle in 1911 in which they were referred to as **'Kachari'**. They were recognised as a Scheduled Tribe after Independence. In the **Ahom Buranjis** (historical account of the Ahoms), the Bodos is referred to as 'Kachari' (Bhuyan, 1951). The European scholars like Hodgson (1880) and Grierson (1903) had used the terms 'Kachari' and 'Bodo' interchangeably to refer to this linguistic group of Assam. Grierson (1903) identified them as Indo-Mongoloid group of people belonging to the Tibeto-Burman language family. At present, the members of this community prefer to call themselves 'Boro' whereas those who are leading the movement for their right of political self-determination prefer to use the term **'Bodo Habitat.'**

Assam is the home of the Bodos. Their main concentration is now on the northern bank of the Brahmaputra River starting from Dhubri and Kokrajhar districts, Goalpara district in the west, to Dhemaji and Lakhimpur districts to the east.

The Bodos are the single largest tribal group in Assam constituting 45 per cent of the plains tribal population of Assam. They have heavy concentration in the Lower Assam region, presently under the Bodo

Territorial Autonomous Districts (BTAD) comprising of four districts, namely, Chirang, Kokrajhar, Baska and Udalguri.

The Census of 1951 has clubbed Bodo-Kacharis including Sonowal Kacharis which stood at 3.64 lakh against 3.46 in 1961. In 1971 census, the total Bodo population stood at 6.10 lakh whereas in 1981 estimated Bodo population in Assam was 7.41 lakh. In 1991, the total population of Bodos stood at 11.84 lakh, which has increased to 13,52,771 in 2001. In 2011 census, Bodo population is recorded as 13,61,735 in Assam. As a result, the percentage of Bodo population to total population of Assam decreased from 4.53 per cent in 1951 to 4.17 per cent in 1971 and then increased to 5.28 per cent and 5.53 per cent in 1991 and 2001 respectively. In 2001 census, the Bodo population was 40.90 per cent to the total scheduled tribe population of Assam and in 2011 census the Bodo population is 35.05 per cent to the total scheduled tribe population of Assam. In 2011 census, there is an increase of 0.66 per cent Bodo population from 2001 census.

The growth of Bodo population as compared to the increase of State's population is reflective of their greater ethnic consciousness and accurate reporting of their numbers in census reports as already stated. Majority of Bodos in Assam lives in the rural areas. As per 1991 population census, out of 11.84 lakh total Bodo-speakers only 21,259 persons were in urban areas, which was only 1.79 per cent of the total Bodo-speakers in Assam. This clearly reflects the basic characteristic of 'isolation' as generally found in any tribal society (Borah, 2006:7). In 2011 census, rural Bodo population is recorded as 96.17 per cent. As regards to sex ratio, census data of 1991 exhibits that males outnumbered females. The sex ratio of the Bodos was found to be 975 females per thousand males as against the state average of 925 in 1991. In 2011 census, sex ratio of the Bodos is recorded as 994 as against the state average of 985. Although Bodo population is scattered all over Assam, their concentration is the highest in four districts, namely, Kokrajhar, Chirang, Baska and Udalguri in the Bodoland Territorial Autonomous District. Apart from these areas, a large number of Bodo populations are found in the districts of Nalbari, Barpeta, Darrang and Sonitpur.

Significance of the Study

The prime concern of our study is to analyse the status of Bodo women in matrimonial spheres. The study intends to explore the impact of modernisation and the customary laws on the tribal women of this region. In terms of its customs and traditions it showcases greater diversity within itself. The tribes have different historical experiences, social organisations, cultural values, religious identities, economic systems and degrees of exposure to modernisation and commercialisation. These forces have defined their identities and influenced women status at different stages of life. So our study makes an attempt to understand the different spheres of discrimination of women in the transitory of modernisation, such as introduction of various constitutional laws and amendments that protects the rights of women after marriage and divorce determining their economic status and various recent changes through a comparison between political and social sphere. In this process we believe that the real impact of modernisation is not totally benefiting the tribal women thereby making them inferior and more conservative within their customs in comparisons to rest of the country.

Objectives of the Study

If the society has identified women in equal to men, then can we truly say that the women are given equal status in relation to men in our society? As we all know that the problems of women are more pertinent in comparison to men in our society, so are all the welfare schemes of the government really benefitting them to improve their status in the society or they are just confined to live as a backbone or a supporting agents of the male-dominated society? These questions are important because the thinking behind tribal development is to bring about a qualitative improvement in their lives. How much of it has been realised and achieved? As the world is rapidly marching towards global modernisation so in this process are the Bodo population especially the women are being left out by choice or by purpose? Is there any way out, to make a positive mark in the age of modernisation, which will truly identify and take along with it both modernisation and status of women hand in hand in the process of gender equality? Having these questions in mind we articulate the following objectives:

1. To assess the transformation in the process of modernisation in order to analyse the status and gender inequality of Bodo women in marriage and matrimonial laws.
2. To understand the traditional customary law of marriage among the Bodos and the changes that have occurred in it because of modernisation in social, economic, religious, educational, administrative and other changes.
3. To understand how these changes have affected the Bodos as a whole and women among them in particular.
4. To determine the processes that affects Bodo women adversely and suggests remedial measures.

Choice of Villages

For the present study ten villages were selected, namely, Tila Para, Dewrigaon, Dolakati, Purani Goraimari, Bajrajhar, Mathanguri, Lechera, Hathinapur, Bakua, Simla. Out of the ten villages, two villages were selected from urban and two from the semi-urban and six from the rural areas. Villages, namely, Tila Para, Dewrigaon, Dolakati, Mathanguri, Lechera and Bokua are rural villages; Purani Goraimari and Simla are semi-urban and Bajrajhar and Hathinapur are urban villages. Table 25.1 shows that altogether 120 samples from 6 males and 6 females of ten villages have been collected for the study.

Table 25.1: Sample Bodo Villages with Gender

BODO

Village/Sex	*Male*	*Female*	*Total*
Tila Para	6	6	12
Dewrigoan	6	6	12
Dolakati	6	6	12
Purani Goraimari	6	6	12
Bajrajhar	6	6	12
Mathanguri	6	6	12
Lechera	6	6	12
Hathinapur	6	6	12
Bokua	6	6	12
Simla	6	6	12
Total	**60**	**60**	**120**

Women and Matrimonial Law

The 2010 Marriage Law Amendment Bill was primarily meant to make divorce easier by the inclusion of irretrievable breakdown of marriage as a new and more liberal ground for divorce in the Hindu Marriage Act, 1955 and the Special Marriage Act, 1954. Women's organisations and groups have, however, opposed the bill on the ground that making divorce easier in the Indian context would adversely affect the interests of women who have extremely limited rights on separation and divorce. At present, maintenance is the only claim that a separated wife and children with her can make. Women's organisations like the All India Democratic Women's Association (AIDWA) and others have pointed out that neither Indian law nor policy recognises the wife as an equal partner in the marriage and that unless women get an equal right to marital property, women's financial situation post-divorce would worsen.

Therefore, the women's organisations have taken numerous steps to strengthen the rights of women after divorce and the consequence of such action was the introduction of the amendment to the Marriage Law Amendment Bill 2012 should be redrafted to make it mandatory for the court to order that both immovable and movable property acquired during the subsistence of marriage be divided equally between the wife and husband. It has also been suggested that the court should take into account any disadvantage suffered by the woman or the children with her and give her a further share of the property (Singh, 2012:17).

Flavia Anges in an article, *His and Her's,* she has discussed at length about how women folks undergo the issues related to the marriage and division of property at the time of divorce. In India, men have been regarded as the primary bread earners whereas women as homemakers. She further says that, in order to facilitate this process, a woman is expected to sacrifice her career and totally dedicate herself to the task of caring him. In this process she is also expected to take the task of homemaking, childbearing, and child rearing, and caring for the sick. Even if she is required or permitted to work, it is mostly to augment the family income. Her earning is treated as thc family's supplementary income (Agnes, 2012:11).

The above critiques show that the contribution of married women as homemaker spouse has no economic and social position in the society. We shall now see what are the customary laws that a woman has to marry and compete with men in a job market? It is to see whether marriage is the cut-off point of the Bodo women. A woman who does not marry may get partially or completely left out of this because of the absence of a cut-off point. It is also to examine the partition of parental property, particularly when linked with an inherited means of livelihood is heavily biased in favour of sons for socio-economic reasons. Lastly, it is to see whether marriage as the cut-off point, the son may rightfully seek partition, and in the process leave the entire responsibility of his aging parents to his unmarried sisters irrespective of her economic resources. She, on the other hand, is unlikely to demand partition as this would sever her from the only family she has. The question of entitlement through marriage does not arise. This is the only deprivation (in addition to the biological one) that is fully known to the woman, and in this respect alone does she make an informed choice. Other economic deprivations mentioned above generally come as bitter surprises gradually over a period of time and a woman is in no position to make an informed choice about them.

Bodo: Matrimonial Laws

The concept of "marriage" is the basic part of the definition of nuclear, polygamous, and extended families and other forms of domestic organisation. Although anthropologists are convinced that marriage occurs in every culture, we encounter great difficulty in coming up with a definition that can be applied universally. Marriage is a relationship established between a woman and one or more person. This relationship assures that a child born to the woman is accorded full birth rights common to normal members of his or her society, provided that the child is conceived, and born under certain approved circumstances.

Sarana (1969: 159-167) in his paper entitled "*Some Observation on the Definition of Marriage*", has discussed about the limitations of definition of marriage given by different scholars. In the Bodo society also, a traditional set of rules integral to marriage along with some impinging factors can be traced. As marriage is everywhere a set of cultural pattern to sanction parenthood and to provide a suitable background for the care and rearing of children. It is, in fact, the major cultural mechanism to ensure the continuation of the family and other groupings based on kinship.

Different social scientists like Beals (1953), Cantlie (1984), Murdock (1967), Barkataki (1967), Majumdar (1980), Srinivas (1991), Lucy Mair (1998) have studied marriage theoretically and also as the integral part of the social matrix in different societies. The Bodos have a pristine set of rules integral to marriage called *haba*. *Ha* means soil or earth and *ba* means to bear something on the back. It is interesting to observe that the Sanskrit word for marriage *bibaha* also has the same etymological meaning.

There are different types of *haba* among the Bodos, which are akin to the Aryan systems of the *asura* marriage, the *paisasa* marriage and the *brahma* marriage (Brahma, 1989; 16). In *asura* marriage, the bridegroom used to get a bride by paying a reasonable price for her. The ideas probably are that it would be disgraceful for a girl and her family if she is given in marriage for nothing. It proves that the bridegroom pays respect to the bride and her family. In olden days, it was compulsory in Bodo society but now-a-days the customary laws are gradually changing among the Bodos and such practices are disappearing from the society. The *paisasa* marriage system is still practiced in Bodo society, where the bridegroom physically overpowers bride in order to make her yield to his passion. The *brahma* marriage is also akin to a Bodo marriage system in which the father of the bride selects his son-in-law and keeps him in his house. This system is known as *garjia lakhinai* among the Bodos. The bridegroom is compulsory to stay in his father-in-law's house after marriage. This system, in fact, is rarely seen among the present day Bodos.

The Bodos have as many as six prescribed marriages. These are: (1) *Sangnanoi lainaihaba* (negotiated marriage), (2) *Garjia Lakhinai haba* (marriage by service), (3) *Kharsonnai haba* (irregular marriage), (4) *Bonanoi lainai haba* (forced marriage), (5) *Donkhar langnai haba* (marriage by elopement) and (6) *Dongkha habnai haba* (widow remarriage).

Sangnanoi lainai haba is solemnised when the parents of the bridegroom select the bride and the marriage is settled after negotiation. In earlier days, this sort of marriage was solemnised at the house of the bridegroom only. Now-a-days, the marriage is performed at the bride's house. Bride price, locally known as *phon* or *phon thaka*, was common in earlier days. Now, it is not compulsory. Chaudhuri (2004:44) states that the bridegroom enjoys more freedom to choose his life partner than the bride does. The educated Bodos, especially the Brahma section of the society was against the *phon thaka* from the beginning. But now bride price has been replaced by dowry. Of course, such cases of dowry are few and confined to the richer section of the society. *Garjia Lakhinai* system on the other hand indicates matrilineal characteristics of the Bodos, where a boy stays in his wife's house after marriage. In this case, husband identifies himself as the member of his wife's family. In this case, the girl inherits her parental property (Brahma, 1989: 21). Now, this system is rarely seen. In *kharsonnai haba*, the bride enters into the house of the bridegroom before the settlement of marriage through mutual understanding. In *bonanoi lainai haba*, the bride is forcefully taken away from the house of the bride to the house of the bridegroom and then marriage is solemnised. This system of marriage was prevalent in the earlier days. It is not a socially approved system of marriage in the present Bodo society. It is almost similar to the *paisasa* marriage of the Aryans (Brahma, 1992: 77). Sometimes marriage by elopement of both bride and bridegroom takes place. This is called *donkharlangnai haba*. In *dongkha habnai haba*, a man lives in the house of a widow as her husband then they are recognised as husband and wife by the society. However, they have to regularise their marriage according to the customary law called *dongkha Habnai*. This type of marriage is also very rare in the society.

Although the widow re-marriage is allowed in the society, there are some restrictions. The society sanctions junior sororate (marrying of a widower with his deceased wife's younger sister) but senior sororate (marrying of deceased wife's elder sister) is restricted. Likewise, junior levirate (marrying of a widow by her deceased husband's younger brother) is permitted but senior levirate is not allowed.

Adoption is popular. Usually a couple adopts a child if she does not conceive within two or three years. Both male and female children are equally preferred for adoption. The adopted children can also inherit their father's property. Customarily, the Bodos are patrilineal and descent, inheritance, succession, authority, and residence after marriage are traced through the male line. After marriage, a girl has to leave her family of orientation and has to live with her husband in the husband's family of orientation or in a neolocal residence. The Bodos practice tribal endogamy and clan exogamy. Endle (1911: 29-30) states that the tribal endogamy is highly favoured and esteemed, though in recent times marriage with the members of other communities is observed. Such alliances are as a rule not looked upon with favour, and the bridegroom in such cases generally to make his peace with his fellow-villagers by providing them with a feast in which rice-beer (*zu*) and pork are certain to take a prominent place. Children born of such mixed marriages become in all cases members of the father. Marriage between a boy and a girl of the same clan is strictly prohibited. Since violation of the customary law is strictly treated the incest taboo is rarely disobeyed. The Bodos are described as a monogamous tribe. Polygamy is strictly prohibited. They allow a man to marry only one and in rare case two, if the first wife is childless. Polyandry is totally prohibited. Traditionally, the practice of polygyny is not favoured. Only among the richer section of the Bodos, polygyny is noted. Only the polygynous marriage is made to overcome the barrenness of the first wife. Child marriage is unknown among them.

The traditional form of marriage is called *hathasuni*.At this marriage ceremony, the bride offers meal to the bridegroom at a function. This form of marriage is very simple. Before offering the meal to the bridegroom the bride offers a little portion of the meal to the God and Goddess of the *Ishing* (innermost room of the main house, *Nomano*). The meal is placed on a banana leaf. While the bride prays the *deuri* chants the mantras (formula), introducing the bride to the God and Goddess.

The Bodos following the Brahma religion perform the marriage ceremony in a reformed manner. Their system slightly differs from the traditional marriage customs called *hathasuni*. In fact, many of the pre-marriage ceremonies are followed by them. Only they have discouraged the use of rice-beer (*zu*) and pork (*oma bedor*) during the ceremony. At present, tea has taken place of rice-beer and the use of pork is not compulsory. Now-a-days, traditional musical instruments like *serja* (four stringed musical instruments), *siphung* (a long flute), *dhula* (drum) and *jotha* are rarely seen in the marriage ceremonies.

During the marriage ceremony among the Brahma religion, the bride and the bridegroom are taken to the altar of the *yanja* which is also called *mandap*. Both the bride and the bridegroom are given seats in front of the fire of the *yajna,* facing towards the east. The priest who is called *puruhit* starts the function of the marriage ceremony. First, the father of the bride prays to God standing before the blazing fire of *yajnahuti* uttering the *mantra* of the *Brahma Gayatri*. After the chanting of the formula is completed the father of the bride offers mixed corns (rice, pulse, sugar etc.) to the fire. After offering the corns to the fire the father of the bride prays to God for blessings to the bride and bridegroom. He declares before all that *ha* has offered (*sampradan*) his daughter to the bridegroom keeping the fire as witness.

The striking feature of the Bodos is that their customary laws of the marriage system have undergone many changes. The Brahma marriage, performed with *Vedic* rites by arranging *yajnahuti* and chanting *gayatri mantra*, has been a dominant system of marriage among the Bodos at the present age.

A section of the Bodos has abandoned the pristine religion and has embraced Christianity. These Bodos perform the marriage according to the rule of Christianity. The educated sections that do not follow the tribal endogamy sometimes perform marriages according to the norms of the bride's community or even prefer a court marriage. The Bodos have to complete the marriage rituals otherwise he or she will not be recognised as husband and wife by the society.

Since the marriages are celebrated according to the customary laws with rigidity and the rules also changes as per time and space. This institution has changed among the Bodos more than the other social institutions. We shall discuss in this chapter the marriage customs of the Bodos and recent changes in them. We shall look at the customs before marriage such as the selection of partners, permission of marriage, role of village elders in the decision of marriage, bride price and the customs after marriage such as residence after marriage, clan after marriage and changes in marriage customs and settlement of conflicts like divorce and family quarrel etc. and conflict resolution mechanisms.

1. Customs and Procedures before Marriage

The area that has changed more than any other is that of selection of partners. Among them marital union of the younger generation appears to have become a personal affairs rather than family and society. Traditionally, the selection of the spouses by the boys and girls was prevalent in their society and it was mutually arranged by both the parents. Now, the choice of mutual consent does not follow the traditional norms. After they take a decision they or their relatives and friends communicate it to their parents. Thus, it is seen that though the society sanctions such marriages yet it seems to be more in the direction of establishing a nuclear family.

Selection of Partners

Adult marriage is the general rule. The girls are married after the puberty rites. When we asked the informants about the selection of partners they replied that in selecting the partners the parents of both the boys and girls used to decide the selection of the partners for their children but now-a-day's they do not do that, the boy and the girl themselves select their partners and the parents also agrees to it. In case of selecting the partners by the parents, the informants said that according to the Bodo customs the boy's family has to approach girl's family if they want to be in the matrimonial alliance. The boy's family takes the president or secretary of the village as witness along with them and they ask the girl/ daughter for the marriage. These days it is mostly love marriage but if it is arranged then both are given time to know each other and eventually decide the marriage day, year etc.

We have asked the informants if a girl or a boy has selected somebody to get marry with, then under such situation whom do they approach first? They replied that the boy or the girl is free with to approach any person first, in most of the cases, it is the mother whom they approach first. After getting the approval from the parents, there is a societal norm which is known as *dharma bhar* in Bodo term and it is also known as *biban*, and while carry out the *biban* with the witness of the Sun and the Moon and then the *biban* is divided into three forms i.e., one is for the girl's family, one for the Society and one for the cow helpers in the field (*loukhar)*. And this is how they approach the bride's family with the proposal. After the proposal, the groom's family sticks a bangle at the entrance roof of the bride's house and if the bride's family accepts their proposal then they happily takes out the bangle from their roof. This is the most important traditional practice that the Bodos are following in their society. Brahma (1992: 83-84) also mentions that this pre-matrriage ceremony is performed by the bridegroom party. Areca nuts and betel leaves (*goi dro pathoi*) are essential for this ceremony. Two earthen pitchers (*hani thinkligongnoi*) are carried to the house of the bride. On the body of the two pitchers the signs of the sun and moon are painted. If the sign is detected to be wrong then the bride-party charges a fine from the parents of the bridegroom. The person who carries the two earthen pitchers is called *barlangpha***.**

After deciding the girl, the boy's parents approach the girl's parents and asked for their daughter's hand. If the girl is free and not engaged with any other boy and if she is willing for the marriage then an agreement is made between both the parents, and they give the girl a gift it may be a ornament or cloth, and this sign of gifting is a form of engagement in the Bodo custom and from that day onwards no other boy can approach her.

Traditionally, Bodo women have a choice or a voice with regard to marriage. Table 25.1 show that two types of selection of partners are found in the sample villages. These are arranged or negotiated marriage and the other love marriage. From Table 25.2, it is found that out of 120 respondents, 116 (97 per cent) said that the selection of partners is made by the parents of the boy and the girl and the rest 84 (70 per cent) respondents said that the love marriage is the norm. Modernisation in the form of education and religion, Christianity in particular has changed their outlook. Even all the changes, the Bodos has made in social and economic life they have not totally given up their traditional mode of arranging their marriages. That is why we have found that 97 per cent respondents are in favour of arranged marriage.

In arranged marriage, selection of the bride not only depends on the beauty but also other factors. Chaudhari (2004:45) in her study observed that the Bodos do not consider the girl with large hip, breast and waist which is considered as fickle-minded. The girl who makes noise while walking is considered as hot tempered. The girl with pointed nose, bright eyes, small teeth, well shaped fingers, bright face and dark thick hair is considered as most desirable. The desirable qualities of a Bodo bride are not confined to her physical attributes. The other quality considered in an ideal bride is expertise in husking, weaving and cooking etc.

Regarding marriage customs of the Bodos in the sample villages, an elderly female said that: "*According to our custom, the boy's family has to approach girl's family if they want to be in the matrimonial alliance. The boy's family takes the president or secretary of the village as witness along with them and they ask the girl's father for the marriage. These days, it is mostly love marriage but if it is arranged marriage then both are given time to know each other and eventually decide the marriage day, year etc.*"

Another elderly male said that: "*The boy or the girl is free to approach the father or the mother for approval. In most cases, it is the mother. After the approval from the parents, there is a societal norm which is known as dharma dhar in Bodo term, it is also known as biban, and while carrying the biban we see the Sun and the Moon and then we divide the biban in three parts i.e., one is for the girl's family, one for the society and one for the cow helpers in the field (gorokhia). And this is how we approach the bride's family with the proposal. After the proposal, the groom's family sticks a bangle at the entrance roof of the bride's house and if the bride's family accepts their proposal then they happily takes out the bangle from their roof. This is the most important traditional practice that we are following in our society.*"

The selection of prospective bride indicates the status of women. It is obvious that brides have little or no say in her selection. She merely dreams of a house where there are granary and cowshed.

Apart from the arranged and love marriages, the forced marriage was prevalent among the Bodos. In this regard, an elderly female said that: "*Earlier, there was forced marriage; if the boy fell in love with a girl then he forcefully brought the girl even she did not like the boy. But in modern days such marriage is not practiced but there is marriage by registration at the court.*"

An elderly male said that: *Earlier, forced marriage was there to a great extend, but now-a-days, it is very rare. If we hear such cases of forceful marriages then the decision is upon the society. It is the society who decides what should to be to such marriage, whether they should be set free or get married in proper custom and tradition. Normally such forceful marriages are invalid in the eyes of the society as it is against the will of the girl and her family. But in today's time we do not hear such cases, it is very rare in our society.*

Table 25.2: Selection of Partners

Selection of Marriage Partners	*Male*	*Female*	*Total*
Arranged	57 (47 per cent)	59 (49 per cent)	116 (97 per cent)
Love Marriage	43 (36 per cent)	41 (34 per cent)	84 (70 per cent)

Multiple Responses; Total respondents: 120

Permission for Marriage

In most of the societies, the mother is first approached for the permission for marriage. Table 25.3 shows that it continues to be true among the study villages, both in love and arranged marriages. It is reported that the mother being the in charge of the family decision especially the marriage matters she is approached first for her consent.

That is why 78(65 per cent) respondents said that the permission for marriage is taken first from the mother. 11(9 per cent) got their father's permission and 34(28 per cent) from both. Here, we found that the permission for marriage is centred round the woman which reinforcing her role as the person in charge of the family.

Table 25.3: Permission for Marriage

Permission for Marriage	*Male*	*Female*	*Total*
Mother	37 (31 per cent)	41 (34 per cent)	78 (65 per cent)
Father	9 (8 per cent)	2 (2 per cent)	11 (9 per cent)
Both	16 (13 per cent)	18 (15 per cent)	34 (28 per cent)

In this regard, an elderly female said: "*Now-a-days, children are very frank with parents and siblings so they openly discuss with them.*"

Role of Village Elders and Council in the Decision on Marriage

The village council plays a role in marriage. Table 25.4 shows that out of 120 respondents, 71 (59 per cent) said that the village elders represent as witness, 59 (49 per cent) said that the village elders keep records of the marriage (bride's belongings), 23 (19 per cent) said that the village elders arrange the marriage function, 49 (41 per cent) said that the final decision of selecting of partners is taken by the village elders, 1 male respondent said that the village elders offer blessing to the married couple and 3 (3 per cent)

Table 25.4: Role of Village Elders/council in Decisions on marriage

Role of Village Elders in Marriage	*Male*	*Female*	*Total*
No role	2 (2 per cent)	1 (1 per cent)	3 (3 per cent)
Represent as witness	35 (29 per cent)	36 (30 per cent)	71 (59 per cent)
Making arrangement	13 (11 per cent)	10 (8 per cent)	23 (19 per cent)
Offer blessing	1 (1 per cent)	0	1 (1 per cent)
Keeps records of the marriage (Bride's belongings)	30 (25 per cent)	29 (24 per cent)	59 (49 per cent)
Final decision on the choice of partners	23 (19 per cent)	26 (22 per cent)	49 (41 per cent)
Resolves disputes/conflicts	1 (1 per cent)	0	1 (1 per cent)

Note: Multiple Responses. Total Respondents: 120.

said that the village council has no role. Among the Bodos, the family referred the marriage plan to the village elders as it is not merely a family affairs but the whole village involved in it. The married couple has to take blessings from the elders and perform some rituals. The members of the Bodoland Autonomous Council (BTC) have nothing to do with marriage as such.

2. Customs before and after Marriage

The marriage customs change according to the tribe. The tradition of most of them allowed the boy and girl to live as man and wife after the village council or the elders give their consent. It continues to be the case among some tribes but is not common. Also the rituals differ according to the type of society. In this section we shall examine and analyse the customs followed before and during marriage and the choice of the clan after marriage in the sample villages.

Customs before Marriage

Table 25.5: Customs followed before marriage

Customs followed before Marriage	*Male*	*Female*	*Total*
Bride price given	2 (2 per cent)	1 (1 per cent)	3 (3 per cent)
Engagement before marriage	45 (38 per cent)	44 (37 per cent)	89 (74 per cent)
Do not Know	5 (4 per cent)	5 (4 per cent)	10 (8 per cent)
Not Applicable	8 (7 per cent)	10 (8 per cent)	18 (15 per cent)
Total	**60 (50 per cent)**	**60 (50 per cent)**	**120 (100 per cent)**

Table 25.5 shows that bride price is not prevalent among them as such the respondents are almost silent in this respect. 89 (74 per cent) respondents said that there is engagement ceremony. Before marriage, boy and the girl are allowed to meet each other. After that they get consent from the village elders, 18 (15 per cent) said not applicable and 10 (8 per cent) said they do not know anything about the engagement. Hence, pre-marital sex relation is not permitted by the society.

Regarding bride price, an elderly female said that: "*We do not practice bride price. But groom bear the expenses of bride's wedding dress, ornaments, etc. The groom's family has to bring tea, biscuits, etc to the bride's place. They also take betel nut and areca nuts too. The groom has to pay a sum rupee of 101-501 to the village elders called 'raij' as the village elders represent as a witness. The village elders gathered and give advice to the newly wedded couple and give blessings. The names of couple are kept in record for future reference and for the proper functioning of marriage institution.*"

In response of the earlier comment, an elderly male said that: "*There is no such compulsory practice of giving gifts to our daughters during marriage. It all depends upon her parent's will and capacity. If the family is economically well off then they prefer to give all the essential items such as furniture, utensils etc to their daughters to start off the newly wedded life. Otherwise there is no hard and fast rule in our customary law of giving gifts and ornaments to the bride during marriage, even there is no such demand from the groom's side. After the marriage ceremony, when the groom's family finally goes to the bride's house to take her with them, then at that time they used to carry biban in three forms, one for the society, one for the gorokhia (cow helpers in the fields), and one for the bride's family. If they fail to carry the biban then the bride's family imposes certain amount of fine upon the groom's family, which is nothing severe but a mere compensation to retain their customary practices. The Bodo society permits marriage outside the tribe; there is no such restriction against such marriage.*"

Regarding changing of selection of the bride and customs before marriage, a female politician said that: "*Now, in the modern days mostly people go for love marriage. Initially boy's side goes to the girl's place, taking along with them some areca nut and betel nut as a sign of respect. There is ring ceremony also we called gothacoini, cut betel nut in the middle and makes them in equal halves. Usually they take negotiators from village. So they play as a witness.The girl's parents give all the household items and boy has to bear the expenses of bride's jewelleries, dress etc during marriage. I was told that in old times there was bride price. Boy's family had to give away a pig to the bride's family and it was killed and the villagers were invited for the feast. Even today, if they want then they give it, or else they give something. While taking away newly wedded bride the groom has to pay 12.50 rupees to the village elders as per* the customs. *If the woman is childless and she is widow then she cannot inherit the land or house of her husband.*"

Thus, we can say that the marriage is an important phase in the life of a woman. She becomes the member of the family of orientation as well as establishes a new family with affinal and consanguine relatives. It represents the link from existing nuclear families to new ones or perpetuation of extended families and acceptance of their economy and social responsibilities. The customs before marriage shows that they maintain clan exogamy with rigidity. In spite of the change of religion their marriage customs have not changed totally. The village elders look after all the rites and rituals of the marriage.

A marriage not only binds two persons but also two households and two groups of people with duties and expectations. The Bodo society has strict rules regarding marriage obligations. In every step of a Bodo marriage, such rules can be easily being observed. Marriage takes place at the bride's house. In case of love marriage and marriage by elopement, the marriage ceremonies have to be performed even after the birth of the first sibling at a convenient time.

The pre-marriage ceremony as mentioned earlier is a kind of negotiation between the bride and bridegroom's house towards the settlement of marriage. It is observed strictly by the Bodos. The ring ceremony also called *gothacoini,* cut betel nut in the middle and makes them in equal halves. Usually they take negotiators from village. So they play as a witness. The girl's parents give all the household items and boy has to bear the expenses of bride's jewelleries', dress etc during marriage. In old times there was bride price and *biban langnai* (carrying two pitchers of rice beer) are important pre-marriage ceremony of the Bodos. The betel nut and betel leaf is important items in marriage which the groom family gives to the bride's family. This indicates the honour to the bride. On the day of making the final settlement for marriage, the bridegroom has to entertain the villagers of the bride's village with betel nut and pork etc. The skins of the areca nuts are usually thrown on the roof of the main house to remain there till the proper marriage takes place. The last stage of pre-marriage ceremony is the assemblance of parents of the bride and the bridegroom at the house of the bride to fix a suitable date of the marriage proper. The ceremony is known as *khabira langnai*.

The system of paying bride-price, locally known as *Phon* or *Phon Thaka*, was customarily followed in the Bodo society. Later on, the paying of *Phon Thaka* began to be disregarded and in the present Bodo society it has become a symbol. However, the paying of *Phon Thaka* is still prevalent among the followers of Brahma religion. But the elders sit together to finalise the negotiation before marriage. It is locally called *Affat/Afad.* In this case, the parents of the boy offer to the father of the bride a pair of areca nuts and betel leaves and also two one rupee coins (*Goijora pathoijora aro Jorase Thakha Gothang*) on a leaf of the banana, after saluting him. The father of the bride accepts areca nuts; betel leaves and returns the two coins. It means he has not accepted the *Phon Thaka* (bride price). In our field investigation also we have gathered information of *Affat* but no *Phon Thaka*. Though the paying of *Phonthaka* indicates higher status of the women yet the Bodos do not practice now-a-days.

We have gathered information that the groom bears the expenses of bride's wedding dress, ornaments, etc. The groom family has to bring tea, biscuits, etc to the bride's place. They also take betel nut and areca nuts too. The groom has to pay a sum rupee of 101-501 to the village elders called *raij* (villagers) as the village elders represent as a witness. The village elders gathered and give advice to the newly wedded couple and give blessings. The names of couple are kept in record for future reference and for the proper functioning of marriage institution.

Residence after Marriage

Table 25.6: Residence after marriage.

Residence after Marriage	*Male*	*Female*	*Total*
To the bridegroom	60 (50 per cent)	60 (50 per cent)	120 (100 per cent)

The residence after marriage of the women indicates the women's status. We shall now examine the change of residence and clan of the Bodo women after marriage. After marriage, the Bodo woman leaves her home and lives in her husband's house with or without his parents. Table 25.6 shows the change of residence after marriage according to the customary law.

The sample study shows that the residence after marriage is patrilocal or neo-local. In both the cases, the girl enters the boy's house and is deprived of her property rights in her ancestral home. The married couple lives in the bridegroom's house whether it lives with the parents or by itself. The couple may begin its life in the parent's house but as early as possible it builds a house on the plot the boy's parents allot to him. Preference is given to joint living and joint cooking in one hearth. The Bodo custom is that all the sons except the eldest one establish separate houses for themselves. The eldest son lives with the old parents in the ancestral house and look after the aged parents. Thus, the Bodos follow the rule of primogeniture in case of inheritance of their ancestral house.

Clan after Marriage

Clan is the most outstanding feature in tribal societies. They trace their descent through the clans. Retaining or losing the can is an indication of an individual's identity. Brahma (1992: 34-44) has mentioned 24 clans among the Bodos. The clans are locally called *ari* or *hari*. Chaudhuri (2004: 107-

108) states that some clans are totemic in nature, some are territorial origin, and some are occupational categories. The Bodos trace their descent from the original ancestors who were male siblings. Here, we shall examine clan in case of women after marriage. Normally, the patrilineal trend is that the wife joins the husband's clan after marriage. The rule of patrilocal residence after marriage makes the woman part of her husband's clan but in case of men this is not changed. Among the Bodos the woman takes the husband's clan name after marriage. As we have seen from the Table 25.7 that all the 120 respondents have reported that women take her husband's clan name after marriage. The children follow the father's clan. It shows that a woman loses her father's identity after marriage and takes her husband's identity.

Table 25.7: Clan after Marriage

Clan after Marriage	*Male*	*Female*	*Total*
To the bridegroom	60 (50 per cent)	60 (50 per cent)	120 (100 per cent)
Total	60 (50 per cent)	60 (50 per cent)	120 (100 per cent)

Changes in the Marriage Customs

From the above analysis, it can be said that the tribal customs of the Bodos have changed in recent years. It has happened due to the conversion of new religion and sanskritisation. This has affected their social set up and influenced their heritage, beliefs, customary laws and practices. As a result, the past traditions are rarely observed in the changed situation. In this transition, every aspect of their culture is new to them. Not all changes favour the married women because some of them such as paying bride price show that the higher status of women but now this system is gradually changing and they are moving towards patriarchy. We shall now analyse some of the changes in their marriage customs.

Table 25.8: Changes in the Marriage Customs

Changes in Marriage Customs	*Male*	*Female*	*Total*
No change	15 (13 per cent)	14 (12 per cent)	29 (24 per cent))
Love marriage	4 (3 per cent)	3 (3 per cent)	7 (6 per cent)
Increase of Bride price	1 (1 per cent)	0	1 (1 per cent)
Traditional customs no longer in practice	36 (30 per cent)	35 (29 per cent)	71 (59 per cent)

(Contd...)

No more arranged marriage	0	1 (1 per cent)	1 (1 per cent)
Abolishment of child marriage	1 (1 per cent)	0	1 (1 per cent)
Shorter marriage process	8 (7 per cent)	11 (9 per cent)	19 (16 per cent)
Influence of non-tribal custom	20 (17 per cent)	25 (21 per cent)	45 (38 per cent)
Abolishment of forceful marriages	0	5 (4 per cent)	5 (4 per cent)

Note: Multiple Responses. Total Respondents: 120.

Table 25.8 shows that out of 120 respondents, 71 (59 per cent) reported that now traditional customs are not followed in marriage. Nowadays, the socially recognised institution of marriage seems to have become more an individual affair than a contract between two families, Most of the respondents said that the consent of the boy and the girl is becoming common rather than the parents. According to the Bodo tradition, marriage has to take place in the groom's house but now marriages are held in the bride's house. 45 (38 per cent) respondents said that their marriage customs are very much influenced by the non-tribal customs. 19 (16 per cent) said that marriage functions have become shorter, 7 (6 per cent) said that love marriages have an impact on traditional marriages, 5 (4 per cent) said that forceful marriages have been abolished. However, some respondents felt that the practice of non-paying of bride price and love marriages have changed the marriage rules in the present day Bodo society.

It is also said that the traditional marriage customs were lengthy and expensive hence these customs are being shortened and love marriages have become more common. Due to modernisation and sanskritisation, non-tribal marriage customs are followed by the Bodos.

The most important aspect of the marriage is that the sanskritisation process has changed the Bodo society to a great extent. The tribal Bodo society, which was outside the realm of Hindu society, came into contact with Hinduism long back and gradually, came within the fold of that society. The influence of Hindu culture on the Bodo society is seen instead of converting to Hindu religion by most of them. The sanskritisation has made the Bodos to give up the beef eating and some of the tribal habits which can be said the influence of Hinduism.

The introduction of the *Brahma* religion in the beginning of the twentieth century has marked a new era in the history of Bodo society. The *Brahma* religion has its root in Vedic philosophy did tremendous transformation in rituals and customs of the Bodo society. The followers of this cult abstain from taking pork and local rice beer which were essential items in their traditional marriage feast. Moreover, the conversion of Christianity also brought a drastic change in their marriage customs.

3. Settlement of Conflicts

The conflicts related to marriage, divorce, remarriage of widows and inheritance of property is usually dealt by the village council. In marriage, the village elders act as the sanctioning authority and dissolve the marriage disputes. In this section, we shall examine the settlement of conflict resolution mechanism of marriage and divorce.

Women, Divorce and Conflict Resolution

Divorce is permissible in the Bodo society. If both husband and wife desire divorce mutually then it is performed by tearing a betel leaf. This is called *pathoi-lai bisnai.* This ritual is usually performed by the priest (*deuris*). If the husband divorces his wife without any reasonable ground then he is to bear the responsibility of her livelihood for a certain period. Brahma (1992:96-97) has stated that the question of divorce is put up in a big gathering of the public which is called *samaj* or *raij* for the settlement of the divorce cases.

Chaudhuri (2004; 46) has stated that extra-marital affairs is one of the most important causes of divorce. To be most specific, when a woman is involved in such an affair, it leads to separation but when a male is involved it leads to the second or the third marriage. This is because polygyny is socially sanctioned. But the members of present generation, specially the women, have started protesting against polygyny. The author further says that a few case studies show how the members of All Bodo Women Welfare Federation (ABWWF) penalised those men who were involved in extra-marital sex affairs.

As a result of separation, the wife loses the right over her husband's assets in case she is found guilty and the husband loses the right over the children if he is found guilty. Social position of the children remains unaffected, though they have to forego the right over their father's assets. Both male and female can remarry after separation. In divorce cases, the custody of the children is normally decided mutually by the couple, and if there is any disagreement between them then the society and the elders in the family decides who will be the custodian of the children. In such situation, it is very important to look into the emotional and financial conditions of both the parents before handing over the custody. Further, if the society and the elders cannot decide over the matter then it goes to the hand of the legal system, and their verdict will be the ultimate solution.

Our result from the study villages on these issues has shown in Table 25.9. Table 25.9 shows that out of 120 respondents, 109 (91 per cent) said that Village Committees have decided the proceedings of the divorce cases, 24 (20 per cent) respondents said that the elders in the family finalised the divorce cases and 2 (2 per cent) said that they have no idea in this matter. Thus, we can say that divorce cases are generally settled amicably by the Village Committee and the elders of the family as it is a family matter.

Table 25.9: Conflicts Proceedings Done by Whom?

Conflict Proceedings: Done by Whom	*Male*	*Female*	*Total*
Elders in the family	10 (8 per cent)	14 (12 per cent)	24 (20 per cent)
Village Committee	54 (45 per cent)	55 (46 per cent)	109 (91 per cent)
Do not know	1 (1 per cent)	1 (1 per cent)	2 (2 per cent)

Note: Multiple Responses. Total Respondents: 120.

Women and Conflict Resolution Meeting

It is customary for traditional societies not to allow women to attend any dispute resolution meeting except when they are parties to a dispute. Divorce proceedings belong to that category and the women are allowed to attend with their family and clan elders. In some society, they are allowed as witness. In this section, we shall study to what meetings women are allowed to attend apart from that of the divorce cases.

Table 25.10: Conflict Resolution Meeting and Women.

Women and Conflict Resolution Meeting	*Male*	*Female*	*Total*
Yes, allowed to attend	42 (35 per cent)	47 (39 per cent)	89 (74 per cent)
Not allowed to attend	0	1 (1 per cent)	1 (1 per cent)
Only to answer acquisitions against them	15 (13 per cent)	13 (11 per cent)	28 (23 per cent)
Only as witnesses	13 (11 per cent)	11 (9 per cent)	24 (20 per cent)

Note: Multiple Responses. Total Respondents: 120.

Table 25.10 shows that 89 (74 per cent) respondents said that women are allowed to attend the conflict resolution meetings, 28 (23 per cent) said that women are allowed to attend to answer accusations against them, 24 (20 per cent) said that the women attend as witness and 1 female respondent said that women are not allowed to attend in conflict resolution meeting.

Regarding divorce, an elderly female said that: "*Divorce is very rare in our society. When it comes to the choice of partners our society is liberal. There is no forceful marriage; it entirely depends on the decision of couple. Maintenance is given to woman as it is already in the state law. There is no maintenance of the divorced woman in the customary law. If a woman needs maintenance then she has to seek the help of the state law. In such case, the custody of the child depends on the couple or the village council. The village council or village committee decides the case. The divorced men and women are allowed to remarry.*"

In traditional Bodo society, women were not allowed to attend the conflict resolution meetings. But now the women are allowed to attend the meetings. This shows a changing trend among them as the women are educated and service holders unlike earlier women who were not so educated and modernised. Education and modernisation of the women have changed their world views.

Conclusion

We have seen many recent changes in the marriage customs of the Bodos in the study villages. Traditionally, their rules, regulations and formalities were elaborate. Some of them have changed. For example, marriage through negotiations was the norm but they have also known marriages by mutual choices and elopement. Some young person's gave it a new form of love marriage which involves a personal choice. At times it is combined with elopement. Not all observe the conventions, taboos and restrictions. Also their rituals have changed. Some respondents have either abandoned or are on the verge or giving up bride price. The *Brahma* marriage is performed with vedic rites by arranging *yajnahuti* and chanting *gayatri* mantra. The Christian follow the Christian rules in marriage. Some discourage divorce and others have made its rules more rigid than in the past. On the other hand, traditional penalties are strictly adhered to. Conflict resolution, even while remaining traditional has become prompt and more effective than in the courts of law.

Three major changes in the study villages that account for this evolution are education, commercialisation and change of religion. All three have affected their social and marriage customs, some of them with a positive impact on women and others negative. Since these inputs keep interacting with their tradition, it has become continuity with change. For example, the *Brahma* section of the society has accepted the new religion at the macro-level but continue to practice their traditions in their daily life. This interaction between the traditional *Bathou* religion and the Brahma religion is seen in the changes in their marriage customs beginning with the permission for choice of partners. It creates some ambiguity both at the macro and micro level, for example, in the move towards a strong role for men. Religion and education have introduced individualism so have the commercial forces and administrative systems. Individualism and stronger patriarchy by and large had a negative impact on women. They have interacted with their traditions such as not including women in decision-making even while allowing them to attend some meetings. Also making the customary laws on divorce stricter can weaken the position of women.

Some other changes such as freedom of choose the life partners and end of marriage at early years are positive moves. Because of commercialisation celebrations have become more expensive than in the past. That has affected their economy and has introduced class formation. If directed properly, the new customs together with education can take their societies towards gender equality. That requires more stress on the freedom that religion propagates and less on their male-dominated system. It also requires a combination of the traditional with the new and creation of a new ideology to support this change.

References

Agnes, Flavia 2012. His and Hers. *Economic and Political Weekly*. XLVII:17: April 28: 11-12.

Barkataki, S. 1967, *Tribes of Assam*. New Delhi: Book Trust of India.

Beals, Ralph and Hozen, Harry 1953. *An Introduction to Anthropology*. New York: Macmillan Co.

Bhuyan, S.K. 1951. *Assam Buranji.* Gauhati: Gauhati University Press.

Borah, K.C. 2006. *The Bodos: A Demographic Profile*. Deptt. of Economics, Dibrugarh: Dibrugarh University.

Brahma, K. 1989. *Aspects of Social Customs of the Bodos*. Guwahati: Saraighat Printers.

Cantlie, Audrey. 1984. *The Assamese*. London; Curzon Press Ltd.

Chaudhuri, Sucheta Sen 2004. *The Bodo Movement and Women's Participation*. New Delhi: Mittal Publication.

Endle, S. 1911. *The Kachari*. Reprint in 1975, New Delhi: Cosmo Publication.

Grierson, G. A. 1903. *Linguistic Survey of India*. Calcutta: Superintendent of Printing. India, Vol. III part II, reprint 1967.

Hodgson, B.H. 1880. *Essay on the Koch, Bodo and Dhimal Tribes*, Calcutta, 1947. Reprinted in Vols. 1 and II of Miscellaneous Essays relating to Indian subjects.

Mair, Lucy 1998. *An Introduction to Social Anthropology*. Delhi: Oxford University Press.

Majumdar, D.N. 1980. *A Study of Culture Change in two Garo villages*. Guwahati: Gauhati University.

Murdock, George, Peter 1965. *Social Structure*. New York: The Free Press.

Sarana, Gopala 1969. Some Observations on the Definition of Marriage. *Ethnos*. 33 (1-4); 139-167.

Singh, Kirti 2012. Towards Achieving Equal Rights in Marriage. *Economic and Political Weekly*, Vol. ZLVII: No. 24: June 16.

Srinivas, M.N. 1991. *India: Social Structure*. Delhi: Hindustan Publication Corporation.

26

Protecting Tribal Cultures: The Role of State Instrumentalities

— *Rupa Barman Borgohain*

Every civilisation, ancient or new, modern or traditional, builds up a distinctive culture of its own over the course of time. So we can say that culture and civilisation are two sides of the same coin. A study of culture reflects whether the particular tribe or race is in the process of progression, regression or annihilation. When the race or the tribe suffers different onslaughts from encroachers and foreigners and other outside forces, then their culture is eroded and diminished and even faces extinction. Normally, a majority culture faces no such threat. Rather, there is a lurking fear that the majority might over-shadow the minority. Ironically, in most instances the minority happens to be the indigenous or first people of the land. To save these indigenous people from physical and cultural extinction, certain statutory provisions are necessary. In India, the Constitution of India through the 6th schedule tried to install certain protective measures and safeguards for the tribal population of the north-east. The question is: how effective have these constitutional measures been?

The 6th schedule is considered as a smaller constitution within the main Constitution. At present the 6th schedule is applicable only in the four north-eastern states of Assam, Meghalaya, Tripura and Mizoram. In Meghalaya, the 6th schedule is applicable in totality, whereas with regard to the other three states certain selected areas are covered by the schedule. According to M.P. Jain, 'The condition of tribal areas of these states is considered to be different from those in the other Tribal Areas. These Tribal Areas are divided into fairly large districts inhabited by single tribes or fairly homogeneous groups of tribes...of the other people in the State.' (Jain 468) The main object of the 6th schedule was to protect the customary tribal traditions cultures with their appealing anthropological significance. The tribes of Assam are considered to have deep roots in their culture, customs and civilisation which is, however, in urgent need of protection and preservation as their own resilience may not be enough in the context of the complex swirl of modernity with its host of conflicting forces. So some amount of self-governance and autonomy was given to these tribal peoples by the Constitution through which they could preserve their identity, culture and script. In this paper attention is drawn to the fact that despite the provisions of the 6th schedule the Bodos are still fighting for their social, political and cultural existence. There has been relentless encroachment on their land which has made their existence uncertain and even perilous. As A.K. Ganguli states, 'The idea of property underwent changes not so much by law, but by the development of human society. Land today, as it has been yesterday, is likely to be a very important kind of property.'(Ganguli 492) We find that the rich and fertile land has been the bone of contention between different classes, castes and tribes. Since the tribal people were the original inhabitants, they had settled in the fertile stretches and it was precisely because of this that they became vulnerable to encroachment leading to their eviction and displacement. 'It's been said that the draft Central government ministry report described the rush for Chhattisgarh's mineral riches as the biggest grab of tribal lands after Columbus.' (Shrivastava and Kothari, 225)

The Sixth Schedule alone cannot solve every problem which these tribes have been facing and there are bound to be some lapses and pitfalls regarding its implementation and execution. The major tribes of Assam are Bodo, Kachari, Mikir (Karbi), Lalung, Dimasa, Hmar, and Hajonj. In this essay the emphasis is primarily on the Bodo community, a strong and proud race which is still facing threats to its identity from within and without. Their pride resides in their many-hued culture and tradition. The Bodos consist of more than 40 per cent of the scheduled tribe population residing in the Brahmaputra valley. Amalendu Guha states that 'on the basis of the census of 1881, in the later part of the eighteenth century the Bodos formed one-third of the indigenous population of the Brahmaputra valley.' (Guha, Amalendu, 26) Unfortunately, we find that the population of the indigenous Bodos has declined in the scheduled Bodoland area. It has been estimated 'that the Bodos constitute not more than 25 per cent of the total population in the proposed Bodoland Territorial Council (and not more than 6 per cent of the total population of Assam). This means that the BTC Accord gives the Bodos a special status under the Sixth Schedule of the Constitution at the cost of 75 per cent of non-Bodo population in the proposed BTC areas'. (Nath, 543) This is still a large minority grouping, with areas of privations and needs calling for special steps of welfare and amelioration, but one presumes that the inclusion of the Sixth Schedule in the Bodo territory was delayed and neglected due to political reasons. This is a clear indication of the lackadaisical, lackluster policy of the Central and state governments towards the tribal people. In analysing the cultural predicament of the Bodos, however, we also need to throw light on aspects like food, occupation, religion and dress which can be considered inherent to one's culture and basic survival.

The Bodo tribal community practices all types of cultivation from rice to tea-plantation. They also rear pig and poultry and are experts in making different bamboo products. Their relationship to the land is however, not confined to agriculture and animal husbandry. Their dwellings are distinctive: 'The mode of living of the Boro-Kacharis in compact villages and putting barriers all around the homestead is a common sight to see. This speaks of their sense of privacy and esthetic beauty.' (Bordoloi, Sharma Thakur and Saikia, 3-4) We find that the Bodos have a great sense of colour combination and they know the natural art of dyeing, using various shades of red and blue. From a very tender age the Bodo girls weave cloth and the conventional dress of the female is called *dokna*. Regarding religion, the contemporary Bodos have adopted diverse religious practices like Bathouism, Hinduism and Christianity. (Many Bodos were converted to Christianity during the British colonial rule). Bathouism is a special kind of worship of the progenitors, better known as 'Obonglaoree'. Here the supreme God Bathou is propitiated through various offerings. 'During the currency of the Baishagu festival the Bodo-Kacharis observe certain taboos, which include prohibition of entry into the household granary, disposal of any property by way of sale, husking paddy or rice, etc.' (Bordoloi, Sharma Thakur and Saikia, 10) The Baishagu festival is also known as Bishu, which is Bihu for the Assamese. Thus, the Bodos have a distinctive culture despite having certain affinities with the Assamese in certain modes of celebration. As Anil Boro points out, 'Notwithstanding the processes of cultural assimilation and fusion, the Bodos have maintained their distinctive identity through the ages.' (Boro, 2)

Though in this age of globalisation the taste buds are undergoing changes and becoming cosmopolitan in the appreciation of 'world food,' many races, castes and tribes still have certain cuisines which are ethnically distinctive or special .The special Bodo dishes are 'Omar Bedor', 'Onla' and 'Narzi', and their conventional drink is called 'Zu Mai' where *zu* means wine and *mai* implies rice. This drink needs to be served in every social function. In their different festivals like Kherai, Garja, and Baishagu different musical instruments like Serja, Jotha, Kham etc. are played as expressions of joy and merriment. As one can see, many of these life-practices and artistic expressions are land-based. They emerge from the rootedness of the Bodos, and are shaped by their intercourse with the land on which they have been living for ages.

The unnecessary delay in applying the Sixth Schedule for constitutional recognition for the Bodos, despite their possession of a rich culture and tradition has unquestionably made them resentful and thus more radical. While some of them sometimes flaunt their distinctive attire such as the *dokna* in public, seemingly gaining a cultural-political victory, in a deeper sense their culture is under siege. What is mere symbolism when faced with harsh facts of land encroachment and loss and fratricidal strife?

The Sixth Schedule was amended by the Lok Sabha on 29th November, 1988 with regard to the states of Mizoram and Tripura by giving far greater power to the governors of the states to fulfill the aspirations and demands of its tribal populace but nothing was envisioned for the plains tribe of Assam, i.e., the Bodos. Hence it was termed 'Constitutional Discrimination'. The plain tribes, i.e., the Bodos were always campaigning for the recognition and granting of their different rights with regard to their land, language etc. both in the post and pre-independence eras. The colonialists, i.e., the British were very much in need of land for tea plantation and then for the expansion of the petroleum industry in the state. To fulfill their aim they enacted the Assam Waste Land Settlement Rules (1838) to make land acquisition easy and feasible. This resulted in huge land alienation for the ethnic communities of Assam including the Bodos and the Kachari tribes. Way back in 1929 the Bodos submitted memorandums to the Simon Commission for fulfilling the demands of their community. This itself reflects an early awareness on the part of the community about the threat of losing their identity, culture and heritage. So in 1933 a convention of the plains tribals gave birth to the All Assam Tribal League (AATL) and this Tribal League rendered support to form the government and as such Mr. Sadullah became the Chief Minister. Unfortunately the government failed to meet the demands of the League and to safeguard the 'Line System' (for the protection of land) which was introduced by the British. The history of the 'Line System' indicates that it was devised in 1916, and was enforced in 1920 in the districts of Nagaon and the sub-division of Kamrup district, compelling the migrants to settle in segregated locations. Under this 'Line System', lands were divided into three categories (1) open to immigrants (2) closed to immigrant and (3) mixed — where a line was drawn there immigrant could settle on only one side of it. The system was reasonably successful in restricting indiscriminate encroachment but immigrants did settle in areas closed or partially closed to them because of apathetic and corrupt settlement officers. As already stated, Mr. Sadullah who came to power in 1939 with the support of the Tribal League wanted the abolition of the 'Line System' to facilitate and encourage the settlement of the Muslim immigrants and to make Assam a permanent base of the Muslim League. On one hand Mr. Sadullah began to administer the state with the support of the Tribal League, but on the other hand their expectation that their diverse and genuine interests would be protected including the right over their land was undermined. Hence we can assume that the Tribal League was given a false assurance. The census superintendent of the year (1931) C. S. Mullan wrote in a report: 'Thither flocks the Mymensingias, without fuss, without tumult, without undue trouble to the district revenue staff, a population which must amount to over a half a million has transplanted itself from Bengal to Assam during the last 25 years.' Mullan feared that 'the outcome of this unbridled immigration would be like wiping out the Assamese race and culture more conclusively than the Burmese invasion a hundred years ago.' (Saikia) If the agenda of the political rulers is only to win elections with the help of the immigrants by underplaying the genuine concerns of the indigenous tribe, then no constitutional provision would be of any help to such a tribe. It is pertinent to note that the mindset of the political class prevalent in the pre-Independence period, i.e., to conceive of the immigrants as a vote bank, still persists.

The Bodos were already feeling alienated because of large scale encroachment on their lands and they expected that some steps would be taken to mitigate the same. But Mr Sadullah failed to fulfill his commitment and brought large numbers of Muslim migrants to settle in the Bodo areas. As the tribal lands were more fertile so the political leaders of Assam encouraged them to settle in these fertile lands, thereby causing displacement of the tribals, particularly the Bodos. Even Mr Gopinath Bardoloi disappointed the AATL (All Assam Tribal League), because as the chairman of the Constituent Assembly's subcommittee dealing with the north-eastern tribals, he chose to ignore the genuine grievances of the plains tribes. The British took farseeing and preventive steps by initiating the 'Line System' which would enable some areas in Assam to remain free from immigrant settlements. But they are also to be blamed as they brought indentured labourers for the tea and petroleum industries and settled them in the Bodo areas. Later we find that successive governments of Assam continued to press for the abolition of the 'Line System'. In 1942, the Sadullah government opened up grazing reserves for the settlements of the immigrants under the banner 'grow more food'. Thus, the 'Line System' which was introduced by the British was offset by the native governments who had no consideration for the plain tribes. If a tribe is encroached upon in their own land then a series of after effects follow such as that the tribe becomes economically poor. Economic poverty leads to the down-gradation of the social status of the tribe and in such a situation the indigenous culture of the tribe also gets wiped out. The Bodos were predominantly agriculturists in the fertile tracts of the Brahmaputra, but because of rampant encroachment they were literally pushed to the remote jungles and had to depend on the jhum cultivation. The violation of the 'Line System' by the officials and interested parties at the local level received protection from powerful lobbies and the local people could not be stopped from selling lands to immigrants in the restricted areas for high prices. Hence the demand for the formation of 'belts and blocks' to protect the tribal lands came up after the independence of the country. According to Jitendra Narayan Dash, 'the state Congress government had created a number of "tribal belts" and "blocks" (around 40 of them) in 1950, in which only tribals and scheduled castes can own land, but the encroachment and land grabbings still continue unabated'. (Dash, 340) The 'belts and blocks' which were incorporated in chapter X in the Assam Land and Revenue Regulation 1886 suffered the same fate as the 'Line System' partly due to the negligence and malpractices of the officials and also because of the drawbacks in the legislation itself. Given that the malpractices were evident and the law had failed to fulfill its primary purpose, the state machinery should have brought amendments to the law or it ought to have replaced the old law by a new one.

Every culture is associated with land and when one is deprived of one's ancestral land then definitely such deprivation would lead to the overshadowing of that culture and the life-style associated with it. Many art forms and customs emerge from primordial rituals related to the soil such as fertility rites. In a way, all human beings can trace their origins back to a *tribe.* In the amended version of the Assam Land Regulation Act of 1886 which was intended to give protection to tribal lands the word 'tribal' was omitted in chapter X. The very purpose of the law is defeated because the main aim of the legislation was to provide protection to the tribal land, and if the word 'tribal' is missing then it nullifies the objective for which it was enacted. Because of these defects it has been estimated that about 60 per cent of tribal land has been encroached upon and consequently the tribes face economic hardships. As early as 1967, the PTCA (Plains Tribal Council of Assam) was formed by some tribals themselves in order to preserve and protect the cultural, social and political identities of the plain tribal. Given the big brotherly attitude of the Assamese (as perceived by the Bodo leadership) the Bodos resisted assimilation with the majority community. As the government was also not sensitive to their needs and not keen on giving any protection or autonomy to preserve the identity of the Bodos, they themselves had to take matters into their own hands. So the stir for the demand for separate Bodoland began in 1987 in a democratic manner with the slogan, 'Divide Assam 50-50'.

Verrier Elwin uttered the following words with great relevance to our topic that Ramchandra Guha quotes in his renowned work *Savaging the Civilzed*: 'We may fight for three freedoms — freedom from fear, freedom from want, freedom from interference. We may see that the aboriginals get a square deal economically. We may see that they are freed from cheats and imposters, from oppressive landlords and money lenders, from corrupt and rapacious officials – the essential thing is not to "uplift" them into a social and economic sphere to which they cannot adapt themselves, but to restore to them the liberties of their own countryside'. (Guha, 170) The original or aboriginal people the Bodos deserve gestures of the kind that Elwin was calling for.

Recognising the language of a particular tribe in a formal way leads to the progress of that race or the tribe because it is in language that the socio-politico-cultural identity of the tribe can be realised, stabilised, formalised and preserved. What can be said or recorded about them in their own language cannot be as well done in some other language. If the particular tribe is miniscule in numbers then it might not find its recognition in the constitution or the statute books, however. But the Bodos were considered as the aborigines and were also substantial in numbers. Hence if such a large segment of the populace speaks the language then the Bodo language ought to have been included in the official language but we find that its inclusion was rather neglectfully delayed by the policy-makers. The Bodos speak the Bodo language which is derived from the Tibeto-Burmese family of languages. It's closely related to the Dimasa language of Assam and the Garo language of Meghalaya and also the Kokborok language spoken in the Tripura state.

The Bodo leaders campaigned for the introduction of Bodo as a medium of instruction in the primary and later in the high schools, through the Bodo Sahitya Sabha (formed in 1952), and we find that the Bodo medium of instruction was introduced in the primary school in 1963. Currently it is used as the medium of instruction at the secondary level and is also considered as the associate official language in the state of Assam. The language is officially written using the Devanagari script, though there is a long history associated with the using of the Roman script. The Bodos have now developed their script which is popularly known as the 'Deodhai'.

The Bodo language with a fairly rich legacy and tradition has been in the Eighth Schedule of the Constitution of India since 2003. Gauhati University has introduced the post-graduate course in Bodo 1996 which is laudable. The Bodos resented the imposition of the Assamese language in part because it is not 'the aboriginal language of Assam' and because it violates the pluralism of the multiethnic society. The Bodos were also very skeptical about the impact the Assam Accord would have on their existence, i.e., culturally, politically and economically. (In fact the Bodo leaders strongly opposed clause 6 of the Assam Accord, which promised safeguards to protect the cultural identity of 'the Assamese people'. Though the leaders of the Assam movement meant by the term 'Assamese people' the composite indigenous population of Assam, the Bodo leaders feared that the clause might give legitimacy to the imposition of Assamese language and culture on the Bodos. As Sanjib Baruah points out, 'During the six years of the Assam movement, ties among Assam's many ethnic groups were significantly ruptured…a somewhat surprising effect of the period was the worsening of relations among the "indigenous" people – the ethnic Assamese and the "tribal" groups, principally the Bodos.' (Baruah, 124)

India is hailed as a country where unity exists despite diversity but the Constitution felt that diversity should be allowed to exist in order to preserve the unity of the country, i.e., the different tribes should be allowed to practice their own vocations, culture, tradition, and customs. In the case of the scheduled tribes in the tribal areas, the law made by Parliament or the law made by the local legislature of Assam shall not apply unless the Governor *extends* that law to the tribal areas. So in order to respect and maintain the autonomy of the tribes, the Constitution of India provided for the establishment of Autonomous District Councils (ADC) which gives elaborate legislative, administrative and judicial powers. The District Councils have been empowered to constitute village councils and village courts, and as stated clearly no law of the centre or the state will be applicable in these autonomous regions without the District Councils' approval. Theoretically it is sound and appropriate but a more pragmatic approach is required from the administrators of the autonomous councils and the state and the central government.

Aware of their precarious position in the matter of land and territory, the Bodos were demanding a separate territory both in pre- and post-Independent India which was, however, never conceded. In the post-Independence period it was expected that the plain tribes, i.e., the Bodos would assimilate with the larger community of Assam. But unfortunately it never quite happened and the Bodos took to the path of different movements at different points for the recognition of their rights. Being poor and underdeveloped in many respects, they could not compete with their non-tribal neighbours. Hence some sort of protection with autonomy was demanded by the leaders at different points of time. Moreover, the homogenous culture was also breaking down as the 'moneyed outsiders' tempted some of the indigenous people to sell off their land at high prices. Hence the topography of Bodo culture saw a sea change. The Bodo accord of 1993 provided a statutory autonomy within the state of Assam by creating the Bodoland Autonomous Council (BAC). The council was to administer 38 subjects and to have its own legislative and executive organs. As the Bodo areas lacked continuity, it was not much of a success. And ultimately in 2003 the Sixth Schedule was made applicable by creating the Bodoland Territorial Council (BTC). The Bodoland People's Front (BPF) is the party in power and in the recently concluded election it has come to power again with Hagrama Mohilary being sworn in as the chief in the BTC area. An in-depth analysis makes one realise that the Constitutional safeguard was belatedly given and the encroached land cannot be given back to the original inhabitants. The provision of BTC Act 2003 states that those residing in the BTAD area at the commencement of the Act would continue to enjoy their rights over the land. This has created a great resentment among the plain tribes and they are resorting to unlawful ways of getting back the land. Thus, large scale violence has erupted between the Bodos and Adivasis and Bodos and Muslims. This has resulted in the violation of Human Rights of the non-Bodos by the Bodos. Of course, the land rights of the Bodos were first violated by the non-Bodos which resulted in the loss of livelihood and the creation of an ethnic crisis. So violation of rights is taking place on both sides. If post-independent rulers had been more aware of the land rights of the Bodos then the massive arson, looting and killing would not have occurred. In Assam, about 3.14 lakhs Bodos and Adivasis were displaced as a result of ethnic clashes between the two communities in 1993, 1996, and 1998. The BPF (Bodoland Peoples Front), the ruling party did not posses much power and it had no jurisdiction over the police which resulted in the clashes often going out of control. So it was functioning as an expanded Panchayat rather than a real autonomous council as given by the Sixth Schedule. We can also raise a point that that the success or the tall claims of the growth fallacy which the political and the permanent executive constantly make need to be subjected to grass-root analysis. This is because the different sub-districts of India, which has a high concentration of the tribal population, are in an abysmally poor condition in terms of income, health, education, nutrition etc. This applies to the tribal population of our state too. It has been estimated that '40 per cent of the 60 million people displaced following the different developmental projects in India are tribal which is not a surprise given that 90 per cent of our coal and more than 50 per cent of most minerals and dam sites are mainly in tribal regions.' (Shah). So we find that the different laws and regulations meant for the different tribes and the sub-tribes to ward off their different deprivations, e.g., ethnic or regional disadvantages, have not been pragmatic or effective enough. We find the same situation in the state of Assam with respect to our tribal population.

The situation in the Bodo areas is uncertain and insecure. Political will and efficiency is needed to make the impoverished Bodos live with dignity. Only then their culture and tradition will exist and perpetuate. If the Bodo rulers and the coteries surrounding them use power to fulfill their own interest, then the Bodos as a plains tribe will perish and no Constitutional safeguards will help in their preserving their 'distinct identity'. It has been claimed that the canker of corruption is also infecting the autonomous council. Everyone should take these charges seriously. The political class should be more accountable and free from corruption.

Through education one can see the light of one's own culture and civilisation. Hence spreading of education should be undertaken on a vigorous scale. The school syllabus should also teach children about their rich cultural heritage. The culture of Common Property Resources should be started in the undeveloped and poor areas which will enable them to have some sort of equity amongst themselves. This concept will further aid in achieving the much needed 'sustainable development' which not only ensures the legitimate utilisation of our resources but also to preserve it for our future generations. Here the role of the *gaon-burah* in the Panchayat is very crucial.

Once the Maharani Gayatri Devi of Jaipur blamed the Congress government for brutally disturbing the cultural ethos of the tribals by taking away their lands, damming their rivers…to despise their tradition. (Guha, 337) We can sum up in Elwin's words that 'Whatever is done, and I would be the last to lay down a general programme, it must be done with caution and above all with love and reverence. The aboriginals are the real swadeshi products of India in whose presence everything is foreign. These are the ancient people with moral claims and rights thousands of years old. They are here first: they should come first in our regard. (Guha, 170) Hence the government, citizens (tribal and non-tribal), non-government organisations and civil society should always recognise the legal and rightful demands of the tribal before we see them disappearing from the face of the earth.

References

Baruah, Sanjib (2001), *India Against Itself: Assam and the Politics of Nationality.* New Delhi: Oxford University Press.

Bordoloi, B. N., G.C. Sharma Thakur and M.C. Saikia (1987), *Tribes of Assam Part - 1*. Guwahati: Tribal Research Institute.

Boro, Anil Kumar(2010), *A History of Bodo Literature.* New Delhi: Sahitya Akademi.

Dash, Jitendra Narayan, 'Udayachal Movement in Assam – A Case of Socio-Political Identity for the Bodos, ' *The Indian Journal of Political Science,* Vol. 50, No. 3. July – September, 1989. 335-42. http://www.jstor.org/stable/41855438. Accessed 20 April, 2015.

Ganguli, A.K., 'Right to Property: Its Evolution and Constitutional Development in India.' *The Journal of Indian Law Institute*, Vol. 48, No. 4 (Oct-Dec 2006). 489-526.

Guha, Amalendu (1977), *Planter-Raj to Swaraj*. New Delhi: Indian Council of Historical Research, p. 26.

Guha, Ramachandra, *Savaging the Civilised*, New Delhi: Penguin Books, 2014.

Jain, M.P., *Indian Constitutional Law*. Nagpur: Wadhwa Publication, 2005.

Nath, Manoj Kumar, 'Bodo Insurgency in Assam: New Accord and New Problems', *Strategic Analysis* (A Journal of Institute for Defence Studies and Analyses), Vol. 27, No. 4 (Oct-Dec 2003). 533-545. www.idsa.in/taxonomy/term/681.html

Saikia, Utpal, 'Immigration, Land-occupation and Identity Crisis, ' *The Assam Tribune* (January 2, 2015).

Shah, Mihir, 'Tribal alienation in an unequal India,' *The Hindu,* 14 July, 2015.

Shrivastava, Assem and Ashish Kothari. *Churning the Earth: The Making of Global India*. New Delhi: Penguin Books, 2012.

27

Tradition and Change of the *Kherai* Dance

— *Rupashree Hazowary*

Methodology

Primary and secondary source is mostly used to collect the data on the origin and use of the traditional musical instruments of the Bodos from the different people specially associated with the musical and social institutions. Few printed books, magazines and souvenirs published by the distinguished publishers and the reception committee of conferences of the Bodo nationalist organisations, internet sources were referred.

Introduction

The Bodos is one of the major tribes of Assam belonging to Tibeto-Burman group of Mongoloid family. They have a rich tradition of their own culture. The culture of the Bodos constitutes not merely physical or material culture; it also comprises mental and spiritual culture. The festivals and ceremonies of the Bodos can be classified as (a) Religious, (b) Seasonal and (c) Agricultural. Among the religious festivals of the Bodos the '*Kherai*' worship or puja and the '*Garja*' worship or puja' are the most important that are observed in different times.

Before going to study on the *Kherai* dances of the Bodos it deems necessary to give short description of the traditional religion of the Bodos which is called *Bathou*. The *Bathou* is the traditional religion of the Bodos that has been practicing since time immemorial and this is a major religious festival or worship of and closely associated with Bathouism. The term *Bathou* has two words-'*Ba*' and '*thou*' i.e. composed of five deep philosophical significance or five principles. These are *Bar* (air), *Ha* (land),

Dwi (water), *Or* (fire), *Okhwrang* (sky). Hindu philosophy is *panchaphut*. According to Bathouists, '*Ba*' means 'Five' and '*Thou*' means deep spiritual things, the unfurling of which needs close introspection. This is embodied in the mantra of the *Bathou* worship:

Thaigir ni Khonga Khongba
Sijouni Siria Siriba
Siphungni Gudunga Gudungba
Bathouni Bandoa Baodwba
Boro Boraini Raoa Phongba
i.e., The Thaigir(ou) fruits has five ridges.
The *Siju* plant has five edges.
The *Sifung* (flute) has five holes.
The alter of the *Bathou* has five rings
So the Bodos have five principles.[1]

Similarly in many cases, the Bodos have the principle of five viz,

(a) The first imaginary Gods worshipped by the primitive Bodo people are also only five: (i) *Hailong* (the god of earth), (ii) *Agrang* (the God of water), (iii) *Khwila* (the god of air), (iv) *Sanjabwrlee* (the god of light) and *Rajkhumbree* (the god of sky). (b) Principles given by the Primitive Bodo man called *Mwnchinchin* are also five –(i) *Saithi* (peace), (ii) *Laothi* (control of mind), (iii) *Nalathi* (co-operation of mind and body), (iv) *Maothi* (achieveness), (v) *Sonathi* (Dearer). (c) The original numerals are also five (i) *Se* (one), (ii) *Nwi* (Two), (iii) *Tham* (three), (iv) *Brwi* (four), and (v) *Ba* (five). (d) The five holy realisations: (i) Realisation of *Siju* (The supreme soul), (ii) Linking of the '*Jiwma*' (human soul) with *Siju*- the supreme being, (iii) Realisation of *Mainao* (i.e. Laksmi, the Goddess of prosperity), (iv) Realisation of the five great elements, viz. Earth, water, Air, Light, or Fire and Sky, (v) Realisation of need of worldly affair. (e) The religion is based on five folds preaching's as: (i) Meditation prayer of God, (ii) Conversing Religious and spiritual matters, (iii) Making charitable gifts to the poor, (iv) Loving the fellow-beings, (v) Doing things unitedly. The '*Sijuo*' tree (Euphorbia splendens) is the living symbol of *Bathou Brai*, the supreme God.

Etymology of the *Kherai*

It is difficult to ascertain the source from which the word '*Kherai*' was originated. There are different meaning of different scholars and writers about the origin of the words '*Kherai*'. The worshippers of the *Bathou* use to believe that the *Kherai* word originates from the sound '*Khe*' and it is added with the '*Rai*', which means enchanting formula before the chief god '*Bathou*' (*kherai Borai*). So, it is also believed that the word '*Kherai*' is derived from a combination like *Khe+rai= Kherai*. There is similarity between the *Kherai* puja of the Bodos and '*Ker*' *puja* of Tripura, the *Khernang* of North Cachar and the *Kheraima* of Nepal.[2]

According to Kameswar Brahma, "The '*Kherai*' worship is the greatest religious worship and festival of the Bodos. There are four kinds of '*Kherai*' worship : (i) The Darshan Kherai, (ii) The Umrao Kherai, (iii) The Phalo Kherai and (iv) The Nowaoni Kherai.[3] The Bodos perform these four worships or pujas on some specific occasion.

(i) The *Darshan Kherai*: This *Kherai* is performed during the first week of the month of *Khati* or *Kartik* (Bengali month). This *Kherai* puja is meant for '*Mainao*' or 'Lakshmi', the Goddess of Wealth and welfare.

(ii) The *Umrao Kherai*: It is held during the month of '*Ashara*' at the end of the '*Amthi Sua*' for the welfare of the villagers as well as of the crops.

(iii) The *Phalo Kherai*: The *Phalo Kherai* is performed during the month of *Magha* (Bengali month), specially on the day of '*Magi Purnima*' or the full moon of the month of '*Magha*'.

(iv) *Nowaoni Kherai*: This kind of *Kherai* is performed by the family when it deems necessary.

According to Liladhar Brahma, "there are five kinds of Kherai worship- (i) *Songsari Kherai,* (ii)*Garja Kherai,* (iii) *Amthi Kherai,* (iv) *Mainao Kherai* and (v) *Bathou Kherai*.[4] Whatever it may be, though the observation of *Kherai* worship is different place to place the purpose of worship is the same. It needs mentioning here that there are two systems in respect of worshipping this age old practice: traditional and modern. The traditional system is with offering and sacrificing animal and modern system is with offering flower and *prasad.* Like other parts of areas two systems of observation are also found available in Kokrajhar district. The worshippers of the traditional system of *Kherai* the *Douri* offers and sacrifices chicken in the name of different deities: on the other hand, modern system of *Kherai* worships the *Douri* offers *Alari bathi* i.e. earthen light and flowers.

Myth Associated with *Kherai Mwchanai* (Dance)

It is already said that the *Kherai* is a religious worship and many kinds of dances are performed here. The same meaning of English term 'dance' in the Bodo word is *mwsanai i.e.* the Bodo word *Mwchanai* means dance. The word '*Mwchanai*' is composed of two words, e.g. *Mwdwm* +

Chanai=Mwchanai. *Mwdwm* means 'Body' and *Chanai* means 'to be twisted'. Thus, the word *Mwchanai* means the twisting of the body in bewitching motion and waves. So '*Kherai Mwchanai*' means '*Kherai*' dance of religious of Bodo.[5] The dances those are performed during the *Kherai* worship are known as *Kherai Mwchanai*. There is a mythical story which narrates and recounts the origin of '*Kherai*' worship and '*Kherai*' dance among the Bodos.

Once upon a time there was an old man. His name was Zara. He had five sons, who were all grown up. During the course of time all the sons of the old man were married. His youngest daughter-in-law named was Mongli. She was not only beautiful but also she was so expert in household activities. (*nokhorni maba mwnse jengna jana noniphrai kharkhwma langw*)). But after big problem of the family she fled away one day early at dawn. Finding her missing, his granary became empty. His youngest son become like a mad. The old man Zara went in search of her and moved from place to place. He could not find out her whereabouts. But he did not take rest. He went on search Mongli. He forgets to take food. He forgets to take care of his dress and health. So people called him *phagla* (a mad man) jokingly, but he was not *phagla* (mad). After 12 years the old man dreamt a dream. An old man appeared before him in dream and told him to perform the *Kherai* puja or worship with the help of the musical instruments like *Khum* (drum), *Cerza* (cerenda), *Cipung* (flute) and *Thal* (cymble). The old man invited all his sons and performed a grand *Kherai* worship in the night of full moon. As the musical instruments were played, a woman appeared there from somewhere and began to dance as the '*Doudini*'. This woman was none but Mongli, the lost daughter-in-law of the old man. This is how the '*Kherai*' was originated. The old man who performed the '*Kherai*' worship was '*MonsingsingBrai*' and old man appearing in dream was '*BathouBrai*'. This mythical tale extant in Bodo culture is a significant one as it narrates the tale of the early fore-father of the Bodos to be accepted as true.[6]

Kheraisali

The place where the *Kherai* is worshipped is known as *Kheraisali*. Before worshipping the place where to be observed is clean and the new *sijou* is planted here with certain rites and rituals. The '*Sijuo*' tree (Euphorbia splendens) is planted in the *Bathou* altar at the centre as the living symbol of *Bathou* religion during the *Kherai* worship.

The '*Kherai*' institution is the prayer institution of '*Bwrai Bathou*'. The '*Kherai*' dances are performed to please the holy '*Bathou Borai*' and other Gods and Goddesses. Two holy persons, a *dauri* and a *doudini*, remain as the holy custodians of worship or puja under of the '*Oja*' (a medicine man) and they performed all the religious rites. The '*Doudini*' is the key dancer during the '*Kherai*' worship and it is the role played by a woman or a girl only. In other words it can be said no male dancer is allowed to role her part. The word '*Doudini*' may be derived as follows-*Dou+Dhi*> *Doudhini*> *Doudini.*

In Rigveda of the Aryans it is found that '*Dou*' means 'Worshipping God' and '*Dhi*' means 'Meditation', thus the word. '*Doudini*' means the female individual by whom 'worshipping God in meditated'. The great philosophers of religions opine that God cannot be felt or meditated without a super-human media. To this concern '*Doudini*' is the media for *Bathouists* while *Krisna* is for Hindus, Buddha for Buddhists, Jesus for Christians, Hazarat Mahammad for Islamists and so on.[7] In ancient India, there were no dedicated auditorium halls or theaters, and dance was usually a functional activity dedicated to worship, entertainment or leisure. Dancers usually performed in temples, on festive occasions and seasonal harvests. Dance was performed on a regular basis before deities as a form of worship. Even in modern India, deities are evoked through religious folk dance forms from ancient time. Classical dance forms such as *Bharat Natyam* use *mudras* or hand gestures also retell episodes of mythological tales such as the slaying of *Kaliya* of *Krishna*. Gradually dancers, particularly from south India, moved from temple to houses of royal families where they performed exclusively for royal.[8]

Role of '*Doudini*' during the '*Kherai*' Worship

There are eighteen types of '*Kherai*' dance-dramas who concepts the theory of eighteen deities, one for each while sixteen for the connectors of sixteen. In addition, there are more '*Kherai*' dances which can be called associated '***Kherai***' dance-drama. All the items of the '*Kherai*' worship are performed by '*Doudini*', while she dances by the mantra or formula of '*Oja*'. Besides, two *Kham* (drum) beaters, two '*Sifung*' (bamboo flutes) players, and two *Zotha* (cymbal) players . From the begging of the worship '*Doudini*' is demonstrated into three stages activities. The first role of the '*Doudini*' is called '*Doudini Onsrainai*' or '*Alongikhangnai*'. She falls into a trance and is converted to a spiritual being and now she can speak in the voices of the Gods and Goddesses. Thus, she started speaking as the representative of gods and goddesses. "In ancient Indian temples Brahmin priests (pundits) used to narrate the stories of Gods and Goddesses through dance came to be known as *Kathakar* (storyteller) and dance came to be known as "*Kathak*."[9] So it is observed that *Doudini* becomes the mediator between the divine and mundane and spiritual. She speaks about the future of the crops and the good and bad days to come in that calendar year. The '*Doudini*' moves round the '*Bathou*' alter and '*Dwi Santhi*' (holy water) sprinkles from a brass pot and dance rhythmic dances as the musical instruments like *Kham*, *Sifung Serza* and *Zotha*. This is the **second** stages of '*Doudini*' dances known as '*Bathou Phwtharnai*'. It is interesting to note here that in the midst of performing '*Kherai*' worship, the male performers make comic gestures and actions while the players of musical instruments play traditional musical instruments. The worshippers also may join in the circle of dancing with *Doudini*.Whatever, it may be, though there are eighteen kinds of dances in the traditional *Kherai*, the modified Bathouist they perform only 16 (sixteen) kinds of dances. As my field work done in Naigaon Bathabari under Kokrajhar district, they do not perform *Dao thwi lwngnai* (drinking bird's blood) and *Thungri sayao mwsanai* (dance on the sword). There are no much difference between the modified and traditional *Kherai* festival in respect of worship. The traditional sacrifice animals and rice beer. On the other hand the modified use flower and holy water. Whatever, it may be.

Description of the Dances of the *Kherai*

While '*Doudini*' dances, she imitates the nature of Gods and Goddesses. She demonstrates as many kinds of different dances.

They use flower and holy water during the worship of each deities of the *Kherai*.

By this time she changes her nature into three stages. **First**, she changes her mood, **secondly**, she assimilates her with Gods and **thirdly**, she imitates the nature of different Gods and Goddesses dramatically. The dances of the *Doudini* during the *Kherai* festival have given birth to specific art form. These are as follows—

(i) Dahal sibnai: This dance is one of the important dances of the *Kherai* worship. Both the traditional and modern system of *Kherai* worshippers performs this dance. This dance is related with the God '*Ailong* deity'. '*Doudini*' holds '*thungri*' (a long sword) and a *Dahal* (a shield) while she dances. '*Doudini*' demonstrates this dance preparation of the battle field and she moves round the altar of the '*Bathou*'.

(ii) Cha gwlao bwnai: The second '***Phathali***' (stage name of Gods and Goddesses) is dedicated to '*Khaji*' deity. Through this dance '*Doudini*' demonstrates the preparation for the battle. This dance compare with the character of '*Samudra Manthan*' of the '*Mahabarata*'. This dance is like tank of war.

(iii) **Khwijwma fonai:** This dance related with the God '*Abla Khungur'* deity. '*Khwijwma'* means amroli insect. '*Phonai'* means to get rid of. Here *khwijwma* is replete with symbolic connotation. With this dance the *Doudini* demonstrate the tactics how to destroy the enemies in the battle field. D*oudini* taking *Gupur Gamcha* (a white towel) by her left hand and holding a '*Thungri'* (shield) by right hand and performed. arw thungrijwng sunai baidi danw. Kwijwmani wngthia jadwng suture. Jwng sutura gaglwba hengtha hwnangou arw pwjwbnangou.

(iv) **Chathraoli:** This is a kind of war dance in the name of '*Agrang'* deity. '*Doudini'* dances holding a sword by right hand (piding piding) and a sword in mouth (khungajwng ornai) and moves dancing round the alter of the *Bathou*. He is believed to be demonstrating the war dance in the name of the Goddesses of war.

(v) **Gandoula Bwnnai:** '*Gandoula'* means dragonfly. '*Doudini'* performs this dance dram form to propitiate the God '*Khwila'* deity. Here also demonstrates the tactics of subjugating the enemies are shown by the *Doudini* through her dance. This dance form tactics of catching a dragonfly with the help of a trap.

(vi) **Dahal –Thungri Sibnai:** The *Doudini* performs this dance form with Dhal (a sword) and Thungri (a shield) in her hands. (thungrikhou daoha nangnai baidi sibw arw suhang khalamna dinthina mwsayw). She demonstrates the tactics of self-defence during the battle in the field.

(vii) **Khamao Barkhwnai:** *Kham* means drum, *Brakhwnai* means climb up. At the time of propitiating this God '*Doudini'* performs this dance climbs up the *Kham* (drum) and dances on it. ('*Rajkhandra'*, grandson of *Baraibatou*, is the God who is performs this dance.

(viii) **Badali Birnai:** This dance is related with the God '*Swanjani Ali Burah* Deity. She imitates the nature of *Badali* (bat) in this dance form. She covers her face with a piece of white cloth and starts dancing catching hold of the '*Khangla'* reads in the *Bathou*. (Arw akhaikhou unthing malaba birnaibaidi khalamw).

(ix) **Mwishw Gelenai:** This dance is a dance form performed by *Doudini* during *Kherai* festival. *Mwisw* means buffalo. So this dance form demonstrates the nature of the buffalo. (khituthing akhai paikrob paikrob mwsayw). The *Doudini* performs this dance form to God ***AiDibaoliya deity.***

(x) **Bathou gidingnai:** *Douini* performs this dance moves round the altar of the *Bathou* for three times dancing slowly in the tune of the *sifung* (fute), associated by the *Kham* (drum), and *Zotha* (cymbals), (hailalai huilalai akhikou udang hogarna giding giding).

(xi) **Nao Basainai:** This dance is dedicated to '*Monasu'* a deity of river. The '*Doudini'* holds a miniature boat made of the shell of a banana tree and goes dancing around the '*Bathou'* trailed by group of male dancers. The underlying philosophy of this dance lies in the explanation that the boat represents the road of God and that the rivers or sea represents the wide world. This road helps a man to renounce evil thoughts acts and designs, and acquire truth and peace.

(xii) **Mufur gelenai:** *Mufur* gelenai (dance of bear playing) is performed by the *Doudini* in the nature of a bear (*mufur*) and dances around the *Bathou*. Other dancers also move dancing along with the *Doudini*. The dance of bear play points out man's desire to subdue his animal spirit and then worship '*Bwrai Bathou'* in the form of *Sijou* (cactus plants).

(xiii) **Mainao Borainai:** This dance is presented to sari *Joumwn Bwrai* deity. The '*Doudini'* herself assume the form of *Mainao* (laxkmi. Riches, health) deity from the world she build altar in a kitchen corner of village worship and related festival. The '*Doudini'* sits on *Gamari* wood which is believed to be holy. After some ritualistic propitiation chanting of mantras or formula the '*Doudini*' performs the dance drama followed by the devotees to tune of the flute and the beating of the drum and rhythm of the cymbal.

(xiv) **Mwsa gelenai:** The '*Doudini'* performs this dance for *Bag Raja* (tiger) deity. As the music of drum, flute, and cymbals flourishes the '*Doudini'*, acting like a tiger, dances around the '*Bathou'*. Some of the dancers trailing her act like tigers and others like dogs. While the tiger's group roar and try to attack the dog's party they run way to protect themselves.

(xv) **Gorai Dabrainai:** This dance is dedicated to '*Basumathi'* deity. In this dance four or five dancers take a stick each and hold the sticks between their legs so as to make themselves appear as if they were riding horse. There is a belief that God basumati is a soldier of *Sibrai*. With a view to propitiating him, the '*Doudini'* performs the '*Goraidarainai'* (horse riding) dance to symbolise the action of the soldiers.

(xvi) Nao Jaonai: The literal meaning of *Nao Basainai* or *Nao Bwnai* is draw the boat. The *Doudini* takes a sword and holding it like an oar while rowing a boat, moves ahead. A few dancers follow suit as if they were helping her in a boat to sail across a river. The helper, at times, steals out of dance in order to create amusement among the audience. Then two or three persons from the audience search for the boatman bring him back and make him row the boat again. Crossing a river by boat involves danger and other kinds of troubles. In spite of this, person can cross rivers by boat safely.

(xvii) Thungri Sayao Mwsanai (dance on the sword): This dance is one of the fascinating and fearful dances performed by *doudini*. This dance is not related to any deities. It seems that *doudini* show her expertise and power through the *Kherai* worship to the gods and goddesses.

The eighteen types of *Kherai* dances who concepts the theory of eighteen deities have also one dance for each deity. But it is yet to study more. The *Kherai* dances without having concern with the deities of *Bathou* family are associated *Kherai* dances which bear an important role at par. These are known as Secondary *Kherai* or *Uphra Kherai,* e.g., *Thwi Lwngnai Mwchanai, Thenthamali Mwchanai, Neolai gelenai mwchanai, Lantha Gurzi, Dawang Buthua, Maoji Mengbrang Gelenai, Jaraphagla, Dawang Buthua, Saoria Daoria* and so on.

Last Phase of the *Kherai* Worship

At the conclusion of the '*Kherai*' the worshippers symbolically receive *Mainao* (Lakshmi), the Goddess of the wealth from the earth through the '*Doudini*'. The *Doudini* sits on the ground in front of the *Bathou* altar without any movement and remains quite silent. The *Oja* or *Douri* and his associates then starts worshipping the Goddess *Mainao*. Then they pray *Mainao* to be always with them, while the *Kham* (drum), *Sifung* (flute), *Jotha* (Cymbal) and *Serja* are played on and produced melodious tune.

At the request of the worshippers the '*Mainao*' becomes satisfied and agree to say at kitchen of the worshippers. She expresses dramatically her willingness to go with them on some conditions. After that '*Doudini*' stand up from her seat and starts to dance.

Dress and Ornaments: The dresses and ornaments worn by *doudini* during the *Kherai* worship are different from place to place. No uniform dresses and ornaments are worn by other assistants of the worship. The performer playing the musical instruments and the dancers taking part in the dance performances all appear in uniforms of colourful and beautiful designed traditional Bodo apparels and garments. The *Doudini* of Kokrajhar and Chirang and Udalguri wear colourful Yellow *Dokhona*, Red Blouse, *Guphur Phali* (white cloth), *janji khanai phalli* and *Aronai* (traditional neck tight). The musical instruments players wear *gamsa, gosla, phagri* and *Aronai*.

Use of Musical instruments: The following given musical instruments are playing during the *Kherai* worship:*Kham*(drum), *Sifung* (flute), *Jotha* (Cymbal), *Thungri* (sword), *Dahal* (shield) and *Raigon* (one kind of bed).

Conclusion

The *Kherai* is the greatest religious worship among the Bodos that had been observing with traditional system since time immemorial. But it has been modified by the educated section of the society's people to suit it in modern times. But few sections are still practiced this age-old worship sacrificing the animal in the name of different deities. They are of the view that they lost and are losing something their valuable heritage because of modifying this age-old tradition. So, this section wants to have all the dances without losing anything else. The follower of modified *Kherai* worship they stop totally sacrificing animal and offer flower, *prosads*. These can be assumed the influence of Hinduism.

It is an arguable too that the modified *Kherai* worshippers cannot perform the two dances such as drinking bird's blood and dance on the sword. It is certainly true to say that the new believers are losing two important valuable dances. Therefore, the scholars of the *Bathou* believers are also thinking and working in this regard to keep all the traditional things without any changing. Whatever, it may be, there is tremendous change in respect of worship, performances, and earlier the *Kherai* dances were performed only in this worship. Now it has been brought and performed on the stages in the public places such as meeting, conferences and so on. Moreover, the dances have got new form in the hands of the modern choreographers in the society.

References

1. Boro, Anil, 2004, '*The Flute and Harp, an Essay on Bodo Culture and Literature*' pp. 37-38, published by Good Books Distributors Publishers.
2. *Ibid,* p. 104.
3. Brahma, Kameswar, 1998: '*AStudy in Cultural Heritage of the Boros*', p. 102, published by Chiranjib Brahma.
4. Brahma, L.2011, *Boro Mwsanai,* The Assam Institute of Research for Tribals and Scheduled Castes, Jawahar Nagar, Guwahati, p. 39.

5. Brahma, L., '*Religion and Dances of the Bodos*', p. 17, second edition, 2003, published by Onsumoi Library.
6. Bodo publication Board, '*Kherai Mwsanaini Santhou*', pp. 22-27, second edition, 1993.
7. Brahma, L.2003, '*Religion and dances of the Bodos*', p. 8, published by Onsumoi Library.
8. Reddy, Smitha, '*Encyclopedia of Indian Dances*', p. 2, Vol. II, by Cyber tech publications, 2014.
9. Reddy, Smitha, '*Encyclopedia of Indian Dances*', p. 4.

28

Women's Space in Performing Arts (Theatre) in Assam: From Jatra to Mobile Theatre

— Sangeeta Kakoty

Gender is a socially constructed definition of women and men. Sex is the biological characteristics of men and women while gender is defined by the functions, tasks and roles attributed to men and women in society. "The Gender approach is distinct in that it focuses on women and men, and not on women in isolation. It highlights the differences between women's and men's interests even within the household and how these interact and are expressed; the conventions and hierarchies which determine women's and men's position in the family, community and society at large, whereby women are usually dominated by men; the differences among women and among men, based on age, wealth, ethnic background and other factors; the way gender roles and relations change, often quite rapidly, as a result of social, economic and technological trends."[1]

Popular Culture is the accumulated store of cultural products such as music, art, literature, fashion, dance, films, television and radio that are consumed by non-elite groups such as working lower and middle class. There are two opposing social arguments in relation to popular culture. One argument is that popular culture is used by elites (who tend to control the mass media and popular cultural outlets) to control those below them because it dulls people's minds, making them passive and easy to control. A second argument is just the opposite, that popular culture is a vehicle for rebellion against the culture of dominant groups.[2] Here, the dominant culture refers to the elites.

Keeping these two definitions in mind, this paper is a humble attempt to look into the space that has been given to women in the field of performing arts in Assam. Since the arena of performing arts is a very broad the study has been limited to the field of Theater from *Jatra* to Mobile Theater.

In spite of one of the principal feature of the tribal culture of Assam being the position of importance that was occupied by women, why were women missing or relegated to a background position as far as performing arts were concerned? The passage of time stands witness to the various trials and tribulations that women has had to go through in a patriarchal set up to be able to carve a niche in the arena of performing arts (in this case, theater). What were the hurdles? What was the mindset of society? How much of it has actually changed? Today, can we say that women hold a position of equality in the field of performing arts (Theater) in Assam?

This paper has been written basically depending upon Primary data (Interviews) and secondary data, that is, relevant books, both Assamese and English, magazines, souvenirs etc.

Performing Arts are those forms of art in which individual people perform separately or together. It includes dance, music, opera, drama, magic, oratory and circus etc. "The history of Assamese drama is very long and old indeed older surely than the drama of any Indian modern language and older than even the regular English dramas by at least a century. The first drama is certainly *Chihna Jatra* (literally a play with painted scenes) and the first theatre is the performance of it in 1468. As a matter of fact, neither introduction of scenes nor the regular drama in Europe in general can be ascribed to a period earlier than the seventeenth century, and in England in particular regular dramatic work really began in the later part in the sixteenth century with such predecessors of Shakespeare as Marlow, and the Globe Theatre which Shakespeare had immortalised was actually established in 1599".[3] "It is said that just as the cradle of European drama rested on the altar, Assamese drama was also born under the shadow of the *Namghar,* and was nurtured for religious purposes. The *Kathaguru Carita* and *Bardowa Carita* mention that, after returning from his first pilgrimage, Sankardeva*, composed and staged his first play against the backdrop of painted scenes of *vaikuntha* or heaven in 1468. It was called *Cihna-jatra*, or play with the painted scenes. The biographies or *carita –puthis* mention that Sankardeva himself painted the scenes of *vaikuntha* on *tulapaat.* It is said the play was divided into seven parts progressing in quick succession, with a Sutradhar and Vishnu. Sankardeva himself is said to have enacted the role of Vishnu and the play seems to have continued for seven days and seven nights."[4] "Mahapurush Madhabdeva followed his Guru Mahapurush Srimanta Sankardeva's footsteps and wrote plays which contributed to the foundation of Assamese drama and stage. These plays created by the duo came to be known as *Ankiyanaat* though neither Sankardeva or Madhabdeva used this word. Both instead used *Natak*, *Naat* or *Jatra.* The elements drawn from the folk form of music, dance and drama not only broadened the range of appeal but also gave *Ankiyanaat* its unmistakable Assamese character. Among the folk forms that influenced him the most were *Ojapali,* a fascinating form combining elements of balladry, dance and drama, *Dhuliyanaach,* a form of group singing and dancing, *Bhaoriya*, a balladry and *Putola naach,* the traditional marionette theatre of Assam. It required a rare sensitivity to mould all these diverse elements and influences into a powerful dramatic alloy, which Sankardeva possessed.[5]

The Acting process or presentation of *Ankiyanaat* is called *Bhaona.* One of the striking feature about *Bhaona* was that the female roles were played by effeminate boys. There was no space for women in this performing art. In fact, women had no space in all the above mentioned folk forms i.e. *Ojapali, Dhuliyanaach, Bhaoriya and Putola naach*. To understand why we will have to look into the social condition of the time. "The process of Hinduisation or Aryanisation of the Mongoloid people began in Assam, as elsewhere in India, under the influence of the Brahmin priests, the Hindu military adventurers and merchants. But this process was a slow and gradual one and even the influence of Sankardeva and his followers in the Satras did not succeed in transforming the cultural base of Assam to give it a predominantly Brahmanical Hindu base. On the other hand, the Hindu culture and religion underwent significant changes under the impact of the Indo-Mongoloid influence in Assam."[6]

A study of the tribal culture of Assam reveals the position of importance occupied by women. "In all primitive societies, women by virtue of their vital role in procreation and in agricultural activities, occupied a position of supremacy. The matrilineal system, or the system of recognising women's rights in the matter of inheritance and of social administration, was the natural outcome of the practice of apportioning to the woman the primary position in social production. It is significant that even after Aryanisation brought about the overthrow of the mother's rights and the establishment of a patriarchal form of society, the matrilineal system continued to be prevalent amongst certain sections of the tribals of North-East, like the Austro-Asiatic Khasis and the Mongoloid Garos."[7] "The increase of wealth inevitably led to the overthrow of the female supremacy in the Assamese society and the establishment of patriarchy."[8] "The final elimination of women from all important positions in the religious and social life of the

Assamese Hindus for over five centuries was effected by the great Assamese Vaishnava saint, Sri Sankardeva (1449-1568). Sankardeva had successfully counteracted the influence of Brahmanical Hinduism and of Tantrism in Assam and had established a broadly egalitarian base for Assamese religious and social life. He made no distinction of caste in accepting disciples from amongst the tribals, Ahoms and even from amongst the Muslims."[9] "But in case of women, his attitude was marked by a strange intolerance. Considering women to be an evil influence on the male devotees, he advised his devotees to avoid attachment to women."[10] "In the ascetic order established by Madhavdeva, one of the greatest disciples of Sankardeva, strict restrictions regarding women were imposed on the monks."[11] "Sankardeva himself was adverse to accepting women, Kings and Brahmin priests as his disciples and though he was himself a twice-married man, he never gave women any position in the whole religious and cultural set-up created by him. In the Satras established by the followers of Sankardeva, women were virtually excluded from all aspects of the religious and cultural life and even the lowliest of duties, like wiping the prayer-hall were denied to women."[12] "Even today women are denied entrance to most important Vaishnava Satras of Assam. The only reference in the history of Assamese Vaishnavism to a woman playing an important religious role is the story of Kanaklata *Ai* who acted as a religious head for some time and deputed twelve apostles to different parts of Assam"[13] "Neo-Vaishnavite literature reflects the attitude towards women. In many places of his composition, he equalises women with a *sudra*, a *Yavana* or any people of so-called low origin, or even with birds and animals. (*stree sudragan adhama javana anujati papi nare-Bhagavat, II, V. 602*; *Stree sudraantya jati adhama chandale-Bhagavat, XI, V. 17649.)* Aniruddhadeva who composed the 5th Skanda of the Bhagavata says, "*Mahantar Seva jana Muktir Dwar/Stree Sangir* Sanga Narak Jaibar" (Bhagavat, V. 514557) meaning serving the Mahanta is the path to salvation while the company of a female is the path to hell. Thus, it is presumable that the social attitude towards women in the Sanskritised society of medieval Assam was in theory, a continuation of what it was in the greater Aryan society of India. The medieval social reformers themselves having hailed from the same cultural group perpetuated the old values rather than trying to abolish them."[14]

"In such a scenario it was no wonder that women had no space in the *Ankiya Bhaona* performances since these plays were an instrument of religious propagation and women had been consciously kept away from the core of this religious movement. The only common women having some attainments in art and culture were the *Natis* or temple girls who were proficient in cultivation of fine arts like dance and music. The fine arts of the period portray female figures as playing on musical instruments and dancing. The references to the *Natis* or *Devdasis* as proficient in these branches of arts in ancient literature or in those of medieval times as Ananta Kandali's *Kumara Harana*, Sankardeva's *Rukmini Harana* and other works like *Yogini Tantra*; and also the rock-cut remains with the female figures bear testimony to this. It is interesting to note that the dancing girls are neither condemned for dancing nor prevented from cultivating the arts. This was because the males of a particular class who could have condemned them, could enjoy their beauty for their satisfaction; in fact the dancing girls cultivated fine arts for the pleasure of man."[15]

"*Jatra* was the most popular regional theater form in rural areas of Bengal and among the Bengali-speaking people of neighbouring Bihar, Orissa, Assam and Tripura. It also holds sway over village audiences in Bangladesh (formerly East Bengal and later East Pakistan) where Bengali is spoken. *Jatra* means 'procession'. The form may have come into existence in the Sixteenth Century as a part of the Vaishnava devotional movement, introduced by Chaitanya, which swept the population into its fold through songs, dances and plays designed to propagate the faith. The earliest extant of *Jatra* scripts (Pala) date from the late Eighteenth Century. Prior to that plays were preserved as a part of the oral tradition of the region. Upto the early Nineteenth Century the *Jatra* plays focused on the religious themes and were instructive and moralistic in tone. Companies of Actors were owned and managed by the Chief Singer or Actor. In the Nineteenth Century, amateurs, mostly sons of bourgeois of Calcutta developed their own *Jatra* groups and chose secular themes for their subject matter. With the coming of the modern theater movement in the Nineteenth Century, "*Jatra*" borrowed the scenic displays of the proscenium-arch stage and imitated the western style of acting and writing that was beginning to be popular among the middle and upper classes of Calcutta."[16]

"Although it is difficult to establish since when and how *Jatra* became popular in Assam, a look into the cultural history of Assam shows that it was with the coming in of the British rule in Assam that *Jatra* began to spread its influence here. With the British came into Assam a flow of people from different parts of India, particularly Bengal. The main reason behind this was the educated Bengalis, as the helpers of the British rulers understood their administrative workings. Moreover, at that very point of time the British had started the Tea Industry in Assam, where they required people who knew English. Therefore, the British preferred the Bengalis. Naturally the Bengalis who came to reside here in Assam brought their culture with them. During festivals like Durga puja and Kali puja and sometimes just for the sake of entertainment these people organised and invited *Jatras,* which at that point of time was gaining a new leash of life and popularity in Bengal."[17] "It was between 1860-1865 that an indegenous *Jatra* troupe under the leadership of Tithiram Bayan was formed in Barpeta following the Bengali model".[18]

Once this trend of *Jatra* troupes started numerous *Jatra* troupes began to mushroom in Assam, particularly lower Assam because of the closer proximity to Bengal. The *jatra* plays presented in Bengali, naturally showcased the Bengali culture. Women had no space in the *Jatra* and all female roles were enacted by young boys. This comes as no surprise considering the patriarchal conservative society we are looking at. The article *Marginalisation of Women's Popular Culture in Nineteenth Century Bengal* by Sumanta Banerjee in Kumkum Sangri and S.Vaid edited *Recasting Women* is a vibrant account of women's space in performing arts in Bengal at that time.

"Together with the Vaishnava influence, Bengali Brahmanism which was introduced in Assam during the reign of the Ahom King Rudra Singha, proved utterly detrimental to the position of women in Assamese Hindu Society. The introduction of Bengali customs and prejudices, only served to strengthen the latent caste prejudices in Assam and to give legitimacy to such evil practices as child-marriage, prohibition of widow remarriage, ill-treatment of widows and seclusion of women."[19] "Modern Assamese Historians, while mentioning the absence of such extremely inhuman practices as 'Kulinism' and 'Sati' in Assam, have not been able to overlook the fact that women were considered as private property of men in the '*khel*' system, or that education of women was considered to be dangerous for society."[20] The positive fact here is, that in spite of this dark picture, the condition of women in Assam, in comparison to other parts of India, was better. The intermixing of the non-tribal society and tribal culture resulted in the Assamese society attaining a unique identity and social evils targeting women like Sati, female infanticide, dowry system and Kulinism could not gain ground in Assam.

"E.A. Gait has eloquently praised the beauty of Assamese women and the social freedom enjoyed by them."[21] "And yet it was only in 1933 that *Abhinayacharya* Brajanath Sarma, one of the pioneers in the field of theater in Assam, dared to introduce co-acting on the stage of Mobile theatre in Doomdooma in upper Assam breaking the shackles of a conservative society. Sixty years after Sarat Chandra Ghose, on the advice of Michael Madhusudan Dutta had introduced co-acting in Bengal by bringing Jagattarini, Elokeshi and Shyama on the stage, Brajanath Sarma took this revolutionary step that etched his name in golden letters forever in the history of Assamese drama."[22] "This was certainly not an overnight achievement and Brajanath Sarma had to work hard for more than three years to make his dream successful. He found support and encouragement when the legendary Phani Sarma joined the Kohinoor Opera Party. Together they went to the Parihareswar temple in Doobi near Pathsala, which was famous for its *Devdasi* dance tradition. Here they met two dancers Savitri and Sajani, who after prolonged discussions agreed to act on stage. All arrangements were made for the ladies to go to Barnagar for the rehearsals but, the shackles of the conservative society proved stronger and Savitri-Sajani changed their mind. The days roled by and Brajanath Sarma's search went on. Finally, after a lot of hard work, from Puranigudam (Nagaon) was found Sarbeswari Das and Golapi Das, from Samuguri was found Phuleswari Das, from Jorhat was found Sailabala Debi, from North Gauhati was found Labanya Das and from Nazira (Sibsagar) was found Binoda Gogoi. Considering the plight of education, particularly for females, it was not surprising that these girls had not seen beyond primary school (It is said Sailabala had completed M.V). As such, it was not possible to present them on stage immediately. A lot of stage, diction, pronunciation etc training had to be given before they were ready. Brajanath Sarma tutored them in all these aspects. At last in November 1933 "*Moran Jiyori*" was staged which inaugurated co-acting in the history of Assamese stage."[23]

The backlash of this daring endeavour was not surprising. Brajanath Sarma expressed the bitter experience thus to Phani Sarma- *"You know very well how I have managed to bring out these girls to the stage from within the interiors of a conservative patriarchal society. By introducing co-acting on stage I have suffered so much humiliation, criticism and bitterness even my own brother and nephew deserted the theatre party. The newspapers have criticised that I am trying to push the society towards destruction by inaugurating co-acting. I am propagating evil. Today, they are not being able to understanding what I am doing but one day people of Assam will understand. I am not destroying the society instead I have taken the culture of Assam and the drama movement fifty years ahead*."[24] Eminent stage actor Uday Bhagawati has mentioned in his book *Jatrar pora Bhramyamanoloi* how a strong protest was staged against Brajanath Sarma and his co-acting in Nalbari.

"This revolutionary step of Brajanath Sarma was not without appreciators. Intellectuals like Chandradhar Barua and Hemchandra Goswami encouraged and inspired him to bring about social reform through the stage. But the societal criticism of co-acting coupled with other management problems saw the closing down of the Kohinoor Opera Party in 1936. With that came to a standstill co-acting on the stage of Mobile Theater. Twenty years later in 1957 co-acting was seen on the Mobile Theatre stage for the second time when Tulika Das acted in 'Surjya Opera' produced by Late Surjya Das of Rangamati in South Kamrup. After that it was in 1960-61 that co-acting was revived on the stage of Mobile Theatre by Purandar Talukdar of Nityananda, near Pathsala and since then, the trend of co-acting has been continuing without any break till now."[25]

"The revolutionary work of Brajanath Sarma had inspired the thoughts of Rupkonwar Jyotiprasad Agarwala who, at that time was busy with the making of *Joymoti* the first Assamese movie. Agarwala sat in elaborate discussions with Phani Sarma (who had assisted Brajanath Sarma in inaugurating co-acting) before searching out actresses like Swargajyoti, Aideo Xondikoi and Mohini Rajkumari and in these discussions the actresses found by Brajanath Sarma, Golapi, Sarbeswari, Phuleswari etc also featured."[26]

Jyotiprasad Agarwala, in an article titled 'Asomor Film Silpa' has written *"in our nation, it is very difficult to get girls to perform in films: more so to select an able actress from among them. During the filming of Joymoti, about 28-30 girls were brought to the camp in Chitrabon. Most among them were uneducated village girls. From among them, only one could be considered for the film. But even then, this girl had to be continuously taught about acting for almost a year...but of course she had the face and talent for acting."*[27]

"In an interview taken by Bobbeeta Sarma (Author of *The Moving Image and Assamese Culture Joymoti, Jyotiprasad Agarwala, and Assamese Cinema.*) on 17 March 1997, Aideu Xondikoi, the First Assamese Film Actress recounted how she, a young girl of 13 years had been duped by her Uncle and taken to meet Jyotiprasad, how she had to live a life of isolation for three years as the village boycotted her family, the painful experience of how her own mother would not let her enter the kitchen, how for a long time she felt she 'had done something wrong' and as a result she never married. Aideu Xondikoi lamented the fact that she was never invited when the film was released. She was abandoned. Even during her life in isolation no one connected to the film came to meet her. She was forgotten. Years later Chief Minister of Assam Hiteswar Saikia gave her a pension of Rs 600 that was later raised to Rs 1000. It was only in 1994 that she saw *Joymoti* and that too, the documentary made by Dr Bhupen Hazarika, as the original reel had perished."[28]

Considering the conservative patriarchal set up that existed at that time it does not really surprise one that Aideu had to face such consequences but what one wonders is why did Jyotiprasad Agarwala forget her? Why a cultural icon of his stature never uttered any protest against the social injustice that Aideu had to face post-*Joymoti*? Why she was not invited even when the film was released? *Joymoti* was no doubt a revolutionary step in the cultural arena of Assam but was Aideu, a young innocent girl, a pawn in the larger scheme of things? Her name is etched forever in the history of Assamese cinema no doubt but Aideu Xondikoi had to pay a high price for it. What had been her fault? Her fault was breaking the norms and shackles of a male-dominated society that decided a woman's position and space and that too, unknowingly at an innocent age.

In an interview by this scholar, the First female Director of *Bhramyaman* (mobile) Theater, Smt. Pushpa Devi, who was also a leading Actress, recounted how she pioneered in this field in "Moon Theater" (The only all-female Mobile Theater) which was created as an off-shoot of Xuradebi Theater. It was an experiment which did not last very long. Pushpa Devi directed four-five plays in this theater around 1983-84. She also recalled how she also directed the popular play "*Xunmoina*" in Malaxmi Theater (1985) and had written the lyrics of many popular songs in Mobile Theater. On being asked about the dearth of female Directors she replied that ladies will have to volunteer to take up this responsibility in spite of the fact that sometimes they are not wanted.[29] Renu Dutta Phukan, the First female Singer in Mobile Theater who later on went on to become the First Woman Police Officer in Assam nostalgically recounted her stint with Nataraj Theater and the hurdles that she had to face as a female pioneer in both fields she chose. "In our society a woman always has to struggle double to prove herself", she said.

Film and Theater critic Nayan Prasad in his interview opined that basically people who come into this field wants to become Actors. Direction is a lesser chosen option probably because it is too much of responsibility. The Director has to look into everything from A to Z. In Assam, the concept of "specialisation" (roping in people to look into the different departments) has still not really come in so it is all the Directors headache. In such a scenario, a woman, with all her family obligations etc probably cannot devote twenty-four seven in the capacity as a Director. As far as the dearth of Female playwrights, he opined that to be a playwright one has to be very close to the stage and know it inside out. Editing is one field where quite a number of females have come in today. This is probably because although it is a very time consuming and taxing job, it does not entail too much of physical labour or moving around. Commenting on the women's space, Prasad said why Assam, if we look at Hollywood and Broadway also, how many women Director-Producers can we count?[30]

Renowned Theater personality and proprietor-producer of Abahon Theater, Krishna Roy in his interview recalled how one Minoti Acharya's play had been staged by Abahon in the nineties. On the point of this being rare he said that women will have to volunteer and must acquire the required knowledge of the stage. Another point he mentioned was that nowadays the Playwrights themselves are Directors so one has to invest a lot of time as well as hard work to keep up with the demand.[31]

As time has progressed things have definitely changed for the better but this has not been without its share of struggle. Women, who were path breakers in all fields had to put up a stiff fight to find their footing. Today when we look at the position of women in the arena of performing arts (theater) in Assam, it is a different scenario no doubt. Acting, singing or dancing whether on screen or stage is a choice which is encouraged and appreciated. Other associated departments like costume designing, choreography, dancing, singing, etc has provided space for women. Yet, somewhere it is still a male-dominated arena as far as decision-making is concerned. Cinema, theatre etc are reflections of the society's thoughts and views. If that be true, let us look how women are still portrayed in Indian movies and television serials. The ideal woman is still the *pativrata* (Radhika Sati image**). A strong willed woman who wants to live life on her terms is always the negative character. Isn't this a reflection of the age old patriarchal set up? How many women Producers and Directors are there? Or for that matter Cinematographers ? When one looks at the history of Mobile theatre, the question arises why in its existence of half a century not even half a dozen female Director or playwright is seen or heard of? Even in the arena of amateur drama how many female directors or dramatists are there? Women are still in the back seat in the vehicle of performing arts (theatre) in Assam. The question is why? Is there a dearth of talent or capacity? Or is it about opportunities not availed or denied?

* The great *Guru Srimanta Sankardeva*, through his multifarious contributions to the society and people, laid a deep and permanent mark in Assam in the fifteenth-sixteenth centuries, which still persists as a dominating force in the minds of the Assamese people. He laid the foundation of a refined culture in all spheres of individual and social life of the people for which he is acknowledged as the father of the Assamese sub-nationality].[32]

** The famous story of *Radhika Sati* who was a low caste woman and could bring water in a *pala (*a fishing tool that has holes all over), from the

Brahmaputra to the *Tembuani jaan* as per the wishes of Sankardeva, only because of her 'pious' and 'virtuous' character.]

Notes

1. Christine Van Wijk and Francis Jennifer, *Setting the Stage: Demand Resp onsive Water Supply, Sanitation and Hygiene,* The Hague, The Netherlands, IRC International Water Sanitation Centre, p. 1.
2. *Ashley Crossman, sociology.about.com/od/P_ index/g/popular-culture.htm)*
3. Dimbeswar Neog, *New Light in Asamiya Literature*, Guwahati: Xuwani Prakash, 1982.
4. Maheswar Neog, *Sankardeva and his Times :Early History of Vaishnava Faith and Movement*, Guwahati, Department of Publication, 1965, Gauhati University, p.108.
5. PoonaMahanta, *Natokor Kotha* Kaustubh Prakashan, Dibrugarh, 2011, pp. 58-60.
6. Tilottama Misra, *Literature and Society in Assam, A study of the Assam Rennaisance 1826-1926*, New Delhi, Omsons Publications, p. 117.
7. Rajmohan Nath, *The Background of Assamese Culture,* Guwahati: Dutta Baruah and Co., 1978 [1948], pp. 3-4.
8. *Op cit,* p. 118.
9. Maheswar Neog, *Sankardeva and his Times: Early History of Vaishnava Faith and Movement*, Guwahati, Department of Publication, Gauhati University, 1965, p. 368.
10. S. N. Sarma, *Neo-Vaishnavaite Movement and the Satra Institution of Assam*, Guwahati, 1966, p. 65.
11. *Op.cit*, p. 329.
12. *Ibid*, p. 338.
13. *Ibid,* pp. 152.
14. Jahnobi Gogoi (Nath), *Social Attitude Towards Women in Medieval Assam* in S.L. Barua (ed), *Status of Women in Assam,* Omsons Publishing, New Delhi, 1992.
15. *Ibid.*
16. James R. Brandon and Ianham, Martin, (ed) *Cambridge Guide to Asian Theatre*, pp. 89-90.
17. H.K. Borpujari, *Oxomot Nobojagoron: Ona Oxomiyar Bhumika*, Jorhat, Assam Sahitya Sabha, 1987.
18. Dhiraj Deka, *"Jatrapora Bhramyamanoloi: Oxomiya Natak aaru Natyo AndolonoloiBiplobi Silpi Braja Sarma'r Abodan"* in Paramananda Rajbongshi (ed), *OxomiyaNatak:Porompora aaru Poriborton,* pp. 90-99, Chandra Prakash, Panbazar, 1995.
19. Rajmohan Nath, *The Background of Assamese Culture,* Guwahati: Dutta Baruah and Co., 1978 [1948], p.145.
20. H. K. Borpujari, *Assam in the Days of the Company 1826-1858*, Spectrum Publishers, Guwahati, 1980, p. 307.

21. E.A. Gait, *A History of Assam*, 6th edn, Guwahati Lawyer's Book Stall, 1994 [1906], p. 149.
22. Dhiren Sarma, *Brajanath Sarma,* Chandra Prakash, Guwahati, 2011 [1990], pp. 43-45.
23. *Ibid,* pp. 44-45.
24. Natyasamrat Chandra Choudhury, Brajanath Sarmar Xilpi Monor xopun in *All Assam Brajanath Sarma Memorial One Act Play Competition Souvenir,* Tezpur, 1983.
25. *Op cit,* p. 53.
26. Rang Birang in *Phani Sarma Rasanawali*, p. 673.
27. J.P. Agarwala, Asomor Film Silpo, in S.N. Sarma, Navakanta Barua, Birendranath Dutta and S.P. Barua (eds), *Jyotiprasad Rasanabali: The Complete Works of Jyotiprasad*, 3rd edn, 1996, Guwahati: Publication Board, Assam, p. 105.
28. Bobbeeta Sharma, *The Moving Image and Assamese Culture Joymoti, Jyotiprasad Agarwala and Assamese Cinema*, New Delhi, Oxford University Press, 2014, p. 124.
29. Interview on 18/04/2015.
30. Interview on 20/04/2015.
31. Interview on 22/04/2015.
32. K.D. Goswami, *Mahapurusa Sankaradeva*, Publication Board of Assam, Guwahati, 2007, p.104

References

1. Agarwala, J. P., Asomor Film Silpo, in S.N. Sarma, Navakanta Barua, Birendranath. Dutta and S.P. Barua (eds) *Jyotiprasad Rasanabali: The Complete Works of Jyotiprasad*, 3rd edn, 1996, Guwahati:Publication Board, Assam, p. 105.
2. Borpujari, H. K., *Oxomot Nobojagoron: Ona Oxomiyar Bhumika,* Jorhat, Assam Sahitya Sabha, 1987.
3. Borpujari, H. K, *Assam in the Days of the Company 1826-1858*, Spectrum Publishers, Guwahati, 1980, p. 307.
4. Brandon, James R, and Martin Ianham, (ed) *Cambridge Guide to Asian Theatre,* pp. 89-90.
5. Choudhury, Natyasamrat Chandra, Brajanath Sarmar Xilpi Monor Xopun in *All Assam Brajanath Sarma Memorial One Act Play Competition Souvenir*, Tezpur, 1983.
6. Crossman, Ashley, *Sociology.about.com /od/P_index/g/popular-culture.htm*
7. Deka, Dhiraj, Jatra pora Bhramyamanoloi: Oxomiya Natak aaru Natyo Andolonoloi BiplobiSilpiBraja Sarma'r Abodanin Paramananda Rajbongshi (ed), *Oxomiya Natak : Porompora aaru Poriborton,* pp. 90-99, Chandra Prakash, Panbazar, 1995.
8. Gait, E. A., A History of Assam, 6th edn, Guwahati Lawyer's Book Stall, 1994 [1906].

9. Gogoi, Jahnobi (Nath), Social Attitude Towards Women in Medieval Assam in S.L Barua (ed) *Status of Women in Assam,* Omsons Publishing, New Delhi, 1992.
10. Goswami, K. D., *Mahapurusha Sankaradeva*, Publication Board of Assam, p. 104, 2007.
11. Mahanta, Poona, *Natokor Kotha*, Kaustubh Prakashan, Dibrugarh, 2011, pp. 58-60.
12. Misra, Tilottama, *Literature and Society in Assam : A study of Assam Rennaisance 1826-1926*, New Delhi, Omsons Publications, p. 117.
13. Nath, Rajmohan, *The Background of Assamese Culture*, Guwahati: Dutta Baruah & Co., 1978 [1948], pp. 3-4.
14. Neog, Dimbeswar, *New Light on History of Asamiya Literature*, Guwahati: Xuwani Prakash, 1982.
15. Neog, Maheshwar, *Sankaradeva and His Times: Early History of Vaishnava Faith and Movement*, Guwahati: Department of Publication, Gauhati University, 1965, p. 368.
16. Sarma, Dhiren, *Brajanath Sarma*, Chandra Prakash, Guwahati, 2011 [1990], pp. 43-45.
17. Sarma, Phani, Rang Birang, in *Phani Sarma Rasanawali,* p. 673.
18. Sarma, S. N., *Neo-Vaishnavite Movement and the Satra Institution of Assam,* Gauhati, 1965, p. 65. Sharma, Bobbeeta, *The Moving Image and Assamese Culture Joymoti, Jyotiprasad Agarwala and Assamese Cinema*, New Delhi, Oxford University Press, 2014, p. 124.
19. Sharma, Bobbeeta, *The Moving Image and Assamese Culture Joymoti, Jyotiprasad Agarwala and Assamese Cinema*, New Delhi, Oxford University Press, 2014, p. 124.

29

Transformative Context of Urbanisation and the Renegotiation of Cultural Heritage: A Case Study of the Karbis of Guwahati

— *Shabeena Yasmin Saikia*

Introduction

Culture heritage as a concept is multifaceted and attention to its various dimensions have caught the interests of experts from various disciplines and fields since a long time, however, with critical indulgence more in the recent times. The essence of culture heritage bears with it the notion of inheritance and perseveration of cultural elements. This has been the dominant aspect of the discourse on culture heritage and as a corollary emphasis had been on tangible elements of culture as intervention on identification, collection and preservation appears convenient over items where materiality is manifested. Even during the time of Renaissance, there had been interests in collection and preservation of antique artifacts of ancient Greek and Roman culture as monuments and things. The focus on intangible elements of culture made popular by UNESCO by the turn of this century opens up and intensifies a broader debate on cultural heritage that range from issues of political appropriation of cultural items, the symbolic relation of heritage with that of culture, agency, power and the processes of appropriation, cultural rights, identity, participation, governmentality, cultural pluralism, appropriating materiality to intangible elements, etc. A critical engagement of these notions to the comprehension of the transformative socio-cultural milieu of an ethnic group can enable us to analyse the dynamics of the players and processes of production and negotiation of cultural elements and its appropriation as cultural heritage by the bearers of a culture. That heritage production and its identification is simultaneously cause and consequence of defining the identity of a cultural group and leads to the ordering or disordering of relations with other groups brings out the intrinsic political character of the process involved and resultantly of the concept of cultural heritage. Hence, a study of cultural heritage needs to take into cognizance the contexts within which it unfolds and the subtexts it unfolds.

This paper explores the processes of production of culture heritage and ethnicisation of the Karbis of Guwahati as part of the larger Plain Karbi identity within the fast changing heterogeneous context of urbanity. The Karbis of Guwahati shares a number of cultural traits, complexes and constitute a part of the social organisation with the other sections of the plain Karbis of Assam and to a certain extent with the Hill Karbis. There is a strong tendency and effort of the Karbis of Guwahati to align their identity with that of the Plain Karbis and achieving this within a milieu significantly different from the one in which the rest of the sections of the Plain Karbis are situated. The city of Guwahati is the oldest urban centre in North East India situated on the southern bank of the river Brahmaputra and immediately north of the state of Meghalaya. This city has thus served as a religious, cultural, economic and political nerve centre of this part of the country which finds mention even in the Hindu scriptures and later in the stone edicts and finally in the Persian accounts and the *Buranjis* (historical accounts) compiled by the Ahoms who arrived in Assam in the early thirteenth century from Central China through Myanmar. The city and its surroundings have been on the route of major migration of people of different ethnicity and religion and served as home for many of them. The Karbis, who according to many ethnographers and historians, have migrated from one part to another and resultantly got dispersed in this region have a strong presence in the city of Guwahati. They lived a rural life in the precincts of the city and as the city gradually expanded and more drastically after the capital of the state of Assam was shifted to this city in the 1970's it engulfed these rural communities within it.

The Karbis of Assam – a background

Karbi is a tribe of Assam and its people are distributed in Karbi Anglong district which is predominantly a hilly region and the rest of the Karbi population are mainly distributed in the Brahmaputra plains within the districts of Kamrup and Kamrup Metropolitan, Morigaon, Nagaon which is adjacent to Karbi Anglong and sparsely also in the districts of Sibsagar, Golaghat, Lakhimpur, Sonitpur and Karimganj in Barak valley in Assam.

The Karbi inhabitants of Karbi Anglong are officially designated as Hill Tribe and constitutionally as a Scheduled Tribe within the Karbi Anglong District and Dima Hasao (erstwhile North Cachar District) under the provisions of the Sixth Schedule of the Constitution of India, while ethnographically the Karbis dwelling in Assam and beyond Karbi Anglong and Dima Hasao are referred to as Plain Karbi tribe but who are officially not designated as Scheduled Tribe. Apart from Assam, the Karbis are distributed in Meghalaya particularly in the districts of East Khasi Hills and Ri-Bhoi and the Jaintia Hills Division and in the Dimapur district of Nagaland. Although the historical connection between the Plains and the Hill Karbis cannot be concretely pinpointed on account of the dearth of archaeological and historical evidences, yet comparative analysis of the culture of both of them suggest a common origin and possibly later migration in to the different ecological zones and wider cultural milieu that gradually led to the differences within their social organisation and culture including economy, religion and local variations of their dialects. While the hill dwellers are known to be predominantly shifting cultivators as their traditional mode of subsistence, the plains dwellers have been practicing wet cultivation and live in settlements surrounded by other communities notably as Tiwas, Boros, Dimasa, Khasi, etc. and the caste Hindus speaking Assamese language.

Theoretical Framework

The social life of the plain Karbis are organised into village communities with an intensive social network amongst them that cuts across these villages through marital, clan, ritual and political relationship ascertaining continuity in its social organisation and culture along this region bolstered by the self ascription as Karbi, also designated as such by the other ethnic groups in their proximity. The frequency of daily interaction and everyday life is more intensive among villages in the same vicinity and the plain Karbis in and around Guwahati thus, tend to share common life engagements. The Karbis of Guwahati tend to live in the same neighbourhood and this can be accounted to their existence as villages before the expansion of the city of Guwahati. The socio-cultural life of the Karbis in Guwahati is of particular importance since it is shaped by similar factors which are significantly different from those to which their other brethrens in the Plains are exposed to. At a systemic level, the Karbis of Guwahati are functioning within the transformative and multidimensional context of urbanisation and urban life. The multidimensionality of this context includes at the same time forces towards a more levelling of aspects of social life as well as forces that counter the same by heightening awareness of one's ethnicity particularly by facilitating the locus of a political and technological hub of social life. Along with these dimensions of this context its extractive and generative elements associated with (in Durkheimian sense) an increasingly intensified 'dynamic density' among its members and increased 'moral intensity' of demands and obligations and progressively linked to a globalising world causing it to be an open system is increasingly becoming transformative. This penetrates into the social systems of the groups within this context.

In examining the cultural life of the Karbis of Guwahati we apply the theoretical and methodological tools: both as concepts and theorising, of agency and structure. The intellectual engagement both in social anthropology and sociology has been marked both by polarity in the application of these tools as well as its complementarities and consequently of a number of viewpoints on social and cultural reality. This paper undertakes the viewpoint that culture and social life are constructed by members within its historical and contemporary context but within a 'structural' framework which tend to be revised, innovated and altered suggesting that the structural framework is not rigid or 'given' but yet has both a limiting influence as well as projecting scope of innovation. Raymond Firth's concept of 'social organisation'[1] addresses this agency-structure duality and provides much leverage towards understanding society and culture both as objective and subjective realities as developed later in the works of Anthony Giddens, Peter Berger and Luckman.

The Context

In understanding culture heritage of the Karbis of Guwahati, we are at once drawn towards the changes the culture and social life of these groups of people have undergone as a response to the forces of urbanisation. These changes have been systemic which could be accounted to the external macro structural forces of change leading to changes within the Karbi society. At one level this could be explained and analysed by focusing attention on the 'existing network of social relations' between the members and the groups of the society/communities. These could be examined in a manner that the formalists have adopted in explaining how members (the Karbis of Guwahati in this case) as individuals and collectives have manipulated means and resources towards desired goals in such a way where effort is made in gaining maximum satisfaction circumscribed by the socio-cultural limitations and possibilities. Resources would include both, material, social and ideational (values and norms). Hence, the same serves to posit points of reference for the members to behave in a situation. The degree of agency of the actor shall depend upon the nature of the system: as to where it could be heuristically placed in the continuum of it being open or close. This could be phenomenologically addressed if we look at how the members view their social and cultural world- as restraining or permissible and the amount of resistance they can overcome and opportunity they can exercise in their activities and ideas. Critical thought argues towards the possibility of changing structures through human agency. Thus, the objective and subjective realities are dialectic and mutual and as such that of the structure and the agency. The cultural elements of the changing Karbi social system of Guwahati could, hence, be understood within this variant of the constructivist perspective.

The Karbis of Guwahati and the other Plain Karbis have been traditionally agriculturists cultivating predominantly for subsistence and interwoven with this have been their ritual and social life that have permeated the social existence of Karbis around and beyond Guwahati. They exhibit cultural elements that they share with the other plain Karbis which are found to persist within their urban milieu, and also as an ethnic group becoming aware of their ethnicity the Karbis have sought to retain elements of their culture as their heritage and ethnic markers. This has been a continuing process of innovation and revision and various mechanisms/means have been adopted towards this end. These revisions and disappearances of certain cultural elements and particularly cultural markers could be associated with the play of agency within a system.

A diachronic treatment of the life of the Karbis of this city from around the time before the transfer of the capital to Guwahati (1973) to the recent would make explicit the extent of land alienation that occurred amongst the people of these Karbi communities due to the interplay of market forces for land and cash economy, the expanding urban population and the cityscape. The same brought them closer to non-Karbi people even within their homestead land in their neighbourhood/community as rooms were rented out to those who came to the city and agricultural land were sold off. The local community has become highly heterogeneous. Urbanisation and concomitant market forces brought the erstwhile Karbi agriculturists and their younger generations into the non-farm sector of the urban economy. Not only that the very composition and cultural component of the closed neighbourhood of these once homogeneous communities have changed drastically and significantly, but also that the labour and the time of the Karbis have been drawn into the city beyond their community neighbourhood both for economic and other engagements. These led to systemic pressures and tendencies providing a framework of action for the members to which could be traced their changing social and cultural life.

Cultural Life- Redefinition and Identity

The Karbis of Guwahati like any other tribal folks institutionally emphasise upon tribal endogamy and clan exogamy. Not only as a heritage of their culture is this invoked by them, but this is consciously associated with ethnic identity becoming a part of manifest structure. This conscious articulation indicates a selection from their kit of cultural resources and has served as a critical decision on their part to preserve these institutions. These are means of maximising their stake in the midst of an expanding amorphous urban culture; for the older generation it is more of asserting and preserving their culture heritage- cultural uniqueness and familiarity within an encompassing alien and unfamiliar culture and for the younger generations along with this, these are attempts at claiming access to resources allocated by the State reflecting, as Clifford Geertz (1963) states, a growing tendency of cultural primordialism in nation state politics where allocation of resources tend to occur on lines of ethnicity where differently situated ethnic groups in a plural cultural set up assert their ethnic identity to circumvent their losing out on accessing resources that tend to be allocated on lines of achievement and citizenship and thus staking a claim on those resources which come to assume significance in the changed politics and economics of the state. Such sentiments of primordialism constituting the subjective domain of the collective is sought to be manifested and objectified in these institutions, norms and practices. These serve as instruments for asserting group identity and for a stake in access to resources. In the process it tends to institute primodial sentiments. Thus, tribal endogamy and clan exogamy as age old institutions of heritage are glorified and upheld at the level of a social ideal. This has been observed both among the Karbis of Guwahati and other plain and hill Karbis. Although as institutions these are not different from that of other social groups but these are crucial in differentiating them from other social and cultural groups and which the Karbis of Guwahati have sought to retain despite the pressures against these. Along with this, there is the knowledge and the awareness that these ought to be preserved for the sake of their cultural identity thus relegating these to the sphere of cultural heritage by the members of the culture bearing group.

Social control on these used to be achieved, in practice, through actual and the threat of excommunication of the violators, invariably in the matter of clan exogamy while instances of compromise and leniency have been reported, both in Guwahati and among the other plain Karbis, in matters of tribe exogamy. In Guwahati, even in case of marriage of a Hindu Karbi[2] with non-Karbi who is not a Hindu, leniency has been reported. Here, the Karbis have now reportedly asserted that they could not afford to reduce membership of their community and their participation in community matters by exercising this means of social control even in those matters of violation of norms that used to invite the penalty of ex-communication. With several instances of tribal exogamy and clan endogamy the Karbis here have sought to resolve it by the prevalent means of fictive kinship whereby the bride is adopted into the clan of the mother of the bridegroom and particularly as the daughter of his mother's brother, seemingly adhering to their ideal of their preferred MBD marriage (marriage of a boy with his mother's brother's daughter). Where, previously, clan endogamy would invariably lead to ex-communication of those few violators, now instead of that, such deviation is normalised through the extension of the application of mechanism so long applied in other instances for normalising social relations. However, the redefinition of this element of their culture heritage occurs only at the level of practice and that too at micro level where particular instances are individually dealt with and normalised and not at the level of their institution which is being preserved amidst the pressures of urbanisation. The rules of clan endogamy and tribe exogamy have not been altered and this aspect of their social structure has been consciously kept intact by them through their agency of traditional village council of elders/*Khel* in the meeting/*Mel* which comprise the locus of their formal decisions on their social and cultural life. Whenever, they are faced with any serious matter that seems to them to threaten their cultural existence, the members of all the village councils/*Khel* of the Karbis of Guwahati would hold a *Mel* where the best recourse to deal with these are decided upon. Often, the term *khel* is synonymously used to indicate the local community under one village/community council. Thus, for addressing the graveness of preserving the institutions of clan exogamy and tribe endogamy such a collective decision has been taken and leaving it unto the local *khel* to deal with the particular instances of violations within the area of the respective *khel*. This definitely leads to special attention being paid by their social collectivity at a macro level and into each individual instance of violation whenever such would happen where the deviants are accepted within the community after adoption into mother's clan and a ritual purification and a punishment handed out to them which would consist of a fine or/and a feast for the *khel* folks. But it is feared even by the village elders that such handling may be able neither to restrict clan exogamy nor tribe endogamy which are considered undesirable. From once being inviolable these have now shifted to being undesirable at a practical plane.

Regarding their dialect, although most of the Karbis of Guwahati particularly the young ones are no longer conversant in Karbi and converse in Assamese except for the usage of few words and phrases in Karbi they consider the dialect spoken by the other *Bhayam Karbi* as their traditional language. Karbi girls from the rural areas married in Guwahati usually can speak that dialect and although no serious effort has been made to propagate it, yet they consider it as their culture heritage. Similarly, even in marriage, the Assamese *Mekhela Chador* is the popular attire for the brides, yet they have identified a variant of their ethnic attire which is different from the ones worn by the Hill Karbis and is similar to the ones worn by the plain tribes.

The Karbi equivalent of the Hindu funeral practice of *Sraddha* is *Silputa* and nowadays they often use the term *Sraddha* to indicate *Silputa* (erection of stones in memory of the deceased, a megalithic practice) ceremony observed within a year of the death as per their convenience. It is performed at the '*Long-ae*', a ground where *Silputa* is performed. On the day of the ritual performance a male kin of the deceased plays the role of a '*Deo*'- the one who guides the rituals. Two stones gathered from the hills are covered with a piece of white cloth known as '*sakatuk*', these are taken to the *Long-ae* and half buried in the ground. On this day the kins and neighbours are invited for a feast usually with pork meat. Boiled rice, boiled potato, fish, fruits, cooked vegetables, betel leaves, areca nut, etc. are laid upon a banana leaf and covered with the *Sakatuk*. These are offered to the Gods. The women folk weep mourning the loss of the deceased. Finally, the guests are given a feast. This festival marks them off from the Hill Karbis who perform the elaborate funeral ritual of 'Chomangkan' which extends for days and is an expensive affair; hence there is hardly any time limit for the observance of this ritual by the family of the deceased.

Agency and Cultural Heritage

The institution of *Khel* of the local community comprises a critical intangible cultural heritage which is undergoing changes and innovation. These are the ones, which are trying to uphold the cultural values and institutions and it is through this agency that the social and cultural practices gain sanction and primacy as critical and important aspects of their culture that needs to be protected and sustained. This is the custodian of their cultural life and group identity playing the dual role of preserving, redefining and constructing their cultural heritage as *Bhayam Karbi*/Karbi of the Plains and at the same time is itself a critical culture heritage element withstanding the urban pressures of change. Without this institution the social structure of the Karbis of Guwahati will change. Within these, the institution of the *Bangthai* gains prominence as the occupant of this position has to serve as the traditional custodian and steward of the religious and ritual life of the Karbis. He is the leader of the *Khel* and along with the other traditional hereditary positions of the village elders namely, *Deka Bangthai, Bisar*

Dhora, Oklengsar and in consensus with the village/community members play the collective role in sorting out the framework of the annual activities of the community ranging from festivals and rituals as johong puja, dehal puja, aai puja, bhel puja, Bihu, etc. observed at community level to recasting where necessary the socio-cultural norms of the community which is undertaken annually at the beginning of the Assamese new year. This is done by each of the community *khels* scattered in the various localities within the city of Guwahati namely, in Narakasur, Hengrabari, Japorigog, Moina Khurung, Saru Sajai and Nalapara and they all meet when required to address any grave issue of their cultural life in Guwahati.

These members of the different *Khel*s of Guwahati also meet to discuss any serious issue that confront their cultural and social life. One such instance had been to discuss on the matter of the kind of penalty to be meted out to the members regarding the different kinds of violations of customs. Where throwing of a feast with pork meat to fellow members had been a custom meted out for violation of any custom, this has now been changed to making payment of a nominal amount of cash to the *Khel* as a form of punishment now and reserving the former form of punishment only in the very severe of cases as violation of clan exogamy, marriage with a non-Hindu and violations as murder, physical assault on parents, etc. Although the function of the *khel* has been reduced due to the agency of the Police and the judiciary the *Khel* still holds its control over the members of the local community. The Karbis of Guwahati are maintaining a community life as a whole.

Although the *khel*s of the Karbis of Guwahati maintain a close network of relation they are not isolated from the Plain Karbis around. In preserving their cultural life the *Khel* members join together and participate in meetings where serious issues are discussed in such platforms as the *Baro Gram Mel.*[3] The members of the different local communities meet together for the observance of certain rituals and festivals and each of the different clans across Guwahati and the neighbouring Karbi villages have their own observance of certain religious rituals and worship which is known as *faidor puja* performed during the time of Bohag Bihu[4] usually in the house of the eldest member of the clan.

The institutions of the Khel and Banghthai have become assertive in articulating an ethnic identity under the umbrella term of *Bhayam Karbi Adorbar* (an association of plain Karbis) and *Karbi Bangthai Axom* (an association of the ritual heads of the Bhayam Karbi of Assam). In this assertion for an identity that is different and unique from that of the Hill Karbis and other, they have adopted a cultural symbol known as *Numpe Armu* and colloquially in Assamese as the *Mudha Khuta* in contradistinction to the cultural symbol of *Jambili Aathon* of the Hill Karbis.

This has given legitimacy also to the *Mudha Khuta* as a culture heritage of the Plain Karbis. Its symbolic significance is not coincidental rather it has been selected from their cultural repertoire. The *Mudha Khuta* is a sacred site associated with their domestic domain which is a crucial aspect of their social life wherein reside the ancestor spirits of the family and also a site for the propitiation of the household spirits and local spirits and the gods. Thus, the construction of any residence is to commence with the building of the *mudhakhuta* amidst rituals in the presence of the members of the Khel and their community. The membership into a community and representation into Mels of the community gains cognizance only through family membership. Family in the worldview of the Karbis of Guwahati comprises of the family members of a household and a household is understood to be one where a *mudhakhuta* is installed. The *mudhakhuta* also ties the domestic with the public sphere of their life. The *Mudhakhuta* being a part of their culture heritage now has been adopted as their ethnic symbol.

Regarding their religious life, the role of the *Khel* has always been significant. While being custodian of their culture and customs which they hail as markers of their identity the *khels* are means of bringing in and giving legitimacy to new kinds of religious practices. The Khel of Sarusajai (one of the localities in the southern fringe of the city near the NH 37) has adopted *Durga puja*- worship of the Hindu goddess *Durga* at the community level as a part of their cultural life. This puja is celebrated with much grandeur and fun in the city particularly by the Hindus and revelled by city dwellers. In observance of this puja by the Karbis of Sarusajai, no Brahmin priest is engaged and offerings to the deity are made as is done for their local gods. Here an amalgamation of animism and Hinduism can be identified. Temples of Hindu gods and goddesses as Siva and Lakhi can be seen in Sarusajai. Although these have not yet been appropriated as their cultural heritage yet they signify the changing cultural domain particularly at the level of social organisation.

Their notion of Pollution and Purity which may be a result of Hinduisation and the different ways of application of this principle is now a mechanism by which they maintain social distance from other groups and seek to maintain their cohesiveness and group identity. This finds expression not only in regard to marriage with a non Hindu and non-Karbi for which they compulsorily have to go through the purification rite *(Porachit)* but also when they stay away of their local neighbourhood into the city and beyond even for a night. Since, this becomes problematic as overnight visits to the city and beyond are a common urban phenomena, the *khel* has reduced the elaboration of this rite making it a simple practice that could be adhered to with ease. Even for reverting back to normal social life after any violation of social norm as well as for participation in any sacred event *porachit* is mandatory for them which has to be performed under the direction and sanction of the *Khel*. The community has redefined socio-cultural norms and practices so that those which they consider as fundamental can be preserved by them in their group life.

The institution of *Khel* is facing certain tensions, yet the people vouch it to be a critical part of their culture seeking to retain it with due alterations they deem necessary to cope within the transformative urban situation. For instance, while attendance to these *Mels* by the male members from the respective locality is necessary, the people could not always attend the same on account of not being able to miss their attendancc in their offices or their other engagements in the city. That is nowadays being accepted as reason for absence, though with regret, and the *Khel* seeks to fix dates for the meeting taking into consideration both the severity and urgency of the situation on the one hand and on the other, the immediate date and time that would be convenient for most members to attend and participate in the proceedings of the *Mel*. The local people are trying their best to preserve this institution through the changing situations of city life. The importance of the *Khel* has not been compromised with in preserving their norms. In one instance the *Burha Bangthai* had violated their basic social rule of not committing any physical assault on ones parents. The *Bangthai* was punished as per custom and had to pay a fine along with giving a feast to fellow members of the community. Again, very few cases of initial defying of the verdict and will of the *Khel* and the customs by Karbi residents have come to light. But ultimately, reportedly, in each of these the will of the people through the *Khel* has been made to prevail and the errant have accepted the will of the *Khel*.

The Burha Bangthai was absent in the recent meet that decided on an offence considered serious of one village family over triple fault of bringing a non-Karbi girl by one of the brothers which necessitated Porachit (general purificatory rite) which so far was one fault and that too when the narikatasuwa (purificatory rite associated with birth) of the eldest brother's child was still pending which compounded to double fault and further complicating the matter was that instead of informing the village khel of these two defaults and under the instruction of the Khel of doing the porachit for both the suwa together (which is the norm) they settled on their own for only the nari kata suwa that too instead of performing the rite in the village stream, which is considered as the proper place, it was done in their residence while the norm was to inform Khel and go for a single solution of both the problems together. In this context, the bringing in of the non-Karbi girl did not yet become an issue but the disregard shown to the Khel was a severe offence and it was dealt in the Mel and a fine of Rs 3500 fixed on the offending family.

This also highlights the solidarity of their collective life which the *khel* is striving to retain.

Conclusion

The paper brings forth the expanding domain of understanding cultural heritage. It sensitises us towards a number of issues that need to be considered to gain a broader understanding of the concept. The relationship between the concept of culture and cultural heritage, the former with a comprehensive meaning and inclusion of 'anything that man does as a member of the group' and the latter with a qualifier of selection of elements and the need to preserved these makes us contend with issues of the forms, processes, agencies and politics of legitimising the elements of culture as worth preserving. Here, it needs to be comprehended that culture heritage are not randomly selected, but emerge from a context rampant with negotiation, power and redefinition and hence may include contemporary cultural items that they deem necessary to preserve. This needs to address the context in which these processes play out. This also leads us to confront the issue of cultural rights and rights of indigenous people and of their identity and how the bearers of the culture identify themselves with those elements of cultural heritage. When it comes to intangible cultural heritage, one has to be particular that there is no such specific check list of items to be referred to as cultural heritage, but would include anything that the bearers of culture identifies themselves with and as such contributes to social cohesion, a sense of common identity and belongingness. It may include items/institutions/beliefs which are not exclusive of that cultural group but serve as boundary maintaining mechanisms as expounded by Fredrik Barth. In a modern state, appropriation of cultural heritage and identity are not simple processes, but rather entails conflict and negotiation between agencies from within the cultural group, the other cultural/ethnic groups and the agencies- political and otherwise who are involved with the formalisation of the same. Thus, the Karbis of Guwahati as part of the Plain Karbi socio-cultural group are striving for state recognition of their tribal status as Scheduled Tribe and the struggle is still going on.

Notes

1. Firth held that "Briefly, by the structural aspect of social relations we mean the principles on which their form depends; by the functional aspect we mean the way in which they serve given ends; by the organisational aspect we mean the directional activity which maintains their form and serves their ends." While

social structure indicates the ideal patterns of the social group, social organisation indicates concrete activity. Social structure essentially means the "social relations which seems to be of critical importance for the behaviour of members of the society, so that if such relations were not in operation, the society would not be said to exist in that form" (p. 31). Social organisation indicates a social process involving exercise of personal choice/evaluations and making of decisions, the former reflective of the "general ends or values of the group range into terms which are significant for the individual" (p. 36). Such actions lead to ordering of social relations involving sequence of allocation of units played out over time within the limited alternatives that are circumscribed by the structure or rather that which people have been considering critical for social continuity. This entails variance and takes account of social dynamism within structural limits but at the same time it would conceptually lead one to account for the cumulative effect of variations stimulated by a number of factors that may change the structure itself. In this theoretical equation Firth's understanding of the role of the individual and his/her evaluations/choices and decisions plays the spotlight on the role of agency in maintaining social structure, modifying it or changing it, which brings us closer to the theory of Structuration by Anthony Giddens and the theory of Social Construction of Reality by Berger and Luckman.

2. The Plain Karbis are the Hinduised section of Karbis while most of the Hill Karbis have adopted Christianity and few in the Hills have retained their traditional animistic belief and practices. Plain Karbis represent an amalgamated form of Hinduism and their traditional animistic belief as is the case with the other Hinduised tribes of this region.
3. Baro Gram Khel is a Council of twelve villages comprising of khel members from any of the twelve villages of the local neighbourhood. It is one of the local higher authorities that can redefine and alter sanctions and customs which are accepted by the people of the area.
4. Bohag Bihu is observed in the mid of April i.e. the Assamese month of Bohag heralding the onset of the New Year and is a celebration of spring and fertility associated with agriculture. It is one of the grandest seasonal festivals of Assam extending for days. Bihu had its origin in the tribal cultures of Assam and gradually culminated as an assimilation of a number of traditions to become the state festival of Assam. Different tribes have their distinctive style of dances, folk songs and observances associated with this Bihu.

References

Arizpe, L. and Cristian Amescua, (ed) (2013), *Anthropological Perspectives on Intangible Cultural Heritage*, London, Springer.

Barth, F. (1998), *Ethnic Groups and Boundaries: The Social Organisation of Culture Difference,* Illinois, Waveland Press.

Firth, Raymond, (1961), *Elements of Social Organisation*, London, Watts and Co.

Geertz, C. (1963), *The integrative revolution: primordial sentiments and civil politics in the new state.* In Old societies and new states: the quest for modernity in Asia and Africa (ed.) Clifford Geertz, 105-157, New York, The Free Press of Glencoe.

Giddens, A. (1986), *The Constitution of Society: Outline of the Theory of Structuration*, Berkley and Los Angeles, University of California Press.

Saikia, S.Y. (2009), *A Study of the Changing Social System of the Karbis of Guwahati,* Unpublished doctoral thesis, Gauhati University.

30

Disappearing Ceremonial Festivals Once Observed and Celebrated by the Garos in Assam

— Tharsush K. Sangma

The Garos are one of the indigenous tribes inhabiting in the state of Assam. They are mostly found in the districts of Goalpara, Kamrup, Karbi Anglong, Udalguri, Kokrajhar, Dhubri, etc. Constitutionally, the Garo people living in the hill districts of Karbi Anglong and N.C. Hills have been categorised as Hill Tribes while those living in the plain districts, have been recognised as Scheduled Tribe (plain) in the state of Assam.

In political, social, education and economic aspects, the Garo people living in Assam are still backward. Professing Christianity now, they have abandoned their traditional religion. As a result, most of their traditional customs, practices, rituals and religious observations have been discarded. Believing these traditional and cultural practices as being contradictory to their newly adopted Christian religion, they pushed it aside and did not care to preserve and enrich it for posterity. During the period before conversion into the fold of Christianity, the Garo people of Assam observe number of ceremonial festivals like Wangala, Mangona or Mangrua, Gure Rodila or Gure Wata, Nokma Gana, Salpang Sima or Salgrua, Marang Arika or Marang Gala, Grengdik Baa or Grengdik Rodila, Memang Dilbaa, Debra Sugala etc. Out of these ceremonial festivals, Wangala has been the only surviving traditional festival of the Garo people living in Assam which is being observed and celebrated with traditional pomp and gaiety. Yet, the celebrations have to avoid many of its original features as the new religion prohibits many of the rituals and other activities connected with the festival.

Some of the traditional festivals of the Garos, which have been abandoned by them or have been fast disappearing from them are briefly described below.

Mangona: It is a post-funeral festival observed by the Garos. The Ambeng, Matabeng and the Chibok sub-tribes of the Garos observed this festival. Before conversion into Christianity, the Garos believe in a number of gods and goddesses some of which are benevolent while some are malevolent. They believe in the supreme creator whom they called *Dakgipa Rugipa Babra* or *Jamani Nokgipa Janggini Biambi*. Babra was the giver and protector of human souls. After death, it is believed that the soul of the deceased go to *Memang Asong* or the land of the Spirits which they identified first with Napak and then with the Balpakram. Both the places are situated in Garo Hills.

Mangona is a combination of two Garo words. *Mang* means body and *Ona* means lay down. Hence Mangona means laying down the dead to rest. In the pre-Christian era, the Garos do not bury the dead. The corpse of the dead is laid down over by spreading number of metal gongs, and was covered with a piece of cloth called *Bara Marang*. There is a Garo folk song that says....

Chengo mande siode, ao gope galjana,
Mangonesa misi rongpindapana.

Which means :

In the days gone by, when a Garo person dies, the body was not buried;

Laying down the dead, the corpse was buried by millets.

When the all the necessary things for the final send off of the soul of the dead are ready and the relatives of the dead man had arrived, the ceremonial rituals would be started and the corpse would be burnt on a pyre. The mortal remains would be collected in an earthen pot and put in a hut called *Delang*. This hut is constructed on the same day when the corpse is burnt.

The Garos believed that a person must accompany the deceased to the next world. This belief on their part demands for another man to accompany the dead to the next world. So, if someone dies, then a stranger would be captured and be killed to accompany the dead man. He would be captured alive and at the time of burning the dead body, the captured man would also be burnt alive. Hence, the corpse of the deceased would be kept without disposing it off till the time when a stranger is finally captured. The final disposal of the dead body is ceremoniously done only when they could capture and bring the stranger to accompany the deceased to the next world.

When such practice of sacrificing human being to accompany the dead man, has been abandoned by them, the Garos substituted a chicken in the place of human being. When a person is died, a chicken would be tied on his toe. This customary practice is called *Dojasi Kaa* or tying of a chicken on the toe of the dead.

The Ambeng and the Matabeng sub-tribes of the Garos called this post-funeral ceremonies as *Mangona* while the Chiboks and the Rugas called it *Mangrua*, meaning dismantling the body of the dead. *Mang* means body, *Rua* means to dismantle hence *Mangrua.* A small hut is built in front of the main Garo house. This hut is called *Delang*. Here the bones of the deceased collected in an earthen pot is kept till it is ceremoniously disposed of. On the occasion of Mangrua, the bones of the deceased are buried and this small hut is burnt down with performance of rituals. The Rugas dance around the Delang while it is being burnt. At the final stage of their performance, they step into the fire and dance over it. This dance form is called *Delang Ga·kimita*.

Like in the Wangala dance, both male and female dancers take part in the Ruga dance. There is a leader in the Wangala dance who alone carries sword and a shield. But in the Ruga dance, each male dancers carry swords and shields in their hands. One male dancer dances in the middle of the dancing group by carrying an umbrella in his hand.

Gure Rodila or Gure Wata: The Awe Garos have the custom of keeping and preserving a spirit whom they called *Gure mitde* or a deity in the form of a horse. In between March and April months, the Awe Garos observe the Gure Wata festival. A bamboo cage is artistically designed and woven giving a shape to that of a living horse. The whole body of the bamboo cage is covered with a piece of cloth called Bara Barang and a metal bell is tied on the neck of the horse. At the foot of the central post of the house of the person who keeps the spirit, this bamboo cage would be placed and the Kamal Tuara, or a priest by performing rituals, invokes the spirit of *Gure Mitde* by breaking an egg. Once the spirit is invoked, one person is made to carry the bamboo cage on his shoulder. It is said that when the spirit descends into the cage, it becomes heavy and it could hardly be lifted to carry it on the shoulder.

The horse is then escorted all through the village roads singing and dancing together by the followers. The dancing with the spirit all along the roads, visiting the neighbouring villages with large number of followers, merry making etc. would continue for some days till the bamboo cage is dipped into a river or a lake. The celebration comes to an end with a community picnic at the site of the immersion. Till the year 1985, the Gure Wata ceremonies were still in practice in Garo villages like Hakumari, Mallang, Gohalkona under Kamrup district and in villages like Moshkuli, Rongchi, Bakrapara, Patpara etc. under Goalpara district of Assam.

Nokma Gana or Gana Ceremony: In the Garo society, there are various kinds of Nokmas such as *Gana Nokma* (Nokma possessing Wealth), *Kamal Nokma* (Nokma who performs rituals, invokes and appeases spirits), *Challang Nokma* (The conqueror in fighting and in War), *Songni Nokma* (The choosen leader of the village to lead and look after the affairs of the local village administration). However, all the Nokmas do not posses or exercise political powers over a definite territorial boundaries called Aking. Only the Aking Nokma has the political and administrative powers over its Aking and its people. So, he is also well respected and obeyed by the villagers.

Someone who possesses wealth or riches and wants to highlight himself as a respectable person in a society, organises and observes a ceremonial festival called *Gana* or *Gana c*eremony. The person who wants to declare himself a Nokma, invites all his *Chras* (Uncles and Brother-in-laws from the wife's side) to his house and fixes up the date for the Gana ceremony. In another instance, the proposal for ordination as the Nokma comes from the *Chras* themselves on seeing that the person has enough riches to be ordained as the Gana Nokma in the locality. To materialise their good intent, *Chras* would go to the house of the man and one of the members of the *Chras*, by carrying a bundle of firewood, place it down on the ground saying, "*I shall bring firewood*"; another member of the *Chras* would say "*I shall bring Jaksil"* (elbow ring); another member would say "*I shall bring a metal gong*": another would say "*I shall bring Kram and Nagra (drums)*" etc. In this way all the necessary materials required for ordination as the Nokma, would be contributed by the *Chras* themselves. But the larger share of the expenses incurred during the *Gana* ceremony, is to be borne by the to be Nokma himself. Necessary preparations will be made for that day by the person concerned like rice beer, cows, pigs, rice etc for offering sumptuous feast to the village people. On the day of the Gana ceremony, the Nokma designate would be allowed to sit in a designated place and offered a metal elbow ring to wear. This elbow ring is called *Jaksil* in Garo language. He would then be offered a turban called *Kotip Nokma;* a sword called *milam* and a *Spi* or a shield by the eldest member of the *Chras*. Since that time onwards, the person will be respected and called as the Nokma in the locality.

Salgrua or Salpang Sima: *Sal* means the sun and *Grua* means undo. So literally, *Salgrua* means to undo or beat the scorching heat of the sun by inviting rain. This is one kind of celebrations of the Garo people to invoke the rain god. This god is believed to have been living in the seas and oceans which the Garo people called *Aema Ditema* or *Sagal Ama Repok Chiga*. His residence on the land is identified with a place called Kosi, a secluded place or a hill where stone monoliths are erected and offer sacrifices; or a jungle abound with trees and other vegetations etc. The place is kept as sacred and no one is allowed to cut down anything from that particular spot. At the time when there has been a drought or a drought like situation with no rain for some days and months, all the members of the Garo village would go to the *Kosi*. A particular spot would be cleared for sacrificing animals like goat, poultry etc. to the rain god. The priest, through chanting of words, invokes the spirit asking him to see the sufferings of the people and relief them off from their miseries by sending them rain so that they could cultivate *jhum* and start afresh their agricultural activities. While the priest was chanting some words, the villagers would bring water from the stream and pour down upon the priest inviting heavy downpour of rain.

Marang Arikgala: It means chasing away the evils. In the months of March-April, the villagers gather together in a place and collect old household things and implements by visiting each households of the village. On the day fixed for observing Marang Arikala in the village, one member of the family joins the group of villagers who would collect the old and worn out household implements and materials and the other members of the family remained in their own house. In some villages, the villagers going through the road, called out *marang..marang* and on hearing the words, a member of the family immediately take their rags, old and worn out household implements etc. and put it in the basket being carried by them. Every household would be visited in this way till all the houses in the village are completed. The collected materials would be dumped in some remote places on the road side and after that the people take bath in a river to wash away all the profanations.

Grengdik Rodila: Dancing with the bones of the dead. Before conversion into Christianity, when a Garo man dies, his dead body was not buried under the earth. The corpse is burnt and the bone remains are collected in an earthen pot. A small hut is built in front of the Garo house called *Nokachik*. The pot containing the bones of the dead is kept in this small hut till it is officially disposed of. A day is fixed for sending away the spirit of the dead to the next world called Me·mang A·song or Balpakram or the Land of the Spirits. On this day, the bone remains of the dead are carried either by a niece or a sister of the deceased and dance around on the threshold. It is then burnt into ashes and the hut called *Delang* is also burnt down.

Memang Dila: It is the practice of leading back the soul of the dead to his birth place. The Garos believe in the theory of rebirth and this *Memang Dila* ceremony is observed to ensure that the deceased in his next birth can have his place in the same family or motherhood. The sister or a niece of the deceased rolls out a string of thread from the bundle all along the way from the house of the deceased to the place where he was born and attained adulthood. This act is called *Memangna Kilding Sringa* or *Memangna Rama mesoka,* meaning showing the way for the ghost of the deceased to come through. Another sister or a niece of the deceased would carry a metal gong with rice and a black coloured cock tail on it. The rice carried on the metal gong is called *Rongjanggi* or the rice containing the soul of the deceased. The things given to the deceased at the time of his marriage by his parents would also be given back by the deceased wife's family on this occasion.

Debra Sugala: It is a customary practice or a ceremony of compensating the parents by a male child with a gift and a sumptuous meal after his marriage with his beloved. No earthly materials can compensate the love and care of the parents to their respective children of the family. A Garo man, after his marriage, go to the wife's house and stays there till he could establish his own separate family. In the case of a *Nokkrom* marriage (marriage with a Garo inheritress), however, the question of separate living out the house of his wife's parents does not arise. Debra Sugala is done to honour and compensate the love and care of the parents. In course of living with his wife and children, a Garo man along with his wife, would come prepared to observe the Debra Sugala at the house of his parents. The relatives from both sides of his parents and the villagers would be invited to the festival. A loin cloth called *gando* will be offered to his father while a woman's wearing apparel known as *Gana* or a *Dakmanda* shall be offered to his mother as signs of love. A grand feast is given to the parents, relatives, friends and the villagers on the occasion.

Conclusion

These social and religious festivals as have been briefly discussed above are now being disappeared very rapidly from the Garo people living in Assam. The immediate cause is the spread of Christianity and the popularity of the Christian religion among the Garo people. Spread of education among them is another reason as they think these ceremonies and festivals are only a part of their superstitions which are contrary to the principles and teachings of their newly accepted Christian religion. Most of the ceremonial festivals and social institutions of the Garo people are directly or indirectly associated with their socio-religious and economic practices. There is a saying "Loss of religion is a lost of Culture. Loss of culture is a lost of identity. This maxim is true in the context of the life of the Garo people living in Assam. As the Garos have lost tribal religion of their own, they have been losing much of their ethnic identities by way of abandoning religion and their unique socio-religious festivals and ceremonies. It is therefore, a high time now, to look into those disappearing socio-religious ceremonies, festivals and other social institutions of the Garo people living in Assam and start doing the works in order to preserve and promote them before they are completely vanish into the air. The Garo Clan Organisations, the Mahari Associations, the Garo NGOs, etc. should work together and strive to preserve these disappearing social events from the society."

Books and References

Mihir N. Sangma : Maniani Bidik
Awensing S. Rongmuthu : Wangalani Bimik
Dewangsing Rongmuthu : Apasong Agana
Prabodh M. Sangma : The Songsarek Philosophy
Harendra W. Marak : Ku·bidik

Index